CHARLES THE BALD

THE MEDIEVAL WORLD

Editor: David Bates

Already published

WILLIAM MARSHAL

David Crouch

CHARLES THE BALD

Janet L. Nelson

CHARLES THE BALD

Janet L. Nelson

LONGMAN
London and New York

Longman Group UK Limited,
Longman House, Burnt Mill, Harlow,
Essex CM20 2JE, England
and Associated Companies throughout the world.

*Published in the United States of America
by Longman Inc., New York*

First published 1992

British Library Cataloguing in Publication Data

Nelson, Janet L.
Charles the Bald. – (The Medieval World)
I. Title II. Series
944.092
ISBN 0-582-05585-7
ISBN 0-582-05584-9 pbk

Library of Congress Cataloging in Publication Data

Nelson, Janet (Janet L.)
Charles the Bald / Janet L. Nelson.
p.   cm. – (The Medieval world)
Includes Bibliographical references and index.
Summary: Discusses the historical and political aspects of the reign of this ninth-
century French king.
ISBN 0-582-05585-7. – ISBN 0-582-05584-9 (pbk.)
1. Charles II, King of France, 823–877. 2. France–History-
-Charles II, 840–877. 3. France–Kings and rulers– Biography.
[1. Charles II, King of France, 823–877. 2. Kings, queens, rulers, etc.]
I. Title . II. Series.
DC76.N45   1992
944' .014' 092–dc20 [B] 91-17355 CIP AC

Set inBaskerville 11/12
Produced by Longman Singapore Publishers (Pte) Ltd.
Printed in Singapore

CONTENTS

LIST OF GENEALOGICAL TABLES AND MAPS

TABLES

MAPS

EDITOR'S PREFACE

As Janet Nelson explains, this book is the first attempt to write a political biography of Charles the Bald. As she also explains, Charles is a ruler who has for far too long been saddled with a reputation as an unsuccessful participant in a process of decline and disintegration. She tackles not only the subject of Charles's abilities, but also the process which has come to be known as 'the decline of the Carolingian Empire'. Charles emerges as a skilful manipulator of circumstances and as an able and effective ruler; he and his brothers Lothar and Louis the German as men who believed themselves to be in control of their destiny, and who, had they been able to comment, would not have recognised the tragic decline in which later commentators have supposed them to have been taking part. The ninth century emerges as a turbulent time, but also as one of opportunities and achievements.

Janet Nelson brings an unrivalled knowledge of ninth-century politics to the task of producing a convincing portrayal of Charles the Bald and his world. She has also drawn upon a vast array of modern scholarship which is rapidly redrawing our picture of the entire Carolingian period. The result is a book which is not only a reassessment of an important ruler, but also an analysis of the nature of Carolingian court politics and the problems involved in sustaining control in the localities where aristocratic rivalries and Viking war-bands pursued their particular goals. This study of the life and times of Charles the Bald is therefore one of central importance to all interested in the medieval period. A reign which has been relatively neglected by historians is used as a vehicle for ideas which are transforming our awareness of the economic, political and social forces which shaped the Medieval West.

David Bates

AUTHOR'S ACKNOWLEDGEMENTS

I have been fortunate to spend my whole teaching-life in the congenial environment of King's College London. During the year's leave that enabled me to complete this book, David Carpenter, Anne Duggan and Diana Webb cheerfully shouldered extra teaching-burdens: my thanks to them and to the rest of my departmental colleagues for their support, and also to the staff of the College Library for their help. A grant from the School of Humanities research fund enabled me to visit Paris to look at manuscripts containing Charles the Bald's capitularies.

To my students, undergraduates and postgraduates alike, I owe a large debt for much inspiration and moral support, not least during the writing of this book; members of my Special Subject classes in particular have opened up many interesting questions about Charles the Bald. My thanks to James Campbell, Karl Leyser and Patrick McGurk for wisdom and encouragement over the years, and to Bob Deshman and Larry Nees for opening my eyes to art-historical evidence. I am indebted to Philip Grierson for offprints of his still-indispensable articles on ninth-century matters: this is the place to record gratitude to him and to the late Michael Wallace-Hadrill, who nearly twenty-five years ago were kind to a nervous PhD candidate. Close acquaintance with the unpublished PhD dissertations of Giles Brown and John Nightingale has taught me a great deal, as have the dissertations and the published papers of Stuart Airlie, Simon Coupland and Julia Smith: my thanks to all of them, and also to Neville Wylie, whose B.A. dissertation illuminated an obscure text. I am particularly grateful to Stuart

Airlie, Paul Fouracre and John Gillingham, all three of whom have commented on the draft chapters of this book; to Wendy Davies and Michael Metcalf who commented on chapter 2; to Tim Reuter and Julia Smith who showed me drafts of their forthcoming books; and, for their scholarship and friendship over the years, to all the above-named, and to David Ganz, Margaret Gibson, Judith Herrin, Susan Kruse, Jan Marsh, Jane Martindale, Rosamond McKitterick, Tom Noble, Susan Reynolds (who also explained about curtains and hems), Lyndal Roper, Pauline Stafford, Chris Wickham, Ian Wood and Patrick Wormald. I am, as ever, grateful to the staff of the Institute of Historical Research, Univeristy of London, for much more than their expertise. I should like to acknowledge the kindness of Florentine Mütherich, who supplied the colour-slide from which the cover-illustration of this book was made, and to thank the Abbey of San Paolo fuori le Mura for permission to reproduce the throne-portrait from the Bible Charles the Bald brought to Rome eleven centuries ago.

In completing this book, I re-register an old debt to my medieval teachers, the late Kathleen Hughes and the late Walter Ullmann, who first made me interested in Charles the Bald. There are new debts too: to David Bates, who expended so much critical skill and patience on an early draft and to the Academic Department at Longman who gave such cheerful and expert help. Without them all this book might never have materialised. (Its remaining shortcomings are mine; and I am keenly aware that in a short book on a large theme, much has had to be left out or thinly covered).

Special thanks, finally, to Chris and Fritz Groothues, Jane and Howard Brenton, Mary Restieaux and Ted White (who insisted, in La Marteille and in London, that this book actually be finished); to my children, Lizzie and Billy, for good-humoured intolerance of my work-schedule; and most of all to my husband Howard who knew (sometimes despite appearances) that CB wasn't the most important man in my life.

A NOTE ON NAMES

I have not managed (any more than ninth-century writers did) to avoid some inconsistency in my use of the name *Francia* : it sometimes means the Frankish heartlands between the Rhineland and the Seine basin, sometimes the heartlands of Charles's kingdom west of the Scheldt. Context, the index-references, will, I hope, clarify which is meant in particular cases. Personal names are given in their simplest form, anglicised where suitable (e.g. 'Louis' for *Hludovicus*, 'Harvey' for *Heriveus*). Given the small stock of Carolingian names and therefore the frequency of homonyms, I have followed medieval writers in using distinguishing nicknames. I have also differentiated Charles the Bald's son as 'Carloman' from Louis the German's son 'Karlmann'. In saints' names, there is no hyphen where an individual is meant: the hyphen indicates a reference to a religious institution (thus: 'Charles was devoted to St Denis'; but: 'Charles spent Easter at St-Denis').

LIST OF ABBREVIATIONS

AAng	*Annals of Angoulême*
AA SS	*Acta Sanctorum*
AB	*Annals of St-Bertin*
AF	*Annals of Fulda*
AFont	*Annals of Fontenelle (St-Wandrille)*
AM	*Annales du Midi*
ASC	*Anglo-Saxon Chronicle*
AX	*Annals of Xanten*
AV	*Annals of St-Vaast*

B.	R.-H. Bautier (ed.), *Actes de Louis II le Bègue*
BEC	Bibliothèque de l'École des Chartes
BISI	*Bollettino dell'Istituto Storico Italiano per il medio evo*

CCM	*Cahiers de Civilisation médiévale*
CMH	*Cambridge Medieval History*

DA	*Deutsches Archiv für die Erforschung des Mittelalters*

EHR	*English Historical Review*

FMS	*Frühmittelalterliche Studien*

GC	*Gallia Christiana*

HZ	*Historische Zeitschrift*

L.	L. Levillain (ed.), *Actes de Pépin I et Pépin II, rois d'Aquitaine*

Lauer	P. Lauer (ed.), *Recueil des Actes de Charles le Simple*
L/G	L. Levillain and F. Grat (eds), *Les Annales de Saint-Bertin*
LM	*Lexikon des Mittelalters*
MA	*Le Moyen Age*
Mansi	J.-D. Mansi (ed.), *Sacrorum Conciliorum Nova et Amplissima Collectio*, 31 vols, Florence 1757–98
MGH	*Monumenta Germaniae Historica*
Capit.	*Capitularia regum Francorum*
Conc	*Concilia*
Epp	*Epistolae*
Fontes	*Fontes Iuris Germanici Antiquae*
Poet.Lat.	*Poetae Latini Karolini Aevi*
SRG	*Scriptores rerum germanicarum in usum scholarum*
SSRL	*Scriptores rerum Langobardorum*
SSRM	*Scriptores rerum Merovingicarum*
SS	*Scriptores*
NCE	*New Catholic Encyclopedia*
PL	J.-P. Migne (ed.), *Patrologia Latina*, 221 vols, Paris 1841–64
RFA	*Royal Frankish Annals (Annales regni Francorum)*
RH	*Revue Historique*
RHE	*Revue d'Histoire Ecclésiastique*
SCH	*Studies in Church History*
SS Spoleto	*Settimane di Studio di Centro Italiano di Studi sull'alto medioevo*
T.	G. Tessier (ed.), *Receuil des Actes de Charles II le Chauve*
WaG	*Die Welt als Geschichte*

FOR HOWARD, LIZZIE AND BILLY

Chapter 1

INTRODUCTION

'La victoire de Charles-le-Chauve sépara la France de
l'empire d'Occident et fonda l'indépendance de la nation
française'.

That was how, in 1860, Frenchmen commemorated the
battle of Fontenoy in 841, fought between the grandsons of
Charlemagne around a windswept hill in northern Burgundy.[1] The issue was mastery of western Christendom,
over which Charlemagne had been crowned emperor on
Christmas Day 800. The victory of Charles the Bald (823–
877) and his brother Louis over their elder brother the
Emperor Lothar resulted in a division of Charlemagne's inheritance that has proved permanent. Charlemagne himself, at once 'French' and 'German', has always been a
powerful symbol of European domination, a model for
both Napoleon and Kaiser Wilhelm II. Modern Frenchmen
and Germans have disputed possession of Charlemagne.
Charles the Bald, by contrast, could be appropriated by the
French in the nineteenth century: hence the erection of
the obelisk at Fontenoy by a group of local patriots. Charles was often to be invoked in the 1860s: Napoleon III's
choice of Compiègne for one of his favourite imperial palaces recalled the French nation's ninth-century 'founder'.
It was an understandable choice in an age of burgeoning
national myths. Caesar's Gaul had been bounded by the
'natural frontiers' of the North Sea and the Mediterranean,
the Pyrenees and the Rhine, and France was its direct de-
scendant – via the 'French' kingdom of Charles the Bald.

1   Inscription on the obelisk erected on the battle-site at Fontenoy-en-
    Puisaye (dep. Yonne): 'The victory of Charles-the-Bald (!) separated
    France from the Empire of the West and founded the inde-
    pendence of the French nation'. For Charlemagne and his de-
    scendants, see Genealogies I and II.

In fact French unity and French nationality were largely post-medieval; and they were *un*natural. For Charles's was a kingdom of manmade frontiers, superimposed on nature. The Carolingians' heartlands, that is, the area where most of their estates were clustered, and where Franks had been settled for centuries, spanned modern Belgium and the Netherlands, northern France, and western Germany, thus lying athwart the 'natural' frontiers of the Ardennes forest, and the rivers Meuse and Rhine. Carolingians also flouted 'natural' frontiers when they divided their lands. In 806, for instance, Charlemagne imagined for his second son Pippin a *regnum* (literally: area ruled over) comprising Italy and Bavaria, which made sense because of historic links between the two regions but overrode the Alps. Charles the Bald's brother Louis, who (though the Frenchmen of 1860 chose to forget it) had fought alongside Charles at Fontenoy, was called *rex Germaniae* ('king of Germany') by contemporaries who knew the classics, because his kingdom was (like Caesar's *Germania*) 'across the Rhine'. But in the ninth century, it was only writers in Charles's kingdom who labelled Louis thus: in his own kingdom Louis was known as 'king of the eastern Franks'. In fact that East Frankish kingdom included lands on the west bank of the Rhine, as well as, further east, regions inhabited by Saxons, Bavarians and Alemans. In the eighth century, as the Franks had imposed their domination over those they called 'subject peoples', Frankish kings had come to rule over many *regna*, not only far west as well as east of the Rhine, but beyond the Alps and beyond the Pyrenees.

Regna were artificial things. Carolingian rulers didn't just receive them as a given: rather, they created, recreated, shaped them for themselves. Aquitaine, for instance, was the name of an old Roman province; but the shape of the Carolingian *regnum* of that name was a Carolingian creation – which also was quite different from Eleanor's twelfth-century duchy. There were some striking continuities in terms of the survival of Roman law and custom and language. But it is easier to show that the Aquitanians' identity as a people was imposed on them rather than felt by them in Carolingian times. The political units of the ninth century were thus very different from those imagined by nineteenth-century patriots. Nowadays, for convenience, modern historians label Charles the Bald's kingdom West Francia. But no-one used that label in the ninth century; nor did Charles ever call himself king of the West Franks: his own royal title was simply 'king by the grace of God'. His contemporaries spoke of 'Charles's kingdom (*regnum*)', and distinguished within it peoples and *regna*: Francia, Burgundy, Gothia (or Septimania) and Aquitaine. This group of *regna* had seldom been ruled by the same person before 840; and after 840, continuing or permanent union was not foreseen. Charles the Bald himself divided his kingdom, as his predecessors had done theirs, between some of his sons, recreating *regna* within his own *regnum*. Throughout his reign, Charles coexisted with other Carolingians (his brothers and nephews) in territories that had once been ruled as an empire, the *regnum Francorum*, by Charles's grandfather Charlemagne and his father Louis the Pious. Thus the same word – *regnum* – was used for the whole and for both larger and smaller parts. For us this is confusing. Why did mid-ninth-century people see no incongruity there? To pose the question is a form of anachronism. Hindsight makes it possible to distinguish ideal from reality, illusion from conceivable outcome. It takes some imagination to share the contradictions, the unrealised hopes, the might-have-beens, of the past. Who in the ninth century could have foreseen modern France?

In Charles's generation, rival Carolingians competed for royal resources within a *regnum francorum* which, however divided, had been, and might again be, one. (The late-twentieth-century history of 'Germany' shows that collective memories of unity can outlast a generation of partition.) Hence Carolingian diplomacy was not like modern international relations, where each state recognises the others' rights to permanent existence and a defined territory. In the ninth-century 'state-system', each component was itself unstable. Just as within a family holding, division in each generation was partly offset by not just accident but longer-term strategies (cousin-marriage; the offloading of surplus heirs into the Church) that restored unity, so shifts in the shape of the royal family, unpredictable but generally divisive in the short run, were offset by a longer-term impulsion to re-form a united whole. The ninth century's ambiguous use of the term *regnum*, therefore, accurately reflects this historic indeterminacy and open-endedness. It was the kings' collective identity as a family, clearly marked out by their distinctive names, that gave the Carolingian world a political unity underlying successive partitions. The interest shown by so many ninth-century chroniclers, wherever they were based, in what was going on in other parts of that world, and specifically, in what kings did, reflects a persisting reality.

Charles's position in the family remained that of younger brother almost throughout his life. Lothar, the eldest of Louis the Pious's legitimate sons, had acquired the title of emperor even before Charles was born, and dominated his generation until his death in 855. Thereafter Louis the German was the senior member of the family: some seventeen years older than his half-brother Charles, he lived to the ripe age of seventy. Charles outlived him by hardly more than a year: his life was thus in a sense overshadowed by Louis, constantly subject to fraternal political pressure, his kingdom twice fraternally-invaded, his ultimate imperial plans beset by fraternal rivalry. Louis's and Charles's careers were intertwined, therefore; and neither can be fully understood in isolation, still less within the frame of a national history. The recent treatment of Charles the Bald alone, or in a 'French' context, by several British historians has tended to obscure this broader geographic dimension of Carolingian familial politics.

Nevertheless, two hundred years after Charles's death, the inhabitants of the lands he had once ruled were identified as *Kerlinger, Carlenses*: 'Charles's men';[2] and in the thirteenth century, when King Louis IX arranged at St-Denis the tombs of the kings who had preceded him, he left two in positions of special honour, the Merovingian Dagobert, greatest of the First Frankish dynasty, and Charles the Bald.[3] The pages that follow will help to explain how this could have come about: how Charles, partly by conscious action, but also in spite of himself, played a crucial part in France's making. That is only a secondary aim of this book, however. My prime aim is to understand Charles in his own times: what he did, what world he moved in, what sort of man he was.

---

2   *Gesta of the Bishops of Cambrai* III, 2, 40, *MGH SS* VII, pp. 466, 481.
3   Hallam 1982; Erlande-Brandenbourg 1975: 79–83.

Evocations of Dark Age kingdoms are often a Grimms' fairy-tale picture of huge dark forests, dwarfing the puny efforts of humankind. For Charles and his contemporaries, the forests were a resource, in part artificially maintained, and certainly systematically exploited.[4] Cultivation of the land was intensive in some areas; and settlement quite dense. For nearly everyone, the countryside was home, not a wilderness or place of exile. Great rivers functioned, in ninth-century reality and in human imaginations, sometimes as arteries, sometimes as boundaries, and political units (counties, for instance) often straddled them. Take the Loire, for instance. Modern travellers going south from Paris are awestruck by its scale (though they cross, conveniently, by bridge). In the ninth century, one poet praised its beauty, while another drowned in it; salt-traders and vintners plied it as a matter of routine; nobles and religious communities with estates on both sides of it had boats ready for regular crossings and landing-stages where their men could send off surplus produce for sale and unload imports for their masters' consumption; Vikings contemplated arduous upstream journeys, but quick getaways; Charles the Bald, worried over strategic problems, planned the river's blocking, and policing, and also exploited the symbolic possibilities of meetings at Orléans, Fleury, Cosne, Meung, Pouilly to which nobles must come from Aquitaine by crossing the river while Charles himself received his visitors on the Frankish side. So, any reading of landscape as evidence needs to take account of the varied meanings as well as uses which people imposed on their environment.

Ecclesiastical geography again shows the ninth-century landscape manmade. The *civitates* where bishops had their palaces and churches were inherited from Roman times. (I use the Latin term to avoid anachronistic associations: though nearly all *civitates* have become modern towns and cities, their urban character in the ninth century is problematic.[5]) The distribution of monasteries and cult-centres in the rural landscape reflected the location of royal and noble estates, and lay patrons' choices of holy men. Religious communities at St-Martin, Tours, or St-Denis near

4   Wickham 1990.
5   See below, Ch. 2: 36–7; Ch. 3: 51.

Paris, had grown up at the tombs of martyrs in cemetery sites outside Roman *civitates*, and by the ninth century housed over a hundred clergy or monks apiece. Other monasteries – St-Riquier near Amiens, and St-Vaast at Arras, for instance – were certainly centres of economic production and exchange in the ninth century. The label 'proto-urban' fits none of these places very comfortably, however. Little ninth-century architecture remains above ground in any of these sites, though a rare surviving ninth-century crypt, as at St-Denis, or still rarer frescoes, as at St-Germain, Auxerre, or (perhaps most impressive of all) the sombre magnificence and elaborately-structured space of Charlemagne's church at Aachen, give the modern visitor a unique insight into the religious experience of Charles and his contemporaries. Even where documents are available, historians need a lot of imagination to reconstruct any kind of Carolingian site. In Britain, archaeology has thrown a great deal of light on the Dark Ages: but British students, when they turn to the ninth-century Continent, are in for a disappointment, for relatively little has been done. Recently, however, in June 1989, the skeleton of Charles's cousin Nithard was disinterred in the graveyard at St-Riquier; and archaeologists are confident of having located Charles's fortification at Pîtres (near Pont-de-l'Arche, dep. Eure) and the ninth-century *emporium* at Quentovic (near Montreuil, dep. Pas-de-Calais): both remarkably extensive sites.[6]

Other kinds of non-written material offer crucial evidence. Coin finds can help in reconstructing the economic history of this period. The material environment of secular life at any social level has to be reconstructed from even less direct evidence, since, unfortunately, very few ninth-century weapons or jewels, tools or items of household equipment, survive. The lists of possessions bequeathed in aristocratic wills – horses, hunting-dogs and hawks, swords and daggers, belts and baldrics, body-armour, spurs, cloaks and furs, bracelets and rings, drinking-cups and silver dishes – allow a glimpse of this world we have lost. The same wills also list the liturgical objects – crosses, plates,

6   Bernard 1989; Hassall and Hill 1970; Dearden 1989, 1990; Hodges 1990a: 212–3.

censers, bells, candle-sticks – that furnished these nobles' chapels, and the reliquaries made of precious metals and precious stones and housing fragments of saints' bones, hair and beards, or even the names of holy men, which the rich and powerful kept in their treasuries, or even wore around their necks.[7] Poor people, unable to privatise the holy in this way, crowded to shrines where they were welcomed by the custodians of miracle-working relics.[8] Books used in the liturgy were holy objects, often encased in jewelled bookcovers, and placed on altars or carried in processions to inspire and impress the faithful.[9] On the other hand, the audience for the images that were sometimes drawn and painted inside such books – portraits of the evangelists, for instance, or (like the picture on the cover of this book) of a royal patron – must have been very restricted.

The written word more generally is another story: its wide dissemination then is very good news for the historian now. An enormous quantity of written material was produced in Charles's kingdom – from huge, splendid documents to crudely-penned words on small scraps of grubby parchment. The relative importance of these items to those who wrote and kept them can't be assessed in terms of size or splendour. Charms, relic-labels, records of land-grants or dispute-settlements often strike modern palaeographers as unimpressive objects. Ninth-century users had their own criteria of utility, and they preferred to use oral alongside written communications in most contexts. Their attitudes to written records can seem cavalier, and contradictory. Even scholars intent on appropriating the classical inheritance did so for their own reasons: Abbot Lupus of Ferrières made his command of Cicero's letters serve as a sort of code in communicating with learned friends, while Archbishop Hincmar of Rheims compiled extracts from the Theodosian Code and then cited them to suit his own book.[10] Still, the Carolingian Renaissance in the mid-ninth century touched far more than just a select clerical few. Charlemagne had begun with the clergy, encouraging them

7　Riché 1981 (1972); cf. Dhuoda IV, 1, pp. 202–5.
8　Head 1990; Geary 1991.
9　McKitterick 1989: ch. 4.
10　Lupus, below Ch. 6: 166; Hincmar, Devisse 1962: 42–62.

to learn and write correct Latin for the liturgy; two generations later, the lay elite in Charles's kingdom used writing
in several different forms, from books of private prayer to
family archives, while many laypeople of lesser rank wanted
documents as evidence of their own property claims and
legal status. Surviving written texts thus reflect (directly or
indirectly) the concerns of a much larger proportion of the
population than we have evidence for in the period before
the ninth century. The amount of material available to provide a context for Charles the Bald is very extensive indeed.

Evidence for political affairs comes in a variety of genres:
some apparently unlikely sources – theological treatises, for
instance, or accounts of the translations (that is, the carryings to new locations) of saints' relics, and collections of
miracle-stories – turn out to hold a good deal of information about (and reactions to) war and politics. This makes
sense: war and politics were perceived by lay participants as
subject to supernatural interventions that could be magically invoked as well as interpreted – hence the important
role of churchmen and their rituals in these areas of public
contestation and conflict, for instance in not just the retrospective presentation but the preliminary 'staging' of battles as Judgements of God.[11] Ninth-century annals and
histories deal directly with public affairs and provide a
more or less reliable framework of political events; but they
too are shot through with perceptions of the miraculous,
and they are, at the same time, highly personal works (as
historical writing usually is), full of bias and image-making,
whether written (as many were) for the king's entourage,
or for an audience far away from the court. But the sheer
quantity of such texts and the variety of their intended
readers and hearers means that some cross-referencing is
possible. This is the nearest ninth-century specialists can
get to methodological rigour: we should have no illusions
about our limitations, nor about some still-enormous gaps
in available evidence. The so-called *Annals of St-Bertin* (so
called simply because one manuscript survived later in the
Middle Ages at the monastery of St-Bertin) were produced
in Charles the Bald's kingdom, more or less contemporaneously with the events they record, throughout Charles's

11   For examples below, Chs 5: 117; 9: 245.

reign.[12] The *AB* do not constitute a court chronicle: successive *AB* authors (Prudentius, then Hincmar of Rheims) had their local concerns, their blind spots, and their own axes to grind. But their unofficial quality brings gains as well as losses: these writers are often passionately involved in the events they record. There is nothing dry-as-dust about their testimony. Further, it can be checked against other contemporary annals, whether produced in Charles's kingdom but giving a perspective very different from the *AB*'s (the brief Annals of the monastery of Fontanelle, or St-Wandrille, near modern Le Havre, for instance, have their own house-based story to tell), or written in another Carolingian kingdom, like the East Frankish *Annals of Fulda* which are just as slanted as the *AB*, but in a different direction.[13]

One type of evidence comes in very much larger quantities from Charles's kingdom than from any other in the ninth century: capitularies – that is, lists of points (*capitula* literally means 'headings') discussed and/or adopted as law by assemblies where king and aristocracy met to settle public affairs. Plentiful capitulary material means that a good deal can be said about Charles as a ruler. But for the politics of the reign, two kinds of material are still more useful – and available in quantity: personal letters; and royal *acta*. The letters of Lupus, for instance, reveal networks of personal connections, links between court and local community, workings of assemblies – and their egocentricity can, again, be turned to the historian's advantage. Royal *acta*, especially charters, but also letters and judgements, allow the pattern of royal patronage to be reconstructed; and incidentally give information on the king's itinerary and sometimes his entourage. Last but certainly not least, all these materials have been expertly edited, and discussed in a great many learned articles, by earlier generations of Continental scholars. Anyone in the late twentieth century who studies Charles the Bald is perched on the shoulders of those giants.[14]

---

12 Nelson 1991a. All references below are to my translation.
13 Reuter 1991b. On these and other annals, see below: 269–70.
14 Among them, the names of Lot and Levillain deserve special mention. See the Bibliography below.

The writing of a biography is simply impossible for more than a few major churchmen and even fewer secular rulers in the early Middle Ages. In the case of Charles the Bald, though, given the rich documentation, and the giants' spadework, the surprising thing (to invert Dr Johnson on women preachers) is not that it's been done badly, but that – with two partial exceptions – it has *not* been done at all. The exceptions deserve attention. Paul Zumthor's short book, published in 1957,[15] is the work of a historian of culture: a dramatic sketch, full of passion and tragedy, brilliant on some ninth-century writers, but with little reference to capitularies or charters, long on psychology, but short on political analysis. This is literary biography at its most stylish. There are no footnotes. At the opposite historiographical pole is the study of Charles's reign projected by Arthur Giry (d. 1899) in the late nineteenth century and pursued by Ferdinand Lot and his young collaborator Louis Halphen in the early twentieth. Giry's models were the volumes of *Jahrbucher* (year-books) which German scholars had produced for the reigns of other Carolingians: strictly chronological accounts conceived quite literally as annals. (Giry had also begun a translation of the *AB*.) Lot was inspired by Ernst Dümmler's *Geschichte des ostfränkischen Reiches*, to write not annals but a history of Charles's reign: 'But we have kept tightly within the frame of our subject: while M. Duemmler, under colour of writing the history of the East Frankish kingdom, has dealt almost as much with the history of Italy, of Lotharingia, of West Francia, we have devoted ourselves uniquely to the study of this last country, seen from a political point of view'.[16] For this kind of history, Lot like Giry thought charters of fundamental importance, and he 'encumbered his footnotes' (his own deliciously ironic phrase!) with charter-analyses. Lot and Halphen's 'volume 1' (1909) covered the period 840 to early 851. It is magnificent, but it is not the kind of historical writing that brings a dead world to life for late twentieth-century students. The projected three further volumes never appeared. Lot confessed that the preparatory work

15 And reprinted in 1981.
16 This and the following quotes are from Lot's preface to Lot and Halphen 1909: iv–v.

seemed 'endless'. I can sympathise with him: but I have not attempted to write his kind of history.

Since my focus is on politics, why write a biography? Studying the past by reigns is certainly artificial, and risks obscuring in this case, for instance, the intimate links between the various parts of the Carolingian world, and the profound continuities linking the mid-ninth century to the immediately preceding and succeeding periods. More seriously, it may be anachronistic to highlight one man as the unit for study – for it could be argued that 'the individual' had not yet been discovered. Instead, early medieval literature and iconography alike focused on exemplars of a type, a group or a status: royalty, for instance, or the royal family.[17] So-called 'ruler-portraits' nearly always turn out to be stereotypes: in the context of Carolingian group-identity, the precise point about images of Charles the Bald was the resemblance to Louis the Pious and Charlemagne, his father and grandfather. We have what sounds like an accurate personal description of Charles: 'of middle height, good-looking, fit for all sorts of exercise, bold, generous, shrewd and good at public speaking'. In the same breath, the writer attributes identical traits to Charles's brother.[18] In other words, both kings are being depicted as kingly. Charles and his contemporaries did not appeal for authority to individual judgement or experience: instead they invoked shared role-models and peer-group pressure. Isolation was a prospect Charles would confront (so Archbishop Hincmar reminded him) terrifyingly in the next world: 'when the soul has left power and riches and the body itself, and is left naked and alone, without wife and children, and without the comfort and fellowship of followers and vassals'.[19] The king's life in *this* world was anything but private.

Yet a royal biography has two great advantages. First, its concern with a king, his personality and his personal relationships, goes with the grain of early medieval politics. The

17 Cf. Dhuoda's view of the royal kin; below Ch. 3: 41.
18 Nithard III, 6.
19 Quierzy letter 858, *MGH Conc.* III, no. 41, pp. 403–27. Hincmar overtly addressed Louis the German, but revealed in *MGH Epp.* VIII, no. 126, p. 64, that he had intended this letter as much for Charles, to whom he also sent a copy.

qualities of individual kings really did shape events, and accidents of birth and death in a royal family could determine not only short-term alliances and conflicts, but the long-term destinies of peoples and regions. A fairly long, extremely active and relatively well-documented royal life like that of Charles the Bald can serve modern students as a thread through the maze of complex power-relations, and at the same time it leads back to the heart of events. Second, an individual's life has an intelligible shape and built-in human interest. 'The affairs of mortals touch our hearts.' Historical biography may be hard to write, but it draws more readers to history than any other genre.

Historical biographers tend to work within their own national boundaries, and to prefer as subjects the Good Kings of national history. Though my 'frame' is a life rather than a realm, I think an understanding of the Carolingian world requires the transgression of modern national boundaries. I certainly do not share the view of Charles Plummer nearly a century ago (when the fate of Napoleon III was still fresh enough to point an implicit moral), that Charles the Bald was 'a typical Frenchman in many respects, intellectually clever but caring only for the outward pomp and circumstance of empire without the strength of character to grasp and hold the reality of power'.[20] I hope that French as well as British and other readers will find Charles the Bald interesting – but not because he was French. Charles has never been cast as a Good King in the nation-building mould of his contemporary Alfred of Wessex: he would surely not have minded – for he was a Frank, not a Frenchman. On the other hand, Charles had an undeniable impact on the subsequent history of France – arguably no less of an impact than Alfred had on the subsequent history of England. What makes all the difference is the perceived nature of the impact. In Charles's case, Montesquieu has a lot to answer for. In *The Spirit of Laws*, Charles's was identified as the reign when 'the whole of the French political state' was changed and weakened. Montesquieu did not omit the deficiencies of Charles's father Louis the Pious, nor the contributory factors of French fickleness and Viking destruction: but he put the chief blame on the 'weak

20   Plummer 1902: 78.

spirit of Charles the Bald' and, in particular, on the heritability of fiefs which Charles had permitted.[21] Thus France after the high ground of the early Middle Ages descended into a trough from which the nation would be raised only centuries later by the great Capetians Philip Augustus and St Louis: feudal monarchs who defused feudalism. This still widely-held interpretation of ninth-century history, and of Charles the Bald as a Bad King, is there in embryo in the final section of Montesquieu's book. It proved remarkably durable – leaving its mark, for instance, on two of the medieval history-books most read by Frenchmen in the twentieth century: Marc Bloch's *Feudal Society* and F.L. Ganshof's *Feudalism*. Yet, at last, in some cases surprisingly recently, most aspects of this picture have been revised. National prejudices have waned; stereotyped 'feudalism' has been demolished; Carolingian government has been newly appraised; reassessments have been offered of Louis the Pious, of the Vikings, even of the ninth-century Frankish nobility. It seems high time that Charles the Bald too was reconsidered.

Charles's nickname has not helped. More than one modern historian has enjoyed wrestling with the question: was Charles the Bald really bald? The nickname was a contemporary one,[22] a means of distinguishing this Charles from other Carolingians with the same name. It may have been not descriptive but ironic (implying Charles was exceptionally hairy). In the ninth century as later, baldness struck some people as funny.[23] Then as later, bald men liked to rebut the jokers by recalling great bald men of the past. Charles the Bald, if he was bald, was no doubt happy to be classed with famous emperors of antiquity. But what mattered more to him was his given name: Charles. He had been named after his grandfather, whose nickname *magnus*, originally meaning the 'elder' or 'senior' one, was already in the ninth century acquiring the connotations of greatness it has kept ever since. Charles the Bald was said to resemble his grandfather physically. The only contemporary image of Charlemagne is on a few of his coins. Nine 'portraits' of Charles the Bald are extant: five depicted in

21 Montesquieu 1989: 672, 701–2, 708.
22 Jäschke 1970.
23 Godman 1987: 180–1.

13

manuscripts; one carved in ivory; two cast in metal; and finally a coin-image.[24] Some of these images may be partly taken from life, not just from stereotyped Carolingian ruler images. Charles is depicted with a distinctive long, thin moustache (not quite like his eldest brother's), a long, heavy-jowled face, square chin and a large nose. He must have been physically fit to survive the punishing schedule to which he submitted himself. The bouts of ill-health occasionally recorded (they were always politically inconvenient) became frequent only during his last years, but even then scarcely diminished the pace of a very active life. (Charles may have picked up malaria in Italy in 875: he was seriously ill from late July to mid-August 876, and from December 876 to January 877.[25])

And his personality? Lupus of Ferrières reveals something of what it was like to be within close range of Charles. Lupus feared his anger and advised others not to provoke it ('I consider it dangerous to obstruct the king's orders'); felt hurt when Charles very obviously 'doesn't care about the things that matter to me'; appreciated Charles's personally 'asking me at Bourges not long ago what I felt about Predestination'; and was well aware that Charles 'has a face that he puts on when he wants to be charming'.[26] Charles the Bald, in other words, had the two-facedness of successful medieval kings: his friendly smile could win loyalty, his frown could terrify.[27] He was a man of exceptional persistence, who confronted his many setbacks with an apparently inexhaustible supply of energy and re-

24 For the manuscript images (incidentally, Charles seems not to be bald in these), see Schramm and Mütherich 1983: pl. 36–8, 40–1 (Tours and San Paolo Bibles, Psalter, Prayer-book, Codex Aureus), and 165–70; the throne-ivory, Nees 1990: 345; the bronze panel of the Ellwangen Casket, Schramm 1968(ii): 110–8 and plate 21; and the Metz rider-statuette (often wrongly taken to depict Charlemagne), Mütherich 1975. For the Bourges portrait coin I am grateful for information and a photograph from Simon Coupland.

25 Decour 1972. Charles had already been seriously ill in 874 however.

26 Lupus Epp. 67, 72, 78 and 52.

27 For examples of Charles's wrath, see below: 139, 171, and 229; for Hincmar of Rheims's rather shocked allusion to Charles's public dressing-down of the bishop of Laon, PL 125, col. 1039. Auerbach 1965: 131 suggests that Charles was 'motivated . . . by sadistic duplicity', and links this with his upbringing 'amid the vilest intrigues'! See below, Ch. 4.

sourcefulness. It was no wonder that Hercules seemed an apt role-model.[28]

In many ways Charles was a man of his time. He was personally devout: participated enthusiastically in the cults of saints, especially St Denis; begged saintly intercession when he had toothache; requested the compilation of an exhaustive martyrology; wanted an explanation of a puzzling passage in the Song of Solomon.[29] He possessed a little book of private prayers, with an image of himself kneeling before Christ on the cross captioned with a prayer that Christ 'absolve my wounds for me' – a reference to sins which also likened the king's sufferings to Christ's. The book's ivory covers depicted, on the basis of Psalms 25 and 27 (Vulgate 24, 26), a biography of David that implicitly was also Charles's own – from secure childhood with the support of 'father and mother', through the assaults of 'wicked enemies' with the support of 'the innocent and upright', to a secure sanctuary with Christ. Charles's personal copy of the psalter (a manuscript designed for daily devotions) also had ivory covers, showing the prophet Nathan's rebuke of David for his liaison with Bathsheba (Ps 51, Vulg 50) and the protection of David's soul (Ps 57, Vulg 56) depicted as a little child on the lap of a kindly angel.[30] Charles's court-scholars often encouraged him to find inspiration and confidence in the story of David.

Charles's relationship with each of his successive wives seems to have been harmonious, and (unlike David's) fitted contemporary conventions. No infidelities are recorded. Charles saw to the liturgical commemoration of his parents and grandparents, his wives and offspring, but not of any more distant relatives.[31] He seems never to have

---

28 Gussone and Staubach 1975.
29 For Charles's devotion to St Denis, see Brown 1989: 330–410; his response to *dolor dentium*, T. 182; his request for Usuard's Martyrology, Dubois 1965; his request for elucidation of the *ferculum Salomonis*, Taeger 1977.
30 Deshman 1980; cf. Bullough 1975; Wollasch 1984.
31 Rouche 1984.

been close to his sister.[32] With his children, he had problems fairly typical of medieval royal families.[33] He could be ruthless, even to the extent of having his own rebellious son blinded. (Contemporaries accepted that violence even within the heart of the family might be a cruel necessity.) But Charles could prove himself a good lord: when his *fidelis* (faithful man) Adalgar was captured by Charles's half-sister (she supported her full brother Lothar in the fraternal conflict of 841) and taken to her stronghold of Laon, Charles rode through the night with a small retinue to achieve Adalgar's release. (A contemporary was equally impressed by the fact that Charles was able to restrain his men from sacking Laon.)[34] Loyal service was recognised when Charles arranged for the commemoration at St-Denis of two particularly close *fideles*, extending to them benefits until then made available only to the king's blood-relatives.[35]

Throughout his life Charles attracted the young and ambitious to his court. In his entourage of personal servants and clients, along with an Irish doctor and scholar-poet (who seems to have stayed for nearly thirty years in Charles's circle), he had a court-jester.[36] The king's sense of humour seems to have been appropriately dark. One possibly apocryphal joke of Charles's own was made late one night 'after many dishes and many cups' at the expense of the Irish poet: Charles leaned across and asked: 'Quid distat inter sottum et scottum' (what separates a drunk from an Irishman?) But that time at least, the Irishman (it was John the Scot) got his own back by replying: 'My lord, only this table'.[37]

---

32 There is no evidence for contact between Charles and Gisèle, his own full sibling, until after the death of her husband Marquis Eberhard of Friuli, in 864 or 865. Gisèle referred warily to 'King Charles, my – if I dare call him so – brother', in two private charters of 869 and 870, *Cart. Cysoing*, nos 3 and 4, pp. 7–8. Her son Berengar opposed Charles in Italy in 875–6; *AB* 875: 188 and n. 6.
33 Nelson 1988b; Schieffer 1990.
34 Nithard III, 4.
35 T. 379. Cf. Ewig 1982.
36 For the Irish doctor-poet (John the Scot) and the jester, T. 75. For Charles's Jewish doctor, *AB* 877: 202. For a Jewish *fidelis* and messenger, T. 417.
37 William of Malmesbury, *Gesta Pontificum* 1870: 392. The story dates from the twelfth century.

Two other traits Charles may have owed to the influence of his father Louis the Pious, though he pursued both a good deal further than Louis. First, Charles was highly-educated (and here he seems to have benefited from his mother's personal concern), not only sharing the interest of ecclesiastical contemporaries in theology and political ideas, but learned enough to pose convincingly as a philosopher-ruler and knowledgeable enough about Roman Law to attempt self-conscious emulation of Theodosius and Justinian in his own capitularies.[38] Second, he had a strong visual sense and a taste for ritual. He made far more play than his father (or other ninth-century Carolingians) with the penalty of the *harmscara* – a public humiliation imposed at the ruler's discretion which involved the victim's carrying a saddle on his back. Charles repeatedly threatened this for those who flouted his authority.[39] He staged lavish spectacles to signify the granting of favour to a subordinate-ruler, again 'in the style of Roman emperors' and made the most of the great assemblies in which king and aristocracy joined to 'maintain the healthy condition of the whole realm'.[40] He also mobilised the resources of Christian ritual (again following in his father's footsteps but going far beyond him) in the royal and imperial consecrations staged not only for himself and his son but for Ermentrude and Richildis;[41] in the development of royal funerary cult at St-Denis and in the lavish endowment of liturgical commemorations of himself, his family and friends, at a number of churches;[42] and in the use of spiritual kinship, especially the godparental bond, in political dealings with neighbouring princes as a paradigm of beneficent authority.[43] All these demonstrations of rulership had an afterlife long after Charles himself had gone. Even when assemblies rarely if ever met and capitularies were no

38 Wallace-Hadrill 1978; Nelson 1989b.
39 *MGH Capit.* II, nos. 259, 266, 270, 273, 275, 281, pp. 269, 287, 299, 319, 335, 358. For what was involved see the capitulary of Louis II of Italy, Capit. II, no. 218, p. 96.
40 Regino 877: 113; Nelson 1986a (1983).
41 Below, Ch. 6: 154–5; Ch. 7: 174; Ch. 8: 210, 219; Ch. 9: 242, 244. Cf. also the marriage-rite of Charles's daughter Judith, Ch. 7: 182.
42 For the broader context of such concerns, Angenendt 1984b.
43 Especially illuminating on this is Smith 1992. See further Angenendt 1984a .

longer read, the idea of the realm survived in myth, symbol and tradition. It was at that level that a thread of continuity linked Charles with his Capetian successors, and his realm with later medieval France.[44] Charles's reign therefore is interesting both in itself and for what came after. This book's purpose is to show Charles as an archexponent of Carolingian political practice in an age when new (as well as old) problems beset all Charlemagne's successors but none more so than Charles. At the same time, this book helps to explain why Charles's exercise of rulership had long-term effects, and why his kingdom lasted.

44 See below Ch. 10.

Chapter 2

THE CAROLINGIAN ECONOMY AND THE STATE

'It was the best of times; it was the worst of times'. Characterisations of the ninth-century Carolingian world have been almost as polarised as Charles Dickens's portrayal of the French Revolution. When Henri Pirenne placed the demise of the antique state, with the collapse of its increasingly ramshackle economic life-support system, in the mid-eighth century, he identified the moment of transition from the sub-Roman world to the Dark Ages.[1] Much subsequent historiography has been in the nature of post-mortem investigation. Some have suggested that the time of death should be postdated to the ninth century, arguing that while the reign of Charlemagne (768–814) saw a last futile effort to revive a state-run fiscal system, *rigor mortis* finally set in with the new barbarian onslaughts of Vikings and Saracens.[2] There is agreement on the fatal symptoms: a stubborn refusal of the population to increase, a hardening of the arteries of exchange, a closing-off of transfusions of bullion from outside western Europe, a sclerosis of the fiscal and administrative body of the state.[3] The process of post-mortem decomposition has been traced through the ninth century. Archaeologists have come up with data at Dorestad, the trading *emporium* through which the Carolingian court had been supplied, showing protracted decline with, allegedly, a sharp downturn c. 830.[4] Some

---

1   Pirenne 1939. See Hodges and Whitehouse 1983; Verhulst 1989: 3–6.
2   Wickham 1984; cf. Bautier 1971: 49–57; Latouche 1961: 218.
3   Fossier 1981, 1986.
4   Van Es and Verwers 1980: 297–8.

numismatists have confirmed the picture of terminal decay: the Carolingians minted few coins, of which still fewer are said to show signs of having been used. In the course of the ninth century, the minting of coins to pay tributes to Vikings exhausted supplies of bullion that were already meagre. The renunciation of any attempt to tax was at once cause and symptom of the state's demise.[5]

Other historians, archaeologists and numismatists, especially in recent years, have offered a radically different view. They do not deny change; but where Pirenne's followers saw decomposition, they detect signs of economic activity of a new kind. They regard it as significant that the eighth and ninth century saw an increasing volume of exchanges not initiated by the state, but 'privately-generated'; and they look for the new wealth-creators among lords and peasants, finding in rural markets crucial mechanisms of exchange.[6] They advance evidence for population increase in the countryside, and for the expansion in agrarian production. They claim, further, that all this stimulated urban development. Against Dorestad's decline (which they attribute to particular local difficulties) they set the origins and/or thriving of Ghent and Bruges, Cologne and Mainz, Nantes and Angers.[7] Some scholars, especially those who have worked on English as well as Continental evidence, have recently been arguing for the role of kingship, if not in initiating, then in profiting from economic activity in both town and countryside. They point out that whereas merchants had always been welcome at royal courts as vendors of precious things, in the eighth century, and increasingly in the ninth and tenth centuries, kings embarked on more ambitious attempts to exploit systematically the resources of their realms.[8] It would follow that rumours of the death of the state have been exaggerated – or, at any rate, that early medieval conditions did not preclude the state's rebirth.

These two views of the early medieval economy are irreconcilable, but they have something in common. Both as-

5 Grierson 1965; Hendy 1988.
6 Duby 1974; Devroey 1985a; Hodges 1989, 1990a, 1990b; Metcalf 1990.
7 Musset 1974; Coupland 1988; Verhulst 1989.
8 Sawyer 1982; Metcalf 1990; Hodges 1989, 1990b; Maddicott 1989.

sume that the nature of government, indeed the existence of a state at all, depends on the type of resources available to a regime, and the ways in which these resources may be transferred. On the first scenario of catastrophic change, a crucial, redistributable, element in the Carolingian king's wealth was acquired largely from *outside* the realm. The king had at his disposal, not tax revenue, but plunder and tribute amassed through warfare. His armies consisted of nobles and their warrior-followings: hence instead of being a paymaster, the king allocated the proceeds of war through a network of personalised, 'privatised' relations of dependence that replaced public agencies of control and exploitation. The options boiled down to two: expand or die. Without constant inflows of *external* wealth through territorial acquisitions or through raiding, royal power could be maintained only through granting out bits of the fisc, that is, of royal estates. Hence the early medieval kingdom was not only fundamentally different from the tax-based Roman Empire, but inherently weak and unstable.[9] On this scenario, Charles the Bald, whose reign (840–77) fairly straddled the mid-ninth century, was doomed to failure: like Charlemagne, he lacked the institutional means to exploit even what wealth there was within his realm, but, unlike Charlemagne, he could no longer lead successful plundering raids against the surrounding peoples, nor keep his aristocracy happy with regular share-outs of loot. Charles's only alternative was to use royal lands to 'buy' support: a long historiographical tradition casts him as the archetypal squanderer of the fisc.[10] It was monarchic suicide: 'the worst of times'. Hence some recent advocates of Charles the Bald's partial 'rehabilitation' have damned with faint praise: the art-historians' artful exponent of royal style remains, for the historians of politics, a ruler without substantial authority.[11]

But the ninth century was neither the worst nor the best of times. It was an age of possibilities. Though Charles the Bald could not evade the type of political problems just outlined, he was predestined neither to success nor to

---

9   Reuter 1985.
10 For Montesquieu's views, see above Ch. 1, 13; cf. Dhondt 1948.
11 Riché 1983: 187–202; cf. Wallace-Hadrill 1978.

failure. He had some room to manoeuvre. So too has his historian, confronted by a growing body of evidence for change in the ninth-century economy. In the rest of this chapter, I shall argue that options were widened for Charles in part because increasing resources could be tapped *within* his kingdom.

The first type of evidence to consider is the polyptychs or estate-surveys.[12] All relate to ecclesiastical estates (church archives have far better chances of survival), but there is fragmentary evidence for similar surveys on royal estates too, and it seems fair to suppose that lay landlords could also have had them made. Given the fundamental importance of demography for any assessment of a pre-industrial economy, it is not surprising that economic historians have pressed the surveys into service (historians of medieval England have done the same sort of thing with Domesday Book) as sources of demographic data. Size of population is the first question: some polyptychs enumerate not only peasant households but individual members of them (as for instance: 'X, his wife Y, and their three children A, B and C have one *mansus* [peasant-holding]').[13] By totting up numbers for one group of estates, adding a notional 22 per cent for unrecorded children under twelve, and a further 25 per cent for other omissions, and then multiplying these for the whole of France, Lot calculated a population for Charles the Bald's kingdom of 26 million.[14] Most historians at the moment would regard that as a wild overestimate. But the polyptychs' data, even if it's unwise to generalise from them to the whole kingdom, may still be taken to show a relatively dense, if patchily distributed, population in the area they best cover, namely, that between the rivers Seine and Rhine. It just so

12 See map in Pounds 1974: 50 (showing the heavy concentration in the area between the Rivers Meuse and Seine); Fossier 1978; Davis 1987.

13 All peasants recorded in polyptychs are tenant-farmers: I am assuming these predominated in Francia proper. Landowning peasants are documented in some parts of the Carolingian world, for instance Italian mountain-zones, from the evidence of charters; Wickham 1981: 110–1; Wickham 1988: chapters 2, 12; cf. Davies 1988. Numbers, and household sizes, are difficult to assess without polyptych evidence.

14 Lot 1921. See criticisms of Doehaerd 1978: 41–2; Devroey 1981.

happens that this region includes the heartland of Charles the Bald's kingdom. A further question relates to possible movements in population size. The subdivision of *mansi* into fractions documented in some polyptychs has been held to suggest the pressure of rising population on land-holding, and evidence of land-clearance and the extension of the cultivated area could point the same way.[15] There is a speculative element here, for such patchy symptoms could be explained in other ways (for instance by increased consumption of cereals, or by the increasing impositions of lordship in some localities). But on the whole, a gradually rising population throughout the ninth century seems an acceptable working hypothesis.[16]

Polyptychs were not made to reveal population statistics. They record dues owed by peasants to landlords; and they are snapshots of particular points in time. Still, it is some-times possible to infer alterations *over* time, and one direct conclusion that can be drawn is that part, at least, of land-lords' rationale was economic: within a situation affected by such non-economic factors as pious donations, landlords organised estates and renders to maximise resources. This was a function of the domanial estate-structure (sometimes known to English-speaking historians as the manorial sys-tem), that is of a central directly-farmed agricultural unit, having peasant-tenements grouped around it and owing la-bour-services on it, and more distant tenements associated with it owing other types of dues and services. This doma-nial regime suited large-scale landlords with far-flung hold-ings (great monasteries were landlords of this type), and by Charles the Bald's reign, it had become general in much of what is now France north of the Loire with some examples also further south in Poitou.[17] The combination of labour-services, other services, and renders in cash and kind needed careful management. Take the example of St-Ger-main-des-Prés on the west bank of the Seine at Paris: here the landlord, the monastic community, organised peasant transport services not only so as to ensure the abbey's food supply but to permit the sale of surplus wine and corn. This landlord was clearly profiting from involvement in the

15 Duby 1974.
16 Doehaerd 1978: 61.
17 Rouche 1990.

market in basic foodstuffs: a market which stray references in contemporary chronicles and letters show to have been lively in the Seine basin during the ninth century.[18] In other words, the great domain, far from being a closed unit, required the market to dispose of its surpluses and to meet its needs for extraneous products. A great monastery might thus in the same year be an importer of quality wine (for consumption by the monks and their noble guests) and an exporter of poor wine (for the other end of the market).

The polyptychs reveal another important feature of economic management: the requirement of cash payments from peasants. How did a tenant acquire the pennies (say, 6d.-12d.) to pay his annual rent? The inference that he did so by selling is supported by the incidental evidence of miracle-stories: one from St-Benoît-sur-Loire, for instance, recorded in the 870s, tells of two 'comrades' (*compares*) at the monastery's weekly market, who quarrelled over the 12d. they had made on their joint transactions; another story of similar date from St-Hubert in the Ardennes has a peasant (*rusticus*) stating quite explicitly that he has come to an annual fair 'to acquire the wherewithal to pay what I owe to my lord'.[19] A charter of Charles the Bald in 875 exempted the peasants of St-Philibert, Tournus, in Burgundy from market dues 'whether they are trading for the abbey or for themselves'.[20] It's true that surpluses were accumulated, and transferred in non-economic transactions, and peasants had non-economic reasons for acquiring cash: at the monastery of St-Riquier c.830, the offerings that came in (and even if the largest of these came from nobles, the majority, to judge from the beneficaries of miracles, were from peasants) were worth 300 lb of silver *per week*.[21] Further, peasants had ways other than involvement in the market of raising cash: there is charter and capitulary evidence for peasants mortgaging, and sometimes selling, land to their local priests.[22] What the polyptychs clearly suggest,

18 Doehaerd 1947; see also Devroey 1984, 1985a.
19 Adrevald c. 35, *PL* 124, col. 941; *Miracula S. Hucberti, AA SS* Nov. 1, pp. 819–20.
20 T. 378.
21 *Chronique de St Riquier*, p. 308; Lesne 1936: 145.
22 Davies 1983; *MGH Capit.* II, no. 273, c. 30, p. 323.

however, is that in areas west of the Rhine, landlords' cash-demands (backed as they were by the threat of force) drove peasants to acquire coin through transactions on their own account.[23] Cash was a preferable form of income when the landlord could not, or preferred not to, consume a farm's primary product directly. Transport services were costly and hard to organise (though in many cases they were extremely carefully organised).[24] But cash might be preferable when surplus artisanal production was not needed by the lord, and could be sold on the spot. The polyptych of St-Germain records one group of 14 women (*ancillae*) who 'if supplies of material are given to them, make shirts'. The next entry lists 19 other women of rather higher legal status (*lidae*): 'All these women either make shirts of 8 *alnae* or they pay 4 pence.'[25] Cash had the advantage of flexibility. Its usefulness presupposed markets where the lord's agents, or the beneficiaries of lordly gifts, could exchange it for consumables. But cash payments could favour peasants too. Once you had gained the pennies due to your lord, any additional profit went into your pocket. You might use such money to buy or lease land, and so increase the holding you had inherited. Whose had been the initiative in settling the 4d. requirement from the *lidae* of St-Germain? How were the surplus shirts sold? By the monks' estate-manager? Or by the women or their kin themselves?

In some localities distant from estate centres, often around the edges of existing tenures, the polyptych-surveyors listed *mansi absi* – literally 'absent manses'. Economic historians used to interpret these as 'uncultivated holdings' and inferred that they represented a total loss from the landlord's standpoint.[26] Recently, however, it has been pointed out that *mansi absi* were often registered as owing dues, which were always in cash rather than labour services.[27] The inference has been drawn that these tenures, often (though not necessarily) on land newly cleared from forest or heath, were offered by landlords as

---

23 Duby 1974.
24 Devroey 1979, 1984.
25 Longnon 1895: 200–1.
26 Latouche 1961: 282.
27 Devroey 1976.

an inducement to tenants to extend their operations, whether through crop-growing or animal husbandry. Hence the *mansi* remained *absi*, in the sense of not having a dwelling on them, since those who worked them came out from existing farms and it was from those that dues were paid. Tenants working *mansi absi* were often registered as 'strangers', that is, they hailed from other villages. So, the sort of man who took on a *mansus absus* might have been an immigrant attracted by freedom from labour services; or a son who feared that his patrimony, or his share of it, would not be big enough to support his family; or a rich peasant with several adult sons and labour to spare. Any temptation to idealise the life of a ninth-century peasant should be resisted. Still, there were opportunities for the enterprising. In Septimania, *aprisiones*, that is tenures on waste or deserted lands, held directly of the king free of rent, were made to encourage settlers.[28] In the Seine basin, landlords created *hospitia*, free tenures, presumably for similar reasons.[29] Neither *aprisiones* nor *hospitia* are documented before the Carolingian period, and they occur more often in the reign of Charles the Bald than previously. As in the later Middle Ages, individual interest won out over class interest in landlords' poaching of peasants from their peers' estates. In 864 a royal assembly at Pîtres near Rouen dealt with the problem (without indicating how widespread it was) of migrant wage-workers in vineyards: clearly some landlords were short of labour at least at harvest-time, and to persuade such migrants to return to their original farms were willing to reassure them that they could keep their earnings. The same assembly also forbade peasants to sell the holdings on which the bulk of their dues were assessed.[30] There is nothing implausible in the argument that peasants, especially better-off peasants, managed their holdings, and their familial strategies, as adroitly as did some people higher up the social scale.[31] Even if *mansi absi*, or *aprisiones*, or *hospitia*, as a proportion of the

28 Dupront 1965.
29 T. 112 (Sellentois, 849), 168 (Etampois, 854), 174 (Aisne, 855), 363 (Sénonais, 872), 399 (Vexin, 875).
30 *MGH Capit.* II, no. 273, cc. 30, 31, pp. 323–4.
31 Cf. Coleman 1971, 1977/8.

total number of holdings in any area, remained small, they were a sign of 'dynamism' [32] particularly visible in the heartland of the kingdom of Charles the Bald.

What was the outcome of all this activity – of peasant responses to seigneurial pressures, and conjunctures of peasant and lordly interests? Did it do no more than keep a subsistence economy running? The whole idea of economic growth in the early Middle Ages is sometimes dismissed as anachronistic. One frequently-cited piece of evidence is that of desperately low yields for cereal crops (even as low as one measure reaped for one measure sown – compare modern farmers' ratios of up to 18:1) suggested by a fragment of an inventory of the royal estate of Annappes during Charlemagne's reign.[33] Quite apart from the dubious legitimacy of generalising from one such fragment, it is uncertain how the data itself should be interpreted. It is, for instance, quite possible that the grain found on this particular estate by the royal surveyors was what was left after the deduction of food-distributions to slaves and other dependents. Yields of 1:1 cannot have been normal – or we should be dealing with a *sub*-subsistence economy![34] But no sort of quantifiable data are available for anything but small, and possibly atypical, areas. A further problem is lack of evidence on farming methods. It is impossible to say whether use of the heavy iron ploughshare or the horse-collar became more widespread during the course of the ninth century in Francia. One technological improvement is a little better-documented: watermills proliferated, with references to them in Charles the Bald's charters, for instance, becoming increasingly frequent as the reign went on.[35] Unfortunately there is hardly any usable evidence on price movements (apart from obvious dramatic rises during famine-periods), though capitularies document the notion of the local or market price.[36] I accept the term 'growth' on the basis of the probability

---

32 Rouche 1990: 201. (The lands mentioned in T. 112 were not in the Touraine, as Rouche infers, but in the Sellentois (i.e. near Senlis).)

33 Duby 1968: 25–6, 363–4.

34 Fossier 1968(i): 237.

35 Tessier 1955, index s.v. *molendinum*. Cf. Lohrmann 1989.

36 *MGH Capit.* II, nos. 216 (Pavia 865), c. 5, p. 93, and 287 (Ver 884), c. 13, p. 375: Doehaerd 1978: 183, 240–1.

that both population and (though this is harder to demonstrate) productivity were rising during the ninth century. Such growth is documented before the reign of Charles the Bald: the polyptych of St-Victor Marseilles dates from the later years of Charlemagne's reign, that of St-Germain (probably) from the earlier part of Louis the Pious's. But those of St-Bertin, St-Remi Rheims, Montierender and Lobbes date from the period between c. 840 and 870, as did the now-lost surveys of St-Riquier, Notre Dame Soissons, St-Vaast, and Hautvillers. Peasants' renders in cash, the proliferation of markets, a growing volume of coinage in circulation[37], are all demonstrable in the reigns of Charlemagne and Louis the Pious. During the reign of Charles the Bald, however, such developments not only continued but showed cumulative effects. *Hospitia* were numerous enough in 866, for instance, for a special rate to be assigned them when Charles 'imposed a payment throughout his whole realm' to pay tribute to Vikings.[38]

Small though the total take was in 866 (4,000 lb of silver), the significant point was not its size but the fact that it was raised in cash through a generalised tax. The king was impinging on the economy in a new way. The courts of Charlemagne and Louis the Pious had constituted major centres of demand not only for peasant surpluses but for items of conspicuous consumption purveyed via *emporia* like Dorestad and Quentovic.[39] But by the reign of Charles the Bald, while the court remained a large consumer, demand had spread more widely among the elite, and cash transactions multiplied in the countryside. The possibility of more generalised exactions on the internal economy became a real one.[40] It was limited in practice by the power of the aristocracy. Some historians have been arguing recently that payments of *census* and *hostilicium* specified in some polyptychs are forms of tax collection and demonstrate the continuity of taxation, and of the administrative structures to exact it, from the late Roman period to the Carolingians.[41] But it seems more likely that ninth-century

---

37   See below: 31.
38   *AB* 866: 130.
39   Wervers 1988; Lebecq 1989.
40   Cf. Devroey 1985a: 485–7.
41   Durliat 1984; Magnou-Nortier 1987, 1989; cf. Devroey 1985b.

landlords, still using (why not?) the old terminology of the Roman fiscal system, were exacting on their own account dues that had once been owed to the state, rather than acting as tax-collectors on the state's behalf. (Had ninth-century rulers really been able to collect a generalised army-tax, their armies would surely have been very much larger than they clearly were.)[42] Ninth-century aristocrats competed with central power for peasant surpluses and commercial profits. True, they had done so in Roman times, but since then the state's institutional decline meant that the terms of the competition had shifted in favour of the regions and the aristocracy. Charles the Bald though he tried to regulate some forms of relations between landlords and peasants was in no position to intervene in those relations extensively.[43] Nevertheless, to raise tribute for Vikings, he did tax, and more than once. In 877 he imposed a levy on both peasants and nobles which discriminated in the peasants' favour and seems to have provoked noble disaffection.[44] Charles had not entirely abandoned the efforts of his father and grandfather to protect the *pauperes*: at the same time, he had done what neither his father nor grandfather had attempted, in imposing public exactions in cash on the economy at large. The polyptych evidence shows that the peasant economy was well able to sustain these royal demands.

As monarch, Charles had other key resources. The church's vast wealth was accessible to the king on a scale denied even to the greatest of landed magnates. Charles exploited it on a scale his predecessors had not needed to try. The church's ideology not only gave powerful support to kingship: it sustained the very idea of the state as a permanent complex of institutions, because therein lay the best prospect of defending ecclesiastical interests. The church was therefore prepared to put its money where its mouth was: churchmen in Charles's reign might complain bitterly of the economic burdens of military service and fiscal exactions borne by their particular churches, but they

---

42 Frankish casualties of 100 men: *AV* 881, p. 50. Viking casualties of 60, *AB* 869: 163; 500, 400, *AB* 865: 127, 128. See France 1985.

43 Pîtres, 864, *MGH Capit.* II, no. 273, c. 29–31, pp. 323–4. See also below, Ch. 3: 49–50.

44 See below, Ch. 8.

never questioned the right and duty of kings to impose these on the church at large in order to ensure the well-being of the Christian people. By its example, and also by its preaching, the church sought to impress these ideas on the laity, including the secular aristocracy.[45] The church's provinces, dioceses and parishes gave it an extensive infrastructure, its carefully-ranked personnel and tiers of assemblies a hierarchy of control into which the king could tap.[46]

But Charles the Bald also had a communications-network of his own: in his kingdom, many Roman roads had survived, with a system of public provision of food and transport at regular staging-posts at least along some routes.[47] Royal agents were equipped with letters of credit to enable them to use these services. It looks as if, in western Francia at any rate, it was possible to reactivate some of the infrastructure of the late Roman state. The evidence for market-control shows how such a system responded to and impinged on new forms of local power and local initiative. Charles's charters include 19 grants (15 of them dating from the second half of the reign) of rights over markets, often specified as weekly markets rather than annual fairs.[48] The Edict of Pîtres in 864 strongly suggests the combination of political and fiscal reasons behind Charles's determination to keep control of markets: others, presumably local magnates, had been setting them up on their own initiative, but the king now decreed that such markets were to be banned unless they secured royal authorisation, and royal agents were told to keep lists of those so authorised.[49] It is a reasonable inference that the running of a market was profitable; so, no doubt, was the issuing of authorisations. Charles's charters include some 25 references (outnumbering those in the charters of other Carolingians put together) to places identified as *mercatus, portus*

---

45 See e.g. *MGH Capit.* II, no. 266 (Quierzy 857), pp. 287–9. Cf. no. 272 (Pîtres 862), pp. 303–7: bishops as social 'doctors'.

46 Hartmann 1989. See below Ch. 3.

47 Cf. *AB* 868: 150 ('per curtes regias in pago Laudunensi consistentes pergens'); 874: 186 ('per consuetos mansionaticos' from Attigny to Compiègne.).

48 T. 60, 78, 117, 178, 207, 247, 248, 304, 323, 326, 344, 354, 357, 365, 370, 378, 401, 425, 439.

49 *MGH Capit.* II, no. 273, c. 19, p. 318.

or *burgus*: all terms that imply some commercial activity.[50] In many cases, these are the earliest references to trading at the places concerned; and in some, the record has been made precisely because the king is granting the right to run a market.[51] There are many incidental references to traders in Charles's kingdom. In 860, for instance, when Charles needed cash to hire a Viking warband, he taxed not only churches and peasants but also 'traders, even very small-scale ones: their houses and all their stock were valued and on that basis a rate was assessed and required'.[52]

The much more varied and extensive evidence for Charles's control of the coinage has important implications for both government and economy. In the last decade or so of his reign, approximately 100 mints functioned (even if not all did so continuously): for the volume of the coinage they produced, only a 'ball-park estimate' can be given – perhaps tens of millions of coins – but the quality of the coins has recently been very precisely determined: whereas before 864 many coins were debased by up to 50 per cent, after 864 a silver-content of well over 90 per cent was secured across the board.[53] Since every coin bears a mint-name, and most hoards containing Charles's coins are dateable to within a decade or so, it has been possible to show that the coins circulated rapidly, soon after they were issued. Total output seems to have increased in the course of the reign; the issuing of a larger proportion of half-pennies after 864 implies a growing demand for a smaller denomination of coin, usable for smaller transactions. The 864 legislation mentions *en passant* in what sounds like an urban context the selling of bread and meat *per denerarios*: by pennyworths (ninth-century hamburgers?) – which may imply more about normal price levels than Charlemagne's decree in the famine year of 794 that a penny should buy 12 two-lb. wheaten loaves.[54] The miracle-stories quoted above indicate that this was a coin-using peasant society: every household wanted coins some of the time – notably

50 Endemann 1964. See below, Map 5.
51 E.g. T. 323, 370.
52 *AB* 860: 92. On traders in general see Johanek 1987: 55–65.
53 Metcalf and Northover 1989; Metcalf 1990: 65.
54 Prices may also have risen generally; see above n. 36.

when it came to Martinmas (11 November), the customary time for paying dues to landlords (as it remained in the nineteenth century). Increasingly widespread use probably accentuated a chronic shortage of coin. In permitting the bishop of Châlons-sur-Marne to set up a mint in 864, the king acknowledged difficulties in suppling the new currency. The cathedral clergy were to take the profits from the mint they ran, but in the short run they were evidently short of cash. They were just the sort of purchasers on whom peasants relied. (It was no coincidence that the bishop's request came in November.) But clergy could have other business too: at Rheims, Archbishop Hincmar found them using the leaves of ancient manuscripts to make envelopes 'in which to keep the pennies they gained from trade'.[55] In issuing coinage on a larger scale, the king was meeting the widely-felt needs of 'private interests'.

He was also suiting his own book. In the first place, the king too was a landlord – the biggest in the kingdom. Cash-rents were exacted on royal estates. Charlemagne's managers were told to present a series of accounts each year in writing, and Charles the Bald's were warned not to have more in their strongboxes than they should.[56] It is no coincidence that a number of smaller mints are located at royal estate-centres, and there was one quite important mint at the palace – that is, within the king's peripatetic household.[57] (An early medieval mint, as recent reconstructions have shown, could be set up, and packed up, within hours by experienced moneyers.) Secondly, the king exacted tolls on trade within his realm.[58] It was worth a monastery's while to gain exemption for its own boats, for instance, and then as now, the great rivers of France lent themselves to bulk traffic. Thirdly, the king had an indirect but extremely effective way of taxing external trade: only his silver pennies and halfpennies were accepted within the realm, so any foreign coins brought to a port, whether by a home-coming Frankish trader as profit or by a foreign trader to

55 T. 277; *Vita Remigii* pref., *MGH SSRM* III, pp. 251–2.
56 *Capit. de Villis*, *MGH Capit.* I, no. 32, cc. 28, 44, 55, 62, pp. 85–9, trans. Loyn and Percival 1975: 67–72; *MGH Capit.* II, no. 297, c.14, p. 437. See also Oexle 1988: 111–16.
57 Cf. Coupland 1986.
58 Ganshof 1959.

purchase Frankish goods, had to be converted into Charles's currency. We know from records of royal instructions that these regulations were made: what the evidence of extant coins proves is that they were actually carried out. In eight major hoards found on French sites and containing coins of Charles the Bald, there are no foreign coins. Yet hoards found elsewhere – in Scandinavia and in northern Britain, for instance, where no such royal controls operated – show that there was plenty of 'international' trade going on in the ninth century. It seems likely that the king profited directly from this by setting a charge for the conversion of currency: you brought in, say, West Saxon pennies containing 20 ounces of silver to the mint at Quentovic, and you got back pennies of Charles containing 19 ounces of silver.[59]

On at least one occasion in his reign, in 864, Charles applied this conversion system to the currency of the realm in an exercise known as a *renovatio monetae*: a renewal of the money. And the money needed renewing: the numismatic proof of the debased state of the currency at this point has already been mentioned. The regulations issued in 864 give debasement, and ensuing loss of confidence, as the reasons for the recoinage. The evidence of the coins again proves that the recoinage was effected. The argument that Charles needed sound money to pay off Vikings[60] is not convincing. It's true that Vikings demanded tributes in good silver. But why not simply pay in ingots? Why bother to make pennies? There is no sign that silver was running short by 864, as it should have done had tribute-payments made huge inroads into the total supply. Not only were the coins issued in 864 and after much purer, but there were considerably more of them. Further, mints continued to issue the new, sound, coins throughout the rest of Charles's reign yet, no tribute is recorded between 866 and 876. When he acquired new territory in 869, some twenty new mints were set up there. This distribution, as Map 4 shows, extended an existing regional concentration of minting in the north-eastern part of Charles's kingdom. Here lay the focus of royal fiscal control.

59 Metcalf 1990, and personal communication.
60 Grierson 1990.

The way in which the coinage circulated can be deduced from the proportions in hoards of coins from different mints. A two-fold pattern emerges. Coins circulated vigorously *within* each of three major regions of Charles's kingdom: Francia between Scheldt and Seine, Neustria between Seine and Loire, and Burgundy between Seine-Yonne and Rhône. Secondly, coins travelled to a rather lesser extent *between* these regions with the flow being mainly from Francia to the other two. It was of course in Francia that over half the mints of the realm were located. Elsewhere, in Aquitaine, the hoards show a very low level of mixing of coins from various mints, suggesting only local circulation around a single centre, and there is virtually no sign of coins entering the region from the north or north-east.[61] It may be that royal involvement here was less intense: Aquitaine contained only five mints of any size, and these did not implement the recoinage of 864. But the fact that Aquitanian hoards contain no foreign or older coins suggests the maintenance of some form of royal control. Though the weight of royal government impinged unevenly, there was no region that did not feel it.

The king expected direct benefits from the recoinage. Since he wanted people to pay him in cash, and to stimulate the transactions that enabled them to do so, it was in his interests to restore confidence in the currency. This was clearly true of peasants on royal estates, which is where many smaller mints were located. Further, though no source states this explicitly, the recoinage, like individuals' conversions of imported coin, presumably gave the king, as well as the moneyer, a cut. In other words, a recoinage was a massive, realm-wide, form of taxation. The first Carolingian king, Pippin I, in 754/5 had specified 'concerning the mint, that of each pound of silver, not more than 22 *solidi* were to be minted, of which one must go to the moneyer and the rest to the lord [king]': since the account pound used in normal business reckoning contained 20 *solidi*, Pippin was in effect decreeing a royal mint charge of 1 *solidus*, i.e. 5 per cent.[62] In the twelfth century, when the issue of coin had in many areas ceased to be a royal prerogative,

---

61 Metcalf 1990.
62 Spufford 1988: 44–73. The *solidus* was a unit of account, worth 12d.

this sort of charge was known as seigniorage – a valuable perquisite of controlling a mint. Then and later, we know that local lords engaged in renewals of the money to make a fast profit. It was a risky game: played too often, it caused widespread loss of confidence in the currency, hoarding, and commercial bottlenecks.[62] Handled skilfully, it brought long-term as well as short-term advantage. The evidence for the continuing large-scale production and brisk circulation of a high-quality currency from 864 to 877 in Charles's kingdom suggests that his recoinage had been, from the king's standpoint, a financial success.

Aristocratic criticism of royal rapacity was a backhanded tribute to that success. Rebels in 875 complained on just this score against Charles; and the amount of treasure he fielded in 876 and 877 bears them out. The complaint was not new: in 858, rebels had accused Charles of extorting 'whatever the Vikings had left'[63]: again, Charles's conduct in the ensuing years – and notably the 864 recoinage itself – suggests that once he had re-established his political grip, he was able to reimpose fiscal demands. The political and the economic were of course inseparable. But they could be seen to be so 'from below' as well as 'from above'. A sound currency is one of the things that people expect from a government that is working well. A revaluation of the coinage could reflect a regime's high morale: it could also, whatever immediate sacrifices it imposed, raise the morale of the ruled. The revalued currency was a remarkable demonstration of political will, and effectively generated user-confidence. It harked back to the world of the fourth- and fifth-century Christian emperors; at the same time it signalled a new world of money-using economic agents including peasants and small-scale traders.

What did Charles do with his money? Some uses were not new: Charles's father Louis the Pious had also minted coins on a large scale and very probably paid cash (as well as bullion) for allies and for imported luxuries. In the reigns of Charlemagne and Louis the Pious, workmen engaged in large-scale construction-projects had been paid in cash, and Charles no doubt hired skilled labour for his am-

62 Barrow 1990.
63 See below Ch. 7: 187.

bitious building-programme at Compiègne later in his reign. Charles had new cash-needs, however. One was to pay off Vikings. Another was to pay hired troops. In addition to his military household, rewarded with 'annual gifts' of clothes and equipment, Charles had to field armies for the sort of warfare that did not appeal much to Frankish nobles – namely, defensive or non-expansionist war; and here the availability of cash stipends may have helped recruit professional warriors (including Vikings). Charles also needed cash to supply his court. Though the direct consumption of the product of royal estates remained important, the extent to which Charles was a migratory king has been exaggerated. Portrayed over the reign as a whole, his itinerary looks extensive; but looked at year by year, season by season, it shows a heavy concentration in the region bounded by Pîtres, Servais, Attigny and Paris, with the great majority of known stays between October and June being at palaces within that quadrangle.[64] In the last years of the reign, Charles was developing Compiègne on the River Oise as his 'capital': his *Carlopolis*.[65] His stays at or near *civitates* were relatively frequent compared with his predecessors'. His increased cash resources, and increasing commercial activity in the Frankish heartlands, made it possible for Charles's household officers to organise the provisioning of the court by buying from local markets. Charlemagne's 'system' of funnelling trade through one or two frontier *emporia*, like Dorestad, was rapidly being replaced by a much more widespread diffusion of commercial sites (denoted in charters by such terms as *portus, mercatus, burgus*) at or near *civitates* in the realm's interior. When Hincmar urged that Charles and his entourage should live off royal estates in the traditional style, he acknowledged – in backhanded fashion – the novelty of Charles's freedom of manoeuvre. In the last 15 years of Charles's reign, at least four winter assemblies were held in *civitates* in Francia.[66] Increased economic activity in these locations can be seen in Char-

---

64 Uncertainties arise from shortage of charters, which constitute the main evidence until 861. After 861 the *AB* record where the king spent Christmas each year.
65 Lohrmann 1976.
66 Senlis, 862; Auxerre, 863; Rheims 870; Senlis 871. Evidence of royal stays suggests the special importance of Senlis: cf. below: 57.

les's grant to the bishop of Paris of the Grand Pont with its mills and, later, of the right to dispose of some newly-built houses; in the mint (with its profits) conceded to the bishop and cathedral clergy of Châlons; in the trading interests of the clergy of Rheims; in the monks of Corbie's intended purchase ('if we have enough money') of pepper at Cambrai;[67] and in the scattered but widespread references to episcopal and monastic building works (not all of them ecclesiastical) and, more rarely, in archaeological traces or architectural remains of these constructions. *Civitas* populations surely grew. In 860 Charles had valued the houses and stock of small traders.[68] In 877, to pay a tribute to Vikings at the mouth of the Seine, Charles demanded cash contributions from 'traders and people living in *civitates* according to their means, in proportion to their resources'.[69] These Viking activities and Frankish responses to them will be looked at later in this book. But here is the place briefly to consider the overall impact of the Vikings on the West Frankish economy. They used the great rivers of northern and western France to penetrate far into the heart of Charles's kingdom. According to one modern historian, their 'systematic destruction of all that had made western Europe a going concern economically' marked the definitive break between the sub-Roman and medieval worlds.[70] Others have cast the Vikings as archetypical 'market-men' (perhaps the literal meaning of the word Viking: *wic*-ing), releasers of hoarded wealth, stimulators of social movement and peasant production: in short, as agents and prime movers of the economic growth which was to characterise western Europe in the High Middle Ages.[71] We are back with the ninth century as a historiographical battleground: 'It was the best of times, it was the worst of times....'

The Vikings certainly did cause extensive damage to property in the short term. But there is no evidence that

---

67 T. 186, 277; Doehaerd 1978: 205.
68 Above: 31.
69 *MGH Capit.* II, no. 280, p. 354.
70 Bautier 1971: 57.
71 D'Haenens 1967, 1970; Duby 1974; Sawyer 1971. For a parody of this view of the Vikings ('little more than groups of long-haired tourists who occasionally roughed up the natives',) and a restatement of the contrary view, Wallace-Hadrill 1975: 220.

they either intended or effected systematic and long-term destruction. Despite repeated attacks on Quentovic in the 830s and 840s, for instance, the output of the Quentovic mint, meagre in those decades (but also in the 820s), became large in the latter half of Charles's reign; in 858, the monks of St-Wandrille fled for safety to Quentovic.[72] The Vikings certainly caused some upheavals in the countryside. In 864, the Edict of Pîtres ordered that peasants who had fled because of the Vikings should not be oppressed by counts or others in the places in which they had found refuge: they were to return home to their original lordships but they should be allowed to keep their earnings from working in the vineyards; on the other hand, if they had married and fathered offspring while resident in others' lordships, the wives and children were to remain with those lords.[73] The legislation makes it clear that peasant migration was no new phenomenon, only that the new bout produced by Viking activity was causing some headaches for landlords. As in the Statute of Labourers in England immediately following the Black Death, a ruling class was attempting to reassert control in a situation where its grip had been temporarily shaken and labour shortage threatened.[74] There is not much sign of peasant migrants escaping seigneurial control altogether. The Edict of Pîtres (unlike the Statute of Labourers) may have been a response to a situation that was only local – confined, that is, to the lower Seine valley. The landholding of few of the great monasteries of northern Francia shows anything more than temporary dislocation. Where lands were lost by churches, as in Aquitaine, the main beneficiaries seem to have been the local aristocracy – who traditionally cast greedy eyes on ecclesiastical wealth.

There is very little evidence for Viking slave-raiding and slave-trading among the peasant population. A reference to Vikings seizing *mancipia* (slaves) may reflect attempts to exploit their labour directly.[75] Much more frequent mentions of *captivi* seem to refer to nobles, and one writer explicitly

---

72 Metcalf 1990: 85, 92; Coupland 1991a; *Mirac S. Wandregisili, MGH SS* xv, p. 408.
73 *MGH Capit.* II, no. 273, c. 31, 324.
74 Bolton 1980: 209.
75 *AB* 866: 130.

says that the reason the Vikings having arrived by boat then used horses was 'so that they would be able to capture some nobles for the sake of money (ransoms)'.[76] An over-land slave-trade from Central Europe to Cordoba via Verdun predated the Viking incursions. Historians who hypothesise large-scale sea-borne slave-trading in this period should give more thought to logistics. Such trade was difficult enough in the seventeenth century. The Vikings' impact on peasant-farmers was two-edged. In the Seine and Loire valleys, for instance, the presence of Viking warbands over fairly long periods may well have stimulated local producers and sellers of horses and weapons and, above all, food and drink. In these same areas, Vikings also caused the kind of short-term, local damage which provoked peasants to flee. Peasants might flee, however, not only from such 'natural' problems as local drought, famine and disease, but from the ravages of their 'natural lords'. A Viking raid, and the passage of Frankish warriors who 'lived off the land', left similar trails. In terms of their material culture and lifestyle, the Vikings were really not so different from the Franks: hence the speed with which they adopted Frankish military and diplomatic conventions, and, where they settled, assimilated with the local population.[77] Historians looking at the early tenth century find it difficult to identify the Vikings any longer as an 'external' force. But in the ninth century too, Vikings belonged in the mainstream of economic activity within the Frankish world. In some places, Nantes and Rouen, for instance, they contributed to commercial activity already under way. Elsewhere, it was not Vikings but local producers and traders and lords who made and benefited from the growth of markets.

If, so far as the Continent is concerned, the Viking impact is essentially a West Frankish phenomenon, that is because the Vikings went where they knew moveable wealth was to be had. This raises one last point about the geographical distribution of the symptoms dealt with in this chapter: each can be found outside Charles the Bald's

76 Aimoin, *Miracula Sancti Germani* ii, 10, *PL* 126, col. 1045. By contrast Saracens were interested in slaves: Archbishop Roland of Arles ransomed for (inter alia) 150 *mancipi*, *AB* 869: 163; cf. *RFA* 807. Nothing comparable is recorded in the northern trading area.
77 Coupland and Nelson 1988. Cf. Bates 1982.

kingdom; but the syndrome of generalised cash-relations in the countryside, the proliferation of markets and mints, extensive activities of traders including small-scale ones in *civitates*, and a pattern of frequent royal residence in or near *civitates*, can be found only there – and specifically in the north-eastern part of the West Frankish kingdom. East of the Rhine in the kingdom of Louis the German, for instance, there were no mints, and there is much less evidence for markets and traders, while in the Middle Kingdom (Lotharingia), the volume of coinage in circulation was much smaller than west of the Meuse. The West Frankish syndrome is difficult to account for unless we assume a measure of sustained interest on the part of Charles the Bald himself. The causes of increased monetary use and commercial activity were largely out of his control: but he knew where and how wealth was being generated, and was intent on exploiting that wealth systematically. A *renovatio monetae* does not just happen: it is conceived of, then planned, and executed by many agents. The next chapter examines the governmental context of Charles's fiscal and monetary methods: his imitation of late-Roman emperors was something more than a charade or a figleaf for impotence.

Chapter 3

THE CONTEXT OF POLITICS

When the noblewoman Dhuoda saw off her fifteen-year-old son William to join Charles the Bald's court in 841, she gave him a book of advice. Most of it was personal and spiritual. Dhuoda thought of the palace as a place of great temptations. She also thought of it as a great household, in which her son could find a favoured place. He would meet many kinds of influential people. Most important, thought Dhuoda, apart from the royal lord himself, were the royal kin: persons to be especially cultivated by an astute and aspiring young man. Then there were great men, the king's trusted advisers: men with much to teach and many ways of helping William. And there were wise priests: William should have dinner in their company and learn from their conversation. Later on, his mother hoped, when William married and set up a household in his turn, he would make it like the royal one, a model of harmonious order.[1]

As Dhuoda sat writing at Uzès in Septimania, another writer, Nithard, was hard at work at the other end of Charles's kingdom, in Francia. His audience may have included William, and since he wrote history rather than moral instruction, Nithard had much more to say than Dhuoda about politics. For him too, the ruler was a central figure, but Nithard was primarily interested in depicting the relationship between kings and their great men. Nithard admired Charlemagne, who had known how to tame Franks as well as barbarians. He also (at any rate while writing the

---

1   On Dhuoda and her work, see Riché 1975; Dronke 1984: Ch. 2; Nelson 1988a: 221–2; Claussen 1990.

41

first part of his book) admired the young Charles, who consulted with his nobles and followed the good counsels of bishops. (Nithard saw no inconsistency there.) Nithard wrote in the midst of war. Shame and honour were what motivated men. To die for your lord was noble, to betray or forsake him was base, while to outlive him in battle brought disgrace, not only on you but on your kin. Good faith was the hallmark of nobility, and it was displayed most clearly in fidelity to your king. 'Horizontally', nobles shared values as well as status.[2]

Nithard also reveals something about 'vertical' relationships between nobles. Though himself the king's cousin, Nithard had another patron too, the king's right-hand man, the seneschal Adalard. In a Carolingian court, a post like Adalard's (the seneschal organised the feeding and accommodation of the royal household) gave access to the king and also control over others' access. Nithard was very probably also a blood-relation of Adalard: kinship could give an extra claim on a magnate's patronage. Nithard thought a good king should be able to handle competing claims fairly, and maintain solidarity among nobles whose rivalries might otherwise tear the realm apart. In making his decisions about gifts or patronage, a king had to bear in mind that his nobles too had clients, and obligations of their own. A noble individual, such as Nithard himself, could reasonably expect his royal lord to look after his interests and reward faithful service with *beneficia* (literally 'good deeds'), meaning grants of lands or of *honores*, 'offices' which carried lands with them: hence the linguistic distinction between *honor* and *beneficium* became blurred.[3] When disputes arose between nobles, or between lay and ecclesiastical landlords, each party would expect 'justice', meaning a settlement, often a compromise, that was acceptable to both parties and seemed fair to others of their rank and status. But nobles within a realm had collective interests too. A king should rein in the aggression of warriors, especially of young men; he should punish crime, keep his court a place of peace. No realm was an island: to those ambitious young warriors, the courts and the largesse of

2   On Nithard, see Nelson 1986a (1985): 195–237; Nelson 1989a.
3   *AB* 839: 45.

neighbouring kings presented a continual counter-attraction. A king therefore had to keep control of his own: he must inhibit opposition within the realm, and exile the faithless, but be sufficiently fair in his distribution of patronage to forestall the defection of valued supporters to other realms. A king had to be able to create a sense of solidarity among his men. Nithard gives more information than any other contemporary about how kings, and especially Charles at the very outset of his reign, measured up to these requirements.

Just four years after Charles's death, Archbishop Hincmar of Rheims, who had been an important political figure throughout Charles's reign (though not consistently close to him), wrote a treatise, *The Government of the Palace*, for the young King Carloman, Charles's grandson, and lent it an air of authority by claiming to incorporate the work of Abbot Adalard of Corbie, who had died nearly sixty years before. What influenced Hincmar most (though his description idealised it a little) was the regime of Charles the Bald, especially its latter years.[4] 'The king, his queen and their offspring', wrote Hincmar, 'are in overall charge.' Here Hincmar touched on the nature of medieval royal government as a family firm. He did not elaborate on the usual roles played by a king's sons, who in fact were expected from an early age to join in their father's business, as envoys and generals, counsellors as long as they remained in their father's household, and rulers of sub-kingdoms as and when *regna* were available.[5] Perhaps Hincmar's silence here was tactful, since Charles the Bald's sons had not distinguished themselves in the traditional roles. Nor did Hincmar say more about a king's daughters: in Charlemagne's later years, the political influence of his womenfolk (mistresses as well as daughters) at court had been notorious, but his successors had either used their daughters in marriage-alliances, or, more often, placed them in convents, either way removing them from the pol-

4   Nelson 1986a (1983a): 103–11. The work is translated in Herlihy 1970: 208–27 (but translations below are mine). The title is not Hincmar's, but has been current since the sixteenth century.
5   For father–son relationships in the Carolingian family, and resultant tensions, see Schieffer 1990. For Louis the Pious's 'family firm', see Nelson 1990c.

itical centre. The queen's central position, by contrast, was an *ex officio* one, and Hincmar therefore highlighted it (c. 22): her most important responsibility was for the 'good order [in both practical and model senses] of the palace, and for the dispensing of the annual gifts, apart from their food, drink and horses, to the king's warrior-retinue' – the latter a quasi-maternal role which enabled the queen to form a network of personal relationships with a younger generation of budding leaders. Hincmar noted too the queen's special tasks in the overall management of the provisioning of the royal household, and sometimes (when the king commanded) in gift-giving to foreign embassies. In his section of the *AB*, Hincmar attributed many crucial diplomatic and political activities to queens:[6] since some were activities of which he approved, and only some queens were credited with such roles, it seems less likely that he obsessively exaggerated the nefarious influence of women (though misogyny was in the air breathed by medieval churchmen) than that he accurately portrayed a feature of Carolingian political life underrecorded by other contemporary writers. The king's wife, like the wives of other *potentes*, often remained at home while her husband journeyed and campaigned: throughout the medieval period, for as long as kings led armies in person, the queen's role in household management could become tantamount to a regency. Hincmar fills out his palace-picture by listing the rest of the household personnel: the apocrisiar, responsible for ecclesiastical business, and the archchancellor, in charge of the notaries (who alone issued valid royal documents).[7] Then come the secular offices: those of chamberlain or treasurer (the treasure was kept in the king's chamber), the count of the palace, who handled legal appeals not heard by the king himself, the seneschal, the butler, the constable and a string of other household officers.

Hincmar confirms much of what Dhuoda and Nithard say or imply about the workings of a political system centred on the court, adding details and assigning plausible

6   See Index s.v. Judith, Ermentrude, Richildis, Engelberga, and 879: 216–19.
7   In the office of apocrisiar, Hincmar invented his own ideal job-description: in fact no such post existed, the palace clergy being headed by the archchaplain; Löwe 1972.

motives and explanations. He underlines Nithard's insistence on what nowadays might be called line-management: he reveals that a manager's problem in the Carolingian palace was the maintenance of good order and morale among the often unruly yet indispensable 'crowd' of young noblemen who were deployed on a variety of tasks and errands, especially of a military sort. The chief officers of the household had to ensure that 'hearts were kept aflame for the king's service'. Hincmar reveals more than Dhuoda about eating arrangements, and, incidentally, about the layout of the palace-complex. The Carolingians had come a long way from the single ancestral beer-hall: the chief officers would invite groups of the young men to their houses (*mansiones*) for dinner, 'not to encourage gluttony, but for the sake of promoting true rapport; and rarely would a week go by without each [youth] receiving one such invitation from someone'. It might be impossible to keep all of the boys happy all of the time, but the majority of them should be 'cheerful and quick to smile', as well as alert. (c. 27)

Hincmar also shows how the chief officers kept 'the confederation of the whole realm glued together with the palace'. (c.17) They should always be available to needy and oppressed persons 'from whatever part of the realm' and of whatever rank, to bring their cases to the king's ear. (c.25) If such an office-holder died, he had to be quickly replaced by a suitable man. (c.26) 'Since the kingdom consists of different regions, officers of the first, second, and indeed any rank should so far as possible be picked from different regions, so that [men from] the various regions should be able to come to the palace with a greater sense of knowing their way around (*familiarius*) since they would know that men who were from the same kin-group (*genealogia*) or the same region held a place there.' (c.18)

Having depicted the palace not just as a multitude of busy people and face-to-face relationships, but as an arrangement (*dispositio*), an apparatus to be efficiently designed and maintained, Hincmar moves on to a second institution, the assembly. Two sessions took place each year: their rhythm suited the seasonal character of early medieval warfare and travel generally. A small winter meeting of select counsellors considered issues likely to arise in the coming year: an example, says Hincmar, is the decision on whether to renew or break a truce on a particular part of the frontier, given that trouble in one part must be offset by stability in another. In summer (usually early summer), a much larger gathering met. Its time and place had been circulated well in advance. It was attended by a 'multitude' of lesser aristocrats as well as by magnates and leading clergy. Its agenda was prepared by the king in a written list under chapter-headings – *capitula*. First, at one or more morning sessions, the counsellors met as a group to consider the *capitula*, discussing each point, sometimes seeking clarification from the king. Sometimes the clerics among them met separately from the laymen. Meanwhile the king held informal discussions with the multitude. If the weather was nice, these meetings took place outdoors. When the counsellors were ready, they met again with the king and agreed their proposals. A plenary meeting (perhaps in the afternoon) involving the multitude as well as the greater men then 'received the proposals, and sometimes meanwhile deliberated on them too, and confirmed them'. At this point, what had been enacted became law. (cc. 29, 30, 35)

Hincmar is perfectly explicit about assembly management (as an archbishop, he had much experience of running synods) and about the crucial need for confidentiality on the part of counsellors. Matters in fact agreed at the winter meeting were kept secret and brought before the summer one 'as if nothing had been previously worked out concerning them'. At summer meetings, a leak from the counsellors' morning session could be especially dangerous. 'For it often happens that in such discussions, in order to promote the common good, talk has nevertheless centred on a single individual.' It was particularly vital that no counsellor mention that man's name 'to a servant or to anyone else: for the individual concerned is all too likely to become very upset, even desperate, or, worst of all, to fall into infidelity. Thus a man who could have done all sorts of good things is rendered useless; and the same sort of outcome could follow in a case involving not one but two men, or a hundred or more, or even a whole branch of a family (*progenies*) or at the same time a whole province – if you're not very careful!' (c. 31)

It would be false to infer (any more than it would in comparable modern cases) that such management made a mockery of the deliberations as a whole. Hincmar suggests that assemblies held the realm together in two main ways. First, in 'vertical' sociological terms: the *minores* were not just being cheated when their consent was called for. Their voices were heard. And their informal contact with the king on such occasions was basic to the whole process of government. Charles the Bald's capitularies were issued 'with the counsel and consent of the people'. That was not just empty rhetoric. Hincmar puts in a significant phrase when he says that the *minores* who 'confirmed' assembly-decisions did so 'not because they were forced to do so, but because they understood them in their own minds and agreed with them'.(c. 29) Hincmar implicitly contrasts this situation with others – common enough no doubt – when men felt themselves coerced or duped. West Frankish dispute-settlements of the mid-ninth century show that lesser landholders were perfectly capable of taking evidence on board, considering it rationally and reaching recognisably fair conclusions; also that they could distinguish between genuine verdicts and frauds. Hincmar may have idealised ninth-century consensus politics; but his picture had a basis in reality. The point is reinforced if we consider the king's personal conduct at assemblies. Hincmar describes how while the counsellors deliberated, the king spent time (outdoors, weather permitting) among the *minores*, chatting with them in a familiar way, listening to their grievances. (c. 35) He was open with them: so men were able to tell him openly about their quarrels and rivalries. They had views on major political issues too: it's no coincidence that well-informed contemporaries mention the existence of an East Frankish 'public opinion' in the context of Carolingian invasion plans in both 858 and 876.[8]

Assembly proceedings also had a crucial function in 'horizontal' geographic terms. Hincmar had already observed that 'because the realm consists of many regions', court officials should be selected from different regions so that provincials with problems would feel confident of a

8   Below Chs 7: 187 (and *AF* 858: 50); 9: 240.

hearing at the palace. A similar point is made now in the context of assemblies: 'When a man came to the assembly from one of the regions, the king was concerned to ask him what news he had brought with him that ought to be reported and discussed, and he would be strictly required before he next returned to the palace to make exhaustive enquiries outside as well as within the realm, getting information from outsiders as well as from his own people, and from enemies as well as from friends, without concerning himself overmuch about how any person questioned had come by his information.' (c. 36) Whereas outside the realm, the king needed warning of any rebellion by subject peoples, or any imminent attack, 'inside the realm [the vital point was to find out] if the people (*populus*) in any part, region or corner of the realm was in a state of disturbance, then what was the cause of it, and if a complaint of the people was becoming serious or if a noise was being made about some injustice about which it was necessary for the general assembly to deal'. What the king did, in other words, was to use the assembly to defuse trouble in the provinces. Rumblings of complaints, of accusations of injustice, were to be dealt with before they escalated into rebellion. Then the assembly could be brought into play as well – as a forum for airing grievances and settling them – and, again, making men feel that their concerns and feelings were being taken into account.

Hincmar in *The Government of the Palace* was writing a prescription for effective rulership. But his choice of detail, and his treatment of practicalities seem to reflect experience. His account of how government worked in the ninth century is plausible, not least because it squares with what we can infer from Dhuoda and Nithard, despite the differences in their aims and standpoints. The crucial point on which all three writers converge is the role of the aristocracy as the collaborators and agents of the king. The point is important, because much of the modern secondary literature on Charles the Bald's reign, and on the Carolingians generally, has depicted the aristocracy as greedy and boorish, incapable of sharing the higher aspirations of kings or clergy, lacking any sense of public interest. Michael Wallace-Hadrill saw their epitome in the 'repulsively realistic...hairy nobleman' depicted in a late eighth-century

Frankish Sacramentary.[9] A variant theme in recent historiography has been that by the mid-ninth century, nobles had
been too much influenced by the church's stress on peace,
and had thus become unfit for military service. Either way
(and the suspicion must be that some historians are determined to have it either way), blame for the collapse of the
Carolingian state is laid at the door of the Frankish nobility. Our three ninth-century writers lend such views little
support. All three, from their different perspectives, and
each with bitter experience, saw the dangers of noble egoism. But all put their confidence in noble service and loyalty as guarantees of the realm's prosperity: this was the
lesson of history, whether sacred or Frankish, ancient or
contemporary. Pope Gregory the Great had spoken of tam-
ing the wild unicorn, symbol of the man of power. These
three ninth-century writers purveyed a similar message in
their own times to audiences made up wholly or in part of
lay nobles. Dhuoda and Nithard wrote at the very beginning of Charles the Bald's reign: Nithard believed the
young king showed promise, Dhuoda that this generation
of Carolingians were predestined by God to rule, and with
His help would shine forth in their success. Dhuoda addressed her 'beautiful boy' where others might have seen
just another hairy Frank. Hincmar in his very first sentence, made clear his assumption that 'great men' could
also be 'wise'. (c. 1) Writing shortly after Charles's death,
he believed that a new generation of both kings and nobles
could preserve the realm so long as they had the right personal qualities. In other words, the descendents of Charlemagne and his faithful men had their opportunity as
Dhuoda put it (iii, 8), 'manfully to rule, defend and govern
their world'.

What Hincmar the theorist skates over lightly (c. 35) is
noted more deliberately by Hincmar the annalist: the presentation to the king of 'annual gifts' by those who attended
assemblies.[10] This too was a kind of taxation, an institution-
alised imposition (in cash, bullion, and kind) by the king
on the lay and ecclesiastical elite. Arbitrariness was surely

---

9   Wallace-Hadrill 1983: 178, apparently referring to Sacramentary of
    Gellone (i): fig. 4, fol. 9v. (cf. (ii): 11)
10 *AB* 864: 118; 868: 151; 874: 186. See Reuter 1985.

involved, the king intimating what size of gift was acceptable. Room for royal discrimination meant grounds for others' resentment. Assemblies were the pivot: so long as the king could secure attendance, he could refill his coffers, exercise patronage, and maintain consensus at the same time. There is just about enough annalistic evidence to suggest that Charles operated this system at least in the second half of his reign.

*

So far, this chapter has dealt with ninth-century perceptions of the working of politics at the centre, through palace-organisation and general assemblies. But how exactly did men 'govern manfully' in the ninth century? How did the king administer his territories at a distance? And how did the aristocracy, whose economic power was based on local landlordship, participate in ruling the realm? Using other kinds of evidence, we must move out to the localities, and the counties. In the lands west of the Rhine, there was in principle, as there had been in late Roman times, a count for each *civitas*, though in practice, one man often held two or more neighbouring *civitates*. Demarcation problems were foreseen if a county court had to deal with a dispute involving men of different counties, or when a 'criminal' fled from one county into another. It is impossible to say, even for the relatively well-documented western part of the Carolingian Empire, how many counts there were at any one time, let alone identify the personnel. (A recent guesstimate suggests '600-700 counties' in the Carolingian Empire as a whole[11] of which perhaps 100 would have been located in Charles's western kingdom; but given the frequency with which multiple countships were held by one man, there can be no straight translation from numbers of counties to numbers of counts.) Quality mattered, in any case, more than quantity. Some countships were more equal than others: a 'greater' count was presumably so called in part because his *civitas* was richer and more important, for instance, as a central place in one of the *regna* (like Angers in Neustria, or Autun in Burgundy). A 'greater' count operating on a frontier or elsewhere,

11   Werner 1980: 191.

called a *marchio*, or 'marquis' would have large military resources, and 'smaller' counts under his sway. In practice,
counts had autonomous sources of local power. Where evidence is available, some kind of hereditary comital succession seems always to have been normal. Studies of the
countships of Paris and Autun in the eighth and ninth centuries show that if a count had no son (or no adult son), a
brother or nephew or cousin would often succeed.[12]
Counts who possessed inherited lands within their counties
(and often elsewhere besides) could grant benefices there-
on to vassals of their own. They kept their own warrior–
followings, companions in hunting and in 'private wars'
(*werrae*) with rival magnates and their men. Counts can be
found as often in big houses on estates in the countryside
as in their *civitas*–centres. In the regions west of the Rhine,
the ascendance of bishops within many *civitates* may have
strengthened counts' preferences for the country life.
There is little sign of comital residences in *civitates*, nor any
evidence of a comital archive being kept in a *civitas* (as
they still had occasionally been in seventh-century Gaul).[13]
Carolingian sources usually refer to counts without spec-
ifying their *civitates* at all (which explains why it is impossible to give a complete list of counts for any ninth-
century county).

In the reigns of Charles the Bald's predecessors, the
count's first main function was to look after royal estates
(fisc-lands) and royal income (for instance from tolls and
fines) within his county. Second, he was expected to lead to
war the king's benefice-holders (*vassi*) from within his
county. Third, he exercised jurisdiction over the *pagenses*
(the 'men of the *pagus*' or county): replicating the assemblies of the realm at local level were the county assemblies
which were supposed to be held three times every year, and
met either in the *civitates* or elsewhere in the county. (Smal-
ler-scale gatherings could be held more frequently at meet-
ing-places in the countryside, at the count's discretion.)[14]

12 Levillain 1937b, 1938, 1941; Lot 1941.
13 Wood 1986: 13. Yet ninth-century counts were expected to keep
    documents; Nelson 1990f: 282–3. T. 139's explicit mention of a
    comital residence (at Angers) is unique among charters of Charles
    the Bald.
14 Werner 1980: 221–7.

All three comital functions are documented in Charles the Bald's reign, though royal instructions have a good deal more to say about the first and second than about the third. Counts can be seen as royal servants; but at the same time they used their position to entrench their local power. Charlemagne had complained, for instance, that some counts held too many assemblies – in order to extract 'gifts' from those forced to attend.[15] When he presided in court, the count was accompanied by a panel of local *boni homines*, 'good men', that is, more substantial landholders with perhaps further qualifications of age and experience and personal prestige, in whose selection an element of peer-group choice was acknowledged. Judgements were given with their collective approval. In practice, counts no doubt often had local *boni homines* in their pockets. Charles the Bald's counts, helping the king, also helped themselves.[16] Their supervision of mints and markets in their *civitates* would give plenty of opportunity for taking a cut. So too would the confiscation of misappropriated royal lands[17], or the dismantling of unauthorised fortifications.[18]

Charlemagne and Louis the Pious had found ways to forestall their losing out too much by such cosy local arrangements. To supervise for instance the selection of 'good men' to serve on local panels, they sent *missi* from the palace.[19] The term is significant: the passive past participle (*missus* literally means 'the sent man') implies a stress on the sender, and it is quite unspecific, again implying an agenda at the sender's discretion. Charlemagne often sent *missi* in pairs, one ecclesiastic (usually a bishop) and one count, on annual tours of duty, each pair given responsibility for a group of counties, their *missaticum*. *Missi* were supposed to hear and remedy complaints against counts and generally to function as direct lines of communication between court and locality, reporting difficult cases back to the king. Who was sent? A contemporary of Charlemagne's observed that a *missus* who lacked local

15 *MGH Capit.* I, nos. 44 (805), c. 16, p. 125.
16 See Nelson 1986c: 48, 62.
17 Nelson 1990f: 275.
18 *MGH Capit.* II, no. 273, additional c. 1, p. 328.
19 *MGH Capit.* I, no. 40, c. 3, p. 115; II, no. 192(829), c. 2, p. 15.

clout would be far too susceptible to local pressures. More effective might be a *missus* sent to his own home-territory where his power was trusted and feared.[20] He would then use his office to pursue his own interests. Well, potency was preferable to impotence. So long as the *missi* remained royal appointees, and in regular face-to-face contact with the king, the substance of royal interests too could be preserved.

Missi were enthusiastically deployed by Charlemagne and Louis the Pious. They continued to be used in the next generation by Charles the Bald. In fact they are well-attested then (in descriptive as well as prescriptive evidence) *only* in Charles's kingdom, especially in Francia and Burgundy, but also in Aquitaine.[21] *Missi* continued to be expected to supervise counts, and to act as vital links between palace and counties. It is precisely in reference to such functions that the issue of royal control arises. For if Charles the Bald profited from the increased resources generated by the ninth-century economy, so too did the aristocracy. Their power grew. But did it necessarily grow *at the expense of* royal power? Montesquieu posed the question in the eighteenth century (it was still topical then) and gave the answer: yes. He saw what he took to be Charles the Bald's institutionalisation of hereditary countships in 877 as clinching his case.[22] In fact, there had been a tendency for countships (and benefices) to become hereditary long before the mid-ninth century: it was inherent in a social organisation where power and property in general were inherited. Nor did that tendency in itself inevitably

20 On *missi* generally, Werner 1980: 191–211. For local magnates as *missi*, Nelson 1986c: 47–8. The Lorsch Annals 802 (English translation King 1987: 144–5) have been thought to imply that Charlemagne used humble men ('poorer vassals') as *missi* until that date, but found them too open to bribery and so appointed magnates thereafter. Hannig 1983, points out that the annalist confuses two sorts of *missi*: humbler men used as agents of the ruler for instance in estate-management, and magnates entrusted with governmental powers. Hannig also stresses the annalist's propagandistic purpose: Charlemagne demanded personal incorruptibility of his leading men.

21 See for instance *MGH Capit* II, no. 260 (Servais): below, Map 7; T. 375; the Perrecy case discussed by Nelson 1986c: 53–5.

22 Above: 12–13.

mean loss of royal control. One crucial factor was whether the king in appointing a count or *missus* had any real choice: for instance, as between kinsmen, or between an outsider and a local man. The evidence from Charles the Bald's reign is surprisingly clear: he could and did intervene thus – on numerous occasions and in counties that were vitally important politically and militarily. The converse, although more difficult, was also possible: Charles could remove a count from whom his favour was withdrawn.[23] Last but not least, he was able to maintain contact with his counts and *missi* through meetings at assemblies.

Counts had their subordinate officers, viscounts and vicars, and beneath them hundredmen (*centenarii*) and (perhaps only in some areas) *Franci homines* ('Frankish men') who were tenants on royal land (hence, royal vassals of a special kind) and owed special obligations of service in return, notably in reporting and repressing crime. Charles the Bald's capitularies presuppose the effectiveness of these local 'agents of the state' in requiring decisions to be transmitted to lower-level 'assemblies in dioceses or counties' and then carried out. Viscounts apparently helped to run mints, while hundredmen received oaths from *Franci homines*.[24] There is a frustrating lack of the sort of corroborative evidence for the carrying-out of functions which we occasionally have in the case of counts and *missi*. Equally scarce is information on royal estate-managers in Charles's reign. Royal charters and letters show, as do capitularies from beginning to end of the reign, the king's keen interest in exploiting landed wealth; but as in the reigns of Charles's father and grandfather, the great bulk of the evidence is prescriptive rather than descriptive. At the end of the day, the efficacy of Charles's control over his local agents must be gauged from the political action with which the rest of this book is mainly concerned.

*

The most influential model of ninth-century political

---

23 For the cases of Bernard of Autun, Hunfrid of Gothia, and Gerald of Bourges, see below: 202, 211–12.
24 *MGH Capit.* II, no. 266, c. 2, p. 286; no. 273, c. 14, p. 315; no. 260, oath-formula p. 274.

change since Montesquieu's has been that of the Belgian historian Jan Dhondt. Charles the Bald remained the villain of the piece. In Dhondt's view, Charles was the arch-squanderer of the fisc, his reign the critical period in the formation of territorial hereditary principalities in what would become France, for it was Charles who allowed the amassing of countships and once-royal estates by great regional magnates.[25] Dhondt had an important point: the ancestors of some of the great houses of the twelfth century are indeed to be found among the recipients of Charles's favour. There is a frequent absence of straight lines between the two periods, however. Take the example of Robert the Strong, ancestor of the Capetians: Robert, Count of Anjou, was killed in 866 and his two sons were disinherited by Charles, only recovering their father's Neustrian *honores* in the 880s, after Charles's death. Dhondt's argument seems to fit Flanders best: but the Count Baldwin (died 879) who held some counties in that region in the latter part of Charles's reign is never called 'Count of Flanders' in any ninth-century text; the hallmarks of entrenched territorial power (systematic fortifications; minting of coins) are not to be found during his lifetime, but rather in that of his son; Baldwin had no monopoly on power in Flanders, for other magnates operated in the same region; finally, no hereditary transmission of the 'principality' can be demonstrated here during Charles's reign but only, again, after Charles's death.[26] Though some of Baldwin's kinsmen found favour with Charles the Bald, there is no evidence that they formed a consistent political grouping – any more than Robert and his relatives did. In the ninth century, members of this magnate stratum, this 'imperial aristocracy', could still move about the Carolingian world; and they moved nearly always as individuals, no doubt with retinues, but not (an exceptional case apart)[27] concerting action with groups of kinsmen.

---

25 Dhondt 1948. For some valuable criticisms, see Martindale 1985.
26 Dhondt 1948: 109; 250. Werner 1978: 155–9 suggests 'a widely-spread clan' on the basis of name-evidence alone. Brown 1989: 18–29 wisely cautions on methodology.
27 *AB* 861: 94–5; below Ch. 8: 200–1 – significantly, from east of the Rhine.

There were two interlocking reasons for this individual mobility. One was that patrimonies were not large enough to maintain several brothers in the style to which they were accustomed: perhaps because the survival of several brothers was becoming more common at this social level, noble younger brothers often had to seek their fortunes far afield, whether in an ecclesiastical or in a secular career. The second reason was precisely that a single Carolingian world still existed, and men of the high nobility moved within it. Kings – Charles the Bald and his brothers and nephews – competed for their talents and support. Charles's maternal uncles and their sons provide good examples of the geographically-disparate fortunes of different descent-lines and individuals within Charles's own lifetime. Younger men sometimes criss-crossed the frontiers of Carolingian *regna*: middle-age brought a tendency to settle down in the *regnum* where closeness to the king (modern German historians have coined the useful term *Königsnähe*) had brought greatest rewards.[28] But a great man, a *potens*, in Charles's kingdom could quit the scene as completely as he had momentarily seemed to dominate it: if he died leaving only young sons, or no sons at all, or if he moved to another Carolingian kingdom, Charles might redistribute his *honores* as he put it, *voluntarie* – 'in accordance with my will'.[29] The king could also transfer such men from one region to another within his own kingdom.[30] They might be given no time to put down territorial roots.[31] It is this footloose quality of so many of the *potentes* in Charles's reign which belies Dhondt's tidy territorial model. Magnate moves were critically affected (if not determined) by the decision of the king, and what bound such men to the king was their dependence on *Königsnähe*: in Baldwin's case, the abduction of that most desirable of treasures, a king's daughter, was the highroad to fame and fortune.[32]

---

28 For Charles's maternal uncles and cousins, see Genealogy IV; for Hubert, Hugh and Hilduin, see below: Chs. 8 and 9.
29 Below: 196. For the cases of Adalard, Robert and perhaps Engelram, see below: 209; 213; 240.
30 For the cases of Odo, Robert, Boso and Bernard, see below.
31 For examples of magnates who failed to establish themselves in the Spanish March, see Collins 1983: 255–8.
32 Ch. 8: 203, below. Cf. Ch. 6: 148 for the comparable case of Giselbert in Lothar's kingdom.

The king derived further freedom of manoeuvre from the existence below this 'imperial aristocracy' of a lower stratum of regional nobility. These men had strong territorial roots, but at local level. Within a region, several noble families competed for influence. The king could intrude on the local scene by bringing in an outsider (perhaps with some local associations)[33] but he also had the option of picking a talented man from a local family to endow with countships or abbacies.[34] There was nothing inherently subversive of royal authority here. On the contrary, such dispositions of *honores* and patronage were, as they had been for Charles's predecessors, crucial instruments of royal power in the regions.

Within the region of the Seine basin where Charles's power was concentrated and where he most often stayed, the counts were of the 'lesser' variety. When Charles sat in judgement, he had a whole entourage of such counts beside him. But it may be no coincidence that counts of Paris, Rouen, Senlis and Rheims are un-documented in Charles's reign.[35] Here in his own heartlands, his home-base, the king alone stood tall among lay *potentes*. He was helped by ecclesiastical wealth and power. Charles the Bald's ancestors, the eighth-century founders of the Carolingians' family fortunes, had taken control of the church and its resources on a massive scale, and systematically: they had incorporated the church into the state. Though some churchmen protested, on the whole they accepted royal exactions as the price of protection and corporate power: they saw that the alternative was the wholly *unsystematic* despoilment and privatisation of church property not only by laymen but by individual ecclesiastics too.[36] (A bishop or abbot might be tempted to put the lands and treasures of his church at his family's disposal.) Archbishop

33 Examples are Odo and Robert in Neustria, Wulfgrin in the Angoumois, and Bernard at Autun.
34 Vivian rather than Lambert in the Loire valley during the 840s, for instance; Ranulf in Poitou; and Rodulf's family (see Martindale 1990b) in Angoumois-Limousin. For Charles's use of such alternative options on the Spanish March, Collins 1990b.
35 Conrad was Count of Paris in 879, *AB*: 217, but is not so identified in *AB* 876: 198. Charles's treasury may have been at Senlis from c. 860.
36 Nelson 1986a (1979).

Hincmar of Rheims endorsed the Christian monarchy whose laws promised both security for ecclesiastical wealth and firm support for the church as an institution with its own hierarchical structure, as well as investing Charles's kingship with new forms of legitimacy, Hincmar, as he wrote proudly to the pope, regularly supplied the military aid he owed to the king.[37] The 'aid' took the form of contingents of warriors maintained on the lands of the see of Rheims, but still available for service at the king's behest. Contingents organised and supplied by churches formed a significant part of Carolingian armies (a proportion that may have grown larger during the ninth century), complementing the king's own military household and the troops led by lay nobles.

A bishop's military resources were also an essential part of his local lordship. Like any other landlord, he relied on his men to coerce his peasant tenantry. The bishop's kinsmen and clients would tend to receive grants of lands belonging to the see, and would appear in lawcourts as the bishop's friends and witnesses. An archbishop was a regional magnate. Hincmar of Rheims wrote to give orders to a neighbouring count who just happened to be his kinsman: it is not hard to see how an archbishop might refer to the local counts collectively as 'his', or the draftsman of a capitulary write in general terms of 'archbishops and their counts'. Such accumulations of local power were not antithetical to royal government, however, but rather its potential agencies. At Rheims, Rouen, Sens or Bourges, the archbishops may well have assumed the functions (and resources) of those 'greater' countships. Again, the vital questions were: could the king appoint archbishops? and could he keep in regular contact with them once appointed? In both cases, the answer was an unequivocal yes.[38]

To reward the faithful service of count or young man in the palace, the king granted, out of the extensive and farflung royal estates, *beneficia* – benefices: the very term, meaning 'good deeds', implied something personal and arbitrary, outwith the normal regulations governing family inheritance. The grant was to an individual, and could be

37 *MGH Epp.* VIII, no. 198, p. 206
38 For episcopal lordship generally, see Kaiser 1981.

revoked if the recipient lost the king's favour; but the son of the original tenant would expect, other things being equal, to 'inherit' the benefice. The king might be happy to comply; on the other hand, he had a strong interest in maintaining his pool of benefices, and sometimes tried to resume a grant on the death of a tenant, especially if the potential heir was a child. If the heir's family or friends objected, they might over time persuade the king, or *his* heir, to a change of mind. A chance mention in a letter written in the 820s shows that one card in a Carolingian king's hand was the existence of a 'solemn custom' whereby any recipient of a benefice had to come to the palace in person and ritually 'commend' himself to the king. Even when a benefice was in effect being inherited, it was accepted that the king's right should be acknowledged at the moment of succession. The worried son of a deceased benefice-holder mobilised two great magnates, one of them well-placed at court, to ensure his succession to a *beneficium non grande* when he himself was prevented from coming to the palace. Plausible excuses had to be offered. ('he is not old but he suffers terribly from gout').[39] From the king's standpoint, the vital consequence was that in each county he had a loyal cadre of men whose services and renders he could call on directly when he chose. According to Notker the Stammerer (whose *Deeds of Charlemagne*, written at St-Gall in the 880s, reveals much of the workings of ninth-century government), 'Charlemagne was very prudent . . . he never gave any count more than one estate at a time . . . unless there were special reasons for doing so. When asked by his closest advisers why he had this habit, he replied: With this income or that estate, . . . I can make as a good a vassal out of some faithful man as can any of my counts, and maybe even a better one'.[40] Counts needing the wherewithal to attract service were likely to cast greedy eyes on royal benefices within their counties: but in the West Frankish kingdom, the earliest evidence of such 'mediatisation' of *vassi dominici* comes only after the death of Charles the Bald.[41]

39 Einhard *MGH Epp.* V, p. 123 dated 833, in reference to a benefice in Burgundy.
40 Notker I, 13.
41 See below, Ch. 10: 261.

What sanctions existed to enforce compliance with the orders of *missus* or count? The king's 'boys' were trained for war, and could in the last resort be used as a sort of flying squad to coerce a recalcitrant local *potens* on his home-ground.[42] But *potentes* too had their squads of trusty vassals.[43] To have such a group under one's roof making their own vociferous demands imposed certain constraints and posed problems of control. The retinue of Count Hugh of Tours, for instance, sang rude songs to mock his alleged cowardice: 'He daren't come out of his own doorway!'[44] When lords met, especially if they spoke different languages, it was expected that their followings might quarrel. Mock battles were quite likely to turn into serious ones.[45] These young men's violence could be unleashed almost at random. *En route* to assemblies or campaigns, they were liable to ravage and steal and rape.[46] An able lord could redirect his men's energies to his own ends in the avenging of a slight, the quest for an heiress or the prosecution of a claim. Such violence was an everpresent threat to, but at the same time always a potential instrument of, Carolingian government. Charles the Bald could warn or punish by leaving a trail of havoc along his line of march.[47] Yet many had a strong interest in the control and positive redirection of violence. This was what kingship promised to the church and to the *pauperes* – the powerless ones who suffered. *Potentes* themselves often preferred a peaceful alternative.

Kings found many kinds of entrée into local politics. Though property-disputes were no doubt very often settled informally, through arbitration by senior family-members,

42   For an example, see *AB* 868: 143.
43   Nelson 1989a.
44   Thegan c. 28, p. 597.
45   Nithard III, 5, commenting admiringly that Charles the Bald and his brother Louis kept perfect control of the military exercises conducted by their men.
46   Injunctions to maintain *pax in itinere* ('on the march') were the staple fare of Carolingian capitularies from the eighth century onwards: e.g. *MGH Capit.* I, nos. 18, cc. 6, 7; 75, p. 168; 150, cc. 16, 17; p. 305; *Capit.* II, nos. 204, *adnuntiatio Karoli* c. 1, p. 71; 260, c. 12, 13, p. 274; 266, c. 9, p. 287.
47   *AB* 861: 96; 866: 136. Cf. above, Ch. 1: 16, for Charles restraining his men when he wanted to.

for instance, and so have left no trace in the written record, some recorded cases arose over property-claims held or transmitted through women, especially widows. The protector of all such 'weak persons' was the king and so such disputes invited royal as well as ecclesiastical intervention.[48] Another common cause of recorded disputes was the 'theft' of church property by laymen. Such thefts often arose from grants of benefices known as *precariae* (from *preces*, the 'prayer' or 'request' which had to be offered by the recipient) on church lands. It was the standard form of patronage operated by ninth-century ecclesiastical *potentes*. In principle, a *precaria* was temporary (often limited to three lives: typically the recipient, his wife, their son). The recipient, however, had a strong interest in reducing the precariousness of his holding: he could hope that, over time, the grant would be merged in his patrimony. Such a neutralising of the grantor's intentions was not something that evolved in Charles the Bald's reign, a degradation of a once-pure system: rather, there was always, from the time when the earliest precarial grants are documented, a tendency for grants to be assimilated to hereditary lands, and then be passed along with those to the beneficiary's heirs. When disputes arose out of such situations, both parties might turn to royal justice.[49]

Royal power worked through the church in more direct ways. Not only archbishoprics but episcopal sees were filled by royal appointment from among the pool of palace clerks.[50] Charles the Bald did this effectively throughout his reign. Lay-abbacies, though not his invention, were deployed by Charles with a new frequency.[51] This entailed a dual arrangement: an ordained regular abbot (i.e. a monk, one who followed a *regula*, or rule) ran the community's liturgical work and day-to-day upkeep from the inside, while, from the outside, a lay aristocrat assumed control of

48 As for instance in the resolution of the divorce-case of Stephen; see below: 196–7.
49 For the case of the Neuilly estate Ch. 9, below: 241. For the Perrecy case, Nelson 1986c: 53–5. On precarial grants and local politics at a slightly later period, Nightingale 1988 is invaluable.
50 Lupus Ep. 26 (dated 842) states this as Carolingian custom.
51 Felten 1980. The best example is Count Vivian at St-Martin, Tours; below: 142, 158.

the community's landed endowment along with responsibility both for the military service owed to the king from the men beneficed on the monastery's lands, and often for hospitality at the monastery for the king and his entourage. In many cases, the community's total landholdings were divided, so that a share known as the *mensa* ('the table') was earmarked for the community's maintenance, the rest being available for the lay-abbot's management and the king's service. Royal guarantees secured such a division. Very similar in practice to a lay-abbot's was the position of a secular cleric (that is, a man in holy orders, often a deacon or sub-deacon, and not a member of the monastic community) appointed to an important abbacy. In both cases the king secured political and military service without the loss of fiscal lands. The secular cleric had the further advantage from the king's standpoint that he was strictly a life-tenant, unable to transmit his abbacy to a legitimate heir. As for the religious communities themselves, they had long since sought the protection of local *potentes* to speak for them as advocates in legal disputes or to put in a word with the king. Lay-abbacies formalised such arrangements on the king's terms. Like all early medieval lordship, a lay-abbacy carried responsibilities. Its holder cared about his reputation in this world and the next, hence often brought protection and prosperity to the community in his charge. Above all, he had to care about satisfying the king, maker and beneficiary of such appointments. During Charles's reign, lay-abbacies contributed significantly to the maintainance of royal power. At St-Denis, from 867 onwards, Charles himself was lay-abbot.

It was to him as king, however, hence as guarantor of all rights, individual or collective, of free men in his realm, that a group of St-Denis tenants came in 861, seeking a royal judgement against the abbey's local representatives. Charles's tribunal sat at the palace of Compiègne. Twenty-three men (including a notary) came from St-Denis's estate at Mitry (dep. Seine-et-Marne) some 60 km away, bringing with them 18 women (including ten 'with their children', because the case turned on legal free status which was transmitted through a mother to her offspring). 'They claimed that they ought to be [treated as] free *coloni* by birth, and that Deodadus the monk [responsible for running the Mitry estate] wanted unjustly to bend them down into an inferior service by force, and to afflict them.' Deodadus naturally contested the claim (the men, he said, were serfs (*servi*), 'hence bound in right (*per drictum*) to inferior service') and won: that is why St-Denis preserved the evidence. There is no way of knowing if other cases were judged by Charles's tribunal in favour of peasant groups complaining against their lords. But the peasant plaintiffs in the Mitry case presumably made the journey to Compiègne believing they *might* win.[52]

Peasants certainly lacked the spatial mobility required for regular participation in the politics of the realm. Yet even peasants, bounded through their lives mostly by their immediate vicinity, could sometimes travel further afield, whether pursuing a legal claim, like the Mitry group, or about their lords' business, like the men of St-Germain-des-Prés who owned transport-services between Anjou and the Paris neighbourhood.[53] Capitularies reveal landlords' anxieties about peasant emigrants who transferred their labour elsewhere; polyptychs show landlords welcoming peasant immigrants onto their lands. On the whole, however, it was the powerful who travelled in the Carolingian world, following the economic and political requirements of the seasons: winter would be spent at a home-base, whereas in summer men took the road when summoned to assembly and/or campaign. The letters of Abbot Lupus of Ferrières allow us a glimpse of his contradictory attitudes to involvement in state affairs. For *potentes* like himself, such involvement was an overriding moral obligation. Yet Lupus, awaiting a royal summons, was torn between hope and fear: attendance (and to ignore an invitation was dangerous) threatened new burdens, yet being with the king (though to appear *un*invited was unthinkable) offered the prospect of benefits.[54] What Lupus could be sure of was that invitations would be sent: the attendance-lists of assemblies are evidence of invitations received and obeyed. A system of post-horses and vouchers for supplies and hospitality ensured that royal messengers and royal agents (including

52 T. 228. See Nelson 1986c: 51–3.
53 Devroey 1984: 572–6.
54 Lupus Epp. 15, 17, 41, 45, 58, 67. Cf. above: 49–50.

Lupus himself) could move around the realm. Information of most political importance, such as news of the death of a king or queen, went astonishingly fast, both within Charles the Bald's kingdom and, over great distances, between Carolingian kingdoms.[55] When Charles left for Italy in 877, among his chief concerns was the maintenance of efficient communications with his faithful men back in Francia.[56] The frequent meetings between Charles and his Carolingian fellow-rulers were co-ordinated between the courts concerned. Of course the transport-technology of Charles's regime, as of any *ancien régime,* had its hazards: once crowns were mislaid in transit (though unlike the baggage of the English King John three centuries later, they were soon found).[57] But the 'miracle' that Nithard saw in the safe delivery to Charles at Troyes of regalia from Aquitaine was in the eye of the beholder.[58]

For the most part, the political history of Charles the Bald's reign which is this book's prime focus was the concern of an aristocratic elite. Though king and magnates depended (as Chapter 2 showed) on the labours of a vast peasant labour-force for the surpluses that sustained and funded their activities, their direct personal contact with peasants seems to have been rare, even within the lands they ruled most intensively. Royal and local government often give the impression of operating independently of each other, on two separate planes.[59] Yet against apparent distinctness of structures must be set evidence of linking, and overlapping, relationships. Lords and peasants shared attitudes and beliefs. The Mitry peasants (like the proverbial cat) could look at a king, and they spoke the same legal language of customary rights and fairness as Charles and his faithful men used in their capitularies. Every coin in those peasants' purses bore the royal monogram and title prescribed by the king. Political events from time to time touched peasants directly: war and external attack

---

55 Lupus Ep. 41 refers to supply vouchers (*tractoriae*). See further Ganshof 1927. For examples of news travelling fast, below Ch. 8: 219; Ch. 9: 221.
56 *MGH Capit.* II, no. 281, c. 25, p. 360.
57 *AB* 865: 127.
58 See below Ch. 5: 113–14.
59 Cf. the fine analysis of the Breton evidence in Davies 1988: 201–10.

harmed their lands and families, while Charles the Bald's fiscal demands affected all levels of the peasant work-force at least on royal and ecclesiastical estates. Quite small-scale landholders, and not only in Francia proper, but in Brittany and the Auvergne too, used royal reign-years, as magnates did, to date their transactions.[60] The vast majority of cases involving peasants were heard in local courts, but the judges in those courts wielded an authority devolved in principle from the king. The ideology of royal power was already widely diffused in Charles's kingdom after centuries of Merovingian rule. Under the Carolingians, churchmen preached it still more intensively.

The religious life of Charles and his contemporaries is not the main theme of this book, but no political study can ignore it. Ritual observances punctuate Charles's story in the chapters that follow; churchmen intervene in politics not only as purveyors of ecclesiastical resources and institutional support but as counsellors and monitors, sometimes interested parties, but sometimes too, as more or less disinterested arbiters and spiritual guides. For the ninth century was a crucial period in the ecclesiastical history of western Europe. At one level, that history was (and remains) one of particular churches caught in webs of local traditions, loyalties and observancies, dependent on local patronage and personnel. Nevertheless, the church had an institutional existence on other levels. It was the 'frail aqueduct' across which late Roman administrative practice, with its geographical division into provinces and dioceses, passed to early medieval successor-states, including the kingdoms of the Carolingians.[61] Charlemagne and Louis the Pious and their counsellors had strengthened the authority of archbishops, and promoted regular meetings of councils of one province or of several provinces: trends that continued after 840, and especially in the kingdom of Charles the Bald. The evidence lies in two imposing series of texts, the records of church councils, and the statutes (regulations for the performance of sacramental and pastoral duties) issued by bishops and archbishops for their lower clergy. In both cases, though some parallel texts survive from Lothar-

---

60 Davies 1988: 201–2; *Cartulaire de Brioude*: 200–1, 203–5, 210.
61 Anderson 1974: 131, and cf. 137.

ingia, from East Francia and Italy, the bulk of the evidence comes from the kingdom of Charles the Bald.[62] A third kind of evidence points the same way: the great collection of canon law known by the mythic name of 'Pseudo-Isidore', the substantial and, despite the inclusion of some forged papal letters, for the most part perfectly genuine residue of the western churches' institutional life over eight centuries, was produced in the heart of Charles's kingdom, in the province of Rheims, about 850.[63] One of its main purposes was to defend the integrity of the church by affirming both its institutional property-rights and its hierarchical internal organisation. The 'Pseudo-Isidorean' team could have accomplished their work nowhere else in the Carolingian world, any more than the series of conciliar acts and episcopal statutes could have been produced anywhere else on such a sustained large scale. For it was in the western part of Charlemagne's Empire that a particular combination of conditions – persisting Roman administrative and legal practices, well-organised provincial churches with longstanding traditions of conciliar meetings and the issuing of legislation, elites long-christianised and committed to their local churches, the written word in a language not too far removed from the spoken vernacular – favoured a particularly strong corporate awareness and activity on the part of churchmen within a group of provinces. Hincmar of Rheims played a crucial role; but alongside him were colleagues with similar training, shared traditions and experience. It makes sense, therefore, to think of the ninth-century West Frankish church, deeply implicated though it was in secular politics, its personnel largely recruited from the indigenous nobility, and often riven by factional rivalries, yet with its own corporate self-consciousness and distinctive goals. Charles the Bald did not simply exploit the church within his kingdom: he had to work with not against the ecclesiastical grain. And, a point of critical importance, he himself had been educated by churchmen and shared, if not their institutional loyalty, then many of their aims and ideals.

Embracing local and provincial churches was the

---

62 Hartmann 1989; Brommer 1985.
63 Fuhrmann 1972: 191–6; Fuhrmann 1990: 224–6.

Church, headed by the papacy. On this level too, there were important changes in the ninth century. 'From below', provincial churchmen in the various kingdoms from time to time demanded authoritative rulings, arbitration, and leadership, to maintain their churches' own new-won institutional integrity, or to fight more particular battles involving the interests of ecclesiastical individuals or groups;[64] and lay persons sought the pope's protection.[65] 'From above', a line of exceptional popes asserted the authority of their office and the universal scope of their pastoral care, willingly responding to appeals from the rest of Christendom. In the 860s, a new bout of jurisdictional conflict with the patriarchate of Constantinople gave Nicholas I an opportunity to speak for 'the Latin Church' against 'the Greeks'. In the 870s, his successors Hadrian II and John VIII exploited an impending imperial vacancy (Louis II of Italy lacked a male heir) to claim for the papacy the right to choose emperors.[66] At the same time, the growing threat of Arab expansion in the western Mediterranean evoked passionate pleas for help from the beleaguered popes. It was no coincidence that these decades saw new programmatic statements of papal ideology and a revitalising of contacts between Rome and all parts of the west. It was equally predictable that these contacts were liveliest with the West Frankish church; and that it was Charles the Bald who responded most strongly, both positively, to papal appeals for help, and also aggressively, to what he saw as papal interference in the West Frankish church's political concordat with his own regime.[67]

*

Ramshackle, held together by a thousand personalised special arrangements, a state existed, still, in the ninth century, capable of being operated by a skilful king. The central subject of the rest of this book is the way in which

64 For the clerks of Ebbo, Rothad of Soissons, Hincmar of Laon and Carloman, see *AB* 866: 132, 865: 123–4. 868: 152, 870: 171.
65 For the cases of Judith and Baldwin, and Theutberga, see below Ch. 8: 203, 215.
66 The significance of these popes was stressed by Ullmann 1962: Ch. vii.
67 See his protest to Pope Hadrian, below Ch. 9: 235–8.

the operation was managed by Charles the Bald. Ninth-century writers when they wanted a metaphor (and a paradigm) for the system at work invoked the *familia*: the patriarchal household, the big house (as Dhuoda called it): – the palace. This too was in some ways a ramshackle world: where rotten beams could give way, hurling king and courtiers to injury or death; where everyone's dinner might depend on the day's hunting; where an often crude and cruel humour mimicked life.

> The king's son had a young man's idea of a joke: he thought he'd test the courage and much-vaunted toughness of Albuin. One evening when they were coming back from the hunt, he pretended to be someone else and, all alone, jumped on Albuin pretending that he was going to steal by violence the horse Albuin was mounted on. Albuin, little knowing he was the king's son, unsheathed his sword and struck him on the head . . . When Albuin realised whom he had struck down, he fled.

Such was the fate of Charles of Aquitaine, second son of Charles the Bald: horribly wounded, he lingered on, to die two years later.[68]

Yet this was also a society with its own code, its own strict tempo of liturgical observances, its own rituals of rank and solidarity, honour and shame. Some acts put a man outside it altogether: at a summer assembly in 846, a man guilty of sodomy with a mare was condemned 'by the judgement of the Franks to be burned alive'.[69] On the other hand, outsiders could be welcomed in if they acknowledged the basic rules: a Viking recruit could 'swear fidelity in his own fashion' or, better still, accept Christian baptism.[70] At the king's table, as in the great processions from residence to chapel that marked the church's great feastdays, men knew their places. When the king held court, nobles in attendance participated in the giving of judgements; brought and received gifts; joined royal feasts or fasts; heard royal speeches. From the palace, they went out to hunt, or to make war, together.[71] At home, their life-style aped that of

68 Regino 870: 101. See below Ch. 8: 209–10.
69 *AB* 846: 63.
70 *AB* 858: 86; 862: 98–9. See below Ch. 8: 206.
71 Jarnut 1985; Nelson 1987.

the royal household: a great magnate had his own jester, his band of retainers who hunted and ate with him, his chapel and his chapel clerks.[72] Because they all spoke the same language of fidelity, of joint interests and common belief, the great assembly could bring men together with their royal lord psychologically as well as physically. This was a court society: not in the sense sometimes imputed to the *ancien régime* of a parade-ground where a despot brought his nobility to heel, but an elite world where within shared conventions political conflict was contained and consensus was continually re-formed and re-enacted.[73] Notker has a story about Charlemagne: 'he had given his brother-in-law Udalric a number of grants of land, but after the queen's death, he revoked them because of something Udalric had done. A jester said in Charlemagne's hearing: "Now his sister's dead, Udalric's lost his lands, those in the east and those in the west". Hearing these words, Charlemagne wept, and he gave back to Udalric all he had formerly held'. Notker thought Charlemagne's reaction showed him a 'just ruler'.[74]

If personal relationships counted for a great deal more than structures in such a world, nobility and kinship gave a man claims on royal favour; and the most influential men – the holders of the key household offices, for instance – were those with special *Königsnähe*. The king retained some freedom of manoeuvre: he could not choose his blood-relatives but when bestowing patronage, especially with more distant kin, he could choose between them. He could choose his wife: her close kin would acquire their own claims on the king; but as Udalric's case showed, a king's in-laws could not count on keeping royal favour. The jester in Notker's story conveys the anxiety of men at the mercy of the king's will. There was the other, fearsome, face of royalty.

---

72 Miracle-stories offer glimpses of this life-style: e.g. *Mirac. S. Benedicti* c. 18, col. 921 for a count's jester; *Mirac. S. Mauri* c. 3, p. 467, for Count Rorico's devotions; *Mirac. S. Germani Autiss.* c. 68, col. 1238, for Vivian's hunting-hawks. Cf. also the aristocratic wills discussed above Ch. 1: 6–7; and see Airlie 1991.
73 Cf. Elias 1983, esp. ch. VI. See further Fried 1982; Nelson 1988a.
74 Notker I, 13. For marvellous insight into Notker's humour, Ganz 1989.

The 830s offer two particularly clear examples of aristocratic dependence. Bernard the chamberlain held his high office for only a few months, in 829–30. He lost both office and influence at court as a result of factional enmity, but Louis the Pious's disfavour ensured that the losses were permanent.[75] Adalard the seneschal is first documented in 831, and apparently kept his post through the 830s. He received the lay-abbacy of St-Martin, Tours; and in December 842 Charles the Bald 'married Adalard's niece Ermentrude . . . in order to win the support of most of the people'.[76]

The antecedents of both Bernard and Adalard had risen along with the Carolingians themselves. Bernard's father, a kinsman of Charlemagne, had been count of Toulouse, and several of his sons had shared his inheritance of land and position in the south-west of Gaul (though only Bernard achieved high favour at the court of Louis the Pious). Adalard's grandfather had been Pippin I's choice as count of Paris, a countship then held successively by Adalard's uncles and his brother. Both Bernard and Adalard were born with prospects of wealth and power in the Carolingian world. Rulers had to reckon with them. But both depended on *Königsnähe*. Both were accused by some contemporaries of pursuing their own interests, cynically exploiting their position, betraying the ruler when it suited them. Yet both defended themselves against the charge of infidelity.[77]

Birth and inherited status played only a part in the stories of Bernard and Adalard. The family connections that some historians have reconstructed, and alleged to explain the rise of both men, are curiously neglected by contemporary sources. Perhaps they were too well-known to need spelling out; but it is just as likely that the personal qualities which contemporaries did stress were what really accounted for both men's influence at the courts of successive Carolingians. Behind the monolithic abstraction 'aristocracy' was a real world of competing noble individuals, often threatened rather than supported by their own

75 See *AB* 831: 23, n. 5. See Genealogy VI.
76 Nithard IV, 6. See Nelson 1986a (1985): 231–3; and Genealogy VII.
77 For Bernard, see Nithard III, 2. His wife was Dhuoda; above: 41. Adalard was probably the author of an interesting letter of self-justification, *MGH Epp.*V, pp 343– 5. See Nelson 1991c: 44.

kin, lacking a strong enough local base, needing royal patronage and support. Even marriage into the royal family only assured such support in the short term. For space close to the king was limited, and few occupied it for more than a decade or so, partly through accidents of mortality, partly through a career-structure in which the holding of high office in the royal household was often the prelude to a provincial post,[78] but most of all through the play of faction around the king. A poet in the 870s imagined Charles the Bald controlling the wheel of fortune, throwing down one man, and raising up another. This was no mere poetic fantasy. A fallen favourite had little to hope for unless he could find an alternative royal patron.

What kept such hopes alive was conflict between royal kin. In the early Middle Ages, every royal family, as generation succeeded generation, seemed to be unhappy in its own way. If a ruler had a brother, or nephews, rivalry was virtually inescapable; if he had an adult son, or sons, tension was likely and open war an everpresent possibility. The women of the family often saw advantage in fomenting such disputes. Charlemagne was lucky in that his only brother, four years younger than himself, died in 771 after a short period of increasingly fraught joint-rule; but it took more than luck to remove that brother's sons – they, and their mother, disappeared when their uncle defeated and imprisoned their protector, the Lombard king. In his own sons, Charlemagne's fortunes were mixed: the eldest rebelled and was incarcerated; the ambitions of the remaining three legitimate sons were contained when each received a substantial part of the empire to rule while Charlemagne remained in overall charge. The illegitimate sons were too young to pose much of a threat during Charlemagne's lifetime. Half-brothers and cousins and in-laws were given large shares in the benefits accruing from *Königsnähe* : they commanded powerful military retinues, and were assigned large shares in the rewards of imperial expansion. Charlemagne used his womenfolk indirectly as

78 Instances of this pattern: Odo the butler, later count of Orléans; Vivian the chamberlain, then count of Tours; Boso, chamberlain (in Aquitaine), then duke of Italy; Theuderic, chamberlain, then count of Autun.

safety-valves for the resentments of male kin, and directly as props to his own authority. As a paterfamilias, Charlemagne did well. Even so, there is a note of baleful realism in his injunction that:

> none of our own sons should in any circumstances cause any [of our grandsons] accused before him to be put to death, or corporally mutilated or blinded or tonsured against his will, without lawful trial and inquiry.[79]

When he succeeded in 814, Charlemagne's sole surviving legitimate son, Louis the Pious, faced a family-situation in some ways more difficult than Charlemagne's. Though Louis had had plenty of time to gain experience of ruling and to form a court of his own in the subkingdom of Aquitaine (he had been king there since the age of three), he had had to wait a long time for his father's inheritance. This meant that some of his own sons were already adult when he succeeded at the age of 35: his eldest son Lothar was nearly 20 – old enough to provide an alternative focus of loyalty for aspiring nobles. The first thing Louis did when he reached Aachen was to clear himself some political space. Inevitably there were losers. Charlemagne's daughters and granddaughters (Louis's sisters and half-sisters and nieces) were sent away to convents, and Charlemagne's cousins to monasteries: Wala to Corbie, Adalard, Wala's brother, to remote Noirmoutier on an island off the coast of Aquitaine.[80] There were also winners. Louis's young half-brothers, the bastard sons of Charlemagne's old age, were recruited into Louis's entourage, joining his own sons; Louis's son-in-law Bego became count of Paris and his foster-brother Ebbo became archbishop of Rheims.[81]

On Maundy Thursday, 9 April 817, while Louis and his retinue were processing from a service in the splendid church at Aachen, the timber roof of a walkway collapsed on them, injuring several men seriously and giving the emperor himself a nasty shock: it was time to think hard about

---

79 Divisio c. 18, *MGH Capit.* I, no. 45, pp. 129–30, English translation King 1987: 255. See Genealogies I and II.
80 Astronomer c. 23; *Epitaphium* II, c. 22, and *Vita Adalhardi* c. 30.
81 Nithard I, 2. For Bego, see Werner 1990: 44–5, 49; for Ebbo, McKeon 1974b.

the distribution of power within the royal family. Louis and his great men deliberated, and decided: at the summer assembly in July, the *Ordinatio Imperii* accommodated Lothar's ambitions by giving him the title of co-emperor forthwith and promising him the whole of Francia on his father's demise.[82] This strategy revived the division-project that Charlemagne had adopted in 806 but never implemented. Earlier Frankish successions from the sixth century onwards had divided the heartlands, the patrimony, between royal brothers as well as assigning whatever acquired *regna* were available: the 806 and 817 projects, by contrast, gave the first-born son the patrimony entire, leaving the younger brothers *only* acquired *regna*. In 817 this meant that Aquitaine went to the 19-year-old Pippin, and Bavaria to the ten-year-old Louis (the future Louis the German). The scheme swept up one problem but shovelled others under the carpet. Lothar was happy; but what what was to become of Bernard, Louis the Pious's 19-year-old nephew, who had been ruling Italy since his father's death in 810? The *Ordinatio* assigned Italy to Lothar 'if God wills that he lives to be our successor' (c.17), without mentioning Bernard. Seeing his own disinheritance as imminent, Bernard rebelled. Louis the Pious reacted with devastating efficiency. The revolt collapsed, Bernard was captured and condemned 'by the judgement of the Franks' to be blinded, and died two days later, on 17 April 818. Bernard's fate was blamed, not long after, on Louis's wife, Lothar's mother the Empress Ermengard. Only six months after Bernard's death, Ermengard too died. Louis's prompt remarriage, in 819, to Judith, daughter of Count Welf, opened up a Pandora's box of possibilities. From the standpoint of Louis's existing sons, it was a provocative act. At about the same time, Louis's young half-brothers were tonsured and sent away from the court to monasteries. It was not long before Judith gave birth to a daughter, named Gisèle after Charlemagne's favourite sister. Louis was reconstituting the royal family, keeping his adult sons on tenterhooks.

The coexistence in Francia of Louis and Lothar as co-emperors was possible so long as Lothar remained unmar-

---

82 *RFA* 817; *MGH Capit.* I, no. 136, pp. 270–3. See Map 3.

ried. But in October 821 Lothar acquired a wife of his own. Two imperial households inevitably caused friction. In 822, Louis sought reconciliation with his half-brothers, pardoned the rebels of 818, and restored Abbot Adalard and probably Wala to favour. Louis then took the occasion of the summer assembly at Attigny 'with the counsel of bishops and magnates' to perform public penance 'for his own and his father's misdeeds'. What motivated Louis was neither political weakness nor a suddenly-discovered conscience.[83] He was posing as a new Theodosius, evoking the 'happy Christian emperor' who had performed penance for a political massacre, made his peace with his critics, and won the praises of St Augustine in *The City of God*. Louis too was determined to wipe the slate ritually clean of recent conflicts, in order to secure agreement for a new disposition of power within the royal family.[84] That Louis's basic intention was to reassert his own control emerged in the immediate sequel to Attigny: he 'sent Lothar to Italy';[85] and he engendered another child by the Empress Judith. That child was to be Charles the Bald.

83 Cf. McKitterick 1983: 135.
84 Werner 1990: 56–61.
85 *RFA* 822.

Chapter 4

823–840: YOUTHFUL TRAINING

Charles was born on 13 June 823 in the palace of Frankfurt
on the Main. The very fact that we have these details is
significant. Birthdays, in the modern sense, were rarely recorded in the early Middle Ages: it was the 'heavenly birthdays' (the earthly death-days) of saints and martyrs that
were celebrated in liturgies. We don't know the exact date
of birth of any early medieval king before Charles (nor of
most for centuries afterwards). There is no direct evidence
at all as to even which year Charlemagne was born; in
Louis the Pious's case, the year (but not the exact date) of
birth was recorded by the Astronomer, his anonymous biographer, because Louis was exceptional as the survivor of a
pair of twin boys. Even the births of firstborn royal babies
were rarely noted by contemporary annalists. High infant
mortality made such events of doubtful political importance. Thus no writer of the 820s or 830s mentioned the
birth of Charles. The Astronomer, writing some twenty
years later, noted its occurrence in 823. It was Charles himself, reviving the practice of Christian Roman emperors,
who arranged for the annual commemoration of his 'nativity in this world on 13 June' at a number of ecclesiastical
centres.[1]

There is a second, and paradoxical, significance in the
birth of 'the first king of France' at a location in 'Germany'. The Carolingian Empire in 823 was at its furthest

---

1   Astronomer c. 38; T. 147 (3 April 852); 246, 247. It was still cel-
    ebrated in the twelfth century at St-Denis, as Abbot Suger reported:
    Oeuvres complètes: 353–6.

extent, and Louis the Pious had numerous palaces in his Frankish heartlands. In the earlier years of his reign he had tended to stay in the central area of Francia proper, often at Aachen, his father's old base, or further west, for instance at Compiègne on the River Oise. From 822 his itinerary shifted eastwards: in 822–3 Louis and his court spent the whole winter at Frankfurt where 'he had had buildings newly constructed for this purpose following his orders'.[2] Frankfurt was to be a frequent residence in the later 820s.[3] The main explanation lies in shifting relationships within and around Louis's family. Louis was determined to assert his own authority throughout the heartlands, and to keep Lothar confined to Italy. Further, Louis's wife Judith hailed from the eastern part of the empire: her ancestors' connections with Alemannia, in particular, offered hopes of support in that region. More generally, it was in the 820s that Louis favoured *transrhenani* ('men from across the Rhine') which gave him a strong network of loyalties in the east, though it came to be bitterly resented in the west.[4]

According to Nithard, Louis was 'anxious' from the outset about the future of the new child, 'because he had already divided the whole empire between his other sons. Then [Louis] asked his sons on behalf of this son. At last Lothar consented on oath that the father should give [Charles] any part of the kingdom he wanted, and moreover that he [Lothar] would be his guardian and protector against all his enemies now and in the future'.[5] This passage was written in 841, and it reflects the hindsight knowledge of events in the 830s. The likelihood of a redrawing of the 817 project had surely been on the horizon since Louis married Judith (especially so if, as seems likely, she had already given birth to a daughter, Gisèle, in 821). What seems more doubtful is that Charles's future share in the realm was overtly discussed in June 823. Curiously Nithard does not reveal at this point (though he does so later) that Lothar stood godfather to his little half-brother. With the Frankish Church's new emphasis on godparental obliga-

---

2   *RFA*. See Map 1.
3   *RFA* 823, 826, 828, 829.
4   Adrevald c. 27, col, 931.
5   Nithard I, 2.

tions, such a reinforcing of a biological kin-tie by a spiritual one became an adroit response to the dangers set out by Charlemagne in the 806 division-project.[6] Lothar, as *primogenitus*, and future family-head, was the obvious choice as protector: he was also the worst threat to Charles's survival – literally, perhaps, as well as politically. The news of Charles's birth must have been exactly what Lothar had feared since his father's remarriage.

By contrast, Judith's influence was considerably enhanced. The sense of relief, and the newfound power, of a queen who has successfully produced a healthy boy emerge in an anecdote told by Charles himself over forty years later: 'In the very hour of my birth, my mother Judith sent a ring to Ebbo [archbishop of Rheims], asking him, since he was an archbishop, to pray for the newborn baby. She also promised that, if he returned the ring to her whenever he was in trouble, she would help him.'[7] Ebbo, added Charles, often took her up on this promise. Before 823, there is no mention of Judith's influence: assorted scraps of evidence thereafter attest her efforts to bolster her own position by collaborating closely (some said, too closely) with her husband's chief counsellors.[8]

No information survives about Charles's infancy. He may, like his father, have had a wetnurse (though his father as one of twins was atypical), and if so he may not have remained with Judith when, for instance, she travelled to Rouen to meet her husband in November 824. For us, Charles makes his first public appearance as a three-year-old, in the bosom of his family. The occasion was the baptism of a Danish king, Harald, at the palace of Ingelheim in June 826. Louis's use of baptismal ritual to suggest his own imperial status vis-à-vis Harald was modelled on Byzantine practice, and Louis was seeking, as his eastern counterparts so often did, to promote imperial interests through intervention in the dynastic conflicts of a barbarian people. Harald, challenged by rival kin, was willing to become the Franks' client. On Louis's part, the offer of patronage was an imaginative strategy for dealing with the Danes where

6   Above, Ch. 3: 72. See further Lynch 1986.
7   Letter to Pope Nicholas I, *PL* 124, col. 873.
8   Ward 1990a, 1990b.

conquest was simply not an option. The rituals of Ingelheim were original too in their extended use of godparental bonds: Louis stood godfather to Harald, Judith was godmother to Harald's wife, and Lothar was godfather to Harald's son.[9]

The brief accounts in the narrative sources say nothing about Charles. The spotlight first falls on the little prince in the verses of Ermold the Black. Aquitanian by origin, Ermold had been disgraced (for unknown reasons) and sent into exile at Strasbourg: a striking intervention by Louis in the affairs of the *regnum* of his son King Pippin of Aquitaine. Ermold wrote his verse biography of Louis to win back imperial favour.[10] For all its bias, such poetry written for a specific occasion has some obvious advantages as source-material. Ermold's final section covering the reception of the Danes at Ingelheim was written within hardly more than a year of the event, and with an explicit purpose: every detail was calculated to please Louis and Judith in 827. The account of the great procession into the palatine church at Ingelheim conveys the splendour and wealth, but also the order and control, of the imperial court. Roles, costume and gesture are meticulously assigned; everyone has his or her place, alongside, or following, the emperor. Just one person in two lines of the poem breaks the formal pattern:

Ahead of his father, the lovely boy Charles, resplendent
  in gold
Merrily goes, pattering with his feet across the marble
  floor.[11]

This could just possibly be accurate reporting of a three-year-old show-stealer. In any event, Ermold assumed that the parents would relish the description of their son, and be amused by the contrast between the adults' formality and the child's spontaneity (though such licence may have been permitted only to under-sevens). Charles's presence in the scene squares with evidence for comparable partici-

9 Angenendt 1984: 215–23.
10 Godman 1987.
11 Ermold ll. 2300–1, p. 176.

pation in public ritual by Charlemagne and Louis the Pious
when aged six and three, respectively. This was a central
part of the training of a prince. Royal parents could also
use the medium to convey a dynastic message: the ritual
role identified the child born to reign.[12]

To return to Ermold's procession: Charles's mother
Judith follows, flanked by the magnates Hugh (count of
Tours and Lothar's father-in-law) and Matfrid (count of Or-
leans).[13] The passage belies Nithard's suggestion that these
two were already in the mid-820s goading Lothar to harm
his young half-brother. Assuming, still, that Ermold wrote
to please, it follows that Hugh and Matfrid must have been
especially close to Judith in 826, which in turn implies that
she had indeed been successfully cultivating Lothar's sympathy for the interests of herself and her son.

Similarly calculated, and again perhaps no mere 'enco-
miastic vignette'[14] but drawn from life, is Ermold's picture
of the little Charles at his father's hunt:

> By chance a little doe with the pack of hounds behind
>   her flees
> Through the shady grove, and leaps through
>   willow-woods.
> See, the very place where the mighty throng and the
>   Empress Judith
> Had been standing, and with them the boy Charles
>   himself!
> The doe swiftly runs past, her only hope in her own feet.
> Unless flight brings her help, see! – she will die.
> Catching sight of her, the boy Charles – see him now! –
>   wants
> To follow his father's model: he asks, he begs for a keen
>   horse,
> Urgently demands weapons, quiver and swift arrows,
> And craves to go chasing after the doe, just as his father
>   himself would do.

12 Charlemagne: *RFA* 753; Louis: Astronomer c. 4. Cf. Alfred of
    Wessex, *ASC* 853; Alfred's grandson Athelstan: Lapidge 1981. For
    the importance of royal names, see Ermold's stress on 'Charles' in
    the passage quoted below.
13 Ermold ll. 2303–4, p. 176.
14 Godman 1985: 47; cf. Godman 1987: 124–5.

He redoubles plea on plea. But his beautiful mother
Forbids him to go, will not give way to his wishes.
If his tutor and his mother had not restrained him
    despite his desire,
The boy, as boys will, would have rushed off on foot.
But other young men go off and capture the fleeing
Little creature, and soon bring it back, unharmed, to the
    boy.
His weapons, specially made for one of tender years, he
    then seizes
And the boy strikes the beast's quivering back.
The glory of boyhood is all around him, embraces him:
The manliness of his father, the great name of his
    grandfather, adorn him:
He shines like Apollo, striding the summits of Delos,
Bringing great joy to Latona his mother.[15]

Echoes of Virgil, and of earlier Carolingian epic, are incorporated in Ermold's poetic offering. In these 21 lines,
where the word *puer* occurs seven times, he contrives to
praise the father in the son, and the grandfather's greatness in the promise of this new Charles. But the hunt is a
setting of more than ornamental significance: when the
young men of Judith's retinue aid the display of the
prince's virtue, they symbolically carry out their political
roles of aides and adjutants.[16]

Ermold depicted scenes of concord in 826. In the years
that followed, the factional conflicts that centred on Louis's
court were coolly observed by Hincmar, the future archbishop, then a young monk at St-Denis, close therefore to
Abbot Hilduin, Louis's archchaplain. Hincmar in The *Government of the Palace* noted the repercussions at court of rivalries in the regions.[17] A good example occurred in
827–8: a noble from the Spanish March, disappointed at
the palace, had gone home and allied with the Muslim
amir of Cordoba[18] to pursue local claims against Count
Bernard of Barcelona. Louis the Pious was Bernard's god-

15   Ermold ll. 2394–2415, pp. 182–4 (my translation, but owing much
     to Godman 1985).
16   Above Ch. 3: 45.
17   Above Ch. 3: 48.
18   Cf. *AF* 826: 24.

80

father (and distant cousin) and had recently appointed him count. Perhaps Louis was also stung by the threatened negation of his own youthful exploits on the March. He sent an army under Counts Hugh and Matfrid to help Bernard; but the two commanders delayed so long en route that Muslim troops were able to ravage the county of Barcelona. It was alleged that the delay was deliberate. At the Aachen assembly in February 828, Hugh and Matfrid lost the counties of Tours and Orléans which they had held since Charlemagne's reign. The court annalist thought it was 'what they deserved'.[19] The distribution of power, regionally in the middle Loire valley, and centrally among the great men at the court, was violently shaken. Louis reallocated Orléans and Blois to the brothers Odo and William, men who were his own mother's kin and also allies of Bernard, and probably Tours to Vivian, one of the local nobility. Judith for her part sought security for Charles and herself in new alliances. The youngest of Charles's half-brothers, Louis the German, was married to Judith's sister Emma in 827.[20] Bernard, count of Barcelona, the most obvious beneficiary of the disputes, in 829 was appointed chamberlain, a post that involved close collaboration with the queen.[21]

At the same time, Louis summoned a series of assemblies involving both bishops and lay nobles. The result was the biggest administrative programme seen since 817–18. Louis's aim was twofold: first, to cope with the tensions that had arisen from the implementation of ecclesiastical reforms, for instance by sending out *missi* to settle disputes between clergy and laymen over the appropriation of tithes; and second, to tighten control of local government, for instance, by asking *missi* to draw up lists of all those liable for military service in each county. Other instructions readjusted local power politics in line with the personnel-changes in 828: on 4 April 829, *missi* were instructed to investigate Matfrid's 'misdeeds' in the county of Orléans, and to encourage complainants to come forward.[22]

19 *RFA.*
20 *AX*: 7.
21 *Government of the Palace* c. 22.
22 *MGH Capit.* II, no. 188, c. 3, p. 10.

Charles the Bald was later to find inspiration in these measures. At the time, what can hardly have failed to make a strong impact on the boy were the great ritual events, including the assemblies, which punctuated the life of the court, and which Charles presumably was brought out by his nurse from the women's quarters to attend: the arrival of envoys from Constantinople at Compiègne in September 827; the public deposition from office of Hugh and Matfrid in February 828; the reception of the relics of SS Marcellinus and Petrus at Aachen a few weeks later. As striking for an impressionable child would have been the earth tremor on 27 March 829 which brought down houses in Aachen and damaged the roof of the palatine chapel.[23] What was the meaning of such an extraordinary event? No doubt his nurse had her answers.

It was at about this time that Charles acquired a tutor and through him began to look out on the world through a learned man's eyes. Walahfrid Strabo, a monk of Reichenau in Alemannia who had spent the years since 825 at the great monastic school of Fulda, was already known to some of the court clergy. In an early poem, he had skilfully enhanced Louis's reputation as a reformer by criticising moral shortcomings inherited from Charlemagne's regime. His plea that Louis stop appointing widows as abbesses may have been a response to the installation of Judith's mother Heilwig as abbess of Chelles.[24] But Walahfrid's most earnest request was for patronage; and Judith had enough political sense (a clever critic was the very man to disarm) and sympathy for a fellow-provincial to offer Walahfrid the post of tutor to Charles. Judith may also have admired Walahfrid's poetry. Certainly it was she, rather than her husband, whom scholars praised for such discernment, and she who apparently took a personal interest in the literary side of her son's education. (None of his half-brothers seems to have received anything like it.) Louis himself, enthusiastic huntsman that he was, no doubt saw to Charles's acquiring of physical skills. But if Charles was the first Carolingian, and perhaps the first medieval king, to show an insider's appreciation of contemporary scholarship, he had (directly

---

23 *RFA* 827, 828, 829; *Trans. SS Marcellini and Petri, PL* 104, cols. 574–9.
24 Visio Wettini: ll. 756–69, *MGH Poet.* II: 328.

or indirectly) his mother to thank. He studied with Walah-frid for the best part of nine years, from 829 until 838.

What did Charles learn? There is little direct evidence. His few surviving letters bear the hallmarks of Hincmar's style, though Charles may have personally dictated some; otherwise no work of Charles's is extant. But from the indirect evidence of books dedicated to him, scholars patronised by him, and texts produced in his name, a picture emerges of a man genuinely interested in learning. To know the Bible was to trace divine and human action in this world through history. It was also the key to understanding the workings of power in the present and the future. Old Testament kings were to be taken as literal models, the measurements of the Temple in Jerusalem as a blueprint for the palatine chapel. To grasp the mystic significance of numbers – for instance, the two poles of Solomon's litter, and the four struts that supported its canopy[25] – was to acquire (as some wielders of power in modern times have done through astrology) a sense of control over the contemporary world: to explain the failure of some policies, to plan and time others more effectively. The study of the Old Testament also had the practical purpose of explaining and justifying the organisation of the Church which was foreshadowed in the history of Israel and now through the sacraments offered all peoples the hope of salvation. Further, to share such knowledge and such assumptions united 'the wise' in a strong bond. What in the case of Alfred of Wessex is explicit can be inferred for Charles too: the inculcation of wisdom among the nobility was designed to strengthen their commitment to the king. Direct shared access to the written sources of wisdom was, for both Alfred and Charles, perhaps the most attractive of the uses of literacy. A king who drew scholars to his court from afar, surrounded himself with them, sought their help in formulating his edicts, used them as his agents and publicists, was following the example of the most successful rulers of antiquity. A learned court was a prestigious court in the eyes of the realm's elites; it impressed Greeks and Muslims too. Learning, in short, was useful because it enhanced the

25 Hincmar's *Ferculum Salomonis* was written at Charles's request; Taeger 1977. See further, Nelson 1991c.

style and substance of rulership. There was also a particular association of such patronage with *Carolus Magnus* – 'senior Charles' who from young Charles's earliest years was held up as a role-model for him.

The conduct of *Carolus Junior* (he seems to have approved this epithet) as king, casting retrospective light on his own formative years, suggests that his teachers vigorously instilled the lesson of wisdom's utility. It lies at the heart of the two-volume world chronicle of Bishop Freculf of Lisieux, who dedicated Book II of these *gesta imperatorum* to Judith, for use in the education of her son. Freculf also sent Charles a copy of the fifth-century military manual of Vegetius, an exercise in practical wisdom.[26] The same lesson can be found in the works of Walahfrid. He made short (and useful) summaries of the lengthy biblical commentaries of Hrabanus Maurus. He produced a practical edition (with chapter-divisions) of Einhard's *Life of Charlemagne*: in his prologue, written after 840, Walahfrid held up for emulation both Einhard's *scientia* and the preference of the 'most powerful and most wise' Charlemagne for the company of wise men. The *Life* made an excellent 'mirror' for a future ruler, and may well have been studied by Walahfrid and Charles in the mid-830s, soon after it was written. That joint reading perhaps lies behind the appeal in Walahfrid's prologue that the quest for wisdom be revived and widened 'in modern times'. The linkage of wisdom with power can hardly have escaped a student-prince. Another work of Walahfrid's, though written after his days as royal tutor were over, lets us guess what tutorials might have been like. *The Origins and Development of Ecclesiastical Equipment and Ritual* is the clear, systematic work of a very good teacher. It explains the ritual practices of the 'modern' church, ranging widely in space and time to assemble comparative data. It also contains an agenda for reform in emphasising the pastoral and teaching services of the priesthood. Finally, Walahfrid demonstrates the workings of two parallel hierarchies of office in church and state: each is animated by the vital flow of communication through it,

---

26 McKitterick 1980: 31. The sending of the Vegetius-manuscript can perhaps be dated to the period of Charles's education too. For Freculf's *Chronicle*, Nelson 1989b: 195.

and each buttresses the other. The work as a whole reflects the experience and preoccupations of a palatine cleric, and it addresses the questions of someone reared in that milieu.

The palace was also Charles's religious school. The cults of the saints were the very heart of its curriculum, and if the translations of relics were highdays and holidays, the liturgical calendar supplied its everyday timetable. Louis the Pious had a particular devotion for St Denis, and he conveyed this to his son.[27] Charles perhaps still more than his father regarded St Denis as both personal and dynastic patron; and though the earliest evidence of this comes from the early years of his own reign, it was surely rooted in childhood habits. Like other boys, Charles almost certainly had the Psalter for his primer, and the Wisdom Books of the Old Testament for further reading: his later ecclesiastical correspondents quoted especially profusely from these texts. But the Psalms were also the basis of private spirituality in the ninth century: Dhuoda recommended daily readings to her son. As a man, Charles possessed his own copy of the Psalter.[28] David, an obvious model for early medieval princes, could have had a special appeal for Charles (as we know he did for Alfred). Charles (like Alfred) was a youngest son, the boy who unexpectedly surpassed his elder brothers.

The Latin Psalter points towards Charles's acquisition of literacy. What language did the boy speak? Though the court of Louis was surely bilingual in Romance and Germanic, Charles's birthplace (and hence the implied origin of his nurse – which may be more relevant here than his mother's), and the likely residence-pattern of his early years suggest (again paradoxically for a future 'French' king) that his native language was, as in Walahfrid's case, a form of German. Tutor and pupil may, however, have spoken Latin to each other. For the Latin that the adult Charles read, and presumably wrote, so fluently, he must have owed Walahfrid a large debt. His taste for poetry too reflects his tutor's skill.

27 Brown 1989.
28 Above Ch. 1: 15.

It is no coincidence that our next piece of biographical evidence, like that for 826, is poetic, the work of Walahfrid himself. *Theodoric's Statue* was written soon after the poet's arrival at Aachen in 829. Its audience was familiar with the statue which Charlemagne had brought from Italy and set up in the courtyard at Aachen. Whatever meaning this image had had in Charlemagne's day, Walahfrid invited his contemporaries to compare and contrast the miserly, heretical, tyrannous Theodoric with the generous, orthodox and merciful Louis.[29] Most modern commentators have seen in this poem intimations of conflict. But only hindsight casts such a shadow. Though the poet, in broad terms, castigates greed and disloyalty, his message is one of optimism rather than foreboding, and his concern is not with general crisis but a particular, personal cause for rejoicing. Walahfrid pictures Louis, the new Moses, with his family and entourage in a procession that aptly symbolises order and unity. First comes Louis himself, followed by Lothar, then Louis the German: each is described in fulsome, if rather conventional terms. Pippin of Aquitaine is mentioned extremely briefly: he was not at Aachen in the summer of 829, says the poet. With Charles's appearance, Walahfrid's tone becomes more specific, warmer and more personal:

I saw too how lovely Rachel led forward
Benjamin, comfort of his ancestors, with her right hand,
  in due order:
His great well-being is for long to nurture someone's holy
  old-age.
For him, a fifth share, which the other one joyfully
  acquired,
Is left over, I think, for he will shine forth with an
  honour of his own:
He himself will create a tribe and a lineage with his pious
  virtue . . .
Happy the line that continues with such a grandson:
grant, Christ, that he will follow in deeds him whom he
  follows in name![30]

29 Godman 1987: 135–44.
30 *MGH Poet.* II, pp. 375–6, ll. 177–88. Cf. Freculf's stress on the name 'Charles' in the preface to Book II of his *Chronicle*.

The 'honour' referred to here is the grant of Alemannia, which Louis conferred on Charles in August 829. An older historiographical tradition depicted Louis as an impulsive weakling, at the mercy of his overbearing wife. This denigration of 'the great emperor's weak son' had a long run for its money.[31] Only recently has Louis been reappraised as an effective ruler in his own right.[32] He had long intended, and prepared the ground for, some landed provision for Charles. Walahfrid's 'other one' who had enjoyed Alemannia before this, must be Louis the German whose marriage to Judith's sister in 827 had created a strong axis of solidarity between this son and his father. The emperor and empress had foreseen and tried to forestall resentment on Louis the German's part at the grant to Charles. There is little evidence of such resentment in 829.[33] Neither the *RFA* nor the Astronomer links the rebellion of Louis's elder sons in 830 with fraternal hostility to their half-brother's 'promotion'. Nithard does so, however, while the author of a curious single annal for 830–1, tacked onto the *Prior Metz Annals* (the last entry otherwise was for 805) makes Judith the central figure in the story, and explains the 830 rebellion in terms of her stepsons' hostility to her and her 'very goodlooking son Charles' who 'they feared might succeed as heir in his father's realm'.[34] No reallocation of the family-holdings could have avoided upsetting someone. The grant of Alemannia, where none of Charles's half-brothers had a prime interest, was the least provocative way of making reasonable provision for Charles's future. As Walahfrid put it, this *honor* remained 'left over'. He glossed over the fact that Charles was also granted Alsace, Chur and part of Burgundy: areas in which Lothar (and his supporters) certainly did have interests.[35] Still, Lothar, who in September 829 had again been 'sent to Italy',[36] was not the leading spirit in the 830 rebellion. Louis the Pious seemed to have

---

31 Staubach 1990.
32 Godman and Collins 1990.
33 Only Thegan c. 35 says that Louis the German as well as Lothar and Pippin were resentful.
34 Nithard I, 3. *Annales Mettenses Priores* 830: 96. This annal was perhaps written at Chelles for Abbess Heilwig, Judith's mother; Nelson 1990e.
35 *AX* 829: 7. Cf. Boshof 1990: 183.
36 *RFA*.

the situation firmly under control when in the autumn of 829 he took the six-year old Charles to make a kind of *joyeuse entrée* into his intended realm. Walahfrid's choice as tutor made perfect sense: it was in his Alemannian 'tribe' that Judith's Benjamin would 'create a tribe of his own'. When Charles visited Walahfrid's old monastery at Reichenau, the poet produced an appropriate encomium:

Due glory we accord
To the power of the Trinity
Which conveyed you here safe and sound
Through the realms of the Franks! . . .
Hail, O holy offspring of kings,
Charles, dear to Christ![37]

But Charles was never to make his home, or his realm, in Alemannia. Instead, his half-brothers' unfilial behaviour spurred Louis the Pious to change his plans.

The standardbearer of the 830 revolt was the second of Charles's three half-brothers, Pippin of Aquitaine. Walahfrid in *Theodoric's Statue* had already hinted at his disaffection: Pippin was not among the family party at Aachen in August 829, but stayed at home. Pippin's grievances had, unsurprisingly, nothing to do with Alemannia but a lot to do with his father's interference in and around Aquitaine which had once, of course, been Louis's own realm (he had ruled it as sub-king from 781 to 814). The instigators of the revolt were Hugh and Matfrid, the dis-honoured of 828: it was Pippin they turned to first; and when Charles's mother Judith was taken from her husband's side, and accused of adultery with Bernard, she was sent to custody in Aquitaine, at Ste-Croix, Poitiers.[38] Lothar then joined the rebels: his great expectations affirmed in 817, he had never reconciled himself to the role of mere 'emperor in waiting', ousted meanwhile from the Frankish heartlands and 'sent to Italy'. Lothar, his sights firmly focussed on Francia, wanted once more to make an immediate reality of his co-imperial title, as he briefly had done in 821–2. Louis the German, by contrast, refused to join the rebels, and played

37 *MGH Poet.* II: 406.
38 Radbert, *Epitaphium* II, 8, p. 69; *AB* 830: 22.

a key part in ending the shortlived revolt.[39] There is no
record of any action taken by the rebels against Charles,
nor of his reaction to these events. When the revolt collapsed and Judith was released, Charles rode out with his
uncle Drogo bishop of Metz to escort her home to a ceremonial reception at Aachen in February 831.[40] The boy
was presumably present when his mother stood before a
Frankish assembly 'declaring her willingness to purge herself on all the charges levelled against her' – and no accuser appeared.[41] Since Charles figured in later medieval
tales as the killer of Bernard to avenge his mother's honour, or, alternatively, as Bernard's bastard son[42], it is worth
stressing that the charge of adultery against Judith is mentioned only in 830 (Bernard is first documented at the palace in 824)[43] and that no contemporary source ever cast
doubt on Charles's paternity. References to Charles's physical resemblance to his grandfather and namesake can be
taken seriously.

The real issues in 830 thus scarcely involved Charles.
The fundamental conflict was between Louis and Lothar;
and its outcome now was that Lothar was, once more, un-
compromisingly 'sent to Italy' early in 831, while his leading supporters, Hugh and Matfrid, were imprisoned and
exiled. With Pippin, his father decided to deal in more
conciliatory fashion. It may have been now that Ermold
was returned to his beloved Aquitaine, and favour at Pippin's court.[44] Louis the German deserved reward for un-
swerving loyalty. At Aachen in February 831, Louis the
Pious's counsellors canvassed a revised division project:
though much of its text was based on that of 806, it
reverted to more traditional Frankish practice in dividing
the heartlands. Pippin was assigned Neustria, but the two
main beneficiaries were to be Louis the German *and Char-*

---

39 Thegan c. 35.
40 *Annales Mettenses Priores* 830.
41 *AB* 831: 23.
42 Lot and Halphen 1909: 99, n. 3.
43 Dhuoda, pref., p. 84, says that she and Bernard were married there
    on 29 June 824.
44 Against the view of Ermold as a 'failure', Godman 1987: 129–30, I
    accept his identification with Pippin's chancellor in the 830s; cf.
    Levillain 1926: xliii.

les, leaving Lothar with only Italy.[45] There is nothing to show that this plan was 'officially adopted': if anything, it was a shot over Lothar's bows. In May, he was 'honourably received' by his father at Ingelheim, and his supporters recalled from exile (though not restored to their lost honours).[46] It was understood that Italy alone was on offer for the time being; but the imperial prospects of 817 were undimmed.

Nevertheless, the revolt of 830 had transformed Charles's prospects: the 831 draft-project for the first time gave him hopes of a share of the heartlands of Francia itself. At the same time Louis the Pious firmly reasserted his power to alter the arrangements of 817. From now on, Charles would have to be taken seriously by his half-brothers as a potential heir to Charlemagne. It was probably now that Charles, at his father's behest, stood godfather (and gave his name) to Pippin's newborn second son.[47] In 831, Charles was assigned a new importance in Louis the Pious's reconstructed family. But the reconstruction was shaky. Pippin too now had new hopes in Francia which seemed to be threatened by his father's rapprochement with Lothar. When Louis summoned, exceptionally, a third assembly in the same year, at Thionville, Pippin failed to appear; and when he did turn up for Christmas at Aachen, there was a family row. Pippin 'fled' back to Aquitaine, and welcomed an unexpected ally: Bernard, who had lost forever any chance of recovering great influence at Louis the Pious's court.[48] A few months later, Louis the German, thinking his loyalty in 830 inadequately recompensed, marched into Alemannia. Louis the Pious, taking Charles with him,[49] moved quickly to reassert his control. Louis the German was forced to withdraw: he would have to be satisfied with his Bavarian *regnum.*

In the summer of 832, Louis the Pious met Lothar at Mainz and again floated the idea of dividing Francia between Lothar and Charles.[50] Apparently no definite arrangement was made. By October, Louis had decided on

---

45   *MGH Capit.* II, no. 194.
46   *AB* 831: 23.
47   *AB* 849: 68 and n. 5.
48   Astronomer c. 47.
49   *AB* 832: 25, implies this.
50   Astronomer c. 47.

immediate action elsewhere: Aquitaine was to be taken from Pippin and given to Charles instead. At a great assembly at Limoges, Charles was presented to the leading men of Aquitaine, who swore oaths of fidelity to their new nine-year old king. Pippin was given a public dressing-down, and ordered to precede his father to Francia; Bernard was deprived of his honours.[51] But Pippin escaped, returned to Aquitaine, and forced Louis to withdraw across the Loire 'in less dignified fashion than was suitable', taking Charles with him.[52] They spent Christmas at Le Mans with the newly-appointed Bishop Aldric, a trusty supporter of the emperor.[53] Nevertheless, Louis's position was dangerous, for inconclusive talks had failed to secure Lothar's support, while both Pippin and Louis the German had turned against their father. Early in 833, rumours were rife of the political conjuncture Louis the Pious had most feared, and hitherto avoided: the alliance against him of all three adult sons. Lothar, back in Italy, had seized his chance, to co-ordinate revolt – and to secure papal support.[54] In June 833 when Louis the Pious, with Judith and Charles beside him, tried to face down his opponents in Alsace, his own supporters quailed at the size of the army ranged against them, broke faith and fled. Within a year or two, the place had become known as 'the Field of Lies'.[55]

Many years later, Charles recalled the defection of 'the whole people', the emperor's capture, the sending of 'his wife' (this, interestingly, is Charles alluding to his own mother) into exile in Italy, and 'the treatment of me, a mere ten-year old, as if I had committed huge crimes'.[56] In this phrase, there is an emotional ring totally absent in Charles's recollection of his mother's fate. Louis was 'made very sad indeed' when Charles was taken away from him and sent to the monastery of Prüm in the Ardennes.[57] There he stayed for some eight months, in the care of Abbot Markward. Separated from his tutor, Charles never-

---

51   *AB* 832: 26; Thegan c. 41.
52   Astron. c. 47.
53   Le Maitre 1980; Weidemann 1989: 185, 188.
54   Fried 1990: 267–73.
55   Thegan c. 51; *AB* 833: 26, n. 1; Astronomer c. 48.
56   Letter to Nicholas I, *PL* 124, col. 872.
57   *AB* 833: 27.

theless found himself in a fairly congenial environment:
Markward was a noted scholar, and Prüm's library was well-
stocked. So too were its larders.[58] Charles is unlikely to
have suffered much in physical or intellectual terms from
his enforced brief stay. More importantly, he was not tonsured: Lothar, perhaps moved by the obligations of a godfather, could not bring himself thus to exclude Charles
from the ranks of the throneworthy. Thirty years afterwards
Charles still felt deeply the humiliation he suffered at this
time; but unlike some little princes in similar situations, he
lived, politically as well as literally, to fight another day. He
also survived psychologically: later in life, his favourite role-
models were David and Hercules whose virtues were indo-
mitable courage and perseverance in adversity.[59] Charles's
boyhood sufferings taught him a patience far removed
from defeatism, reinforcing Christianity's message that to
be humbled was the prelude to triumph.

Only five months after Ebbo and a handful of episcopal
colleagues in the church of St-Medard at Soissons had ritually deprived Louis of weapons and insignia, he was restored to power.[60] Looking back from the 860s, Charles saw
this as the direct result of divine intervention. More mun-
dane reasons were growing rifts in the ranks of the rebels
and Lothar's overall loss of control. Before the end of February 834, Charles was reunited with his father at the abbey
of St-Denis, and Lothar was on the run. Charles had almost
certainly not witnessed his father's effective deposition, but
he now looked on while 'faithful' bishops reclothed the
emperor in his royal robes and rearmed him with his weapons. By May, Judith had been rescued, and restored to
husband and son. Walahfrid wrote a poem to celebrate the
virtues of Ruadbern, the young *fidelis* who escorted Judith
home.[61]

The last years of Louis the Pious have been seen (where
they have been 'seen' by historians at all) as a period during which Judith gained an increasing ascendancy, as the
old emperor lost his grip. It is often said that no political
recovery from the trauma of Soissons was possible. Louis's

58 Cf. Kuchenbuch 1978.
59 Above, Ch. 1: 15.
60 *AB* 869: 161; Charles to Nicholas, *PL* 124, col. 872.
61 *AB* 834: 30; Walahfrid, *MGH Poet.* II: 388–90.

own behaviour belies such a gloomy diagnosis. The bewildering swings of fortune in 833–4 had in fact resulted from shifting calculations of self-interest and public interest on the part of magnates, and fractures of aristocratic consensus that could be healed. As Walahfrid put it, 'the glory of ruler and state were always reparable'. During the six years that followed his restoration, Louis put together again the coalition of ecclesiastical and secular support that had sustained him in the 820s. He reigned alone in the Frankish heartlands, and prevented filial or factional hostility from coalescing into any major revolt. The future of Lothar and his supporters was settled when Louis met them at Blois in September:

> The emperor sat in his pavilion which was set up in the middle of a wide field on a hill where the whole army could see him, and his faithful sons [Pippin and Louis] stood beside him. Lothar came and fell at his father's feet. His father-in-law Hugh the Fearful followed him, then Matfrid and the other ringleaders in crime. They all confessed their great wrong-doing.[62]

The upshot was that Lothar was sent to Italy, 'never to leave it unless on his father's orders'.[63] In reasserting his paternal authority, and finding his old political touch, Louis showed himself in his last years a conspicuous success.

Charles was old enough now to begin to play a hand of his own. Unfortunately there is no direct evidence from this period about his personal relationship with either of his parents. In 835, his influence with Louis was being solicited by Hrabanus Maurus:[64] not yet a man, Charles was already a *potens*. His mother's friends at court became his: in time they included, along with Walahfrid, Lupus of Ferrières (welcomed by Louis and Judith at Frankfurt in autumn 836),[65] the palace clerics Prudentius, Wenilo and Berno,[66] and the seneschal Adalard. In 835 and 836, Charles

---

62 Thegan c. 55. Louis's Loire-valley nominees had been slain: Nithard I, 5.
63 Nithard I, 5. See Nelson 1990c.
64 *MGH Epp.* V, p. 521.
65 Lupus Ep. 11.
66 Lupus Ep. 26.

presumably itinerated with his father, joining in the autumn hunting in the Ardennes and in the forest-area around Frankfurt, wintering at Aachen. He learned at first hand the economic geography of the *regnum francorum*. At Louis's side, he saw how to meet Viking attacks by diplomacy and a mixture of force and guile. To watch his father conduct assemblies, disgrace and dismiss incompetent commanders, was the most useful kind of political training.[67]

Louis was determined that Charles should have a share in the Frankish heartlands. At a Christmas assembly at Aachen in 837, having carefully built up aristocratic and episcopal support, and secured the agreement of Pippin (whose own ambitions in Francia now looked blighted) and Louis the German, Louis solemnly conferred on Charles 'a part of the *regnum*', with the following boundaries:

> the greater part of the Belgic provinces, in other words, the whole of Frisia from the North Sea and Saxon frontier as far as the frontier of the Ripuarian Franks, and along the latter, the counties of Mulekewe, Ettra, Hamarlant and Maasgau; then all the territory between the Meuse and Seine as far south as Burgundy, including Verdun; and going from Burgundy, the counties of Toul, Ornois, Blois, Blaisois, Perthois, the two Bars [i.e. Bar-le-Duc and Bar-sur-Aube], Brienne, Troyes, Auxerre, Sens, the Gâtinais, Melun, Etampes, the Pays de Châtres, and Paris; then along the Seine to the Channel and up the coast as far as Frisia again: within these, all the bishoprics, abbacies, counties, fisclands, and all pertaining thereto. At the emperor's command and in his presence, the bishops, abbots, counts, and royal vassals holding benefices in the above-mentioned places, commended themselves to Charles and confirmed their fidelity with an oath.[68]

The real resources of the area from a royal standpoint are implicit in the listing of 'bishoprics, abbacies, counties, fisclands and all pertaining thereto': in other words, all

---

67 For these events, *AB* 835–839.
68 Nithard I, 6; *AB* 837: 38. Cf. Map 3.

rights over moveable and immoveable property involved in royal lordship of churches and in direct or indirect royal exploitation of fisclands, as well as in the disposition of countships. The prime agents of royal control were the men bound by oath to a particular king: the bishops, abbots, counts and *vassi dominici*. Nithard names two of the great men who took these oaths in December 837: Abbot Hilduin of St-Denis, most royal of western Frankish abbeys, and Count Gerald of Paris, a city which had once been a residence of Merovingian kings. Hilduin and Gerald had both been appointed to their posts by Louis; though their loyalty had wavered in 833, both had soon recovered imperial favour. Hilduin's kinsmen held important ecclesiastical posts in the heart of the empire. Gerald enjoyed *Königsnähe* with the Carolingians several times over: his wife and Lothar's wife were sisters, and his brother was the seneschal Adalard.[69] These were the men to underwrite Charles's new status in the region north-east of the Seine.

Why did two contemporary annalists call this 'the best part of the *regnum francorum*'?[70] The answer is that it included particularly rich concentrations of royal resources: Dorestad with its *emporium* and mint; major churches, including the metropolitan sees of Rheims and Sens, and rich abbeys like St-Denis and St-Wandrille, on whose endowments the Carolingians had laid their hands; a number of royal palaces, and many royal estates and forests, both Carolingian patrimonial lands around the lower Meuse and old Merovingian ones in the Seine basin, especially along the Oise; and last but not least, good communications, including a surviving Roman road-network. All this turned out to have long-term significance for Charles the Bald, for much of this region was to be the central zone of his future kingdom.

The identity of those annalists is important too: they reflected the views of Lothar and of Louis the German, whose interests were adversely affected by this grant to their young half-brother. Lothar had designs on Frankish lands west of the Meuse. Both he and Louis the German had hoped to get their hands on Frisia, and on Dorestad.

69 On Hilduin, Brown 1989; Gerald, below, Genealogical Table VII.
70 *AF* 838: 28; Agnellus c. 172, p. 389.

In 838, both reacted to Charles's promotion by plotting against the old emperor; and when Louis the German answered his father's summons to an assembly at Nijmegen in May, there was another unseemly row, which ended in the son's being formally deprived of all he held outside Bavaria.[71]

The evidence for the years 838–40 scarcely ever allows us to differentiate Charles's political activity from his father's. But perhaps Charles's realm was intended to be rather more than a prospective one. He did not yet have a chancery of his own, but it seems he did have his own chapel, that is, a team of household chaplains (presumably equipped with relics). Twenty years later, Charles reminded an assembly of how 'a part of the realm was assigned me by my lord and father . . . and in it the metropolitan see of Sens then lacked a pastor. For its good government, I committed it to Wenilo, who was at that time serving me as my clerk in my chapel'.[72] It was a good choice: Archbishop Wenilo was to be one of Charles's key supporters in the critical period after 840.

In mid-August, 838, with Louis the German now in disgrace, Louis the Pious summoned his summer assembly to Quierzy on the River Oise. Charles had had his fifteenth birthday just two months before, reaching the Frankish age of majority. Now his father 'conferred on him weapons and a crown and the part of the kingdom between the Seine and the Loire', that is, the region known in the ninth century as Neustria.[73] The event was doubly significant: first, as a sort of dubbing to knighthood, the ritual demonstrated publicly that Charles as a grown man was now able to rule and ready to fight. (There is no evidence that he had yet gained any military experience.) Presumably now, if not before, he was given the wherewithal to maintain a military retinue of his own. He no longer needed a tutor: Walahfrid was paid off with the abbacy of Reichenau, where he could help hold Alemannia against Louis the German. Charles now journeyed independently of his father, and with his own men, to Le Mans, to receive the oaths of the people

71 *AB* 838: 39.
72 *MGH Conc.* III, no. 478, p. 464.
73 *AB* 838: 39; Nithard I, 6. Cf. Nelson 1989a.

he was to rule. Further, the 'kingdom' he now acquired, with Le Mans as a key-place (and Bishop Aldric a strong supporter), was one that carried exceptional prospects. It contained a large number of royal estates: perhaps a third of those which have been identified in the Carolingian Empire.[74] As a political unit, it was a Carolingian creation. Pippin, the first of the line, had destined it for his first-born, the young Charlemagne in the 750s; Charlemagne had assigned it in 790 to *his* son Charles, later labelled *primogenitus* and designated heir to the *regnum Francorum* (though he predeceased his father in 811).[75] Lothar's marriage, and some of his activities in 833–4, suggest that he had designs of his own on Neustria. In making this grant to Charles, Louis the Pious was asserting this son's special status within the family: though the last-born, Charles was now, so to speak in the *primogenitus* slot.

It was necessary to bolster his position elsewhere too, however. In 838, Louis the Pious assigned Charles a *bajulus* (literally, guardian, or superviser), Atto, who held a countship in the Rhineland near Mainz and (along with his two brothers) was now being promoted hard by the emperor to keep Louis the German in check.[76] Charles needed Atto's help: the emperor was clearly anxious about his future in the heartlands of Francia. All three of the boy's half-brothers had had claims there. The risk of denying all of these at once had been painfully clear in 833. Louis's age – he was sixty in 838 – made it urgent to find a succession-settlement that had a good chance of sticking.

> It seemed to [Judith] that the emperor's good physical condition might not last much longer, and his death would threaten danger to herself and to Charles unless they could win over one of Charles's elder brothers to work with them, and they calculated that none of the emperor's sons would fit this role so well as Lothar.[77]

---

74 Brunterc'h 1985: 74.
75 Werner 1985: 36–7.
76 Cf. Werner 1990: 77, n. 275; Airlie 1990: 192, and 196.
77 Astronomer c. 54.

The Astronomer enters this under the year 835; but his chronology goes awry from 835 onwards, and the developments described in this passage seem in fact to belong later. Nithard puts them in 839:

> Charles's mother, and the magnates who had worked on the will of his father to promote Charles's cause, fearing that if Louis were to die before matters were settled, they would risk incurring the hatred of Charles's brothers to their own ruin, advised that the father should choose one of those sons to be his helper so that, even if the others refused to remain at peace after their father's death, these two at least would have been so firmly united that they would be able to withstand the hostility of their rivals.[78]

There was nothing sinister in Judith's role in all this. 'She counted for a great deal in the palace'[79] in the sense that she had privileged access to Louis and thus could be a helpful patron. She had her own circle of friends and clients at court. She had a strong and (as the years passed) increasing interest in securing her own future through that of her son. On the other hand, there is enough evidence to show that Louis the Pious remained in personal control of political and military affairs. His grip on his episcopate was secure. It was his arrival at Nijmegen in 837 that made the Vikings withdraw, and his leadership of the Rhineland campaign in the winter of 838–9 that caused the rapid collapse of Louis the German's revolt. Despite Viking attacks in 834, 835, 836 and 837 on Dorestad, Louis's coinage issued from that mint in increasing quantities in the years 834–40 was of consistently high quality and output.[80] No contemporary source attributes Louis's firm dealings with Lothar, Pippin and Louis the German to the designs of Judith rather than to the emperor's own wishes. The picture of a pathetic old man in the hands of a scheming young woman is the fantasy of nineteenth-century, not ninth-century, historians. Charles too had a voice: the Astronomer credits him as well as Judith with the idea of a

78 Nithard I, 6.
79 Lupus Ep. 11.
80 Coupland 1990.

new rapprochement with Lothar. But as Nithard went on to observe, the policy had originally, back in 823, been that of Louis the Pious himself.

In 839 several things helped revive it. Lothar had suffered from an exceptional mortality-rate among his leading supporters in 836–7. A terrible epidemic in Italy in the Astronomer's phrase 'widowed Francia of her nobility'.[81] These were noble Franks who had followed Lothar into exile. The dead included Lothar's three closest counsellors, Lambert, Matfrid and Hugh, his father-in-law; and Lothar himself was so ill that his life was despaired of. These losses, politically damaging, and bad for morale (they were seen in Louis the Pious's entourage as divine retribution on former rebels), weakened Lothar's resistance to his father's pressure. Changes in the configuration of the royal family had a similar effect. Lothar's attempt to form an alliance with his brother Louis the German against their father had failed dismally in 838. When in the winter of 838–9 Louis the German rebelled openly, the emperor crushed him completely in a swift campaign, and sent him back to Bavaria. The *bajulus* Atto may have failed to uphold Charles's cause in the Rhineland as the emperor had intended: no more is heard of that guardianship. Better prospects had by now opened up for Charles elsewhere with the death of Pippin of Aquitaine in December 838. Louis the Pious decided to disinherit Pippin's sons, though the older, also called Pippin, was by now fifteen. Here, two sets of values conflicted. Louis was within his legal rights, for he had never relinquished his reserve powers over *regna*; and there was no doubt of his grandparental position as head of the family.[82] Nevertheless his action seems to have struck contemporaries as flouting legitimate filial expectations: there was a flagrant contrast with his treatment of his own 15-year old, Charles. But when Louis showed his claws, Lothar knew he meant business. Aquitaine was back in the pool of available *regna*. Thus, in 839 the emperor was in a position to offer to divide the whole empire (save only Bavaria) between Lothar and Charles. It was an offer Lothar could not refuse.

81 Astronomer c. 56. Cf. *AB* 837: 37.
82 Nelson 1990c: 151.

The division made at Worms in 839, unlike the grants to Charles in 837 and 838, was prospective only. The emperor told Lothar to define the two parts, and let Charles choose which he wanted; alternatively, said Louis, 'we'll divide, and the choice of parts will be yours'. Lothar having tried for three days to do the dividing, said he 'could not do so because of his ignorance of the places involved' and so finally left that task to his father.[83] The boundary-line was drawn northwards from Italy, via Geneva, the Jura and the Meuse valley to the North Sea. 'Lothar chose the eastern share, then the emperor gave Charles the second part. After the emperor had received all sorts of oaths from Lothar, he let him return to Italy.'[84]

What did this division mean to the people involved? One way to answer is to look at the interests converging in two marriages probably dateable to 839. The first was that of Gisèle, daughter of Louis and Judith (hence Charles's only full sibling), with Eberhard, duke of Friuli in north-east Italy and a leading supporter of Lothar's regime. The offer of Gisèle as bride was a spectacular gesture: legitimate daughters of Carolingians were usually placed in convents. In choosing Eberhard as a son-in-law, Louis and Judith expressed their confidence that he would help reinforce their entente with Lothar; at the same time, Eberhard gained access to Gisèle's generous dowry of estates in Francia.[85] The second marriage united Judith's brother Conrad with Adelaide, who was Lothar's sister-in-law. Conrad was securing his own interests in Alemannia while acquiring, it seems, Adelaide's dowry in the region of Auxerre.[86] Judith was constructing another axis of alliance for herself and Charles within the wider imperial family-circle. At this point in Louis's reign Nithard comments: 'the emperor could now feel confident that the aristocracy would not desert him for the rest of his life'.[87] Eberhard and Conrad, leading members of that aristocracy, had each acquired landed interests in more than one of the *regna*. They had invested for the long term, if not in imperial unity (and significantly, noth-

---

83 Nithard I, 7.
84 *AB* 839: 45–6 with details of the division.
85 Grierson 1939b: 442. For the date, Nelson 1990c: 152.
86 Louis 1946: 32–4; Borgolte 1986: 166–7. See Genealogy IV.
87 Nithard I, 6.

ing was said at Worms about emperorship or empire), then in the coexistence of Lothar and Charles in the *regnum francorum*. Everyone had hedged bets.

For Charles, this division was a mixed blessing. He was to retain the valuable regions already granted him, and though he would in the future have to share the heartlands with Lothar, still, for a last-born son, he had done rather well. The immediate problem lay in Aquitaine, where some of the nobles who had been close to the defunct Pippin I, had refused to accept the 'disinheritance' of Pippin's son and instead recognised him as their king. Charles had to make good his own claims at once, and so, significantly, he gained his first experience of war in campaigning against, not foreign foes, but a Carolingian rival. Though some contemporaries based in Francia (Nithard, and the Astronomer, for instance) seemed to regard Aquitaine as a faraway country of which they knew little, Charles did not share that view. Aquitaine was, after all, *his* father's former realm, hence could be regarded as Charles's inheritance. It was known to Charles too, for in 832 he had been installed as king there, briefly, at Limoges. In 839, some powerful Aquitanians supported him: they included Bishop Ebroin of Poitiers, thanks to whom Charles was well-informed about the region's political geography.[88] He went directly from Worms to Chalon-sur-Saône: Louis had summoned a host there for the beginning of September. Joined by both his parents, Charles advanced to Clermont, where his Aquitanian supporters came to affirm their allegiance 'with their accustomed oaths'. From here, while Louis took personal command of operations against strongholds held by Pippin II's supporters in the Auvergne and Quercy, Charles and Judith moved north to establish their base at Poitiers.[89] Bishop Ebroin certainly, and possibly also the local count, were committed to Charles's cause. To that part of north-western Aquitaine can probably be assigned Count Rainald, and several other counts and *vassi dominici* who witnessed a document in April 838 as Louis's faithful supporters.[90]

88 Astronomer c. 61.
89 *AB* 839: 46–7.
90 Oexle 1969: 163, 176.

Just what kind of opposition did Charles face in Aquitaine? It is not only shortage of contemporary evidence that makes the question hard to answer. The reconstruction of the eleventh-century historian Ademar has been eagerly accepted by twentieth-century historians predisposed to believe in the existence of an Aquitanian national identity in the ninth century. Ademar's evidence is demonstrably unreliable, however;[91] and without it, there is nothing to show that Pippin II's support was at all widespread. The *regnum* of Aquitaine was the Carolingians' creation. Its aristocracy included a large infusion of Franks, whose kinties and political interests drew them often towards Francia. Pippin I's recurrent problem had been the meddling of his father, ex-king of Aquitaine. The personal loyalties of the aristocracy were torn. Not long before his death, Pippin I had married one of his two daughters to a noble whose support he must have been especially keen to hold, Count Gerard.[92] Crucial evidence on Gerard's conduct after Pippin I's death is supplied by a letter of Lupus of Ferrières written in July 840: Gerard, it says, 'the former prince and favourite (*princeps et carus*) of Pippin [I]' was now one of Charles's right-hand men in Aquitaine.[93] Lupus was in a position to know. A substantial contingent of men from his abbey had been among Louis the Pious's forces in Aquitaine since the previous autumn, and when they returned to Ferrières in July 840, they brought first-hand news of Gerard's appointment as commander of Charles's garrison at Limoges.

One other supporter of Pippin II can be identified with some certainty: that was Bernard, the former chamberlain, whose downfall in 830 had been so dramatic. He had never recovered his position at court (perhaps that was not surprising, given the rumours that linked his name with Judith's in 830). After appearing in Pippin I's entourage in 832, Bernard had incurred the emperor's lasting disfavour. Later in the 830s, Bernard had improvised a career in Septimania, outside Pippin's kingdom, abandoning his old base in Barcelona for a new one in Uzès, where his wife

91   Gillingham 1990.
92   Astronomer c. 61. Cf. Nelson 1986a (1985): 234.
93   Lupus Ep. 17.

Dhuoda was installed, and acquiring resources by appropriating local church lands in the Narbonnais.[94] Louis the
Pious had done all he could to oust him by encouraging
opponents in the region. Bernard spent little time at
home.[95] The developments of 839 cast further doubt on
his future. There was unlikely to be a place for him in a
reconstituted kingdom of Aquitaine that included Septimania and was ruled by Charles the Bald. Bernard therefore
turned to Pippin II, not because of residual devotion to
Pippin's father, still less from a sense of Aquitanian identity,
but because he needed a Carolingian alternative to Charles. From Pippin II's standpoint in 839, *any* support was
welcome; and Bernard had useful contacts, through kinsmen and inherited lands, in Septimania and in Burgundy.

Two charters survive given by Pippin II as 'king of the
Aquitanians' in 839 and 840.[96] One was issued from the
monastery of Figeac; its beneficiary was the abbot of Solig-
nac near Limoges. The other's beneficiary was the *fidelis*
Rodulf whose lands also lay in the Limousin. (His father
was the count of Turenne.) The basis of Pippin's support
was narrow, but its geography meant that Louis's autumn
campaign against him had to be fought in difficult terrain:
this part of Aquitaine was a region of hills and crags, dee-
ply-wooded, and crossed by great rivers that impeded
north-south communications. Warfare in this region was always about sieges. Louis did well to take Carlat, its fortifications natural as well as man-made. But before he could
besiege Turenne, sickness among his men caused him to
withdraw.[97] He spent Christmas at Poitiers with Charles and
Judith. But in February he returned to the Rhineland to
deal with yet another raid by Louis the German there (this
time the emperor drove his son out so forcefully that he
had to seek refuge with the Slavs before making his way
back to Bavaria). Charles was left for the first time to conduct his own strategy in Aquitaine, no doubt with Judith to
help him. Perhaps it was now that he appointed Ebroin,
himself an able military leader, to be his archchaplain. In
the four months following the emperor's departure,

94 Astronomer c. 47; cf. Thegan c. 58 ; T. 47, 54.
95 Dhuoda X, 4, pp. 350–2.
96 L. 49, 50.
97 *AB* 839: 47–8 gives these details.

Charles's military moves are unknown. By July, however, he was in control of three strongpoints that straddled central Aquitaine: Clermont, Limoges and Angoulême.[98] Numbers of his opponents had been captured or come over to him. Lupus summed up the situation: 'everything had gone well'.

Lupus exaggerated. Pippin II was still at large and still had supporters. Charles opted, realistically, for negotiation, and sent envoys to offer a meeting at Bourges in July.[99] Bernard seems to have been one of those who swore that Pippin would come. But before Charles himself got to Bourges, he received news from the Rhineland: his father had died, on 20 June, near Ingelheim. Charles and Judith had been in Louis's thoughts as he lay dying: he had left Charles a share of his treasure, and despatched crown, sword and sceptre to Lothar 'to have on condition that he should keep his faith to Charles and Judith, and guarantee to Charles the whole share of the realm which with God and the leading men of the palace as witnesses, Lothar with his father, and in his father's presence, had assigned to Charles'.[100] But (as Hobbes observed), 'promises without the sword are but words'. Charles was soon to find out what Lothar's words were worth. And that would depend, in turn, on whether other men kept their word to a dead emperor.

98   Lupus Ep. 17.
99   Nithard II, 2.
100 Astronomer c. 63.

Chapter 5

840–843: WINNING A KINGDOM

The death of a great ruler is a shocking event. In the early Middle Ages it often meant kaleidoscopic change on the political scene but the new pattern (unlike a kaleidoscope's) took some time to form. The 839 succession-plan was too recent and contentious to provide much of a guide for action in the summer of 840. 'Men were driven by greed and terror' in their quest for a new lord.[1] For Louis the Pious's following, the choice was painfully hard. Some preferred to lie low for a while. But most staked their future on making a new commitment swiftly. Nithard was one of the latter sort. He was with Charles at Bourges in July (and had perhaps brought Charles the news of his father's death). Most of Louis's entourage, and most of the Frankish elite, jumped the other way – in the direction of Lothar. Since Lothar had been summoned to meet his father at Worms at the beginning of July, he was already in the far north of Italy en route to the Rhineland when news of the emperor's death reached him. He moved slowly, according to Nithard, 'wanting to know which way things would go before he crossed the Alps'; only when it had become clear that plenty of support would be forthcoming did he decide to claim 'the whole empire'. Quite what that meant is unclear and perhaps was unclear then (the terms of the 817 *Ordinatio* would have needed updating anyway since Pippin I had died); but the one thing that was perfectly clear was that Lothar was abrogating the 839 division-plan.

---

1   Nithard II, 1. For fuller reflections on Nithard's work, see Nelson 1986a (1985).

This can hardly have surprised Charles: even before he knew of Lothar's decision, it seems, he had sent envoys to remind him of the previous year's sworn agreement; of the protection owed by older brother to younger brother and by godfather to godson; and (by way of quid pro quo), of the obedience owed by a younger son to the *primogenitus*. Lothar's reply was cautious: his intentions towards Charles were benevolent, he said, but he asked Charles to 'spare Pippin [II] until he [Lothar] might have a chance to speak with him'. The threat was scarcely veiled; and Lothar had probably been in touch with Pippin already as an obvious ally against Charles.[2]

It is a curious fact that, thanks to Nithard, we know far more about the years 840–42 than about any other phase of Charles's reign. Nithard of course misleads. He is consistently hostile to Lothar, and that means he has almost nothing to say about Lothar's case or about those who 'bought' it. Had a piece of Lotharian history survived for these years, it would have told a different story. Still Charles's biographer should not look Nithard's gift-horse in the mouth! Without his *Histories in Four Books* we should know virtually nothing of what happened in the months following Louis the Pious's death, and, more importantly, we should have had to guess at the motivations of those involved. Nithard was one of the two envoys Charles sent to Lothar in July 840; he completed Books I and II in October 841, Books III and IV by summer 843. His work has all the advantages (as well as the drawbacks) of a participant's testimony. Even his elisions and silences are revealing. It's significant too that, especially in the later Books, Nithard expresses increasing admiration for Louis the German. Relatively poorly documented up to this point, Louis's career already showed promise: his conduct during the revolt of 833–4 had proved his capacity for independent thought and action, and his restiveness thereafter was understandable, given his father's evident preference for Lothar as guarantor of young Charles's claims. After their father's death, it was Louis whose interests proved more closely aligned to Charles's. In Bavaria during the

2   Pippin's charter L. 50 (29 July 840) is dated 'in the first imperial reign-year of Lothar and the second year of Pippin'.

830s, Louis had established a firm power-base for an enlarged kingdom, and his epithet 'the German', though meant by contemporaries to convey simply that he ruled east of the Rhine, would turn out curiously apt in terms of modern state-geography. During his long reign Louis was to prove one of the most effective of early medieval rulers. His and Charles's lives were to run closely parallel – brothers who could never ignore each other, whether as colleagues, or competitors. Nithard already seemed to sense that bond.

Nithard's main focus was on Charles; but in July 840 the eyes of most of the elite were on Lothar. Those based east of the Meuse, in lands that had always been destined for Lothar, readily answered his summons to a great assembly at Ingelheim in August. For Louis the German, this venue posed an immediate challenge. In the meantime, he had to accept Lothar's control of the enclave on the west bank of the Rhine, including Ingelheim, Mainz and Worms, on which he himself had had designs since 831. But in Franconia Louis the German clearly had a good deal of support, and his power-base in Bavaria held firm: no churchman from there attended Lothar's assembly at Ingelheim.[3] Charles's position was far more precarious. Support was fraying at the edges of the realm promised in 839: the bishop of Toul, and the archbishops of Besançon and Tarentaise with their suffragans, all acknowledged Lothar in August 840. There were ominous signs of crumbling in the heart of the Frankish kingdom assigned to Charles in 837. Here all ten bishops of the province of Rheims agreed to the reinstatement of Ebbo, the fallguy of 834–5. For Ebbo, after five years in custody at the monastery of Fleury, Louis the Pious's death unlocked the prison door: the abbot of Fleury brought him to Ingelheim, where Lothar took him under his wing. The Ingelheim attendance list unfortunately does not include laymen; but Nithard says that 'all those living between the Meuse and the Seine' sent an urgent message to Charles in Aquitaine, 'telling him to come before they were taken over by Lothar'. At least one count in this region, Odulf, had already defected.[4]

---

3   *MGH Conc.* II, no. 61, p. 793.
4   Nithard II, 2.

Charles now found himself in a situation that would often recur: he had important unfinished business in Aquitaine, but his presence was required in Francia. It was the sort of dilemma faced by any ruler of a composite state: different *regna* posed simultaneously conflicting demands. This was something Charles would learn to live with. Now he showed a keen sense of priorities, and, as vital, an ability to delegate. In August 840, his decision to move swiftly north to Quierzy to bolster the nerve of his supporters, leaving his mother to take care of Aquitaine, was surely the right one in principle. What hampered him in practice was lack of manpower. Judith simply did not have enough troops to secure her position. (She was probably at Bourges.) When Charles got wind of a threatened attack on her by Pippin and his men, he returned southwards with unexpected speed, fell on Pippin's force and put them to flight.[5]

But Charles's fundamental problem was Lothar. He was threatening to *dis-honour* anyone who refused to come over to him: in other words, the price of continued loyalty to Charles would be loss of estates granted by previous kings (whether as benefices or as lands associated with office-holding). Even before the Quierzy meeting, some of the aristocracy in the region between the Charbonnière Forest and the Meuse had defected from Charles. When Lothar himself crossed the Meuse, probably late in September, and announced that he would advance as far as the Seine, Charles's support in Francia collapsed. Abbot Hilduin of St-Denis and Count Gerald of Paris, key supporters of Charles's Frankish *regnum* from 837–8, went over to Lothar, taking with them many, perhaps most, of the nobles with *honores* in the region.[6] Among the defectors was one of Charles's kinsmen: his cousin-once-removed, Pippin, 'son of King Bernard of the Lombards' (Nithard identifies him very carefully at this point). 'They preferred to break their faith, the way serfs do', comments Nithard scornfully of this whole group, 'rather than part with their lands for a while'. This of course was just what Nithard himself had *not* done: he had been willing, instead, to see his lands confis-

5   Nithard II, 3.
6   Nithard II, 3. Cf. above Ch. 4: 95.

cated by Lothar and, no doubt, regranted to one of Lothar's men. Nithard pointed out that what Lothar had done to him was just what he planned to do to Charles. This passage, in revealing Nithard's own personal concerns and hopes, also points clearly towards his audience. He says in the prologue to Book I that Charles in May 841, asked him to produce a record of recent history, 'because, my lord, you know that you and your men have suffered undeservedly the persecutions of Lothar . . .' *Vos vestrique*. Nithard wrote of what he and his companions had suffered; and he wrote for them as well as for Charles – significant evidence for Charles's own constituency.

Charles's fortunes seemed to reach their nadir in October 840, when Lothar (having *en passant*, though Nithard does not say so, re-installed Ebbo at Rheims)[7] pushed westwards across the Seine, aiming to gain control of Neustria. Some of the nobles in that region were reputed to be wavering; and Lothar had support in Brittany as well. What was Charles to do? 'He summoned a meeting, where a simple plan was very simply found: since they had nothing left but their lives and their bodies, they chose to die nobly rather than to betray and abandon their king'.[8] In fact no such agonising choice confronted Charles's men: Lothar himself recognised that his own position was dangerously exposed; and winter was close. No-one wanted a fight. Instead, at Orléans in November, a truce was agreed until another meeting at Attigny the following May. Charles was meanwhile to keep Aquitaine, Septimania, Provence and part of Neustria. Lothar promised to attack neither Charles nor Louis the German – which suggests that Charles and Louis were already in touch. Lothar believed that all he needed was time. Already, in the *regna* assigned to Charles at Orléans, a number of important men had declared for Lothar. According to Nithard, he set about 'soliciting' Charles's supporters more insistently than ever, in the hope of 'dissipating his realm'.

The monastery of Ferrières offers a good example of the sort of dilemma now faced both by individuals and by communities. Ferrières itself was south of Paris, between Sens

7   *MGH Conc.* II, no. 61, p. 792.
8   Nithard II, 4.

and Orléans, both sees whose bishops were supporting Charles; but its rich dependent house of St-Josse near Quentovic was in the area that fell under Lothar's control in September 840, and Lothar lost no time in handing it over to one of his own clerks. Odo, the Abbot of Ferrières, explained his difficulties to Abbot Markward of Prüm: 'We are placed betwixt and between – and we float uncertainly. If general opinion favours Lothar, and if you are in a position of influence with him, please don't forget us, and drive the wicked designs of bad men away from us, as far as you can.'[9] A few weeks later, the monks of Ferrières wrote as a group to beg Lothar to return St-Josse to them: 'incited by this *beneficium* (literally, 'good deed'), we would pray God more attentively for you and for your offspring'.[10] On the other hand, potential new beneficiaries were all too glad to accept *beneficia* like St-Josse. And, on the other side, one outcome of the Truce of Orléans was that Charles took the abbacy of Ferrières away from Odo and gave it to a member of the community whose chief recommendation (with still more pull than his fine scholarship) was a readiness to commit himself to Charles. The new abbot was Lupus.

Thanks to Lupus's letters and Nithard's *Histories*, it is possible to identify a dozen others who threw in their lot with Charles during the difficult first months of his reign: from Francia, Counts Adalgar (of Thérouanne) and Egilo, and the Seneschal Adalard (whose brother Count Gerald of Paris had defected to Lothar – perhaps the brothers had agreed to hedge their bets). An important ecclesiastical recruit was Louis, a bastard grandson of Charlemagne and Louis the Pious's archchancellor since 835, who had transferred his post and his loyalty to Charles without hesitation in June 840. Louis was also a monk of St-Denis. When Abbot Hilduin of St-Denis defected to Lothar, Charles promised Louis that abbacy. Southwards of Paris, the loyalty of Archbishop Wenilo of Sens and Bishop Jonas of Orléans probably helped Charles to install his men in the key abbacies of Fleury and (as we've seen) Ferrières, when the previous incumbents left to join Lothar. Further west, the

9 Lupus Ep. 18.
10 Lupus Ep. 19.

adherence of Count Rainald of Herbauge was vital for Charles's prospects not only in the region of the lower Loire valley but in Aquitaine, where in July 840 Rainald commanded the garrison of Angoulême. Count Gerard, in command at Limoges, and Bishop Ebroin of Poitiers, Charles's archchaplain, also maintained their support in Aquitaine. Finally, from Burgundy, Charles early in 841 received two valuable recruits: Count Warin, and Bishop Theutbald of Langres. The men whom Nithard terms the 'sharers of Charles's counsels' included some magnates of first-rank importance who were clearly willing to stake their own futures on Charles's success.[11] These supporters were fairly well-distributed in Charles's *regna*, and, most crucial of all, their loyalty was to stand the test of open conflict in 841.

A worrying hole in Charles's position in Aquitaine had appeared late in 840 when Pippin II was able to install his *fidelis* Rodulf, son of the count of Turenne, as archbishop of Bourges. For Pippin, this was a major coup (the silence of Francia-based writers reveals a chronic failure to appreciate the significance of events in Aquitaine), which extended his range far to the north of the Limousin-Quercy area.[12] Charles came to Bourges in January 841, hoping to meet Pippin. Instead, Bernard appeared bearing excuses. Charles was probably justified in suspecting bad faith: he and his men made a swoop on Bernard, who narrowly escaped with his life, leaving his men to be killed or captured and his baggage-train seized. It is a telling comment on ninth-century political practice that this humiliation, according to Nithard, brought Bernard into a more accommodating frame of mind. Promising to be loyal in future, he begged Charles for another chance to 'deliver' Pippin.[13] The sequel to this episode suggests its impact on contemporaries. A visit to Le Mans enabled Charles to reestablish the control there of his supporter Bishop Aldric and brought welcome new adherents in Neustria. The Breton leader Nominoë promised to abandon Lothar. Charles's

11 Nelson 1986a (1985): 234–5.
12 Levillain 1926: clxxvii and n. 6; cf. above Ch. 4: 103. Coupland 1989 gives numismatic evidence for Pippin's control of Bordeaux at this time.
13 Nithard II, 5.

position in Aquitaine and in Burgundy was strengthened. By March, support seemed to be flowing in 'from all sides'.

The qualities these men admired included guile alongside bravery. Nithard and his companions had sworn to the truce at Orléans 'because they all had a lot of confidence in [Charles's] cleverness'. But they were fairly sure that Lothar would persist in *his* old tricks, and in that case, as Nithard candidly admitted, 'they would have to be regarded as absolved from the oath they had sworn'. The truce, in other words, was merely a breathing-space. Lothar immediately sent emissaries into the *regna* assigned to Charles 'so that they [i.e. leading men there] should not accept Charles's lordship', while Lothar himself moved south-east 'to receive those who came to him from Provence'.[14] It followed that Charles and his men were no longer obliged by the truce-terms.

Nithard presented Charles as doing everything possible to avoid battle and to reach a settlement with Lothar. Yet the record of Charles's actions demonstrates the very opposite: his determined pursuit of his own right to a kingdom in Francia set him and Lothar on a collision course. They had agreed to meet at Attigny on 8 May. To get there, Charles had to turn eastwards and to cross the Seine. But he moved towards Paris in late March: everyone knew that it did not take six weeks to get from Paris to Attigny. Lothar's new supporters east of the Seine, including Count Gerald of Paris and Archbishop Guntbold of Rouen, determined to stop Charles crossing the river. They were helped by a Spring tide which caused extensive flooding and rendered all the fords impassable. To these natural obstacles they added man-made ones, damaging or sinking available boats and destroying the bridges. Charles was equally determined to confront the men who had so recently betrayed him. He moved rapidly down-river to Rouen where a number of merchant vessels had been driven in by the exceptional tide, and requisitioned twenty-eight boats. The crossing of the Seine, on 31 March, was carefully planned. Messengers were sent on ahead with a manifesto: Charles was coming to make good his rights; there would be an amnesty for all who now came over to him; those who re-

14 Nithard II, 4.

fused to accept his God-given rule would have to quit his kingdom. Fixing to his boat's prow the cross on which the oaths of 839 had been sworn, Charles led his flotilla over the river. Gerald and the rest on the opposite bank watched their approach: 'when they recognised the cross, and Charles, they fled'.[15]

Only a delay in getting his horses across deflected Charles from instant pursuit. Instead he went to St-Denis to offer thanks, and from there to St-Germain-des-Prés. Despite the absence of Count Gerald, Charles did not enter Paris (perhaps it was fortified against him). En route for Sens, he was joined by Warin and Theutbald from Burgundy. From Sens, on 13 April, he pressed on eastwards by night through the Forest of Othe: he had heard that Gerald and the rest were there, and hoped to fall on them unawares. Unfortunately for Charles, they were warned just in time, and escaped. Again, Charles was unable to pursue the fugitives: horses and men needed a rest-day, before Charles could arrive at Troyes on Good Friday, 15 April. Next day,

that very Easter Saturday, a truly wonderful and most notable thing happened. For neither he nor anyone in his following had anything at all apart from the clothes they stood up in and their weapons and horses. Charles was just getting out of his bath and was about to put on again the same clothes he had taken off beforehand, when suddenly, there at the gates were envoys bringing from Aquitaine a crown and all the royal gear, and everything needed for holy rites! Who can fail to be amazed that so few men (and virtually unknown men too), could carry such a huge quantity of jewels unharmed over so great a distance? Even more amazing is how they managed to arrive at just the right place, and at just the right day and hour required, when not even Charles himself knew where he and his men would be. It seemed that this could only have happened by God's grace and with his approval. And through this, Charles inspired awe in those who fought along with him and encouraged

15   Nithard II, 6.

them all to a confident hope that things would go well for them. And Charles and his whole exultant cohort devoted themselves to celebrating Easter.[16]

This story derives its resonance from its specific timeframe. The correct royal and liturgical equipment was required for the greatest feast of the church's year: its arrival from so 'far away' (in fact, from northern Aquitaine) was timely in every sense. It was hardly even a coincidence (Charles had told his Aquitanian supporters little more than a fortnight before to follow him northwards, and envoys from Lothar found no difficulty in locating Charles at Troyes on Easter Monday, 18 April). But Nithard invited his audience to invest it with the quality of a near-miracle. Perhaps echoing the ritual reality of an annual Easter reclothing of the royal retinue, the episode as recounted six months later to Charles's camp signified his political 'resurrection' and the collective cleansing and rededication of his followers. In his handling of the event at the time 'to inspire awe in those who fought along with him', Charles again showed a talent for exploiting symbols.[17]

The appearance of the Aquitanian envoys also revealed more material resources. They had evidently been sent by Judith: she had been in control of the treasure they brought with them, and, interestingly, of Charles's regalia. She was also mustering troops, and planned to lead them northwards to join up with her son. Charles urgently needed reinforcements. Not only had Lothar consolidated his position west of the Meuse; he had heavily defeated Louis the German's forces in the Rhineland and driven Louis back to Bavaria. All this was bad news for Charles, despite his own hopeful move towards Attigny. When Lothar's envoys arrived at Troyes, they told Charles to advance no further, and were unimpressed by his complaints about the treatment of Louis. For Lothar, the Attigny meeting had become irrelevant: Charles should be finished off quickly before he could implement the now-obvious policy of joining forces with Louis the German.

16   Nithard II, 8.
17   Nelson 1989a.

Lothar and Charles spent the next six weeks in manoeuvre and countermanoeuvre. Neither as yet had a large enough force to risk battle. Each feared the other's surprise attack before reinforcements arrived.[18] Both pumped out 'information' – and feared 'false rumours'. Morale counted for much. Men on both sides were jumpy; but the cause was not cowardice. After all, Frankish nobles were trained from youth, as Charles had been, to ride and to wield weapons, through hunting, wargames, and fights over property and honour in which, according to at least one contemporary canon lawyer's opinion, killing was no sin.[19] True, the great days of Frankish imperial expansion had ended a generation before; but the 830s had seen campaigns against Bretons, Danes and Slavs. Those who read history-books (and some laymen did) knew that the Franks had grown mighty by conquering 'external peoples': not since the battle of Vinchy in 717 had Franks slaughtered Franks in 'civil war'.[20] The style of 'internal' Frankish politics had involved many confrontations, many feints and pursuits, many rituals of rebellion, but all previous potential conflicts between rival Carolingians had in the end been resolved by talk and compromise, and rituals of conciliation like shared acts of worship. Early in 841, Lupus was urging Charles to seek 'a bloodless victory' over his brother, in traditional Carolingian fashion.[21] But by May, bloodshed was beginning to look inevitable. Like all civil wars, this one would pit brother against brother, each with a recognisable 'right' on his side. For the truth was that both Charles and Lothar had good arguments, in law and in morals. There were no absolute rules governing the succession to the *regnum francorum* or its division between royal heirs; and precedents pointed in different directions. One oath could be overlain by another; obligations could conflict when a man had acquired successive lords – as so many had between 837 and 841. Men could examine their consciences, and still opt for different sides. Nithard, hav-

---

18 Nithard II, 8, 9.
19 Nelson 1989a.
20 Vinchy was recalled by Hincmar for Louis the Stammerer, *PL* 125, col. 986. For lay readers of Frankish history, McKitterick 1989: 239, 247.
21 Ep. 22.

ing chosen his, wrote for those still undecided, or agonising over the consequences of their choice. That is why Nithard's account of the parleying of May–June 841 had to be lengthy. His audience wanted to believe that battle had, in the end, been unavoidable.

What did the rival Carolingians themselves believe? Were all the sendings of messengers, offers and counter-offers, a propaganda exercise, a charade? Such an interpretation places the propagandists, as it were, outside the thought-world of those they addressed. Charles and Lothar were not simply deceiving each other; still less did they try to deceive their own followers. Realities were not so simple, men neither so cynical, nor so naive. Charles had decided on battle as the only way to cut through the competing loyalties and quite literally, reduce the number of Carolingian competitors: thus, as the only way to secure himself a kingdom that included Aquitaine along with the lion's share of Francia (as promised originally in 837); but also, as the only way to secure an outcome all would accept as definitive – a Judgement of God. He made this decision, to be sure, because he thought he could win. By mid-June, two things had crucially altered his prospects of victory: first, at Châlons, Judith arrived with men from Aquitaine; second, Louis the German and a small but experienced force met up with Charles near Auxerre. On 21 June, says Nithard, the two armies, of Charles and Louis on the one hand, of Lothar on the other, 'were within sight of each other'.[22] Charles and Louis did not attack straight away. Instead, they set out rules: the battle was to be 'without any fraud'; it was to be preceded by fasting and prayer. Next day, Lothar withdrew southwestwards, to Fontenoy. Charles and Louis followed, to encamp at the village of Thury, just over 7 km to the south. On 23 June, Charles and Louis sent envoys with final offers: the Frankish heartlands should be divided three ways, but Louis would give up his claims to the Franconian lands west of the Rhine, around Ingelheim and Mainz, while Charles would yield his claims to the region between the Charbonnière Forest and the Meuse. These offers were meant to demonstrate that the two younger brothers had gone to the very limit of reason-

22   Nithard II, 10.

able concessions, and hence would bear no guilt for the casualties of battle. But they surely did not expect Lothar to accept these terms. For they knew perfectly well that Lothar was waiting for one thing to happen before engaging in battle: one thing which would make him too feel he could win. Lothar was awaiting the arrival of Pippin II and his men from Aquitaine. Contemporary Frankish writers are explicit in making the timing of the battle of Fontenoy dependant on Pippin's appearance.[23] It was Pippin's help which ensured that the ensuing battle would be fierce, Pippin's arrival that made Lothar feel so confident that that night in his camp Archbishop George of Ravenna (an Italian supporter who had invested hugely in Lothar's cause) promised him that 'Charles should be tonsured tomorrow' – hence, excluded forever from kingly power.[24] Why had Charles and Louis also been willing to wait? The only possible answers are that they wanted to ensure that Lothar would not evade the battle, and that the battle would be decisive. Lothar, the moment Pippin had joined him, flung down the gauntlet: he alone was to have imperial power, he said, and the interests of his brothers no longer mattered to him. The issue was clearcut, and there could be only one response to a Judgement of God.

Even the date of the battle was not wholly fortuitous; nor did it lack significance for those who fought in it. On Thursday 23 June Charles and Louis had announced a timetable: next day, 24 June, they would celebrate the Feast of St John the Baptist's Nativity; they would join battle on 25 June at 8 a.m. (Nithard, quite exceptionally, repeats the day twice and the hour three times.) There are two themes in the liturgy of the Feast of St John: the first is of release – the opening of Anna's previously barren womb and of Zacharias's dumb mouth, the washing away of sin; the second is of salvation – of baptismal rebirth, foreshadowings ended and prophecies fulfilled through the Coming of Christ.[25] Fontenoy too was designed to be a watershed – washing away the detritus of the past, opening up a clear future.

23 Nithard II, 10; *AB* 841: 50. Both use the ablative absolute: 'Pippino accepto'.
24 Agnellus c. 174, p. 390.
25 Typical of the liturgy then current in Francia, Sacramentary of Angoulême: 153–4.

The battle, in Nithard's account, went according to plan. At dawn Charles and Louis moved northwards with about a third of their troops to occupy the wooded hill overlooking Lothar's camp at Fontenoy itself. Nithard's statement that they waited, as agreed, until 8 a.m. before joining battle, has been rejected by some modern historians, who think that Charles and Louis instead swooped *before 8* on Lothar's sleeping camp. All that is known of medieval warfare suggests that Lothar and his men would not have been sleeping after dawn – least of all when they *knew* that battle was imminent – and that Lothar's scouts would have kept him well informed of his brothers' moves. Furthermore, no contemporary writer, even one who supported Lothar, alleges that Charles and Louis won this battle by a surprise attack (though that tactic was of course standard military practice, and quite familiar to Charles). I think we can accept that Charles and Louis played by the rules they themselves had set. The battle took place on three distinct sites.[26] In the first, hard-fought, sector of the battle, Louis put Lothar to flight; in the second, Charles had swift and complete success; conflict was fiercest, and most protracted, in the third sector, but 'in the end, everyone on Lothar's side fled'.

Nithard leaves out Fontenoy's crucial Aquitanian dimension, which is recorded, fortuitously, in Italian sources drawing on the eye-witness accounts of Archbishop George of Ravenna and his men. Andrew of Bergamo says that 'great slaughter was made especially among the nobles of the Aquitanians. . . . To this day [he is writing c. 860] so wasted is the nobility of the Aquitanians that the Northmen take their land and they have no strength to resist'.[27] Agnellus of Ravenna begins by stressing the large size of Lothar's army and Lothar's personal valour ('had there been ten men like him on his side, the empire would never have been divided'). Nevertheless, Charles, helped by Louis, was victorious. 'But then Pippin king of Aquitaine came up

---

26 By the Brook of the Burgundians, where Lothar engaged Louis; at 'Fagit' (site unidentified) where Charles fought a second body of Lothar's supporters; at Solmet, where other allies of Lothar (unidentified by Nithard) confronted a third section of Charles's and Louis's forces commanded by the Seneschal Adalard.

27 Andrew of Bergamo *Historia, MGH SRL*, p. 226.

with relief for Lothar's army, and battle was rejoined. A number of Charles's men were killed because they had strayed out of formation. When Charles's troops had re-formed, battle began again. More than 40,000 men fell on the side of Lothar and Pippin'. Archbishop George was taken prisoner and, with his clergy scattered, the wealth of his church looted and lost, was brought before Charles. The king threatened permanent exile, but his mother Judith (her presence at Fontenoy is otherwise unrecorded) counselled mercy. As George grovelled at his feet, Charles, resplendent in full armour, publicly condemned him:

> Why did you have to ruin your own church, to lose in a single hour all that your predecessors acquired? Believe me, you won't get any of it back if you live to be a hundred! . . . Weren't you saying in the tent only yesterday: 'When Charles has been beaten and stripped of his weapons, I'll personally tonsure him as a cleric and take him back to Ravenna'? Why deny your own words? Look here – you've done wrong twice over: what you said was wrong in the first place; but then you failed to carry out your promise! God will give you your just deserts. For my part, I'll let you go – as my mother tells me to. Back to Ravenna with you![28]

This scene may give a rare glimpse of Charles's personal style as king. The hard-headedness and the sardonic humour seem true to life; and Judith's role sounds as plausible as her son's wry acknowledgement of her influence and his own youth. As for Agnellus's account of Fontenoy, if his casualty-figure is fantastic, his statements about Pippin's role, and his side's heavy losses, look factual. Though we have no contemporary report from Aquitaine, tenth- and eleventh-century writers there complement the Italians' information by assigning a key role to 'the men of Aquitaine' on Charles's side, with two Aquitanian counts named as among the slain.[29] In short, Fontenoy was a

28 Agnellus p. 390.
29 *Chron. Aquit. MGH SS* II, p. 252; Ademar III, 17; *Mirac. S. Genulfi, MGH SS* XV, p. 1208.

battle between Aquitanians, as well as between Franks. On Pippin's side there was also a crucial non-participant: Bernard 'though he was only about 8 km away from the battlefield, gave no help to either side'.[30] Lothar's supporter Angelbert who wrote a lament over the fallen, may have had Bernard in mind when he attributed his own side's defeat to the last-minute defection of certain 'commanders'.[31]

Was Fontenoy decisive? Charles and Louis saw it as a divine Judgement, confirming their claims to a share in the Frankish heartlands. For Charles it may have meant political survival, for perhaps he really would have been tonsured had he been defeated. Certainly he would have lost Aquitaine. Victory meant, conversely, that in all the negotiations of the subsequent two years, Charles's claims to Aquitaine were never in dispute. In that sense, though Pippin lived to fight another day, the future composition of Charles's kingdom was settled after June 841. Victory also brought an immediate windfall of loot when Lothar's camp fell into his hands: Charles was able to offer gear from Lothar's travelling chapel in thanks to St-Benoît, Fleury.[32] Yet the fact that no Carolingian contender was a casualty meant that Fontenoy failed to resolve the central problem of the imperial succession. Lothar's supporters implicitly recognised this when they tried to postpone the battle's political impact by spreading rumours that Charles had been killed and Louis wounded.[33] Lothar's survival allowed his side, anyway, to reject the notion of Fontenoy as a Judgement of God. Lothar still hoped for 'monarchy', in other words the whole inheritance of Francia. Charles's and Louis's conduct after the battle was conciliatory: they allowed fugitives to escape, and buried the dead on both sides. Pippin was expected to capitulate; but there would have to be a settlement. Charles while still at Fontenoy welcomed into his following a new recruit – Bernard's 15-year old son William.[34] (It was for him that Dhuoda, far south in Uzès, now began her book of moral guidance. She still dated by Lothar's reign-years: it was not clear in whose

30 Nithard III, 2.
31 Godman 1985: 262–3.
32 *Mirac. S. Benedicti c.* 41, *PL* 124, col. 946.
33 Nithard III, 2.
34 Nithard III, 2.

kingdom Uzès might end up.) Bernard himself sent promises, this time with greater credibility, that he would 'deliver' Pippin on Charles's terms.

While Louis the German went eastwards to the Rhine-land, after agreeing to another meeting at Langres in September, Charles's first move after Fontenoy was westwards into Aquitaine. Pippin eluded him (though some of his followers came over to Charles). The problem, again, was shortage of time: Charles had to return with Judith to Francia to make the most of the expected strengthening of his position in the heartlands between Seine and Meuse. Lothar's defeat, and his departure to the Rhineland to launch an attack on Louis, had left his more westerly supporters demoralised. Charles's men gained control in Paris, Soissons and Rheims (whence Ebbo was again driven out). There were prestigious recruits: Hugh, an illegitimate son of Charlemagne and abbot of the great monasteries of St-Quentin and Lobbes, Immo bishop of Noyon, and perhaps other Rheims suffragans. Most encouraging for Charles were new supporters from the Meuse valley region, won over 'more by love than by fear'[35] (in sharp contrast to Lothar's 'terror-tactics'): Giselbert, count of the Maasgau, and Count Odulf (whose adherence had to be clinched by the grant of Ferrières's rich dependency of St-Josse – which did not please Abbot Lupus!).[36] After a stay at Attigny, not far from the Meuse, Charles returned to Paris early in September.

Lothar, in a last bid to shore up his power in western Francia, made a foray to the Seine. Charles withdrew to the west bank at St-Cloud; Lothar stayed at St-Denis and sent envoys to talk of peace while still trying to reconstruct an alliance with Neustrians, Bretons and Pippin of Aquitaine. It was too late. His former supporters turned their backs. 'He spent the whole winter in wasted effort',[37] while early in the new year his Rhineland *civitates* too fell to Louis the German. On 14 February Louis and Charles and their followings met at Strasbourg to agree a strategy for forcing real and permanent concessions out of Lothar.

35 *AB* 841: 51.
36 Lupus Ep. 32. Lupus received a confirmation of Ferrières's privileges, however (T. 3).
37 *AF* 841: 33.

This meeting is famous for reasons not strictly historical. Not only does Nithard say in which vernacular languages the two kings addressed their men (though he records the addresses in Latin), but he gives the ensuing oaths in vernacular texts that are among the earliest examples of Old High German and Old French.[38] Louis in the *lingua teudisca*, Charles in the *lingua romana*, purveyed an identical message: Lothar had rejected the Judgement of God, and he was responsible for the continuing sufferings of 'our people'. Only through 'firm fraternity' would Lothar be brought to acknowledge 'justice', that is, the just claims of his brothers. Louis then swore in the *lingua romana*, so that Charles's men would understand him:

For the love of God and for the Christian people and for our common salvation, from this day henceforth, as far as God grants that I know and can, I shall so help this my brother Charles with my aid and in all things, as every man ought in right to help his brother, on condition that he does the like for me. And I shall never accept [the offer of] any meeting from Lothar which, with my will, may cause harm to this my brother Charles.

Charles then swore an equivalent oath to Louis in the *lingua teudisca*.

Charles's following (*populus*) then swore 'in its own language, the *lingua romana*': 'If Louis keeps the oath which he swears to his brother Charles, and my lord Charles for his part does not keep his, if I cannot make him refrain [from that action], then neither I nor any other whom I can make refrain will give him any aid against Louis'. Louis's men then swore an equivalent oath in the *lingua teudisca*.

Clearly, everyone present had to understand what commitments were being entered into, and not everyone knew Latin or was bilingual in Romance and Old High German. This suggests that *all* in the kings' followings, lesser men as well as great nobles, were involved in the action, and played a *collective* role in underwriting the kings' commit-

38 Nithard III, 5.

ments. In other words, the sanction holding Louis and Charles to their promises was the aristocracy's power to withdraw their loyalty. Nithard went on to speak of a 'pact' (*pactum*) between the two royal brothers and the *primores populi,* that is the 'leading men' who presumably swore the oaths in person. The maintenance of a united front between Louis and Charles was the only way to bring Lothar to negotiate the secure peace that would benefit everyone. At this point in his narrative Nithard inserted a joint-vignette of Charles and Louis: 'Both were of middle height, good-looking, physically fit. Both were brave, generous, prudent and eloquent. Even more important than all these noble qualities was the holy and respected concord between the two brothers. They nearly always ate together; they gave each other all they had that was especially valuable; they shared the same house, slept under the same roof.'[39] Nithard's aim here was not accurate physical description but the symbolic underlining of shared commitment. The account ends with a vivid picture of military exercises, first involving feigned flights performed by two equal contingents drawn from peoples of the various *regna* – Saxons, Gascons, Austrasians and Bretons, then the 'putting to flight' of all these by the two kings and their followings (*omnis iuventus*) on horseback, the whole thing characterised by 'so many noble participants, such superb control'. The control impressed Nithard, for such exercises, he noted, often ended in real fights.

Once Lothar had again spurned his brothers' messengers, and come southwards from Aachen to the Moselle, apparently seeking battle, the scene was set for a final showdown. Louis moved down the Rhine by ship from Worms, Charles with his horsemen travelled overland across the Hunsrück ('a difficult route' on which the benefits of hard training showed),[40] to meet up at Koblenz on 18 March. Lothar fled – first to Aachen, where he plundered the imperial treasury, and then southwards, leaving Aachen, the 'first seat of Francia', to be occupied by his brothers. This was, as Nithard put it, 'the end of Lothar's second contest'. This time the victory was bloodless – but

39 Nithard III, 6.
40 Nithard III, 7.

123

its outcome confirmed that of Fontenoy. Louis and Charles would have their shares of Francia.

At first, they gave every appearance of being determined to exclude Lothar from the Carolingian heartlands altogether. A large assembly of bishops and priests declared that Lothar lacked 'the knowledge of how to govern the state', and had fled 'by a just Judgement of God, first from the battle-field and then from his own realm'. God had thus clearly transferred the realm to his brothers, whom the bishops now invited to take it up.[41] Perhaps Charles's hand can be seen behind this remarkable foreshadowing of a new style of king-making ritual. The maintenance of both morale and consensus among his and Louis's supporters was especially critical now. The two-way division agreed at Aachen in March 842 is best seen as a way of putting pressure on Lothar, convincing him that this time he had no alternative to opening negotiations in earnest. The terms of this abortive treaty (gaps in Nithard's text seem to suggest that details were never agreed) are therefore less significant than the way it was drawn up. Charles produced a panel of twelve commissioners (one of them was Nithard) and Louis did the same. 'This division was adapted not so much to the fertility or equal territorial extent of each share, as to the family connections (*affinitas*), and the interests and commitments (*congruentia*), of everyone involved' – that is to say, not of the kings alone, but of all twenty-four commissioners and beyond them, of their comrades, kin, friends and clients.[42] This short passage makes crystal-clear the role of the aristocracy in Carolingian politics, and explains why Charles now and later worked so hard to carry his followers with him.

The sequel proved the wisdom of the brothers' strategy: within weeks, Lothar sent envoys to reopen negotiations, this time talking in far more accommodating tones than ever before. But consensus had its limitations in practice. Louis and Charles proposed to split Francia proper into three, giving Lothar all the lands between the Meuse and the Rhine. 'Some people already thought this was going beyond what was fair and suitable.'[43] But Lothar then ex-

41 Nithard IV, 1.
42 Nithard IV, 1. My reading owes much to Classen 1963.
43 Nithard IV, 3.

tracted a further concession, 'since he would not have, he said, in the share [of the *regnum*] they were offering him the wherewithal to make good to his own supporters that which they had lost. The envoys – I do not know by what trickery they were deceived [here Nithard bursts out into the first person] – thus increased Lothar's share of the *regnum* so that it extended as far as the Charbonnière.' There seems little doubt that a personal disappointment dictated Nithard's reaction here, and the natural explanation is that Nithard's own lands lay within the newly-conceded region, that is, between the Scheldt and the Meuse. Charles therefore failed to carry Nithard's full-hearted support in the further detailed negotiations after June 842. On the other hand, disappointment did not drive Nithard to defection: Charles had nicely calculated, just as Lothar had done – and this surely was a prime requirement of successful kingship – whom he could, and could not, afford to disappoint. Similarly, despite Lupus's heartful pleas, Charles decided to leave St-Josse in the hands of Odulf whose continuing fidelity it guaranteed. Charles knew that Lupus's stern warnings to 'avoid the company of the wicked'[44] relieved his feelings without actually compromising his loyalty.

Once a three-way division had been agreed in principle, each of the three brothers spent the rest of the summer in consolidating his position where it seemed weakest. Lothar remained in central Francia, perhaps tightening his grip on the region east of the Charbonnière. Louis had a serious revolt in Saxony to quell. Charles as usual faced conflicting priorities. Vikings had just sacked Quentovic, probably in June 842, taking advantage (as other Vikings had done in 834) of conflict between Carolingians. The raiders were bought off, perhaps by a locally-organised rather than a royally-directed payment. Recognising a more serious problem in the fact that Pippin II remained at large in Aquitaine, Charles moved across the Loire, this time penetrating much further than before into the south-west, where Pippin's adherents were evidently still to be found. On 23 August, Charles was at Agen on the Garonne, with men from Burgundy under his command.[45] 'He put Pippin

44 Lupus Ep. 31.
45 T. 10.

to flight',[46] but again failed to capture him. Before the end of August he was turning north again leaving affairs in Aquitaine to be looked after by Duke Warin and by Egfrid, whom Charles seems to have installed as count of Toulouse shortly before.

The three brothers had agreed to meet at the beginning of October, at Metz, where their father was buried. There they were to leave commissioners, forty picked by each brother, to work out a detailed division of the heartlands. If the choice of site was intended to reinforce fraternal solidarity, it failed: Lothar's palace at Thionville was too close for comfort, and his brothers still mistrusted him so much that they demanded hostages from him to guarantee the security of their own negotiators. In the end they agreed that the 120 commissioners should hold their meetings in the church of St-Castor at Koblenz, lodging each night on opposite sides of the Rhine 'to forestall outbreaks of fighting between the commissioners' men'.[47]

The negotiators immediately ran into a problem: no-one on Louis's and Charles's side had a thorough knowledge of the whole 'empire' (*totius imperii*). They would have to send out *missi* to make detailed descriptions, they said – otherwise they would be violating the oath they had taken, to make a fair division. A second problem arose when Lothar objected to the delay. Bishops were again brought in to arbitrate; but they did not see eye to eye. The bishops on Lothar's side declared that the involuntary sin of an oath thus broken could be expiated and that a speedy division would prevent further damage to the Church. The bishops on Charles's and Louis's side, taking a firmer line about oaths, asked why anyone should have to sin in this case, and repeated the proposal that a complete survey of the empire be made. When the full meeting of commissioners also failed to agree 'without the authority of their lords', they made a truce until 5 November and reported back for further instructions.

At the three courts of Lothar, Louis and Charles, the *primores populi* agreed on one thing: there was to be no repeat

---

46 Nithard IV, 4.
47 Nithard IV, 4 and 5.

of Fontenoy. A poor harvest in 842, and the imminence of winter, strengthened their determination. Louis and Charles conceded a tactful point to Lothar by sending their envoys to him at Thionville, but on the main issue they had their way. A *descriptio* would be made, and the final division would follow after 14 July 843. The three parts would be determined and then Lothar should have first pick.

Nithard's account hardly goes beyond this point. I have followed it through closely because it shows the kind of diplomacy which, though no comparable evidence survives, has to be assumed for subsequent relations between Charles and his brothers (and later his nephews) throughout his reign. Nithard reveals the contradictory values and expectations which otherwise have to be surmised. He shows conflict in the very heart of the royal family, injunctions to 'brotherly love' constantly at odds with manifestations of brotherly hate. He shows commendable 'guile' not far from deplorable 'trickery', the force of lordly authority belied by followers' barely-controlled violence. He shows the struggles of individual aristocrats to reconcile public and private concerns, personal claims and collective duty to lord or king, competing obligations towards kinsmen and clients. He shows genuine episcopal devotion to 'the Church's welfare' crosscut by the commitment of individual bishops to their political masters.

On 13 December 842, at the palace of Quierzy, Charles married Ermentrude, niece of Adalard, because 'he thought he could thereby win over to himself [the support of] the majority of the lesser aristocracy (*plebs*)'. This is virtually Nithard's last word; and he offers an explanation of Adalard's power: 'Caring little for the public good, he devoted himself to pleasing everyone. He persuaded [Charles] to distribute privileges and public revenues to private individuals for their own use; and, since he caused to be done what everyone wanted, he reduced the [resources of] the state to absolutely nothing'.[48] Adalard, in other words, had acted as a *potens* was expected to; what Nithard resented was his own absence from Adalard's honours list. His sour grapes should not be mistaken for an accurate impression of the flavour of Charles's court in December

48   Nithard IV, 6.

127

842. Clearly Adalard's influence was great (Nithard was not alone in identifying Ermentrude as 'Adalard's niece' rather than as the daughter of Count Odo of Orléans, Adalard's brother-in-law, though an obvious reason could have been that Odo had died eight years before, perhaps leaving Ermentrude in her uncle's care).[49] As lay-abbot of St-Martin Tours, Adalard occupied a key strategic position in the Loire valley. Charles came to stay at St-Martin in February 843.[50] In 841–2, the prominent position of Adalard's brother Gerald at Lothar's court may have eased the route to a settlement between Charles and Lothar. Charles's marriage probably further enhanced Adalard's influence, at least in the short run: about a year later, Lupus used the 'cooperation' of this 'most weighty man' (*amplissimus vir*) in pursuing Ferrières's interests at Charles's court.[51]

But Adalard was not the only influential man in Charles's entourage at this time. Vivian first appears as chamberlain in February 843.[52] He hailed almost certainly from the region of the lower Loire, where a close kinsman (perhaps his father) had been killed fighting for Louis the Pious in 834[53] and already before 842 another probable close kinsman, Rainald, was count of Herbauge and *dux* of Nantes. Since queen and chamberlain had to work closely together *ex officio*, Vivian's promotion looks more like a counterweight than a complement to Adalard's. So too does the position of Duke Warin, another *potens* in 843.[54] True, Lupus exhorted Charles 'not to subject himself so much to the influence of one man so that he did everything according to that man's will'.[55] But the subtext of Lupus's letter was disappointment at Charles's withholding of St-Josse, and so the veiled reference here was evidently to Odulf. Later in the same letter Lupus's warning had a plural object: 'Fear not the *potentes* whom you yourself have made'.

49 *AB* 842: 54 and n. 12. See Genealogy VII.
50 T. 20. Cf. Werner 1958: 274.
51 Lupus Ep. 20. Cf. T. 30 (27 Dec. 843) – a confirmation and restoration in favour of Ferrières.
52 T. 19.
53 Nithard I, 5; *AB* 834: 30 – the same battle in which Ermentrude's father had been killed. See above 81, 93, n. 62.
54 Below Ch. 6: 139.
55 Ep. 31.

Potentes of course played key roles at court: Lupus himself was happy to seek, and use, their 'cooperation'. Charles in fact avoided his father's tendency to rely on a single favourite: no-one was ever labelled (as Bernard had been) *secundus a rege* in Charles's reign. Instead he took care to spread his special favour among several men. His youth had perhaps exposed him to charges of being too much under the control of guardians (*bajuli*)[56] but none is documented after Atto in 838.[57] Charles had perhaps depended quite heavily on his mother's support in 840–1. His marriage was a declaration of independence: of personal and political maturity. There is a noteable contrast with Pippin II who (so far as is known) never married. Charles now placed himself on a par with Lothar and Louis the German (whose teenage sons had recently begun to play an active political role themselves). Without waiting for the empire's division to be formally signed and sealed, Charles gave notice of his intention to father a progeny – his own royal line.

There is little evidence about Ermentrude herself at the time of the marriage. She may have been aged as young as 12, the legal age of maturity for women (her parents' marriage can perhaps be dated to 829) and so about seven years younger than Charles. He gave her dower-lands in the Amienois, near Corbie.[58] There is no evidence of what lands, if any, she brought her husband as dowry. She had a (?younger) brother named William.[59] The fact that his life is totally unrecorded until 866[60] need not suggest that Ermentrude's own influence was limited, but shows that a royal marriage did not necessarily bring honours to the bride's close kinsmen. Charles was free to grant or withhold the rewards of *Königsnähe* even to his own brother-in-law. Adalard's enjoyment of Charles's favour was cause rather than consequence of his niece's match.

Within weeks of her marriage, Ermentrude was already on campaign with her husband in Aquitaine. Her unique

---

56 Lupus Ep. 31. Lupus quoted I Cor. 13, 11–12 at Charles.
57 Above Ch. 4: 99. Atto had sided with Lothar, Nithard III, 7.
58 T. 13 *bis*.
59 Presumably named after his uncle, killed alongside Odo in 834, *AB* : 30.
60 Below Ch. 8: 211–12.

closeness to the king gave her the influence of a special *potens*, to whom others appealed that she 'suggest to the king' on their behalf.[61] Such appeals, fairly consistently spread over the twenty-seven years of her subsequent married life, constitute indirect evidence of an untroubled personal relationship with Charles. Ermentrude faithfully performed the crucial function of a royal wife in producing a total of eleven children, and as late as 866, she was still ready to produce more. Little more than a year after her marriage, Ermentrude had given birth to her first child, Judith. The fate of the grandmother after whom the baby was named confirms the *ex officio* importance of the queen. According to the author of the *Annals of Xanten* (he had been Louis the Pious's court librarian and perhaps a protégé of the emperor's wife in the 830s), 'The Empress Judith, Charles's mother, died at Tours, having had all her wealth taken from her by her son'.[62] It seems likely that, as in other early medieval kingdoms, there was room for only one queen at Charles's court. His marriage therefore meant Judith's enforced retirement. 'Her wealth' may have consisted in part of lands earmarked for the queen: now she must relinquish them. Judith, perhaps already ailing at the time of her son's marriage, may have accompanied him to Tours in February 843. She died there on 19 April and was honourably buried at St-Martin's. Charles later saw to her commemoration at thirteen other churches too.[63] Yet there is nothing in the wording of any of these charters (any more than in Charles's later recollections of his mother) to suggest special affection. He wanted both Louis the Pious and Judith commemorated because they were his parents and because their imperial status rubbed off on him. These arrangements thus say more about Charles's developing conception of his office than about his feelings as a son.

The timing of Charles's marriage suggests a further political dimension. Adalard was not Ermentrude's only close relative. Another was a young man named Odo. Allied to him by region and (later) marriage, was Robert. Ermen-

---

61 E.g. Hincmar Ep. 5. See further Hyam 1990.
62 *AX* 843: 13.
63 T. 147, 153, 162, 220, 246, 251, 299, 300, 307, 338, 355, 364, 378, 379, 441, 444, 460.

trude's father had originally come from the Worms area, but he had made his career, thanks to imperial favour, in the west. In the next generation, Odo and Robert followed suit, receiving Charles's favour in the form of lands that in fact belonged to the church of Rheims (the see's continuing vacancy since Ebbo's second departure in 841 had left its property at the king's disposal). When exactly did this happen? The only evidence is a statement of Hincmar's forty years later, that the grants were made 'when the three brothers Lothar, Louis and Charles divided the *regnum* between themselves after their father's death'.[64] This could refer to the period just after July 843, when the division was finalised, or, more probably, to a slightly earlier date, during the negotiations. Either way, the westward move of Odo and Robert and the distribution to them of lands in the Rheims area, can be linked with Charles's marriage to Ermentrude. Perhaps Charles met Odo and Robert during his visit to Worms in November 842. The marriage, and the recruitment and endowment of the two Rhinelanders, had the same purpose: Charles wanted to strengthen his general position in the part of Francia which was to constitute the northeastern sector of his kingdom. To secure that share of the Frankish heartlands, Charles had fought Fontenoy, and faced down Lothar at Koblenz. To stake out part of his frontier he had spent Christmas 842 with Abbot Hugh at St-Quentin, and then moved on to Valenciennes. During the spring of 843, the commissioners did their job of surveying the royal resources in Francia. It was time, in July 843, for Charles to attend the long-planned meeting with his brothers to divide the *regnum* in the light of that survey. He and his men took the road to Verdun.

64 *Vita Remigii, MGH SSRM* III, p. 324.

Chapter 6

843–849: CHALLENGE AND RESPONSE

When Charles and his brothers met up with their commissioners at Verdun in July 843, their aim was a short-term one. They worked within the constraints of dynastic politics and a royal family in constant process of reconstruction. What was wanted was a three-way division of the empire that could secure (where a sequence of abortive projects had failed to do so) the consent for the time being of three rival Carolingians and their war-weary supporters. The details of the division were certainly inscribed in a document, but no copy has survived. Like other inter-Carolingian pacts it probably began with an appeal for divine legitimation, and went on to urge love and peace between the brothers, and between uncles and nephews. The fact that 120 important men participated in the settlement made it widely acceptable. Few at the time took the longer perspective that comes naturally to historians. A generation's span was brief: Lothar had two sons, Louis the German had three, and in each case the eldest was already near manhood, while Charles and his young wife were likely to produce another Carolingian progeny. Verdun could only deal with the short term.

Verdun was significant in what it did *not* say. Its most welcome silence, from Charles's standpoint, was evidently on Pippin of Aquitaine, whose claims Lothar agreed to drop, tacitly accepting Fontenoy's 'judgement'. Unlike the *Ordinatio* of 817, the 843 agreement does not seem to have assigned the *primogenitus*, Lothar, any rights to intervene in his brothers' kingdoms. Nor is it clear whether it made any provision for the future integrity of each kingdom via a single line of succession in the next generation.[1] But it is unlikely that anyone in 843 thought of the three part-kingdoms as permanent. It was this very provisionality that made Verdun acceptable. It provided a framework within which the rivals could continue to manoeuvre, to compete, but also, sometimes, to cooperate. It would be a prelude to further meetings: a kind of congress system. It did not create three Frankish kingdoms, but preserved one, within which a variable number of *regna* (contemporaries called those 'kingdoms', never 'Frankish kingdoms') could be formed and re-formed.

It is not just a coincidence therefore that no 'official text' of the Treaty of Verdun has survived. The geographical boundaries of Charles's kingdom can, however, be reconstructed from later evidence.[2] In the northerly sector, it followed the line of the Scheldt, from the coast to Ghent, then via Tournai and Valenciennes it swung rather sharply westwards towards Arras, embracing the county of Ostrevant but leaving the counties of Lomme, Hainault and Cambrai in Lothar's kingdom; then an eastward shift via St-Quentin brought it very close to the Meuse to a region where a number of counties straddled the river. The line then went southwards, to the east of Attigny, and Ponthion, leaving to the east a string of counties that straddled the Meuse. South of Ponthion another abrupt westwards swing of the line left the county of Bassigny to Lothar, then the frontier went through northern Burgundy east of Langres, again coming very near the Upper Meuse, and embraced the county of Chalon which straddled the Saône. South of Chalon, the line then went sharply west again before turning finally south, to leave all the counties straddling the Rhône, from Lyons to Uzès, in Lothar's hands. Westwards of the Rhône delta, all Septimania was included in Charles's kingdom, giving him the Spanish March with the county of Barcelona in the far southwest.

Some of the details of this boundary suggest the influence of individual magnates. In the northern sector, for

---

1   On this point, the agreement of Meersen in 847 refers back not to Verdun but to 806; *MGH Capit.* II, no. 204, c. 9, see below: 149. Note that both Lothar and Louis the German already had more than one son.

2   See map 3.

instance, Abbot Hugh of St-Quentin surely played a key role in securing that abbey for Charles, while further south, the inclusion of the counties of Langres and Chalon in Charles's kingdom reflects the importance of Bishop Theutbald and Count Warin as Charles's consistent supporters since 840.[3] On the other side, particular interests helped keep the monastery of St-Vaast, Arras, an enclave of Lothar's within Charles's territory. Lordship and loyalty intersected with geographical factors to explain why particular counties, sees and abbacies were on one side or the other of the boundary-line. There was intersection too between the interests of kings and aristocrats, as Charles no less than Lothar secured 'the wherewithal to reward his followers'. That fundamental political concern explains why Charles was determined to ensure that the entire Seine basin with its exceptionally rich cluster of palaces and royal estates remained within his kingdom.

Another kind of cement was provided by the church: Charles's kingdom comprised seven whole ecclesiastical provinces: Rouen, Tours, Sens, Bourges, Bordeaux, Eauze[4] and Narbonne. It also included the whole province of Rheims except for the see of Cambrai, and the four suffragan sees of Lyons – Autun, Langres, Chalon and Mâcon – though the metropolis of Lyons itself was in Lothar's kingdom. Though extensive, Charles's grip on his churches varied a good deal in intensity. In the provinces of Rouen, Tours and Sens the king could have a large say in episcopal appointments and hence in the disposition of diocesan resources. In 843, the temporal goods of the see of Rheims itself were administered directly by the king, and there had been a vacancy (apart from Ebbo's brief return in 841) since 835. Rheims' suffragans (except for Cambrai) were also within close and direct range of royal intervention. Further south, royal influence over church personnel or property was patchier; in the province of Narbonne evidence on episcopal appointments is lacking for any phase of Charles's reign, though there are occasional signs of

3   Classen 1963: 10.
4   This metropolitan see was transferred to Auch (dep. Gers) sometime in the ninth century. Gascony is almost undocumented in this period; Collins 1986.

continuing royal interest in church property and in the political benefits of episcopal support. But bishops and dioceses were not the whole church: just as important (and in many localities much more so) were monasteries. The position of Hugh at St-Quentin was critical for Charles's northeastern frontier, for instance. Even in the south some monasteries maintained close relations with the king: Pyrenean abbots would journey 800 km to the other end of Charles's kingdom to have their houses' privileges confirmed.[5]

How had Charles fared compared with Louis the German and Lothar? On parchment he had not done badly. True, Lothar had gained the lion's share of the heartlands (though he lost to Louis an important region on the west bank of the Rhine, from Mainz south to Worms and Speyer). But – and this was the most significant thing about Verdun – the heartlands had been divided, so that Lothar was never to have the preponderance over his brothers that Charlemagne and Louis the Pious had had over their sons. Charles's kingdom was large. Its five *regna*: Francia, Burgundy, Septimania, Aquitaine, and Neustria contained quantities of royal resources, with, at Melle in Poitou, the only big silver-mine in the Carolingian Empire, and, at Quentovic and Rouen, major mints and trading-places opening out onto the northern world.[6] Charles's kingdom was compact, with relatively good internal communications by river and in many regions by still usable Roman roads. There were also possibilities for extracting plunder and tribute in the frontier regions of Brittany and the Spanish March.

On the ground, Charles's position was more fragile. Aquitaine's future was uncertain as long as Pippin II and his brother remained there. Charles had campaigned successfully early in 843 but when he moved north again, old problems reappeared. At some point between early summer 843 and spring 844, Toulouse, where Charles had left Count Acfrid (Egfrid) in charge,[7] passed to supporters of Pippin. More clouds loomed on a more distant horizon.

5   E.g. T. 166 (854), 221 (860), 289 (866), 340 (870), 415 (876).
6   Coupland 1990a, and 1991b, and above Ch. 2.
7   Nithard IV, 4.

The Spanish March had suffered heavy incursions in 841–2 from Musa ibn Musa, lord of Zaragoza and Tudela, and scion of a family who, following the eighth-century Muslim conquest of Spain, had converted to Islam and since the 790s dominated the Ebro valley.[8] Musa's regional ambitions had caused problems also for his nominal overlord, the amir of Cordoba, 'Abd al-Rahman II (822–52). In 843, the amir's resounding defeat of Musa and his ally, the king of Pamplona, did not destroy Musa's power-base; and, from the Franks' standpoint, while it signalled a respite from Musa's raids into Septimania, it threatened danger from the Cordoban regime itself. In future, Charles would have to find some way of exploiting these conflicts on the Spanish March rather than falling victim to them.

Charles had more serious worries over another marcher region, the lower Loire valley. Early in 843, 'the Breton Nominoë and Lambert, who had recently defected from their allegiance to Charles, slew Rainald duke of Nantes'.[9] Rainald's origins were in northwestern Aquitaine, just across the Loire from Nantes, though his career had taken him further south in Poitou in the 830s (where he successfully fought off Viking attacks), and, in 840, to central Aquitaine. He had been trusted by Louis the Pious, and loyally supported Charles. He was a natural choice as count of Nantes, probably in 841. Lambert, his killer, was the son (or close kinsman) of an earlier Lambert who had been count of Nantes in the 820s, had joined Lothar's rebellion and been dis-honoured and exiled by Louis the Pious, and had died in the Italian epidemic of 836–7. In 840 Lambert Junior was in western Neustria. He supported Lothar, then switched to Charles in 841. Early in 843 he defected again.

Adrevald of Fleury (writing in the 870s) described the conflict between Lambert and Rainald as a 'duel between marquises', meaning great lords of the (Breton) March.[10] Adrevald put his finger on the regional nature of the quarrel. Though Lambert's ancestors had been outsiders from the Rhineland, installed in Neustria by Charlemagne, Lambert himself was a third-generation local man with *hereditary*

---

8   Sanchez-Albornoz 1969; Collins 1983: 190–1.
9   *AB* 843: 55.
10   *Mirac. S. Benedicti* c. 33, *PL* 124, col. 936.

interests in the lower Loire region. Rainald's roots were in neighbouring Poitou. His appointment to Nantes was sound strategy from Charles's standpoint. But it was probably the choice of Rainald's kinsman Vivian as chamberlain[11] which drove Lambert to defect early in 843. Lambert's fellow-defector was 'the Breton Nominoë', another former supporter of Louis the Pious who, after some havering, had come over to Charles in 841, at the same time as Lambert.[12] His cooperation with Lambert in 843 illustrated once again the interconnectedness of local concerns with high-level Carolingian politics. Both Nominoë and Lambert stood to lose out in western Neustria if Rainald's local clout was backed by Vivian's at court. The duel of marquises was also a confrontation between *congruentia* and *affinitas.*

An already complex situation in western Neustria was further complicated by a force of Vikings. This was not the first time that Vikings had exploited Carolingian disputes. From 834 to 838, raids on Quentovic had become an annual event. A warband under a chieftain called Oskar came up the Seine and sacked Rouen in May 841 (within weeks of Charles's activity in this very area). Quentovic had again been raided in 842.[13] Local Frankish disputes also presented Vikings with attractive targets. Lambert's newly-won position was still precarious when a Viking force (perhaps under Oskar) attacked Nantes on St John's Day (24 June) 843, sacked it, killed the bishop, and went on to ravage the western coast of Aquitaine.[14] Rainald's death had exposed 'his' region to attack. The situation invited royal intervention.

In August, as soon as his business at Verdun was finished, Charles set off westwards, picking up Neustrian supporters en route. At Germigny near Orléans in early October, the archbishops of Rouen and Tours were present, with a clutch of Neustrian bishops.[15] By mid-November

11 See above, 128.
12 Nithard II, 5. See further Smith 1992, Ch. 2.
13 *AFont* 841: 75; Nithard IV, 2.
14 *AB* 843: 55–6 and nn. 1 and 2.
15 *MGH Conc.* III, no. 1: Sées, Rennes, Lisieux, Coutances and Bayeux.

Charles was at Rennes,[16] having issued threats of vengeance against those who 'opposed the royal power with contumacious and puffed-up spirit'.[17] His presence at the Neustrian frontier may have had little military purpose: serious campaigning did not usually happen in the winter months. The object of the exercise, instead, was a political demonstration. For Charles was worried about the explosive rivalries among his own leading men in the Loire valley region: Vivian would have to settle scores with Lambert, and his and Adalard's regional interests were also difficult to reconcile. Charles withdrew to Coulaines near Le Mans, where he and his men took counsel. The pact that ensued (it may well have been drafted by Lupus) was between three parties: king, clergy and lay nobility. Charles himself guaranteed the *honor* of the church and the *honor* of the *fideles* (faithful men), while clergy and *fideles* undertook to maintain the royal *honor*.[18]

Lot and Halphen saw the agreement of Coulaines as proof that 'monarchy [had] descended from its throne': here, already at the outset of Charles's reign, was the beginning of the end for West Frankish royal power. More recently, and more constructively, Elisabeth Magnou-Nortier has hailed the birth of a new style of 'contractual monarchy' and a new 'constitutional' basis for Charles's exercise of power.[19] In fact the alleged novelty was not really new: Charles evoked a traditional theme of consensus between king and *fideles*. He still spoke from the throne, and would wield his authority ruthlessly when it was politic to do so. The real threat was that of faction within his camp. Charles met this threat in two ways: he emphasised the duty that bound lay *potentes*, 'illustrious men', to the service of the royal power, the *respublica*, and at the same time he guaranteed the 'law and justice' of 'all faithful men', that is, of the lesser aristocracy as well as the magnates. Coulaines was a response to Lupus's recent advice: 'Do not fear the *potentes* whom you yourself have made and whom, if you wish, you can diminish'.[20] Charles was ad-

16 T. 28.
17 *MGH Capit.* II, no. 293, cc. 13–16, p. 402.
18 *MGH Capit.* II, no. 254, pp. 253–5.
19 Lot and Halphen 1909: 95–6; Magnou-Nortier 1976: 98–108.
20 Ep. 31.

dressing an immediate political problem, not theorising for posterity. He needed both Adalard and Vivian, and he still hoped to reconcile both Lambert and Nominoë, but he needed to offset their power. A note prefacing the capitulary in the earliest manuscript says that it was drawn up 'with the consent of Warin and the rest of the magnates and the other faithful men'.[21]

The coexistence of three Carolingian rulers after Verdun was called by Halphen 'the regime of confraternity'.[22] But beneath the honeyed words of repeated diplomatic exchanges through the 840s, and underlying Charles's problems in both western Neustria and Aquitaine, was Lothar's persisting hostility – pursued not with military but with political weapons. Lothar encouraged Lambert and Nominoë, and kept Pippin II's hopes alive. He also exploited the lingering sympathies for Ebbo of some bishops in the province of Rheims. Coulaines was a message to all these, and to Lothar, that Charles's regime could withstand these pressures. Charles himself sent a copy of the pact to Louis the German. The 840s were to be dominated by Lothar's continuing challenge – and by Charles's sustained response.

The year 844 began well for Charles. After spending Christmas at St-Martin, Tours, (in the company of both Adalard and Vivian) he took the chance of the exceptionally mild winter to move once more against Pippin II.[23] Charles was at Limoges early in February 844 with an army probably drawn from the Loire valley region.[24] Most plausibly associated with an assembly at Limoges is the episode recorded in the *AB* as the first event in 844:

> Bernard count of the Spanish March had for a long time now had grandiose designs and thirsted for the heights of power. He was found guilty of treason by the judgement of the Franks, and was executed in Aquitaine.[25]

The further information in the *Annals of Fulda* that Ber-

---

21 For this manuscript (Hague 10 D 2), see Nelson 1986a (1983a).
22 Halphen 1977.
23 T. 30; *AB* 844: 57.
24 T. 32 (the beneficiary was the bishop of Angers).
25 *AB* 844: 57. Cf. Malbos 1970.

nard was 'taken unawares and when not expecting enmity from Charles' suggests that Bernard had attempted to repeat his ploy of 841, offering to 'deliver' Pippin II.[26] If so, it was a fatal miscalculation. Charles would not be conned again. He made sure that Bernard's sentence was collectively agreed by members of his following, and legally carried out. Charles acted *pour encourager les autres*. Other Aquitanians may have been 'made humbler', as Bernard himself had been by Charles's rough treatment of him in 841. One who was not was Bernard's own son William: he deserted Charles and turned to Pippin II.[27] There is no evidence of other defectors.

By early May Charles was besieging Toulouse (there is no information as to who was holding it on Pippin's behalf). His HQ in the monastery of St-Sernin, just outside the walls of Toulouse, became a busy court. No fewer than 20 extant charters were issued here between 11 May and 30 June.[28] The beneficiaries came mainly from the Spanish March[29] and Septimania,[30] but Archbishop Rodulf of Bourges and the abbot of Estrées came from Berry, and the abbot of Castres from the Albigeois. The bishop of Toulouse was also in Charles's camp.[31] Charles seems to have taken south in his entourage a monk and priest from St-Denis, Hincmar, who surfaces in the evidence now for the first time in Charles's reign.[32] The former faithful servant of Louis the Pious had no doubt recommended himself to Charles already, and now did so further because of his kinship with prominent nobles in Aquitaine.[33] Hincmar's hand may be seen in a capitulary protecting the clergy of Septimania against the depredations of their own bishops[34]: a neat parallel to the charters affirming the rights of Spanish immigrant *fideles* [35] against the encroach-

---

26 *AF* 844: 34. Cf. above Ch. 4: 111.
27 See below: 141.
28 Including T. 51. T. 72 and T. 286 (both undated) should perhaps be included too. *MGH Conc.* III, no. 4, pp. 20–3, was also issued.
29 T. 36–39, 45, 47, 49, 53 and 55.
30 T. 41, 43, 44, 46, 48, 49, 54.
31 T. 42, 51, 33.
32 T. 57.
33 Flodoard III, c. 26, p. 543.
34 Cf. above n. 28.
35 Holders of *aprisiones*; see Ch. 2 above: 26.

ments of Septimanian nobles. Here, Charles's assertion of royal protective authority went hand- in-hand with the bolstering of the regional authority of Sunifred, whom Louis the Pious had appointed count of Urgel and Cerdanya. Charles now named Sunifred as *marchio* in Septimania[36] – thereby underscoring the fact that Bernard had been eliminated.

Charles had gone south with a relatively small force, recruited from Neustria and Aquitaine. The host was summoned by Charles's leading men in Francia, as usual, in early summer. As it travelled to join Charles at Toulouse, Pippin and his forces, led among others by William son of Bernard, fell on it 'unexpectedly' in the Angoumois on 14 June and 'scattered it completely'.[37] It was the sort of ambush of which early medieval commanders dreamed. Among the dead were Abbot Hugh of St-Quentin, Abbot Richbod of St-Riquier, Counts Eckhard and Hrabanus, and Nithard (whose skull shows the sword-cut that felled him).[38] Those taken prisoner included Bishop Ebroin of Poitiers, Bishop Ragenar of Amiens, Abbot Lupus of Ferrières and a number of counts and important nobles. Shock-waves spread through the Frankish ecclesiastical world at the news of the abbots' deaths, and Pippin wept over the naked corpse of his great-uncle Hugh, pierced by a lance-thrust.[39] The extent of the church's military contribution to this Frankish army was very clear.[40] By August Charles was going northwards again via the Auvergne towards Francia, having abandoned the siege of Toulouse. Suddenly, his prospects had clouded.

The cloud's one silver lining was the opening of some opportunities for patronage. At St-Riquier, for instance, Charles's cousin Abbot Louis of St-Denis, and Charles's uncle Rudolf were ready to replace Richbod and Nithard. Lupus had been ransomed, and was back at Ferrières, three weeks after the battle – not soon enough, however, to forestall Charles's offering his abbacy to someone else. Lupus, anxious that 'someone might be able to harm me

36   T. 40.
37   *AB* 844: 58–9, with list of those killed or captured.
38   Above, Ch. 1: 6.
39   *MGH* Poet. II, p. 139.
40   Cf. above ch. 3: 58.

with the king', wrote hastily to Abbot Louis to remind him of their *amicitia* (friendship).[41] Lupus kept his abbacy, but seems to have been chastened by the realisation of his own expendability. (He still had not secured the return of St-Josse.) For Charles, however, all this was small comfort. The defeat in the Angoumois had damaged severely his position in Aquitaine, where Pippin II's claims were now firmly back on the Carolingians' agenda. Setbacks elsewhere compounded Charles's problems. Already before 14 June (to judge from the *AB*'s sequence of events) Lambert and some Breton allies had ambushed and killed Harvey son of Rainald in northwestern Aquitaine, not far south of Nantes.[42] In western Neustria, Nominoë needed no special inducement to raid far into Maine; only a sudden Viking attack forced his withdrawal. Lambert and Nominoë presented themselves as natural allies for Pippin II. For Charles, an equally natural defender presented himself: Vivian, a kinsman of Rainald and Harvey. By the end of 844, the countship of Tours, and the lay-abbacy of St-Martin, had been given to Vivian.[43] What then happened to Adalard, the previous tenant of these key *honores*? K.F. Werner has suggested a neat scenario: Adalard received the recently-vacated lay-abbacy of St-Quentin, himself vacated St-Martin, and everyone was happy.[44] There is no evidence for Adalard's holding St-Quentin's before 863, however; nor for his residence in Charles's kingdom between 844 and 861. When Lupus, in the late summer of 844, wrote of Adalard 'on the point of departure', he was referring, I think, not to a campaign the previous winter, but to a recent decision to switch lords.[45] If, then, the defeat in the Angoumois had made Adalard move east to the Middle Kingdom, this was perhaps, for Charles, its most disturbing effect. Though not overtly a hostile move, Adalard's departure threatened a whole network of loyalties in Charles's Frankish lands too.[46] 'Brotherly love' was not likely to be uppermost in Lothar's response to these developments.

41 Ep. 36.
42 *AAng* 844.
43 T. 60–63. It is not clear that he retained the post of chamberlain.
44 Werner 1958: 275.
45 Ep. 36.
46 Cf. the links suggested by Nithard III, 2.

Charles pressed for a 'confraternal' meeting at Thionville (Diedenhofen, also known as Yütz, near Trier) in October 844. From it, envoys were sent, in the names of Lothar, Louis the German and Charles, to the three 'sowers of discords', Pippin, Lambert and Nominoë. They were to show themselves 'obedient *fideles* of Charles' without delay: otherwise the brother-rulers would 'manfully muster' (the force of this phrase is a little weakened by the preceding words *tempore oportuno* – 'at a convenient time'!) and take revenge on their infidelity.[47] The assembly was well-attended by churchmen: it may have been Lupus, engaging in some special pleading of his own, who inserted into its decrees a fierce diatribe against lay-abbacies. Neither secular nor ecclesiastical rhetoric had much discernible effect. It was Vivian's lay-abbacy at St-Martin, Tours, that promised to thwart Charles's opponents in the Loire valley.

As for Pippin II, his success in the Angoumois enabled him to set his own terms. The diplomatic groundwork for a settlement was laid during the winter of 844–5 by two episcopal middlemen: Ebroin of Poitiers and Rodulf of Bourges.[48] In June 845, Charles and Pippin met at the monastery of Fleury (St-Benoît-sur-Loire). Archbishop Rodulf probably hosted the occasion: he seems to have exacted control of the abbatial resources of Fleury as his reward for services rendered.[49] 'Pippin swore oaths of fidelity to the effect that he would be faithful as a nephew ought to be to his uncle and would give him aid to the best of his ability whatever needs might arise. Then Charles allowed him lordship (*dominatus*) over the whole of Aquitaine, except for Poitou, Saintonge and Aunis.'[50] Charles had salvaged something from a weak position. He had managed to reaffirm his grip on northwestern Aquitaine, and therefore over regions of strategic importance: Neustria and the Breton March could not be controlled without Poitou. They were also uniquely valuable in economic terms, since within them were coastal saltpans, further

---

47 *MGH Conc.* III, no. 6.
48 *Translatio S. Germani c.* 5. Both attended the Council of Ver, December 844, *MGH Conc.* III, no. 7.
49 T. 89; Conc. III, no. 47a, p. 461. Cf. above, 62.
50 *AB* 845: 61 and n. 5.

south the rich city of Saintes, and inland Melle with its sil-ver-mines. Neither party (unlike some modern historians) thought of the 845 frontiers as hard and fast, however. *Dominatus* was an elastic concept: that was why it had been chosen. Charles reserved his own rights of overlordship, rather as his father Louis the Pious had done vis-à-vis Pip-pin's father; but where Pippin I had ruled Aquitaine as king, Charles never admitted that title in the case of Pippin II. It was surely always Charles's intention to reassert his power throughout Aquitaine as soon as circumstances allowed.

The scene in Aquitaine after 845 was more complex and eventful than the narrative sources show. The sequence of Pippin's charters resumes (there had been a gap in the list since 840) in December 845, with a grant to the monastery of St-Chaffre near Le Puy in which, while himself using the royal title, Pippin called Charles *patronus noster*.[51] Pippin's subsequent charters, of which ten are extant, make no mention of Charles whatsoever. Pippin minted on a small scale at Bourges and on a rather larger scale at Dax, Bor-deaux, and Toulouse. But he soon operated beyond the northwestern bounds set at Fleury, 'soliciting' Charles's supporters within Poitou and as Simon Coupland has been able to show, minting at Melle.[52] It was no secret that Pip-pin received help from Lothar.[53]

Viking warbands once more exploited Carolingian dis-putes. There were repeated attacks on the western sea-board: one flotilla came up the Garonne as far as Toulouse in 844 arriving, hardly by coincidence, just after Charles's besieging forces had left; and the raiders who sacked Sain-tes in 845 and killed the Gascon *dux* Siguin then wintered in the Saintonge. Significantly, the latter event was at-tributed by Charles's supporters to the division of Aqui-taine, and hence blamed on Pippin.[54]

After the Fleury meeting, Aquitaine for a while ceased to be Charles's priority. He was preoccupied with consolidat-

51 L. 51.
52 Coupland 1989: 213–5.
53 Implicit in L. 54, for the archbishop of Trier; explicit in c. 4 of Louis the German's statement at Meersen in 847, *MGH Capit.* II, no. 204, p. 70.
54 Lupus Ep. 44. For Viking activity, *AB* 844, 845: 60, 62.

ing his position in Francia. Here the most important decision of 845 was the appointment of Hincmar to the see of
Rheims (he was formally elected in April). As archbishop,
Hincmar was to prove a permanent mainstay of Charles's
regime. Genuinely committed to Charles as his king and
lord, Hincmar put his enormous practical talents and energy at Charles's disposal. He would be able to boast to
Pope Nicholas in 866 that he had conscientiously rendered
the military service due from the church of Rheims whenever the king called for it.[55] Hincmar would also play a
leading role in the great church councils whose business
included so many matters (ranging from social policy to
treason-trials) of critical importance to the king. If Charles
had an eye for public displays to demonstrate and reinforce his power, it was Hincmar who designed the rituals.
Law as ideological and political instrument was of passionate concern to both men. Hincmar's hand can be seen in
many of Charles's capitularies and diplomatic correspondence. From Rheims, Hincmar directed a stream of legal
treatises and advice to the king, sometimes criticising royal
conduct, often supplying justification for royal policy. But
Hincmar would often be at the king's side, for war ('when
we were at Neaufles on campaign against the attacking
Northmen')[56] or for a great religious occasion (as when
Charles attended the consecration of Hincmar's new
church at Rheims in 862)[57], or for a more intimate discussion in the second-floor solar at Charles's palace of Servais.[58] Hincmar's sheer staying-power (his only
health-problem was a poor digestion – for which the medi-
cal advice was abstinence from salads)[59] meant that over
the years the network of his friends and clients spread far
and wide through Charles's realm. Hincmar could put a
word in the king's ear to defend himself against false
friends at court,[60] and could secure the appointment of the
episcopal candidates he favoured, including that of his own

55 Above ch. 3: 58.
56 *MGH Epp.* VIII, no. 131, p. 72. Neaufles (dep. Eure) overlooks the
    River Epte near Gisors.
57 *AB* 862: 102.
58 Mansi XVI, 606b.
59 Contreni 1990: 282.
60 *MGH Epp.* VIII, no. 105.

nephew to the strategically key bishopric of Laon. Later, when he and that nephew had quarrelled bitterly, Hincmar recalled a summer evening (in 870) when he and his friend Odo, former abbot of Corbie, now bishop of Beauvais, stood by a hall-window, discussing how to resolve the dispute: this was at the royal palace of Attigny.[61] Charles and Hincmar would have their quarrels too, but they were never far from each other for long.

Hincmar's tenure of the see of Rheims was to have long-term significance. For Hincmar had a vision of Frankish history with Rheims, not Aachen, as its focal point. He looked back to St Remigius and his entente with Clovis as the foundation of the Frankish realm: the fifth-century bishop of Rheims had baptised, and thus consecrated, the first Merovingian king. That special relationship between Frankish kingship and the successors of Remigius was now to be revived. While the metropolitan province of Rheims had been just one among several in the great empire of Charlemagne and Louis the Pious, it more or less coincided with the heartlands of Charles's kingdom. Hincmar's Rheims-centred vision fitted the time. His deeds and writings, and perhaps most of all, his ritual innovations, helped to endow it with long-term actuality. In 1825, Charles X, the last of the Bourbons, was anointed at Rheims with the holy oil which Hincmar had been the first to record as heaven-sent; and the coronation-prayer used was Hincmar's.

Charles the Bald's choice of archbishop had short-term political motives too. The new incumbent of Rheims could be counted on to resist persistent attempts on Lothar's part to reinstate Ebbo (thus calling into question the validity of Ebbo's deposition at Louis the Pious's behest in 835). If Hincmar was ever tempted by Lothar's promises to secure for him a papal vicariate,[62] the thought of Ebbo deterred him. Hincmar's installation was thus a blunt response to Lothar. Charles could not have made a better choice. The newly-appointed archbishop led his suffragans to join those of the province of Sens, with Archbishop Wenilo and also

---

61 Mansi XVI, 858–9.
62 *MGH Epp.* V, pp. 609–11; cf. Hincmar Ep. 15, *MGH Epp.* VIII, p. 6.

Rodulf of Bourges, at a great assembly at Meaux in June 845, to offer counsel to their 'most devout prince'.[63]

From Meaux, Charles moved westwards to Neustria where by autumn, with Vivian's support, he seemed to have the situation well in hand.[64] He was already moving to winter-quarters at Tours when news came that a faction of Bretons had turned against Nominoë.[65] Charles decided to risk intervention with a small force, though some of his men refused to follow him. On 22 November at Ballon near Redon, he was beaten by Nominoë, and withdrew to Le Mans. In military terms, this was a setback rather than a major defeat.[66] Politically, it brought Charles some benefit. Lambert, fearing Nominoë's ascendance, decided to switch sides. Christmas time 845 saw Charles with Lambert and Vivian round the same table at St-Martin, Tours.[67] In summer 846, Charles and Nominoë came to terms. The countship of Angers, and lay-abbacies in and around that city seem to have been given to new appointees of Charles.[68] At Nominoë's request, a countship was found for Lambert further east, perhaps at Sens.[69] Charles conceded Nominoë the 'official' title of *dux* in return for recognition of his own authority over Brittany. Nominoë must be placated, for behind him was the more distant but much more serious threat of Lothar, whose rule continued to be invoked in the regions around Rennes and Nantes by Bretons and Franks alike.[70]

Charles continued to be on close terms with Louis the German.[71] He needed that alliance as much as ever, for Lothar's efforts to destabilise his regime increased in 846. Charles responded by bolstering support near the frontier with Lothar's kingdom[72] and continued to use lands belonging to the church of Rheims as benefices for an im-

---

63 *MGH Conc.* III, no. 11, p. 83.
64 Implied by T. 73, 74, 77.
65 Lupus Ep. 44.
66 Lupus Ep. 45.
67 T. 81. See also Adrevald c. 33.
68 *AFont.* 847: 79; cf. T. 105, 106.
69 Lupus Ep. 81; T. 100–102, 116.
70 See Smith 1992 for the evidence of private charters dated by Lothar's reign-years.
71 *AF* 846: 36.
72 Three stays at Servais are recorded in 846/7: T. 85, 98; Lupus Ep. 58.

portant group of noble supporters, including Richwin, Odo and Robert.[73] When he held his main assembly in 846 at the Rheims estate of Épernay, and preferred 'the faction of certain men to episcopal admonition' Hincmar may have felt insult had been added to injury.[74] Charles knew that Hincmar in the last resort could not afford to desert him. The archbishop needed Charles's support to keep his see more than Charles needed Hincmar's to keep his realm.

A new cause of conflict between Lothar and Charles occurred at this time: the abduction and marriage of Lothar's daughter by Giselbert, 'a vassal of Charles'. Louis the German immediately came to visit Charles so that both could disclaim any responsibility. Where Charles was concerned, however, 'Lothar could not be pacified'.[75] Like Charlemagne and Louis the Pious Lothar had preferred to keep his daughters unmarried, hence to remove precisely the threat which Giselbert's action represented: aristocratic appropriation of legitimate Carolingian blood. Had Lothar himself died in 846 or 847, with his only adult son far away in Italy,[76] Giselbert would have a strong claim at least to a regency in Francia. Who knew what Carolingian *progenies* Giselbert might father? And he was 'Charles's man'!

Lothar's wrath, and his brothers' responses, also throw retrospective light on Verdun. Clearly several important men from Middle Francia had moved their careers and residence westwards during the years 840–3 – 'the time of troubles'.[77] Odulf was still (to Lupus's chagrin) in control of St-Josse. Adalard had already had second thoughts and moved back east. Giselbert, who had formerly been Count of Maasgau[78] and come over to Charles only late in 841, had an obvious temptation to return eastwards: his abduction of Lothar's daughter indicated ambitions in Lothar's kingdom. These men could not lose interest in the patrimonies they retained in Lothar's realm, nor in their for-

---

73 T. 75. See above 131.
74 The notice added to a Rheims manuscript of the decrees of this assembly seems to represent Hincmar's reaction; *MGH* Capit. II, no. 257. See *AB* : 62–3.
75 *AF* 846: 36. The *AB* do not mention the affair.
76 Lothar's son Louis II had been king there since 840.
77 So called in *AB* 853: 77. Cf. below 170 for an amended translation.
78 Nithard III, 3.

mer *honores*. Their 'amphibious' existence was a constant reminder of the provisional character of the 843 frontiers. The continuing ferment of the mid-840s showed that sedimentation had not yet occurred. Hence while the Giselbert affair frightened Lothar, it also worried Charles. The result was a meeting of all three brothers (Louis remaining the conciliator) at Meersen on the Meuse in February 847.[79] In the ensuing capitulary, reaffirmations of concord and unanimity preceded more specific points. 'No-one henceforth is to commit an abduction' [c.8]; and 'the sons of the kings are to retain a legitimate inheritance of the *regnum* according to the portions defined as at present' [c.9].These clauses answered Lothar's requirements, but c.9 now had a specific reference for Charles too: his wife Ermentrude had given birth to their first son, Louis, three months before.[80]

The general aim was to make permanent what had been agreed at Verdun. Hincmar made sure that a copy of the Meersen agreement was kept. It preserves the speeches of the three royal brothers, each with its distinctive political style. Lothar's is brief, vague and disingenuous ('Thank God! we are ready to act as brothers rightly should'). Louis's is detailed, practical and much more revealing: all three brothers jointly had sent envoys to Pippin, offering him certain named counties in the meantime, and a safe-conduct ('for as long as God wants to keep him safe') to a projected assembly at Paris where his future would be settled. Louis added that Lothar had ordered his men 'who up to now had been acting to thwart Charles, henceforth to stop doing so'. Charles struck a more sententious note ('we have been offending God in these misdeeds') but went on to talk of fundamentals in language borrowed from his grandfather Charlemagne: 'Every free man in our *regnum* is to receive a lord, whomever he wishes, amongst us and our *fideles*' [c.2]; 'no man is to leave his lord without just cause, nor is anyone else to receive him' [c.3]; and

---

79 *MGH Capit.* II, no. 204, pp. 68–71. Note that Meersen lay in the Maasgau.
80 On 1 November. The future Louis the Stammerer commemorated his own birthdate in charter B. 12. Cf. Lupus Ep. 58. No contemporary annalist mentions the birth.

(with a veiled warning): 'We want to agree [to do] what is right to our *fideles*; and we urge you *fideles* to do the same for your men'.[c.4][81]

Meersen exposed problems without resolving them. On the frontier between Charles's and Lothar's kingdoms, tension remained high: Lupus advised certain monks of St-Amand in June 847 not to fail to appear at Charles's assembly that summer: 'I'm sure it's dangerous to disobey the king's commands – especially at this time'.[82] Lothar was soon making serious efforts to detach Louis from his alliance with Charles, though Louis 'cleverly declined his skilled persuasion'.[83] The projected Paris assembly never took place. Lothar continued to support Pippin and may have had Pippin's younger brother in his household at this time as another useful card to play against Charles.[84] The evidence of Pippin's charters suggests an upswing in support for him in 847 and early 848.[85]

Nevertheless, in 848, Pippin's position in Aquitaine collapsed. For this remarkable fact, the rest of this chapter will offer some explanations. One lies in the murky politics of the Spanish frontier. Charles seems to have hit on the 'pincer' method to grapple with Aquitaine. He angled for an alliance in the far southwest, with Musa, lord of Tudela, inveterate rebel against the amir 'Abd al-Rahman II in Cordoba. Pippin would be caught between enemies. At the same time, Charles was happy to be cast in the role of protector of Spanish Christians who feared persecution. The amir took this seriously enough to send an embassy to Rheims early in 847 'to seek a peace and draw up a formal treaty'.[86] Pippin had his own entrée to Cordoba, however – via 'Gulyalim ben Barbat', alias William son of Bernard who appears in an Andalusian source leading an embassy

81 Note echoes here of cc. 10, 7 and 8 respectively of the 806 *Divisio*, *MGH Capit.* I, no. 45, pp. 128–9. Cf. also the wording at Coulaines, above: 138.
82 Ep. 67.
83 *AF* 848: 37. The author shows his usual sympathy towards Louis.
84 For this brother, see above ch. 4: 90; and for his protection by Lothar, below 156.
85 L. 53, 54, 56, 58, 59, 61. Note also Pippin's employment of notaries 'Gulfardus', Hilduin and Joseph in 847–8, perhaps enlarging his staff.
86 *AB* 847: 64. Löwe 1988: 168–9.

in 847 to 'Abd al-Rahman: 'the amir loaded him with gifts and told him to return to the March and fight the king of the Franks [Charles] and those among his compatriots who were rebelling against the authority of Cordoba'.[87] Andalusian diplomacy was played by the same rules as its Carolingian counterpart. For Charles in 847, the game was difficult and so far inconclusive.

The decisive shift in the situation came from another quarter. The activities of the Vikings pepper the annals of the 840s, yet little reference has so far been made to them. It is high time to bring them fully into the picture – but also to get them into perspective. That means going back to the beginning of the decade and the 'time of troubles'. If Vikings had exploited Carolingian disputes,[88] Carolingian disputants in their turn exploited Vikings. Lothar used his Viking ally Harald against his brothers in Frisia in 841.[89] Charles himself seems to have helped another Danish warlord, Ragnar, install himself at Turholt in Flanders, perhaps as early as 840. 'Not long after, he earned the king's wrath and lost . . . all that he held from the king, nor was he able to return thereafter into his former favour.'[90] In 845, a Viking fleet came up the Seine and attacked Paris. The commander on that occasion was Ragnar, whom I identify with Charles's former ally. The author of the *Translatio* of St Germanus (St Germain), the only source of detailed information on the 845 attack, writing within five years of the event, gives no prehistory of the villain of his piece: he begins with 'the division of the empire of the Franks after which the sins of the people grew'. The Danes who appeared in March 845 at the mouth of the Seine were instruments of God 'chastising us as He chastised the Israelites in Babylon'. The story of Viking atrocity that follows is grisly enough. (111 captives are said to have been hung in full view of the Christians.)[91] All the blame for the Franks' failure to resist is laid on the Frankish forces who ran away. 'Seeing what had happened, the

---

87 Sanchez-Albornoz 1969: 30, nn. 64, 65. The source, Ibn Hayyan, is eleventh-century, but draws on earlier material.
88 Above 125, 137.
89 *AB* 841: 51. Cf. Wood 1987.
90 *Vita Anskarii* cc. 21, 36, 38, pp. 46, 71, 73. The author Rimbert came from Turholt.
91 *Trans. S. Germ* c. 12. Vogel 1906: 104–15.

most noble king Charles, though ready to die for the Holy Church of God, griefstricken and beating his youthful breast, withdrew'. He withdrew to the monastery of St-Denis, whose body he had refused to let be 'translated'. There he swore to defend his special patron to the death. The Vikings went on to attack the monastery of St-Germain-des-Prés (on the west bank of the Seine, just opposite the Ile-de-la-Cité) where they were struck down by an epidemic of dysentery. Their warchief, now named as Ragnar, came to Charles to talk terms, and agreed to leave Charles's kingdom. The author of the *Translatio* credits St Germain with smiting the heathen, and says nothing at this point about the large payment which contemporary annalists reveal was the price of Ragnar's departure.[92] The climax of the *Translatio* is the saint's vengeance on Ragnar after his return to Denmark (the author claims to have these details from Count Cobbo, an envoy of Louis the German who happened to be at the court of the Danish king Horic at this time and subsequently visited St-Germain-des-Prés):

When [the Northmen] reached their own land, Ragnar came before the king of the Northmen [Horic]. He showed him a lot of gold and silver which he had carried off from the land of the Christians, and told him how he had captured the city of Paris, entered the monastery of St-Germain, which was the most splendid in that country, and subjected the whole of King Charles's kingdom to himself. When the king disbelieved this tale, Ragnar ordered a beam from the monastery of St-Germain and a bolt from the gate of the city of Paris to be brought to him as proof. He described to the king what a good and fertile land he had found, full of riches of all kinds, such as he had never seen. Yet he had found the people there more fearful and cowardly than any others he'd seen . . . The only one who had resisted was – an old man called Germain! Even as he spoke these words, he fell to the ground . . . and three days later swelled up and burst, thus dying a horrible death.

92 *Trans. S. Germ.* c. 20. See below.

Stripped of hagiographic bravura, the text's historical interest lies in the glimpse it offers of the political scene in Denmark as the context for the activity of Viking warlords. It shows who Ragnar wanted to impress back home. It omits, though, the surely crucial point that Ragnar had previously been Charles's man. The attack on Paris was perhaps an attempt to re-establish that relationship. For Ragnar and his men, depicted in the *Translatio* as sudden intruders from an alien North, were no strangers to the Frankish world. Neither was King Horic, whose high-handed treatment by Louis the Pious in the 830s had given way, in the next decade, to more cautious handling by Louis's successors, as Count Cobbo's embassy suggests.[93] The Franks were becoming increasingly concerned about the Northmen's aggressiveness. Ragnar's attack, unlike earlier raids, struck into the heartland of Charles's kingdom, and the payment made to Ragnar was the largest tribute Charles would ever have to raise at one go: 7,000 lb of silver.[94] A new era of heavy Viking exactions both in Britain and on the Continent had begun. The underlying cause probably lay in the reorientation of an ambitious Danish elite, its enrichment from trading and raiding in eastern Europe and around the Black Sea suddenly foreclosed by the movements of warring peoples in those regions.[95] Charles the Bald was among the first to pay heavily for changes that were far outwith his control.

Nevertheless in 845 the required sum was apparently raised in three months. Charles's strategy of buying off attackers was affordable by the king of 'a rich and fertile kingdom'. The holding of a series of episcopal assemblies at Paris in 846, 847 and 849 suggests that the *civitas* and its region had not suffered too much devastation.[96] The outcome of Ragnar's expedition had discouraged imitators:[97]

---

93   *Trans. S. Germ.* cc. 17, 30. For Louis the Pious's dealings with Horic, see *AB* 836, 838: 35, 40. Envoys sent by 'Northmen' to Louis the German, *AF* 845: 35, and to Horic by Charles and his brothers at Meersen, *MGH Capit.* II, no. 204, p. 70, asked him to restrain his people from attacking Christians.

94   *AB* 845: 60. *AX* 845: 14: 'many thousands of pounds of gold and silver'; *AF* 845: 35: 'much money'.

95   See Randsborg 1980: 152–62; Sawyer 1982.

96   *MGH Conc.* III, nos. 11, 13, 19.

97   Ragnar's death is confirmed by *AX* 846: 14.

certainly no more Vikings attempted to come up the Seine in the later 840s. Instead Viking attacks in 846–8 were concentrated on less risky targets. Frisia in Lothar's kingdom was taken over by Viking warlords in 846–7, Lothar acquiescing in the occupation of Dorestad. In Brittany Nominoë suffered a heavy defeat and bought off the attackers with 'gifts'.[98] In Aquitaine, there were coastal raids, and in the winter of 847–8, a Viking force besieged Bordeaux.[99]

For Charles, these Viking activities spelled good news. It can be no coincidence that in 847, with Nominoë preoccupied by vain attempts at military resistance to the Vikings, there was no Breton campaign into Neustria; nor was there in 848. As for Aquitaine: it seems clear that the Vikings' impact here played a crucial part in the collapse of Pippin II's regime. Toulouse had suffered Viking attack already in late 844. The siege of Bordeaux in 847–8 damaged another centre of Pippin's support; and here the Viking threat gave Charles his opportunity to snatch a victory at Pippin's expense. Like his father, Charles could move very fast when necessary. At Compiègne in December 847 (and probably for Christmas),[100] Charles must have heard of Bordeaux's plight. He had moved south to Tours by 24 February, thence in early March via Poitiers to the Saintonge, where, according to the normally laconic *AB*, 'he attacked part of the Viking forces that were besieging Bordeaux and manfully defeated them'.[101] A less colourful account, probably based on a participant's report, says that 'he captured nine Danish ships on the River Dordogne'.[102] This did not save Bordeaux. But the *AB*'s adverb 'manfully' (*viriliter*) accurately represents the propaganda effect of Charles's gesture. Though Bordeaux fell ('Jews betrayed it', according to the *AB*) once Charles was back in Francia,[103] he had been seen to defend his realm. It was enough. 'The Aquitanians were driven by Pippin's inactivity and incompetence to turn to Charles instead. At Orléans nearly all the high nobility, along with the bishops and abbots, elected Charles as their

98 *AB* 846, 847: 62, 64.
99 *AB* 847, 848: 65.
100 T. 100–102.
101 *AB* 848: 00.
102 *AFont* 848: 81.
103 *AB*: 65–6.

king and then solemnly consecrated him with an anointing of holy chrism and episcopal benediction'.[104]

This consecration was made possible by support for Charles south of the Loire, and that in turn was linked with Charles's action on the River Dordogne. Other campaigns were needed the next year to capture Pippin's brother and mop up Pippin's supporters in Toulouse; and Pippin himself eluded his enemies till 852. But no charter of Pippin's survives from later than March 848; and no more coins were minted in his name. Never again did he look a credible king of the Aquitanians. Their turning to Charles 'instead' meant that Aquitaine was once more linked with Francia. It was this wider realm that supplied a further dimension for the 848 ritual. For Orléans lay on the north bank of the Loire, in Francia, and Charles's consecrator was the local metropolitan, Wenilo of Sens. Hence the 'high nobility' and clergy of the *AB*'s account consisted of Franks as well as Aquitanians. Ten years later, Charles depicted his consecration with 'the consent of all my faithful men' as an inauguration to his whole realm: at once a symptom of growing political strength and a source of symbolic strengthening. If Hincmar's liturgical inventiveness lay behind the formal proceedings, the substantial impetus surely came from Charles himself.[105] No previous royal anointing of a Frankish king by his own bishops had occurred within living memory, and perhaps never since the single extraordinary precedent of the first Carolingian's consecration in 751. Neither Lothar nor Louis the German had been 'anointed to his realm'. Charles alone was the new David – the chosen youth who patiently awaited the appointed time for his power to be manifest. Charles intended the ritual at Orléans to mark a kind of new beginning for his reign. In two charters issued for St-Martin, Tours, early in 849, Charles has the title 'king of the Franks and Aquitanians'. The *regna* won at Fontenoy and confirmed to him at Verdun were now indeed his. Charles's own perception of his rulership was evolving.[106] Per-

104 *AB* 848: 66.
105 Nelson 1986a (1977a), (1977b).
106 T. 113, 114. Perhaps the presentation by Vivian of the famous Tours Bible (Paris BN lat. 1) with its striking throne-image of Charles, should be linked with this; see below: 158. Alibert 1989 dates the Bible's production to 846, however.

haps there was already an imperial tinge in Charles's reception of Irish envoys who reported 'their king's' victory over
Vikings, and brought gifts and a request for alliance.[107]

There was some justification for such confidence. In
January 849 Lothar came to Péronne, just within Charles's
northeastern frontiers, and there the two brothers 'bound
themselves by the law of friendship, and exchanged
gifts'.[108] The meeting constituted an acknowledgement by
Lothar of Charles's improved position. The appearance of
Pippin's younger brother in Aquitaine 'having left Lothar'
may have signified Lothar's abandonment of a potential
tool. Alternatively, Lothar was making another attempt to
rekindle trouble: if so, he failed. Pippin's brother was soon
captured by Vivian, and brought to Francia, where Charles
the Bald subjected him to a show-trial and, 'though he
deserved death for his perfidy towards his uncle and godfather', had him tonsured, hence effectively eliminating
this other possible rival for Aquitaine.[109]

Charles had been able to follow up the assembly at Orléans with another campaign against Pippin – the first
since 844. In August or September 849, Charles held an
assembly at Limoges, and was received 'with the greatest
enthusiasm' by the leading Aquitanians, including Archbishop Rodulf. Charles then moved southwest once more
to besiege and capture Toulouse in late September. He lav-
ished rewards on Odo 'our beloved count and our servant'
whose siege tactics had helped secure this success.[110] Count
Fredelo of Toulouse, presumably Pippin's appointee, was
left in post after capitulating and giving oaths of loyalty to
Charles. After stays at Narbonne and Albi, Charles went
north again. He was at Bourges for several weeks, from December through to January 850: it was the first Christmas
he had spent in Aquitaine since 840.[111]

Charles had faced severe problems in realising the
parchment gains of Verdun. Lothar had persistently tried

107 *AB* 848: 66.
108 *AFont*: 81. Cf. *AB* 849: 66–7.
109 *AB* 849: 67; *AFont* : 81. He was sent to Corbie.
110 T. 119. See also *AFont*, apparently deriving from an eye-witness-
     account: the Abbot of St-Wandrille also played a leading part in
     the campaign.
111 *AFont* : 83; T. 123, 124.

to subvert Charles's control wherever solicitations could penetrate: in Neustria, in Francia, in Aquitaine. Lothar's hostility was still not overcome in 849, despite the pleasantries of the Péronne meeting. The fact that Nominoë resumed his attacks on Neustria in the early summer of 849 suggests that Lothar may again have been encouraging him.[112] There is certainly no positive evidence of Lothar giving Charles political help during 849. Louis the German, on the other hand, in that year displayed his continuing support for Charles more fully than ever. That axis of solidarity between the two younger brothers continued to provide the counterweight to Lothar's predominant power in Middle Francia. Louis and Charles met, perhaps in May, to reaffirm their alliance in the strongest possible terms: 'each publicly handed over to the other a staff, and each commended to the other his realm, wife and children, whichever should outlive the other'.[113] 'On se serait cru revenir aux beaux jours de Strasbourg, sept ans auparavant.'[114] The evocation of Strasbourg is à propos: for this *bilateral* meeting between Charles and Louis in 849 was the first since 841. The likeliest reason for the new affirmations of solidarity (Lot and Halphen are silent on this) was shared fear of Lothar. Charles's anxieties in 849 were the greater, moreover, because his Aquitanian campaign would expose the northeastern part of his realm to Lothar's attentions. Charles might have believed himself back in the terrible days of winter 840–1, when to move into Aquitaine was immediately to risk losing Francia. The likeliest location of the meeting between Charles and Louis was thus (as in 841, and *pace* Lot and Halphen) on the borders of Louis's kingdom, not Charles's. For it was Charles who had most to gain from a long and tricky journey, necessarily through Lothar's kingdom. (It would remain a notable feature of Carolingian diplomacy that such journeys were made by the rulers and *fideles* of both east and west across the Middle Kingdom.) Once assured that Louis would safeguard his home front (and only then), Charles could move south across the Loire. Thereafter he needed Louis's further reassurances, which explains why Louis's trusty Count

112 *AB*, 68.
113 *AB* 849: 67.
114 Lot and Halphen 1909: 202.

157

Cobbo chose this moment to make a pilgrimage to St-Martin, Tours (stopping en route at St-Germain to tell the monks about the horrid end of Ragnar), and why on 18 August Charles's former tutor Walahfrid, abbot of Reichenau, 'bearer of a response from the lord king [Louis] to his brother Charles, was crossing the Loire and drowned':[115] a victim of Carolingian diplomacy.

By the close of this first decade of his reign, Charles's position in the south was thus stronger than it had yet been, and this in turn secured his regime further north as well. Though he had not got Pippin II under lock and key, there was every prospect of a swift follow-up to the capture of Pippin's brother. Viking raids on the Continent had significantly increased since 840, but they had impinged (so far) much more painfully on Charles's enemies than on Charles himself. Thus the net effect had been to strengthen Charles. Pippin's downfall, in particular, was the chief bonus for Charles in 848–9. That, together with the removal of Pippin's brother from the scene, left Lothar without a plausible alternative candidate in Aquitaine. Without Pippin as an effective ally there, Lothar lost his best chance of sabotaging Charles in Francia and so undoing Verdun. For his part, Charles had clung firmly to his alliance with Louis the German – who had not failed him. In the Loire valley, Breton aggression had been checked, again by Viking raiders, Charles's inadvertent allies; and Charles had retained the services of a mixed team of powerful men, including the 'outsider' Odo from the Rhineland[116] and the 'local men', Vivian and Lambert. The importance of this region and of such supporters in this early phase of Charles's reign was aptly symbolised in the output of the scriptorium of St-Martin, Tours. It could produce at Charles's behest a fine Gospel-Book for presentation to Lothar probably in 849.[117] For Charles himself, and on the order of 'the hero Vivian', the community's lay-abbot, it produced a Bible fit for a new David, a new Josiah, a king who 'renewed the authority of his father, grandfather and greatgrandfather'. Here at St-Martin, the community believed that 'the change of so great a king' would

115 Ermenric, letter to Grimald, *MGH Epp.* V, p. 564.
116 Charles appointed him count of Châteaudun: Werner 1959b: 152.
117 Schramm and Mütherich 1983: 161.

mean the triumph of the Evil One, and that it was Charles's 'righteousness' which kept destructive forces at bay.[118] The perception, and the optimism, had a basis in contemporary reality. Charles the Bald had proved he had the personal qualities required of a king. Challenges remained, but there could be no doubt now that he would offer an effective response.

---

118   The quotations are from the manuscript's dedicatory poem, *MGH Poet.* III, pp. 251–2. Cf. above 155 and n. 106. See Godman 1987: 174.

Chapter 7

850–858: COMPETITION AND CRISIS

The story of the 850s is an equivocal one. Its climax, in 858, was a major rebellion, coinciding with unprecedented Viking pressure, and an invasion of Charles's kingdom by his brother Louis: threats which together presented Charles with the greatest challenge of his reign. Historians have tended to be more impressed by the scale of this crisis than by Charles's remarkable success in surviving it.[1] The crisis has often been seen as inevitable – the outcome of a steady build-up of pressure on Charles's dwindling resources, and of his gradual losing of control over the regions of his realm. Historians have tended to pin the blame on Charles, certainly, but also on greedy nobles, and equally greedy Vikings. The argument of this chapter will be that the crisis of 858 should be understood in terms of competing political interests and values rather than of moral shortcomings; that both nobles and Vikings are best treated in terms of individuals and their alliances rather than lumped together; that the Vikings' role, though important, was secondary; that far from being inevitable crisis was nearly averted; and that until 858, Charles coped resourcefully with a range of problems, retaining the loyalty of most of his magnates, and nimbly exploiting tensions within the wider Carolingian family. Crisis there certainly was in 858, and Charles's own actions were in part to blame for it: two particular decisions will be identified as politically inept. Both arose, however, not from irredeemable weakness but from the king's overplaying his hand, and neither need

1 Devisse 1975–6: 281–354; Halphen 1977: 253; McKitterick 1983: 178.

have been disastrous in itself. It was partly a chance conjuncture in 858 that rocked Charles's regime.

To take up the threads of the late 840s means being led first far away from the Frankish heartlands. For it was on the frontiers of the southwest, in Septimania and the Pyrenees, that Pippin II remained at large, and, as long as he did so, posed a threat to Charles. Thanks to the accidents of surviving evidence, these marcher regions are better documented than Aquitaine itself. The southern sector, including the Spanish March, had been more or less stable since the 830s under the domination of Count Sunifred whose authority in the region Charles had recognised in 844.[2] Late in 848, however, William, son of Bernard, had captured Barcelona and Ampurias – perhaps removing Sunifred in the process.[3] Like his father, William had sought to exploit the benefits of *Königsnähe*, and found himself ensnared in Carolingian conflicts. But when Pippin seemed a lost cause, William did not (like other Aquitanians) 'turn to Charles instead'. Was he driven by fidelity to his father's memory? Had he burnt his boats through his part in the battle of the Angoumois? William no doubt made for Barcelona, where his father had once been count, because he could claim lands and clients in that area. Yet his move, and his quest for Muslim allies, have an air of desperation. Charles sent a pair of trusted supporters to regain control of the March.[4] William, abandoned by his allies, was killed while vainly trying to take refuge, once more, in Barcelona. His personal effects seem to have included the Manual his mother Dhuoda had written for him when he came of age only nine years before. She had urged him to put devotion to his father (as she herself had put devotion to her husband) above all other earthly loyalties. Perhaps William had paid too much heed to his mother's counsel. Most men had no difficulty in being faithful to father and king at the same time. William's younger brother was to show more talent for reconciliation.[5]

2   Above: 141.
3   Collins 1990a: 173.
4   *AB* 850: 69; *AFont* 849: 83, naming Count Aledramn of Troyes and Count Isembard son of Warin.
5   Below: 211.

Further north on the frontier in the Pyrenean zone, Charles pursued an indirect strategy. His old ally Musa rebelled against Cordoba again in 850.[6] At the palace of Verberie, Charles received envoys from two Navarrese magnates allied with Musa.[7] Charles had long hoped that help from this quarter would deliver Pippin into his hands. The trap closed in 852. Count Sancho Sanchez, a former supporter of Pippin, seems to have changed sides after being defeated by Musa in Navarre, in 851, and then handed Pippin over to Charles.[8] This coup, apparently at or near Angoulême, in September 852, helped Charles efface the memory of his army's defeat near there in 844.[9] Pippin was taken to Francia, where Charles 'after consulting Lothar, ordered him to be tonsured in the monastery of St-Medard'.[10] The consultation was significant: Lothar, the family-head, and long-time upholder of Pippin's claims, had finally, definitively, abandoned him, recognising Charles instead as king of Aquitaine. It was a striking acknowledgement of Charles's success.

Why had Charles been so determined to keep, or recover, Aquitaine? The answer that comes most readily to a twentieth-century mind is an economic one. The mines of Melle in Poitou were important as a source of silver: Charles had insisted on his right to that region in 845 and, despite a Viking raid on Melle in 848 (perhaps linked with Pippin II's brief seizure of the mint), Charles continued to issue coins there on a considerable scale for the rest of his reign. For the state of the economy of Aquitaine after the 840s, the numismatists' findings offer equivocal evidence, and the impact of Viking activity has yet to be properly assessed. (If, as some historians have argued, the Vikings 'ruined' Aquitaine, no explanation has been offered as to why the outcome here was so different from that elsewhere.)[11] Nevertheless, the rarity of Aquitanian coins in hoards found north of the Loire suggests that commercial contacts between Aquitaine and Neustria or Francia were

---

6 Collins 1983: 233–4.
7 One was Inigo, half-brother of Musa; Sanchez-Albornoz 1969: 24–5.
8 Sanchez-Albornoz 1969: 35–6.
9 *AAng* 852. T. 149 (6 September 852) was issued at Angoulême.
10 *AB* 852: 74–5.
11 Wallace-Hadrill 1975. Cf. Metcalf 1990: 78–9; Coupland 1990b.

weaker than in the reign of Louis the Pious; and it is clear from the distribution of royal estates and of markets as well as mints that the bulk of Charles's resources lay in Francia.

Charles's primary interest in Aquitaine south of Poitou was political and dynastic. His first concern was the pursuit of his own filial inheritance from Louis the Pious, since the legitimacy of his whole rule depended on his heirship to Louis. It was the kind of claim that noble contemporaries understood and admired. He also wanted inheritances for his own sons – and by 852, he had three sons to provide for. Almost certainly, he already intended Aquitaine for the second of them, Charles the Younger, born in 848 or 849. There was another requirement to meet: Charles had to provide an 'empire' in which magnates, ecclesiastical as well as lay, could deploy their interests. Charles's grandfather had exported Frankish nobles to the *regna* acquired by Frankish conquest: writing in the 870s, Adrevald described how Charlemagne made his infant son king of Lombard Italy and 'put commanders in charge of the subdued realm and people, to enforce the authority of laws and cause the custom of Francia to be observed. Thus it came about that the palace was emptied of the leading men of the people and of its commanders because [Charlemagne] gave over to his son many Franks of noble family who were to watch over and rule with him the realm he had just received.'[12] By the mid-ninth century, when acquiring *regna* was no longer feasible, a similar function was to be performed *within* Charles the Bald's composite kingdom by Aquitaine, Septimania and the Spanish March. These are the regions where a series of great magnates made their careers at the king's behest.

These political reasons for making good his claim to Aquitaine also implied ways of ruling it. Charles meant Aquitaine to become a sub-kingdom, ruled by his son along with a number of *potentes* whose regional power Charles himself had created or enhanced. It has been argued that such arrangements inevitably led to a reduction in Charles's own power, and a weakening of the bonds that held Aquitaine to Charles's heartland of Francia.[13] These

12 Cf. Adrevald c. 18, p. 486, translated Nelson 1987: 148.
13 See Martindale 1990a.

were certainly dangers; but Charles found ways of averting them. Within the *regnum* of Aquitaine, for instance, the Spanish March and Septimania constituted a distinct zone whose nobility and ecclesiastical communities already had their own direct ties with Charles. That had been very clear in 844 when Charles held court at St-Sernin, Toulouse.[14] After the establishment of a sub-kingdom, Charles could cultivate such ties, and so contain the power of the Frankish nobles he appointed to regional office as counts and marquises. Secondly, and still more important, Charles could maintain links with the regional magnates themselves. Early medieval kings often achieved this by travelling around their realms. The alternative, preferred by Charlemagne and Louis the Pious, was to let the magnates do the travelling. When Aquitanians appeared at the palace and the assembly, they acknowledged royal power and the benefits that flowed therefrom. Areas unvisited by the king could thus remain within his political grasp. The king might cut his losses by relinquishing royal lands in those areas to the men on the spot. But, again, the build-up of regional powerholding did not preclude further royal intervention.

Thirdly Charles could use his relationship with the church throughout his kingdom to exploit structures of ecclesiastical government and to deploy ecclesiastical patronage south of the Loire. Aquitanian archbishops and bishops were regularly summoned to attend assemblies in Francia, and could be used themselves as royal agents and emissaries.[15] As his reign went on, Charles became increasingly able to attract ambitious clerics to his court, and rewarded them with abbacies and bishoprics in the *regna*. Ecclesiastical appointments functioned in this way as royal access-routes to provincial centres of power. As long as he could trust his regional magnates, could remove as well as approve them, could keep open such multiple lines of communication with the regions: then a distant king could rule in fact as well as in name. It was an extensive rather than an intensive kind of rulership, well suited to early medieval conditions.[16]

14   Above: 140.
15   Cf. Map 8.
16   For these terms see Gillingham 1971.

164

Of course such methods were not always easy to apply. Every *regnum* presented its own testing-ground. In Neustria, the Bretons offered a standing invitation to the discontented to defect altogether. In 849, Charles had reinstated Lambert on the Breton March to deal with renewed attacks from Nominoë. But Lambert (perhaps counting once again on Lothar's backing) defected again the next year and joined the Bretons in fierce attacks all along the frontier. Rennes and Nantes fell into their hands; Maine was ravaged. Meanwhile Nominoë had summoned a synod, Carolingian-style, and deposed all five Breton bishops, replacing them with his own appointees. In 850, Bishop Actard of Nantes was driven from his see: he, and two of the other ousted bishops sought refuge in Charles's kingdom. The orchestrated protests of West Frankish bishops, even with papal backing, had no effect.[17] Nominoë's sudden death in March 851 seemed to offer Charles a golden opportunity. He invoked St Denis's help[18] and mounted a summer campaign into Brittany against Nominoë's son Erispoë. On 22 August at Jengland near Redon, Charles suffered a serious defeat.[19] Vivian was killed, along with Charles's count of the palace Hilmerad 'and many others'. The detailed account of Regino of Prüm, written up in the early tenth century and based on Breton sources fiercely hostile to Charles, presents him as a coward who after two days of Breton guerilla attacks fled at night leaving his men to their fate next morning.[20] It is plausible enough that Charles should have decided on a tactical retreat from terrain that gave the Bretons all the advantages. Charles could move very fast, even riding at night,[21] and Vivian and Hilmerad may have commanded a rearguard hampered by the slowness of Charles's hired Saxon footsoldiers. The allegation that Charles deliberately abandoned his men smacks of Breton propaganda and is not borne out by other evidence of his conduct of war. His failure against the Bretons finds parallels in Frankish defeats at the hands of Basques and Saxons. The marshes of the Vilaine valley, like Ronces-

17   *MGH Conc.* III, pp. 202–7. See Smith 1992: ch. 6.
18   T. 135.
19   *AFont; AAng.* This defeat is unmentioned in *AB.*
20   Regino s.a. 860 (for 851): 79. Cf. Leyser 1982: 27–8.
21   Cf. the episode described above, 16.

valles, were a graveyard of Frankish prowess.[22] Regino's description of the Franks' bafflement in face of Breton tactics helps explain the savage irony of Lupus's allusion to the defeat as 'a most splendid feast': Lupus echoes Cicero's bitter reference to the 'fine feast' on the Ides of March where 'there should have been no left-overs . . .'[23]

Jengland was a humiliation. Charles extricated himself as best he could. If the Bretons could not be beaten, they must join him. Erispoë was 'received by Charles and gave him his hands and was endowed with royal vestments and his father's power, and in addition Rennes, Nantes and the Pays de Retz'.[24] Erispoë seems to have agreed to Bishop Actard's reinstatement at Nantes; and a Frankish bishop remained at Rennes.[25] Subsequently, Erispoë remained loyal, perhaps fearing rivals in Brittany. In 852 his cousin Salomon became Charles's *fidelis* and seems to have been 'given' the very lands conceded to Erispoë the previous year.[26] If the rituals of 851 lent legitimacy to Erispoë, they also allowed Charles to maintain face by representing his own rulership as a superior one. To dispense 'royal vestments' was to assert a position above regality as overlord of plural *regna*.

As for Charles's Frankish *fideles*: Lambert had cut his own political throat, and Vivian was dead. Into this power-vacuum Charles placed his *fidelis* Robert, a recipient of benefices since 843 and a favoured man at court.[27] Now Robert became lay-abbot of Marmoutier and count of Angers, moving into the circle of leading magnates.[28] For the remainder of his career, he would remain a key figure in the politics of Charles's kingdom. According to Regino of Prüm, Robert was formally given the 'duchy' of Neustria, at an assembly at Compiègne in '861'. With the date corrected to 852, this has been taken as a statement of fact.[29]

---

22 Cf. *AB* 845; and, for the Basques' defeat of Charlemagne's rearguard at Roncesvalles, *RFA* 778: 56.
23 Ep. 83. Marshall ed. no. 85, p. 85 notes Cicero's allusion to the murder of Julius Caesar in *Epp. ad Familiares x*, xxviii.
24 *AB* 851: 73.
25 Hincmar, *PL* 126, 218; Smith 1992: ch. 6.
26 *AB* 852: 74, with the suggestion of Smith 1992: ch. 4, n. 68.
27 Lupus Ep. 66 seems to refer to him.
28 T. 147; *MGH Capit.* II, no. 260 (Servais), below: 316.
29 Werner 1959a: 113. The other events dated under 860–2 by Regino belong to the early 850s. Cf. e.g. n. 20 above.

But the anachronistic location of the assembly at Compiègne (no royal stays are recorded between 847 and 860, though this was to become a frequent residence later in Charles's reign) betray Regino's back-projection of the position occupied by Robert's son (and namesake) in the early tenth century. There is no doubt that Charles was relying on Robert to guard the lower Loire; but that was not the same thing as making him a new kind of territorial prince.[30] Charles's plans for Neustria necessarily included provision for his own eldest son Louis, who would soon require a sub-kingdom of his own. Meanwhile, Robert was to share regional power with others, including magnates already ensconced in Neustria.

This is clear from the list of *missi* appended to the Capitulary of Servais in November 853. The roll-call of *potentes* in the *regna* of Francia, Neustria and Burgundy supplies important testimony to Charles's political strength at this time outside Aquitaine. Twenty-two lay magnates in all are named, plus 11 bishops and 6 abbots. Within each of twelve *missatica*, Charles appointed a consortium of *missi*. For southern Neustria, Robert was paired with Osbert as lay *missi* in Maine, Anjou and Touraine, while Herloin and Harduin were to serve in northern Neustria between the Cotentin and the River Risle.[31] The content of the Capitulary of Servais is significant too. It dealt mainly with the repression of violent crime and public disorder, tackling these problems at grassroots level. Hundredmen (*centenarii*) and local landholders with special obligations of military service to the king (*Franci homines*) were not new royal agents, but the Capitulary of Servais is more explicit than any other piece of Carolingian legislation about their responsibilities for reporting and hunting down criminals.[32] The use of the written word was another feature of Carolingian government whose application Charles now sought to extend. Each hundredman was to swear 'to you *missi dominici*' that he would supply an accurate list of *Franci homines* 'in my jurisdictional area' (*in meo mynisterio*). Missi lacking 'the capitularies of our grandfather and father'

30 For Regino's term *ducatus*, and the equivalence of *dux* and *marchio*, see Werner 1980: 216.
31 See Map 7.
32 *MGH Capit.* II, p. 274.

were to get copies made, at their own expense, 'from our archive' (*de scrinio nostro*).[33] Here and elsewhere, this text shows, for the first time in Charles's reign, clear evidence of the use of the collection of Charlemagne's and Louis the Pious's capitularies made by Ansegis in 827. The draftsman at Servais was, almost certainly, Hincmar of Rheims: he was placing Charles in the legislative tradition of his Carolingian predecessors, and, beyond them, of the Christian emperors of the fourth and fifth centuries. Claims to a new kind of exalted status had already been implicit in Charles's dealings with Erispoë in 851, and in the arrangements Charles made in April 852 for the liturgical commemoration of his own birthday – a practice clearly modelled on that of imperial Rome.[34]

Charles assumed another traditionally imperial role in 853 when he attempted to settle a major theological dispute which had racked the Frankish church for several years. In 848, the teaching of the Saxon monk Gottschalk on Predestination – that some were predestined to Heaven, others to damnation – was condemned by bishops in both East Frankish and West Frankish kingdoms. More than theology and canon law was at stake here. As Archbishops Hrabanus and Hincmar perceived it, the issue had clear social and moral overtones: Gottschalk's view seemed to remove an individual's responsibility for his own conduct, and, still more dangerously, to challenge the power of the Church to mediate the means of salvation to the faithful. Bishops, centrally concerned with that mediation, were likely to oppose Gottschalk; monks might be attracted by the spiritual elitism inherent in his theology. In fact opinion was less tidily split: Bishop Prudentius of Troyes as well as Lupus of Ferrières, for instance, showed some sympathy for Gottschalk.[35] There were further complications: those who had supported Ebbo of Rheims tended to side with Gottschalk, since both groups opposed Hincmar.[36] There were also political dimensions: the bishops of the Middle Kingdom (they included Ebbo's nephew and name-

---

33 Ibid., c. 11.
34 Kantorowicz 1946: 67–8.
35 Ganz 1990a. See also Nineham 1989.
36 Hincmar himself linked the two issues in *PL* 125, 386.

sake, the bishop of Grenoble) chose this issue to take a collective and distinctive stand on, pitting the theological expertise of Lyons against Rheims. Charles probably had a strong personal interest in getting the matter settled. It was he himself who requested expert opinion from Lupus,[37] from John the Scot, from Hincmar, and from several other theologians.[38] A king who apparently gave John house-room in his palace for over thirty years surely had a genuine interest in ideas for their own sake.[39] But his over-riding interest was in getting an agreed formula, a collective episcopal line. He could not afford to have his bishops at loggerheads.

In early summer 851, Charles and his brothers met for a second time at Meersen, and agreed on joint action against 'the enemies of God'.[40] Later that year, the death of Ebbo removed a major stumbling-block. It was Charles alone who eventually took action. A pair of assemblies in 853 were intended to settle the Predestination debate and at the same time to clear up the aftermath of Ebbo's checkered career. At Soissons in April, 44 bishops retrospectively confirmed the validity of Ebbo's deposition in 835 by declaring the invalidity of all ordinations performed by him after that date; at Quierzy in June with considerably fewer bishops in attendance, Hincmar and Charles between them secured a kind of consensus which ensured that the whole issue, if it did not lie down, at least caused no major rifts within the West Frankish episcopate thereafter. A four-point formula was agreed on, affirming belief in single Predestination, in man's free will, in God's desire for universal salvation, and in the universal meaning of Christ's atonement.[41] This was very much Hincmar's formula. Charles must have hoped that it would also provide a basis for accord within the Frankish church as a whole, and that the Lotharingian bishops would fall into line.[42]

By 853, Charles and Lothar had established a close entente. The measures announced at Servais in November

37   Ep. 78.
38   Marenbon 1990.
39   Above Ch. 1: 16.
40   *MGH Capit.* II, no. 205, pp. 72–4.
41   *AB* 853: 76–7. Cf. *MGH Conc.* III, no. 28, pp. 294–7.
42   In fact they stuck to their own line; Hartmann 1989: 262–6.

had been agreed beforehand with Lothar.[43] Nevertheless, modern historians may oversimplify in assuming that rapprochement between Charles and Lothar automatically meant the alienation of Louis the German.[44] In 853, the *AB*'s statement seems to come out of the blue: 'Louis was bitterly angry on account of certain agreements that had been made between him and Charles during the time of disturbances'. Calmette commented that this expression is 'quite vague'.[45] In fact it is quite specific; for it refers, surely, to the agreement enshrined in the Strasbourg Oaths in 842, when Louis and Charles had undertaken never to plot with Lothar behind each other's back.[46] What had happened to make Louis so angry? On 9 October, St Denis's Day, 852, a Viking fleet again entered the Seine and came up nearly as far as Paris. One of the leaders of these Vikings was Godefrid, son of the Danish king Harald and a former *fidelis* of Lothar, who had recently defected.[47] Perhaps this was why Lothar joined Charles to counter Godefrid's attack. For some weeks Lothar and Charles campaigned together, they celebrated Christmas together, then came to a joint-agreement with Godefrid, spent Twelfth Night feasting 'with great joy' at Quierzy and sealed their alliance when Lothar stood godfather to Charles's daughter.[48] More directly relevant to the estrangement between Louis and Charles was the fact that in the autumn of 852, Charles had got Lothar's agreement before having Pippin II tonsured.[49] Since 840, Carolingian politics had effectively involved four principals, not three. At Fontenoy, it had been two against two. Now Charles had finally destroyed Lothar's old entente with Pippin, eliminating that fourth party; and there had been no consultation with Louis over Pippin's fate.[50] Other specific acts of 'spying' and 'soliciting' that may have further embittered relations between Louis and Charles will be considered presently.

43   At Valenciennes, *MGH Capit.* II, no. 206.
44   Calmette 1901: 21; Werner 1984: 414. Cf. Dümmler 1887–8(i): 382.
45   Calmette 1901: 22.
46   Above Ch. 5: 122.
47   *AB* 852: 75 and n. 9. Cf. above Ch. 6: 151.
48   *AB* 853: 76. Apparently the fact that Lothar was Charles's own godfather was no obstacle.
49   *AB* 852: 74.
50   Note that *AF* consistently called Pippin II 'king' of Aquitaine.

By 853, Lothar was 57. His wife had died in 851 and he had not remarried. The shape of Lothar's own descent-line was thus clear and Charles bid fair to assume the role of sole 'protector' of Lothar's offspring. Louis responded immediately: while Lothar and Charles were together on the Seine late in 852, Louis met with some of Lothar's magnates at Cologne.[51] They seem to have agreed that Lothar's Frankish realm should survive intact after his death, and that it should be ruled by Lothar's second son and namesake. Charles's hopes of extending his kingdom east of the Charbonnière were once again to be denied by the aristocracy of Middle Francia, who wanted a king of their own. This time, however, the continued existence of that Middle Kingdom was guaranteed, not by Lothar, but by Louis the German.

It must have been because they were well aware of Louis's anger against Charles that 'Aquitanians' hostile to Charles late in 853 'sent envoys to Louis bringing their own submission, and with hostages'.[52] The senders had another reason in mind: while Louis's firstborn son would obviously inherit the patrimony of Bavaria, his second son and namesake (born c. 835) was now beginning to look for active employment and a realm of his own. These Aquitanians wanted an alternative to Charles, and would be equally happy, they said, with Louis or his son. It was a classic case of aristocratic king-making by invitation.[53] A new Carolingian generation had outgrown the regime of confraternity.

The *AB* are typically unspecific about 'Aquitanians'. It is the *AF* who reveal *which* Aquitanians appealed to Louis. They were the kindred (*cognatio*) of Gauzbert whose execution on Charles's orders in March 853 had 'very greatly offended' them.[54] There is no information as to why Charles acted thus, but there is a clue in Regino's statement that Gauzbert was beheaded (*decollatus*) for this was the penalty for treason.[55] It is striking that other ninth-century condemnations for treason were done by the judgement of

51 *AF* 852:42.
52 *AB* 853: 77.
53 Nelson 1990d.
54 *AF* 854: 44. *AAng* gives the date of Gauzbert's execution (but no mention of his kin).
55 Cf. *AB* 866: 134.

the Franks and perhaps it was Charles's failure to secure that judgement in Gauzbert's case which caused such 'offence'.[56] Gauzbert's identity is uncertain. The annalist of St-Wandrille distinguished between 'Count Gauzbert' who fought Lambert in 850; 'young Gauzbert' (*iuvenis*) who was killed fighting for Charles at Jengland; and 'little young Gauzbert' (*iuvenculus*) who killed Lambert in 852 and who seems to have been Charles's victim in 853.[57] It is probable that the three were related. The third Gauzbert, anyway, had kinsmen powerful enough to sound persuasive at Louis the German's court, and clearly located in Aquitaine. One of them was probably Bishop Ebroin of Poitiers, usually assumed to have remained loyal to Charles, and to have died defending Poitiers in 854.[58] He is not documented after 850, though. If he died before 853, then Charles underestimated how important he had been in holding Poitou. If, on the other hand, Ebroin led the Aquitanian rebels in 853–4, that would have represented a severe threat to Charles's control of northwestern Aquitaine.[59] Sheer lack of evidence makes it impossible to judge the extent of political miscalculation in Charles's killing of Gauzbert. The total silence of the Capitulary of Servais on Aquitaine may not be coincidental.

The damage to Charles's position was reparable, however. Early in 854, when Louis the German's son 'came to Aquitaine, wishing to see if the promises made by that people's envoys to his father were true, [Young Louis] was not acknowledged by anyone except by that one kindred whom Charles had greatly offended through the killing of their kinsman Gauzbert . . . The rest declined to come to him, and he judged his coming superfluous. After taking counsel with his men, he returned to Francia in the autumn [of 854]'.[60] Clearly the rebels had been unable to 'deliver' their promise of a kingdom. The East Frankish annalist neglects Charles's counter-measures: he had first neu-

56 See Nelson 1986a (1983a): 102 and n. 56.
57 *AFont* 85, 87, 89. *AAng* dates Lambert's death and implies that Lambert's killer and Charles's victim were identical. For Ademar's conjecture that Gauzbert was count of Le Mans, see Gillingham 1990: 44–5.
58 Levillain 1923.
59 Oexle 1969: 189–91
60 *AF* 854: 44.

tralised Louis the German by encouraging Bulgars and Slavs to attack his eastern frontier,[61] then held repeated meetings with Lothar to secure his continued alliance in 854, and finally addressed himself to driving Young Louis out of Aquitaine. By then the situation had been complicated by the escape from captivity of Pippin II who made straight for Aquitaine. It looks as if Young Louis suffered more from this new intervention than did Charles, and it is possible that Charles took the risk of actually engineering Pippin's escape.[62] According to the *AB*, 'the greatest part of the people of the land flew to [Pippin]'. Yet within months, the same annalist has '[the] Aquitanians' again turning to Charles, requesting that his second son be designated their king, in October 855.[63] No doubt conflict *between* Aquitanians (which the *AB* annalist ignored) underlay these apparently erratic shifts. *Some* Aquitanians supported Charles, perhaps consistently, and in the course of 855, they had the upper hand. A private charter of January 855 suggests a Poitevin-Angoumois group centred on Egfrid and Ranulf and loyal to Charles,[64] while an attack on Poitiers by Pippin in 857 indicates that that *civitas* was then held by Charles's supporters.[65] Other Aquitanians supported Pippin, though, and in 856, staged a king-making for him, thus implicitly rejecting the validity of his enforced tonsure.[66]

Charles's recreation of subkingdoms within his composite realm followed traditional Carolingian practice. Louis, born in 846 (contemporaries were to nickname him 'the Stammerer'), would have Neustria, the appanage of the firstborn: he seems to have been given, perhaps early in the 850s (possibly in his seventh year) a Neustrian tutor.[67]

---

61 *AB* 853: 77.
62 So, Muhlbacher 1896: 484, inferring from *AB* 854: 79. The *AB's* wording allows this interpretation. Cf. their unambiguous report of an escape a few lines later; see below: 179.
63 *AB* 855: 80.
64 *Cartulaire d'Angoulême* no. 52, p. 82, dated 15th year of *Carolus minor*. T. 174 (855) was requested by Count Raymund, possibly an Aquitanian (cf. below n. 70).
65 *AB* 857: 84.
66 *AB* 856: 81.
67 For Joseph, ex-notary of Pippin II, subsequently a canon of Bayeux, see T. 182 and above: 150, n. 85. For Louis's speech-defect, Regino s.a. 878.

Aquitaine was destined for the second son, Charles. The third son Carloman, born 849/50, was tonsured as a cleric at the age of 4, in 854, and hence clearly removed from consideration as a potential king.[68] This exclusion of a legitimate son, using exactly the same means applied to Charles's nephew Pippin two years before, was a new kind of Carolingian strategy. Charles was determined to avert conflict between his sons, and in the early 850s, only two subkingdoms were his to bestow. He may have intended to wait until his two elder sons reached manhood before installing them; but in 855, the Aquitanians' request forced his hand. They wanted a king of their own. Being young, that king would need *bajuli* (guardians) on the spot, and the likely candidates for such posts were Aquitanian magnates. Equally, Charles would try to keep hold of the reins of power, just as Charlemagne had done when he set up his little son, the future Louis the Pious, as subking in Aquitaine. In 855, Charles organised an imposing royal inauguration for his son at Limoges, perhaps erecting an equestrian statue to mark the occasion. The Aquitanians attended *generaliter*.[69] There is no evidence as to who Young Charles's *bajuli* were; likely candidates are Archbishop Rodulf of Bourges and Bishop Stodilo of Limoges, along with two lay *potentes*, Counts Raymund and Hugh, who may well now have sealed their common political cause by arranging the betrothal of Raymund's daughter to Hugh's son Stephen.[70]

The complex politics of the years 853–8 must be looked at as a whole. Historians have happily accepted a well-tried guideline through the tangle. For over a century, this phase of Charles's reign has been seen as dominated by the struggle between two 'parties', or 'clans', consisting essentially of the kin of Charles's wife Ermentrude, daughter of Odo, on the one hand, and the kin of his mother Judith, daughter of Welf, on the other. Historiographical fashions change: Werner's 'Odo-Group' is Calmette's 'family of

68 *AB* 854: 79. See Nelson 1988b. A fourth son, Lothar, was lame and was tonsured; *AB* 861: 94. Two still younger sons were placed at St-Amand, presumably tonsured; *MGH* Poet. Lat. III, pp. 677–8.
69 *AB* 855: 81; Orlowski 1987.
70 T. 170, 174, 178; Hincmar Ep. 136. Auzias 1937: 305–6 identifies Raymund's county as Limoges but it was probably Toulouse; below: 202.

Ermentrude' in a new guise. The labelling of 'the Welfs' has been more consistent, probably because the fame of their putative descendants in the twelfth century and later, tended to strengthen unconscious assumptions of much earlier family identity.[71] Comparison with the limited numbers, and local role, of the *cognatio Gauzberti* suggests that such large-scale gatherings of the clans may be out of place in the ninth-century west.

What has lent reinforcement to these 'clan'-constructs in German historiography since the 1950s has been the influence of the historians of the 'Freiburg School' led by Gerd Tellenbach and Karl Schmid: the large groups of names recorded in *Libri Memoriales* (books associated with the liturgical commemoration of the living and the dead) convinced the 'Freiburg' scholars that large sprawling kingroups were the collective actors and real forces in early medieval politics. It is thanks to 'Freiburg' work that the early medieval world depicted in current textbooks is peopled with 'the Rorgonides', 'the Etichonides', 'the Hunfridinger' – and of course 'the Odo-group' and 'the Welfs'. There is no denying the importance of extensive family-ties in the context of religious practice. Over the past twenty-five years or so, however, a number of British and American historians, led by Karl Leyser, have questioned whether 'clan' cooperation underlay political action. Recently, Constance Bouchard, Stuart Airlie, and others have been focusing, via the narrative and charter evidence, on individual careers, 'small families' and conflicts between kinsmen.[72] A fresh look at the politics of the 850s is timely.

Charles had married Adalard's niece in December 842; and clearly that uncle–niece relationship had been of paramount importance to Charles at the time of the marriage. There is nothing to show, however, that it remained so for very long, nor that it formed the core of a 'party' which still flourished in the 850s. Close kin certainly sometimes made joint arrangements for commemoration in prayer:

71 For 'the queen's party', Calmette 1901: 41–2 (and McKitterick 1983: 185–6); Werner 1959b: 155–6, and 167, with references to the nineteenth-century ancestry of this analysis. For 'the Welfs', Tellenbach 1957; Schmid 1968.
72 For a fundamental critique, Leyser 1968. See further Reuter 1978; Airlie 1985; Bouchard 1986, 1988.

175

Adalard, for instance, apparently on a brief return to Charles's court in August 853, associated Ermentrude in the spiritual benefits when land was transferred to the monastery of Fossés, a house patronised by the ancestors of both.[73] But Adalard's fleeting appearance in Ermentrude's company in 853 did not alter the fact that he had resided for years in Lothar's kingdom and would remain there throughout the 850s. Ermentrude's influence (which was not exceptional for a medieval queen)[74] cannot be correlated with that of her uncle or of any other kinsmen. In the 850s, another man named Adalard was Abbot of St-Bertin and an important figure at Charles's court, but the supposition of close kinship with Ermentrude's uncle rests solely on likeness of name, and no source ever links the abbot with the queen.

Given the relatively small size of the Frankish elite and the amount of intermarriage between its members, kin-ties between political allies can sometimes be surmised (far less often demonstrated) from the evidence of naming patterns: there may, for instance, have been a close kin-tie between Queen Ermentrude, daughter of a Count Odo (d. 834) and Odo count of Troyes, though no contemporary writer says as much.[75] This second Odo was perhaps related by marriage to Robert, who named his second son Odo (though Odo was a fairly common name); certainly the two men both appear as recipients of benefices from Charles in the early years of the reign. But kin-ties did not necessarily make political allies. Brothers might attach themselves to rival kings, as in the case of Adalard and Gerald who fought on opposite sides at Fontenoy. Conversely, close allies were not necessarily related by ties of blood or marriage. Bishop Pardulus of Laon and Robert, for instance, were allies, but there is no evidence that kinship was involved at all. Queen Ermentrude was obviously very close to Pardulus in the early 850s (as, it should be added, was the king) but nothing suggests any kin-tie. No-one can be assigned with confidence to a 'queen's party' at Charles's

---

73 T. 157.
74 Stafford 1983; and see Hyam 1990.
75 The significance of naming-patterns as evidence for biological kinship is clear; but patron–client relations or spiritual kinship could also be relevant factors.

court in the 850s. Further, the alleged members of her 'group' pursued different interests in those years. Robert was in rebellion against Charles from early 856 for the rest of the decade, yet Abbot Adalard of St-Bertin continued to be a *potens* at Charles's court for some months at least after Robert's defection; Robert's alleged 'ally' Odo seems to have remained loyal to Charles until early 858. In short, modern notions of party or group centred on Queen Ermentrude postulate a shared identity and collective action for which no firm evidence exists and which individuals' conduct belies.

'The Welfs' are equally chimerical. Charles's uncle Rudolf, and his brother, Conrad were brothers of Charles's mother Judith, 'daughter of Welf', but neither man is identified in contemporary sources as 'son of Welf'. They had chosen divergent paths after the time of troubles, and there is no evidence at all to link their careers thereafter. Not even books of liturgical commemoration show their names together. While Conrad (presumably the older brother) remained in his lands and *honores* in Alemannia, Rudolf sought his fortune in Charles's kingdom. Before 857, there is some contemporary evidence for Rudolf as a *potens* [76] but none that links him with the only other 'Welfs' modern historians have been able to identify, namely his two nephews Hugh and Conrad junior. Furthermore, the fortunes of these men seem to have risen and fallen independently of each other. When Hugh was expelled from Charles's kingdom in 862, his brother remained count of Auxerre, and his uncle count of Troyes.[77] Werner explains this away: 'When there was a political change-around, of course not all members of the family forming the core of the defeated party lost their *honores*. But that doesn't alter the general picture'.[78] The general picture indicates, though, that Charles's favour was conferred, or withdrawn, according to individual performance. Both Rudolf and his nephew Hugh were loyal to Charles in 858, and were rewarded with grants of confiscated *honores*. But this proves

---

76 E.g. he was named a *missus* for the Blois-Evreux region in the Capitulary of Servais; see below: 316. But he features in only two royal charters (T. 111, 183). See Genealogy IV.
77 T. 248, 261, 256.
78 Werner 1959b: 155, n. 38.

neither 'the Welfs' triumph' nor their long-term opposition to the 'Odo-group'. Hincmar at the close of 857 told Rudolf he was being accused of 'sowing discords between the king and certain of those subject to him' and treated these rumours as an attack on Rudolf by the king's 'false friends'.[79] This reveals rivalries around the king, but hardly the eclipse of a 'Welf party'. The art of government included the ability to exploit such rivalries and to dominate them by keeping the rivals' ambitions firmly focused on royal favour. Rudolf and Abbot Adalard acted *together* as Charles's trusted agents in July and September 856[80] and *both* Rudolf and Adalard, the ex-seneschal, did so in 863–4. The idea of one 'party' excluding another from power is clearly anachronistic. As for solidarity between 'Welfs': true, Hugh had been given the abbacy of St-Germain, Auxerre, and Conrad junior the countship of the same *civitas*. But the brothers may well have competed rather than cooperated: certainly Conrad kept his countship through the period 862–5 when Hugh lost Charles's favour, and the two men's careers show little connection thereafter.[81]

Why and when had Hugh and his brother come west? The answers to these questions may take us nearer to the heart of Carolingian politics than the 'clan' model or the 'party' line. Kinship was refracted, in diverse and complex ways, by kingship, that is, by royal favour or disfavour. Kings competed for the support of their own kinsmen. Men competed for the favours of their royal kin, and manoeuvred between one king and another. What drew 'the sons of Conrad' from home was the quest for the rewards of *Königsnähe:* their (?elder) brother Welf remained with the patrimony in Alemannia. What brought them to the west was not their uncle Rudolf's presence there but royal business: 'Louis (the German) had sent them', according to the *AF*, 'on the grounds that they were his *fideles*, to spy on and report back on the doings of Charles. But they belied Louis's trust and joined Charles.'[82] A glance at the family tree shows that Hugh and Conrad had thus sought patron-

79 Hincmar Ep. 105, *MGH Epp.* VIII, p. 51.
80 *MGH Capit.* II, nos. 262, 265, pp. 279, 284.
81 The 'sons of Conrad' who killed Hubert in 864 were Conrad Junior and Hugh, however; see *AB* 864: 121 n.32.
82 *AF* 858: 51.

age initially from an uncle-by-marriage, Louis the German. But in joining Charles, their cousin, they picked up on a still closer kin-tie; in opting to remain in the west, they followed where many ambitious young Franks had gone before them; and in looking to Auxerre, they may also have pursued an inheritance from their mother.[83]

When did Hugh and his brother make their move? Was it in 853: the date when Hugh held from Charles the abbacy of St-Germain, Auxerre[84] – and also the date of the estrangement between Louis and Charles? The *AF*'s story of the brothers' defection is entered under 858. Historians, accepting that date, have found it necessary to postulate a *sequence* of defections, with Hugh (and Conrad) first joining Charles in 853, then defecting back to Louis at some point before 858, then defecting to Charles again. But suppose the *AF* entry is referring back here to something that happened five years before? That would make the conduct of Hugh and Conrad less bewildering; and Louis the German's 'bitterness' against Charles in 853 more explicable.[85] It would also produce a perfectly plausible scenario for Charles's action: he seized the opportunity of his cousins' 'visit' to poach them from Louis, and then granted them *honores* in northern Burgundy where their parents already had long-established links with Auxerre. Louis the German used similar tactics himself. He was probably behind the springing of Charles son of Pippin (brother of Pippin II) from his monastic gaol at Corbie in 854. Some members of the Corbie community had perhaps been disaffected since Charles had enforced the 'retirement' of Abbot Paschasius and installed a favourite cleric, Odo, in his place;[86] and in 854, the disaffected tended to look for consolation from Louis the German.[87] It was from him that the fugitive Charles son of Pippin sought a welcome, and soon, suitably

---

83 See above Ch. 4: 100.
84 T. 156.
85 Cf. Sassier 1991: 31; and above: 170.
86 This had happened by April 853; Grierson 1935: 162.
87 The *Epitaphium Arsenii* seems have been written shortly after Paschasius had been removed from the abbacy of Corbie in 852. The papal privilege obtained by Corbie in 855 doesn't mention Charles the Bald; but this may be through error, Ganz 1990: 33.

exalted ecclesiastical patronage in the shape of the arch-bishopric of Mainz.[88]

The death of Lothar, in September 855, significantly changed the configuration of the Carolingian family. During Lothar's lifetime, a conjuncture of power and authority had persisted as under Charlemagne and Louis the Pious: the emperor and the *primogenitus* in the senior generation had been one and the same man, and that man controlled the core of the Frankish heartlands. After 855, the Carolingians had, for the first time, no imperial paterfamilias. Instead, new conflicts arose from new disequilibrium. Both the imperial title, and the core of the Frankish heartlands, had passed from the senior to the junior generation, and title and heartlands had passed to two different junior members. There was no longer a coincidence between power and authority, or between different types of authority, within the family. Competition between Lothar's sons was immediately translated into a quest for avuncular patrons, which fuelled the contention between the uncles, Louis the German and Charles the Bald.

Lothar on his deathbed had been attended by his second son Lothar, to whom he bequeathed Middle Francia, and his third son, Charles, not yet fifteen, for whom a kingdom consisting of Provence and the lower Rhône valley was now created with the support of the leading regional magnate, Count Gerald of Vienne.[89] In September 855, Lothar's eldest son, Louis II, was far away in Italy, where he had in effect ruled autonomously since 844 and been consecrated co-emperor in 851. Late in 855 he tried to claim a share in the inheritance north of the Alps as well. But Louis the German had already made contact with magnates in Middle Francia[90] and it was to him that Lothar II now turned. This explains why Lothar II was consecrated king of the Middle Kingdom not at Aachen but at Frankfurt-on-the-Main.[91] He tried but failed to prevent the establishment in Provence of his younger brother Charles; but

88 *AF* 856: 46. Itrabanus had died in February.
89 The former count of Paris had abandoned Charles for Lothar in 840, and received a series of *honores* including Vienne. See DD Loth. I 68, 126, DD Loth II 23; Louis 1946. See Map 2(b).
90 Above, 171.
91 *AF* 855: 46.

the boy already suffered from epilepsy and was unlikely to live long.[92] By 857, Charles the Bald had drawn Lothar II into alliance. Louis the German retaliated by switching to Louis of Italy. Thus 'the regime of confraternity' yielded to a new two-generational pattern, as Louis the German and Charles the Bald sought political advantage through intervention in their nephews' affairs.

In 858, the uneasy equilibrium broke down when Louis invaded his brother's kingdom. In the modern historiography, this has been labelled (with some justification) the great crisis of Charles's reign. It has been argued that the die was cast in 853: that thereafter Charles never recovered control of his own rebellious aristocracy and never managed to staunch the outflow of support in the direction of Louis the German. The *AB*'s statement, under 858, that 'those counts of Charles's realm who for five years had been inviting Louis finally induced him to come', has been taken literally. In fact the rebels of 858 were not the same men as those of 853. Between the two dates, the graph of support for Charles shows fluctuations that reflect political successes as well as failures, and also regional variations.

These years saw an increasing number of Viking raids, not only in Aquitaine and the Loire valley, but via the Seine far into Francia itself. In 854, terrible conflict had torn apart the elite of Denmark: King Horic 'and other kings' and 'nearly all the nobility' were slain.[93] What followed was a marked increase in Viking activity, as warlords with an eye on the power-vacuum back in Demark amassed booty and bidded for followers. In mid-August 856, Vikings came up the Seine and built a stronghold at Jeufosse (hardly 60km from Paris as the crow flies), mooring their ships alongside. From here they launched raids into the Vexin and the Perche. This was altogether too close for comfort. Charles summoned forces against the attackers 'and smote them with very great slaughter'.[94] Though the Vikings settled down at Jeufosse to overwinter, this effective resistance showed Charles determined to protect his heartlands.

92   *AB* 856: 81; cf. 858: 87; 861: 96; 863: 104.
93   *AB* 854: 80.
94   *AFont.* 856: 91.

For part of this campaigning season, Charles had a prestigious companion: King Æthelwulf of Wessex. The previous year, Æthelwulf en route for Rome had been warmly
received by Charles and given an imposing escort through
his kingdom. Now, on the way home, Æthelwulf was bound
still more closely into a West Frankish alliance, when after a
three months' stay at Charles's court, he married Charles's
eldest daughter Judith.[95] Though Æthelwulf no doubt welcomed the prospect of support against increasing Viking
pressure on his own kingdom, the initiative behind the
match surely came from the Frankish side. The rebellion of
Æthelwulf's eldest son during his father's absence had provided Charles with a perfect opportunity for diplomatic intervention on his own terms.[96] Æthelwulf's entourage
colluded, assuring the Franks that the title of queen had
hitherto not been customary among the West Saxons, and
lending Hincmar a king's consecration *ordo* on which to
base a special new one for Judith.[97] Æthelwulf in 856
needed an infusion of Carolingian wealth and prestige:
Charles as his father-in-law (though probably a younger
man) could assume the senior position in an extended
family of kings. Ritual confirmed the asymmetry of the alliance when it asserted the status of the crowned and consecrated Carolingian bride.

Charles's alliance with Æthelwulf, and his assertion of
symbolic seniority, need to be set alongside events earlier
in the same year, 856. Charles's son Louis the Stammerer,
the *primogenitus*, had been invested with rulership of Neustria and installed at Le Mans.[98] At Louviers in February,
Charles had betrothed his son to the daughter of Erispoë.
The Frankish king and the Breton leader thereby became
'co-fathers', but again, Charles's senior position was clear.
His intentions for the Neustrian subkingdom are worth
clarifying. It is often said that Charles was a centraliser who
never meant to set up 'traditional' subkingdoms for his
sons, but instead was always determined to retain control in
his own hands. His tactics in 856, though, present a tradi-

95   *AB* 855: 80, 856: 83. See Stafford 1990: 142–51.
96   Enright 1979.
97   So, Nelson 1986a (1980).
98   *AB* 856: 81–2.

tional blend of palace intervention and locally-recruited power. The appointment of the experienced royal notary Joseph as the boy's tutor, implies that Young Louis was to have a chancery of his own. One official document, a summons to an assembly at Neaufles in the Vexin, appears to be issued in the name of Young Louis as well as Charles, and shows the bishop of Sées, in the very heart of Neustria, acting as *missus*.[99] A second named *missus*, Betto, seems to have been a *fidelis* of Charles,[100] picked for his son's entourage. The man most clearly designated to underwrite Young Louis's regime as the nine-year-old's protector was Erispoë himself.[101]

The establishment of Louis's Neustrian subkingdom with Erispoë in the role of *bajulus* was bound to upset the distribution of power in the region of the Lower Loire. A divide and rule policy founders if any of the sharers in the division rejects the ruler. In 856, Charles seems to have underrated the threat to Robert's interests, or failed to provide sufficient compensation in the form of additional *honores*. French historians have had problems with Robert: the hindsight knowledge that he died fighting Vikings and that his descendants were to be kings of France has caused him to be idealised, where other nobles have been denounced for egoism; yet Robert's career offers particularly good examples of rebellion and of exploiting Viking allies against local rivals. Robert should be seen, in other words, as a fairly representative (if unusually well-documented) figure. Like other magnates, he had his regional position to protect, but he could not do without *Königsnähe*. When that position seemed threatened by Erispoë's new role as prospective father-in-law to Young Louis, Robert in the early summer of 856 joined with other disaffected counts[102] and some 'Aquitanians' to renew the invitation to Louis the German. The defectors were reconciled with Charles when the East Frankish king failed to appear promptly; but it was

---

99 *MGH Capit.* II, no. 263, issued from Bézu, dep. Eure, refers in cc. 4 and 5 to *dominus et genitor suus*. Hadobrandus is unidentified by the *MGH* editor.

100 T. 185.

101 T. 180, 181, 182, associated with the Louviers meeting, are for Neustrian benficiaries.

102 *AB* 856: 82 surely exaggerates in saying 'nearly all'.

a straw in the wind. Robert had not come to terms with a Neustrian regime backed by Erispoë; he still provided a potential rallying-point for others' disaffection. Charles had to find a basis for a genuine reconciliation.

Charles was a king who inspired fear.[103] So long as wrath was carefully controlled and respected the limits of legitimacy, it was a prime royal asset. It could become a liability if its effects were perceived as arbitrary or unjust. A fate like Gauzbert's sent shivers of insecurity down the spines of noble Franks. Charles seems now to have grasped the link between his previous misjudgement in the case of Gauzbert, and Robert's defection: to restore morale he must re-establish his credibility as king. He sent a series of prestigious emissaries, including Count Rudolf and Abbot Adalard, to 'those Franks and the Aquitanians who had defected' offering them some specific assurances. He would not seize any man (c. 2), and would always take counsel in future before acting against an individual (c. 7). 'Reasonable mercy' would be shown to those who 'humbled themselves and wished to mend their ways'(c. 3). No-one need henceforth be worried about his wrath or fury, but they would seek together (*communiter*) to define what was and was not within the scope of the royal office (c. 8). Charles admitted that he had imposed heavy burdens in the past and promised to set up a complaints procedure for those who had been squeezed (c. 6). A pact (*pactum*) united him with all his *fideles* whatever their rank or status(c. 10): if he had accidentally breached this, they should let him know and he would rectify the situation. Should a faithful man breach the pact, the king might deal with him *familiariter* – informally; or, if the offence were more serious, the king would send the man before a tribunal of his peers (*pares*) for judgement.[104] A persistent rebel would be 'expelled by all from the fellowship of all of us and from the realm' by a collective decision. Anyone who wished to seek another lord could leave with Charles's permission, as long as he went peacefully. The envoys guaranteed safe-conducts for those who came to discuss matters with Charles in person.

103 Hincmar Ep. 105; Lupus Ep. 67.
104 *MGH Capit.* II, no. 262, pp. 279–80. There are notable parallels here to Magna Carta cc. 39, 52.

Some of the terms of these manifestos – *barnatus*, for instance, as a collective noun meaning 'baronage' – are documented here for the first time. But they can hardly have been new inventions. Rather, oral, vernacular discourse was being given (perhaps thanks to Hincmar) written Latinised form. Charles struck the traditional Carolingian chords of good lordship and security. There was no question, any more than there had been at Coulaines, of monarchy having 'descended from its throne'. Rather, that throne's solidity was being confirmed. When it came to essentials, Charles reserved his powers to hire and fire. 'For the meantime, you remain in your *honores* and your allodial lands – except for whatever *honores* [the king] our lord has granted you'. By implication, the latter were at Charles's disposal.[105] A virtually identical programme was to form the basis of a more lasting settlement in the next decade; and it was complemented by measures taken at Quierzy in February 857 to repress crime and impose accountability on royal agents in Francia proper.[106]

In 857, old and new problems combined to endanger Charles's position in ways that defied even his resourcefulness. It was this combination – topped up by a final measure of bad luck – which caused the crisis of 858. The old problem was the presence (since 856)[107] again in Aquitaine of Pippin II. The new problem was the simultaneous presence of substantial Viking warbands on the Seine as well as the Loire. Those at Jeufosse had not been dislodged by Charles's campaigning in 856: from that stronghold they raided Paris on 28 December. In late summer 857, Paris was raided again.[108] At the same time, the situation in the Loire valley was increasingly menacing. 'Certain Franks', who surely included Robert, persuaded some leading Aquitanians to revive the cause of Pippin II. One of the Aquitanians was probably Stephen, son of Count Hugh: his choice of this moment to try to break off his betrothal to the daughter of Count Raymund may well have reflected a political rift between the two men.[109] Soon Pippin had

---

105   *MGH Capit.* II, no. 265, p. 285. For allods, cf. below: 195.
106   *MGH Capit.* II, no. 266, pp. 285–91.
107   Above: 173.
108   *AB* 857: 83, 85.
109   Hincmar Ep. 136, p. 89.

recruited Viking allies and with them attacked and burned Poitiers. Finally in November, Erispoë, apparently after a period of disputes (which may explain why he failed to offer resistance to Robert or to the Vikings) was killed by his cousin Salomon.[110] This left Charles's Neustrian policy in ruins. Within weeks Robert had found 'Breton allies' and driven the young Louis the Stammerer and his followers eastwards and out of Neustria altogether. Meanwhile, to add insult to injury, a Viking force late in 857 repeating the previous year's tactic came up-river from Jeufosse, raided St-Denis and carried off as captives Abbot Louis (Charles's cousin) and his half-brother Gauzlin.[111]

Charles showed, as ever, energy and determination. First, he had to secure himself by diplomacy against Louis the German's intrigues with Lothar II. At Quierzy in March 858, Charles met Lothar and reaffirmed their alliance.[112] Second, Charles had to restore consensus within his realm. Also at Quierzy, he gave renewed assurances on oath, and in turn took new oaths of loyalty from key *fideles*, including the Burgundian Isembard, seven leading men of Francia proper, and three from northern Neustria who thus distanced themselves from the rebels in the Loire valley. Among the bishops were Hincmar, and also his nephew and namesake, the newly-appointed young bishop of Laon.[113] Third, Charles took measures to deal with the Vikings. With funds raised largely from his *potentes* together with a huge contribution from the treasury of St-Denis itself – 688 lb of gold and 3250 lb of silver[114] – Charles ransomed Abbot Louis and Gauzlin. He had already induced a Viking force under Sidroc to quit the Seine before the close of 857[115] and those who remained withdrew down-

---

110   *AB* 857: 85.
111   For the date, Coupland 1987: 47–8.
112   *MGH Capit.* no 268, pp. 293–5, March, Quierzy – clearly a riposte to Louis the German's meeting with Lothar in February (*AF* 858) unmentioned in *AB*.
113   *MGH Capit.* II, no. 269, pp. 296–7, lists Engelram, Ratbod, Hunfrid, Odalric, Engiscalc, Rudolf and Odo from Francia, and Hungar, Osbert and Herloin from Neustria. Wenilo of Sens was absent through illness, but signed later; *MGH Conc.* III, no. 47.
114   Coupland 1987: 163. These amounts are specified in a marginal note to a ninth-century manuscript.
115   *AFont* 855 (for 857), pp. 90–1.

river from Jeufosse to Oissel, 15 km upstream from Rouen. This was bad news for those within striking-distance in places like Evreux, Bayeux and Chartres,[116] but an immense relief to the Paris region and so, to the king and his entourage. Early in 858, Charles also won over a Viking warlord, Bjørn, and recruited him and his men into his own following.[117] By July, Charles managed to detach Pippin from his alliance with Robert and the other rebels: though Charles admitted Pippin's lay status and offered him 'counties and monasteries', Pippin seems to have paid the more substantial price of acknowledging Charles's son (Young Charles) as king of Aquitaine.[118] What Charles now needed was a substantial military success. Northern and eastern Neustria were suffering from Viking raids on an unprecedented scale. Could Charles now repeat the propaganda triumph of 848? Would victory over the Vikings bring another political renaissance, this time in Neustria? With Young Charles and Pippin in his retinue, he was joined by Lothar II at Oissel, where the combined Frankish forces proceeded to besiege the Vikings from July through to 23 September.

By then however, Charles faced another threat from within the circle of his own *fideles*. Count Odo of Troyes and Abbot Adalard of St-Bertin decided to throw in their lot with Robert, and went as emissaries to Louis the German to invite him to supplant Charles as king in the West.[119] 'They said they could no longer bear Charles's tyranny. Anything that was left to them, after the pagans from outside had plundered, enslaved, killed and sold them off without even a show of resistance, [Charles] destroyed from within with his evil savagery. There was now no-one left in the whole people who still believed his promises or oaths, and all despaired of his good faith.' The envoys said that if Louis could not come to liberate them, 'they would have to seek protection from the pagans, with great danger to the Christian religion, since they could not

---

116 Ermentarius II, prol., p. 12. The bishop of Bayeux was killed by Vikings in 858, possibly while resisting, *AB* 859, 91; the bishop of Chartres drowned while fleeing, *AB* 858: 85.

117 *AB* 858: 86.

118 *AB* 858: 87.

119 *AF* 858: 49–50. *AB* names no envoys.

get it from their lawful and orthodox lords'. Through the *AF*'s dramatic invention resounds the authentic tone of aristocratic outrage, not about Charles's weakness, but about the forcefulness of his government and the methods by which he met the Viking challenge. Though the information for 857–8 is lacking, it seems clear from the evidence of the 860s that those methods were fiscal: the departure of Sidroc in 857, the recruitment of Bjørn in 858, can only have been obtained for a price, and Charles had passed on the cost to his own aristocracy through generalised exactions. They in turn expressed their resentment, if they did not rebel, by absenting themselves from his court. The near-total lack of extant charters from the year 858 means (at the very least) that far fewer individuals and communities than usual were seeking Charles's patronage or largesse. In November 858, Hincmar himself registered a strong plea that the realm 'which is being ransomed from [the Vikings]' should be 'rescued from undue tribute'.[120] Though the policy achieved its short-term object, and Sidroc and Bjørn, once paid off, kept their side of the bargain, touching the pockets of *potentes* was always a risky business for medieval kings.

During the critical period of the siege of Oissel, Charles fell ill – a piece of bad luck that under the circumstances rapidly turned into disaster. By the time the Oissel campaign was abandoned, Louis the German had entered Charles's realm, and moved quickly via Sens to the Loire valley, where near Orléans 'he received those Aquitanians, Neustrians and also Bretons who had pledged themselves to come over to him'. Archbishop Wenilo of Sens went to meet the invader, offering crucial military support.[121] Lothar II hastily departed to his own kingdom, while Charles sent envoys to offer peace-terms, which Louis spurned. On 12 November, when battle-lines were drawn up near Brienne, Charles realised he lacked the forces to win, and withdrew to Burgundy.[122] Louis moved northwards to Rheims, where he tried unsuccessfully to pressure Hincmar

---

120 *MGH Conc.* III, no. 41, c. 6, p. 412.
121 *MGH Conc.* III, no. 47B, c. 7, p. 466. As 'Ganelon' in the *Song of Roland*, he later typified treachery.
122 *AB* 858: 88.

and his suffragans to follow Wenilo's example, and perhaps to organise a consecration of himself as king in Charles's place. Hincmar's response was evasive: it was a time for fence-sitting.[123] For Louis's position in the west was in fact quite vulnerable. In Burgundy Charles mustered his still-considerable support. At Auxerre early in January, he personally ordered and took part in a *translatio* of St Germain's relics to a new and more imposing shrine.[124] Once again ritual was to prove an effective morale-raiser. The occasion signalled a political turning-point – from defensive to offensive, and from insecurity to strength.

---

123 *MGH Conc* III, no. 41: letter sent to Louis by Hincmar on behalf of the bishops of the provinces of Rheims and Rouen.
124 T. 200; *Miracula Sancti Germani Autiss.* c. 101, *PL* 124, col. 1254.

Chapter 8

859–869: PROSPECTS OF POWER

On 15 January 859 at Jouy near Laon, as Charles later recalled, 'when my enemies had been scattered and brought low before the face of the divine power, the King of Kings, acting with us, restored me to my kingdom'.[1] Charles's own action (as he himself modestly implied) had had a good deal to do with this restoration. Burgundy had been a good place to rally support: no doubt from trusted men like the bishops of Auxerre and Autun, Count Conrad of Auxerre and Abbot Hugh of St-Germain.[2] In Francia, former dissidents are documented on 13 January as having come over again to Charles, leaving a hard core of active rebels confined once more to Neustria and the Breton March.[3] Charles's bishops (except for Wenilo) had not abandoned him; and the newly-appointed young Bishop Hincmar of Laon (nephew of Archbishop Hincmar) had given active service.[4] Meanwhile Louis the German, perched on the edge of Charles's kingdom, saw the dangers of his own position. Jouy was thus the mirror-image of Brienne, two months before: this time it was Louis the German who had to withdraw.[5] John the Scot celebrated Charles's *reditus* in tones appropriate to a Roman triumph.[6] At Auxerre, they credited Charles's 'bloodless victory' to St-Germain.[7]

1   T. 246, 247.
2   Nelson 1986a (1979): 87–8.
3   Levillain 1937a, 163–4, 236–7.
4   Hincmar of Rheims Ep. 126, p. 64.
5   Hincmar, PL 125, col. 963.
6   *MGH* Poet. III, p. 528. Cf. McCormick 1986: 373. Cf. *Vita S. Remigii, MGH SS*RM III, pp. 239–40.
7   Heiric, *Miracula Sancti Germani* II, c. 102, *PL* 124, col. 1255.

For Charles the turn of fortune signalled a wholesale political recovery. In February Lothar II 'hastened to his uncle Charles' at Arcis-sur-Aube to give assurances of his support.[8] On 28 May, the bishops of Lothar's and Charles's kingdoms assembled at Metz to agree the terms of Louis the German's 'absolution'. Hincmar of Rheims led the delegation that conveyed these to Louis at Worms. When Louis's court clergy urged, 'Do what our lord asks! Spare him!', Hincmar answered that while he could willingly have forgiven a personal hurt, evil had been done to his church and people. Forgiveness could therefore only be granted on strict terms 'and not otherwise'.[9] Charles could afford to wait for Louis to agree.

Just as the extent of Charles's difficulties in 858 is hinted at by the near-total absence of charters for that year, so the 16 charters preserved for 859 – the residue of output on a scale not seen since the mid-forties, and mostly confirmations and/or restitutions of property or privilege – suggests a kind of new beginning to the reign: a Restoration. The beneficiaries came from Francia, Burgundy, Septimania and Aquitaine. Only Neustrians are wholly absent, confirming that Neustria had been the epicentre of revolt in 858. Some beneficiaries are identified in terms that seem especially significant: the monks of St-Germain Auxerre and Abbot Hugh *karissimus nobis*,[10] Bishop Erchanraus of Châlons *nobis gratissimus*,[11] Wulfad *karissimus nobis abbas et ministerialis*,[12] and Hunfrid *carissimus nobis comes ac marchio*.[13] Charters are normally fairly dry documents, yet genuine feeling resonates in these phrases. Hugh, Erchanraus, Wulfad and Hunfrid were members of Charles's new inner circle of trusted men who emerged from the crisis of 858–9. Charles's uncle Rudolf can be added to the list with some reservations: Hincmar recommended him at this time as a man 'who holds you and your realm dear' whom 'you [Charles] have told to help you'.[14]

---

8 *AB* 859: 89.
9 *MGH Capit.* II, p. 446.
10 T. 200, 214, 215.
11 T. 212, 213, requested by Queen Ermentrude.
12 T. 202. Wulfad was perhaps Pippin II's ex-notary, above 150 n. 85.
13 T. 203, 208, 209, 210. Hunfrid was *marchio* of Gothia (Septimania).
14 Hincmar Ep. 126.

The distribution of *honores* was an effective and sensitive instrument of political control. Charles's Restoration Settlement involved short-term or permanent loss of *honores* for some of the most prominent rebels of 858. Wenilo of Sens the archdefector was denounced by Charles himself, and threatened with deposition in June 859 but made his peace with Charles later that year.[15] At Bayeux and Langres, where attempts had been made to intrude bishops favourable to Louis the German, Charles used his *principalis potentia* to exact guarantees of loyalty in the one case, and repel the intruder in the other.[16] Odo was permanently deprived of the countship of Troyes; Abbot Adalard lost St-Bertin (though he later recovered it). In Aquitaine, Stephen lost his *honores* when he fled the kingdom in 859.

For the king, it was equally essential that the holders of *honores* should attend assemblies when summoned (but only when summoned):[17] failure to attend was a sign of rebellion. When the Aquitanian Stephen 'evaded two assemblies', he knew that this meant 'discord between my lord the king and myself.'[18] A series of well-documented synods and councils shows extensive participation during the years 859–62 when Charles was re-establishing his position within the Carolingian political system. At Savonnières (near Toul) in June 859 where the three kingdoms of Charles, Lothar II and Charles of Provence were represented, 8 archbishops, 32 bishops and 3 abbots attended, of whom 28 were from Charles's realm.[19] A similar tripartite meeting in November 862, again at Savonnières was attended by 'nearly 200 *consiliarii*, bishops and abbots along with laymen' meeting under one roof.[20] The only list surviving from this series of assemblies to name lay participants is considerably shorter: when Louis the German, Charles the Bald and Lothar II met at Koblenz in June 860, 33 laymen 'negotiated the terms, accepted the *capitula* as to be observed by all' and heard the speeches of the two senior kings.[21] Among Charles's *fideles* present on that occa-

15 *AB* 859: 90.
16 *MGH Conc* III, no. 47A, pp. 459, 460.
17 Lupus Epp. 72, 74.
18 Hincmar Ep. 136, p. 89.
19 *MGH Conc.* III, no. 47, pp. 447–63.
20 *MGH Capit.* II, no. 243, 159–65, with note at 165.
21 *MGH Capit.* II, no. 242, p. 154.

sion were Rudolf, Ratbod, Conrad (count of Auxerre), Richwin,[22] Widric,[23] and Hunfrid.[24]

Ecclesiastical personnel are much better documented, and a series of appointments to key posts at about this time shows Charles fully in command of this area of government. Both Wenilo of Rouen and Hincmar of Laon got their bishoprics in 858, perhaps after service as palace clerics. To the see of Auxerre in 859, Charles appointed Christian, subsequently one of his key negotiators with Louis, and about the same time, an Aquitanian, Frotar, was chosen archbishop of Bordeaux.[25] In 861, the see of Troyes went to Folcric, a royal notary,[26] while Odo, abbot of Corbie became bishop of Beauvais.[27] All these clerics were to serve Charles loyally thereafter as emissaries and agents.

Through the year 859, Charles's political position continued to improve. Yet Vikings remained on the Seine, and a new warband appeared on the Somme, attacking St-Valery and Amiens. How could royal authority and Viking activity increase at the same time? There was no single 'Viking factor' operating as an external force. It had been very clear in 858, as earlier, that various Viking warbands had entered the fabric of Frankish politics, sometimes collaborating, sometimes competing and offering themselves for hire as allies to the warlords they encountered among the Franks. The Carolingian world, with its royal rivals and factional conflicts, presented vertical fault-lines along which Vikings could work. Pippin II allied with a Viking force in 857: Charles the Bald himself had played the same game in the 840s, as had Lothar.

What was new in the later 850s was the concentration of several Viking warbands on the lower Seine valley, and hence on northern Neustria and Francia proper. Their

22 Werner 1959b: 160, n. 57.
23 T. 220. See Brown 1989: 113–5.
24 *MGH Capit.* II, nos. 262, 264, 265, pp. 279, 283, 284.
25 Christian was of Alemannian origin, *Gesta of Bishops of Auxerre* c. 38, *MGH SS* 13, p. 398. Frotar may have been a kinsman of Rodulf: cf. *Cart. Beaulieu*, no. xxxiv, p. 68. T. 199 may be a clue to the timing of his appointment.
26 Tessier 1955: 71–3. Eleven of Charles's sixteen charters issued in 859 were written by Folcric.
27 Grierson 1935: 166–7.

raids threatened the economic resources of Charles's heart-lands; and their availability as allies for rebels further threatened his political control – as the envoys to Louis the German in 858 had made clear.[28] Charles could trade on the Vikings' own differences, however. In 858, he had de-tached Bjørn's contingent and isolated the group at Oissel; and the appearance of a new force, probably led by We-land, on the Somme in 859 enabled Charles to recruit their services against the Seine Vikings before the end of that year.[29] Moreover, the Vikings opened up horizontal fault-lines in the structure of social power within Charles's kingdom. Two episodes in 859 show this process under way. In the first, the peasantry of the region between the Seine and the Loire formed a sworn association to organise resist-ance against the Vikings on the Seine, whereupon the local *potentiores* slew the resisters. The nobility, in other words, saw their social control endangered; and that was a higher priority than defence against potential rival-exploiters of the peasantry.[30] In the second episode, 'Vikings attacked Noyon by night and took captive Bishop Immo and a num-ber of other nobles, both clerics and laymen'. The bishop, perhaps because he attempted resistance or escape, was killed 'on the march'.[31] The message to the nobility was that they should hang together or they would hang separ-ately. The bishops already understood this. In 859, Immo's death, and that of his colleague Ermenfrid of Beauvais (perhaps defending a fortified residence), offered vivid re-minders of the church's need for protection. Charles had always been willing, and in the 860s was increasingly able, to organise defence, and to exact his price for it.

His most pressing problem in June 859, however, was the persistence of rebellion in the Loire valley; and the heart of the problem was the alliance of the Breton Salomon with Robert in Anjou. From Savonnières, a letter was sent to the Breton bishops: they were told to recognise the auth-ority of the archbishop of Tours, and to get Salomon to recognise the authority of Charles. A second letter went 'to the good sons Robert, Odo, Harvey . . . and the rest

28 Above Ch. 7: 187.
29 *AB* 860: 92.
30 *AB* 859: 89.
31 *AB* 859: 91.

joined in alliance with you' wishing them a 'wholesome change of heart'.[32] Despite this conciliatory tone, Charles was determined to impose his own conditions on the rebels. When he went to Andernach to meet Louis the German in July (such was their mutual mistrust that they met on a boat moored in the Rhine), discussions were 'lengthy and inconclusive' – because Louis 'could not secure for those men who had broken with Charles the previous year and become his [Louis's] men, that they should have back their *honores*'. In a final bout of negotiations at Koblenz in June 860, Charles won on points. A detailed account of proceedings survives. Louis made a unilateral acknowledgement of guilt:

Using the *lingua theodisca* (the Germanic vernacular) he declared:
"Now we want to behave towards our brother as a brother rightly should, and towards our nephews as an uncle should".
Turning to Charles he said:
"Now if you please, I would like to have your word concerning those men who came over to me."
Charles then said in a loud voice in the *lingua romana*: (the Romance vernacular)
"Those men who acted against me . . . I forgive their misdeeds, for God's sake . . . Provided that they have made a firm commitment to be peaceable in my kingdom and to live there as Christians ought to live in a Christian kingdom, I grant them their allods by inheritance or by acquisition [*alodes de hereditate et de conquisitu*] and what they had by grant of our Senior [i.e. Louis the Pious] – but not what comes from any grant of mine: all this I do on condition that my brother likewise grants to my faithful men, who have done no misdeed against him, and who helped me when I needed it, the allods they have in his kingdom. Concerning those allods which [the rebels] held as a result of any grant of mine, and also concerning their *honores*: I shall discuss these more fully with him

32   *MGH Conc.* III, no. 47G, pp. 482–5.

[Louis], and towards those who turn themselves back to me I shall act as I will [*voluntarie faciam*]."[33]

This was, of course, to uphold his own royal freedom of manoeuvre where *honores* were concerned, hence leaving Robert and the rest at the royal mercy. Within the few months after the display of Charles's strength at Koblenz, 'nearly all those who had lately defected to Louis returned to Charles'.[34] They included both Adalard (who recovered his abbacy on 25 July 861)[35] and Odo former count of Troyes (who after a while seems to have received the countship in Burgundy instead).[36] But they did not include Robert. Charles decided to revert to the policy of 856. As his son Louis the Stammerer entered his fifteenth year in November 860, Charles gave him the lay-abbacy of St-Martin, Tours, thus signalling the revival of Louis's Neustrian subkingdom. Some Neustrian magnates, perhaps long-standing opponents of Robert, were willing to support this.[37] By summer 861, Robert decided to make his peace with Charles. He kept the countship of Angers; but he and Louis the Stammerer would have to coexist after all.

This settlement in part was made possible by Charles's improved position in Aquitaine, where previously Robert had found allies. Already by the close of 859, Charles had re-established his second son and namesake there, and reneged on the previous year's agreement with Pippin II.[38] Who underpinned Young Charles's subkingdom? Some light is thrown on Aquitanian politics by Hincmar's little treatise on the marital problems of Stephen, written late in 860.[39] Evidently earlier in the year, Stephen had been readmitted to Charles's favour and recovered his *honores*: as part of the deal, he was to go through with his marriage to the daughter of Count Raymund. Within months, Stephen was

---

33 *MGH Capit.* II, no. 242, p. 158.
34 *AB* 861: 95.
35 Folcuin, *Gesta of the Abbots of St-Bertin* c. 66, *MGH SS* XIII, p. 620.
36 *Miracula Sancti Mauri, MGH SS* XV, p. 472.
37 *AB* 860: 94; 861: 95.
38 *AB* 859: 90.
39 *MGH Epp.* VIII, Ep. 136, addressed to Archbishops Rodulf of Bourges and Frotar of Bordeaux. See above: 174, 185, for the beginning of this story.

trying to escape this commitment. But if a man wooed a noblewoman for her powerful connections, he repudiated her at his peril. The breach between the *viri potentes*, Stephen and Raymund, threatened Aquitaine with 'scandals and seditions'. Hincmar's brief was to come up with some respectable canon-law arguments which would justify what Stephen wanted but which Raymund, his friends and kinsmen (who included Hincmar),[40] could accept. Stephen's claim that he had never slept with his bride supplied just the argument Hincmar needed. Raymund's daughter could be assured that as an intact virgin (though it was not yet known whether she would in fact uphold Stephen's claim, let alone whether anyone else would believe it) she remained 'free to choose' between the convent and another marriage-partner. Hincmar suggested, 'in lieu of the compensation' prescribed by Roman law for breach of marital contract, 'she should be returned to her father along with the bride-gift Stephen had given her', even though the marriage had not been consummated.[41] The Aquitanian archbishops were now to help the 'prince of the land', meaning the Young Charles, and the other magnates, resolve the dispute.[42] Raymund had been offered a face-saving formula and a material inducement: he was invited to persuade his daughter (whose chilling treatment by all the men concerned, not least her kinsman Hincmar, seems to have escaped previous commentators on this case) to corroborate Stephen's story. For the time being, it seems, Archbishops Rodulf and Frotar had some success in getting the settlement agreed. Hence, even though Pippin had resumed his old alliance with Robert and the Bretons,[43] this no longer posed the same threat as before. Hincmar had done what Charles wanted, yet secured the best deal he could for Raymund. Raymund's daughter was expendable; Young Charles's subkingdom was not. It looks as if Stephen was already earmarked by Charles the Bald, or perhaps chosen by the Young Charles himself, as the mainstay of the new regime in Aquitaine. The subkingdom's political centre was now to be Bourges, better pro-

40   Above Ch. 5: 140; Nelson 1991a: 11, n. 44.
41   Ep. 136, p. 98. Hincmar was aware of the logical inconsistency here.
42   Ibid. p. 106.
43   *AB* 859: 90.

tected than Poitiers from the Viking warbands who remained active on the Loire and down the western coast.

Stephen's case demonstrates the crucial importance of what we tend to class as 'private' family matters in the public affairs of an early medieval kingdom. Another marital dispute at just the same time caused repercussions throughout *all* the Carolingian kingdoms. For in this case the husband was a king. Lothar II 'as a youth still in his father's house' had an acknowledged relationship with Waldrada, a noblewoman from Alsace.[44] Perhaps the pair were married according to custom: in Carolingian Francia, canon lawyers were still in the process of clarifying just what procedures they would accept as constituting a valid marriage. Waldrada produced two daughters and a son, Hugh.[45] But Lothar I's death in September 855 had left Lothar II in a very dangerous position, vulnerable, in particular, to the hostility of his older brother, the Emperor Louis II of Italy. This explains why Lothar II late in 855 sought security in a marriage, with unequivocal church approval, to someone else – a woman with precisely the political connections he urgently needed. Theutberga, who now became Lothar's queen, had a brother called Hubert, a cleric in minor orders (though his enemies alleged he kept hawks and hunting dogs and enjoyed the company of actresses).[46] He held the abbacy of St-Maurice in the Valais and so controlled the Mons Iovis Pass (the modern Great St Bernard). The short-term benefits of the marriage were as obvious as the main route between Francia and Italy on a map of the Carolingian world.

By 860, though, Lothar II no longer envisaged much danger from his older brother: it had become clear that the 'emperor of Italy' was just too far away to intervene in Francia. Instead, it was Louis the German and Charles the Bald who especially after they had made peace in 860 threatened their nephew with the proverbial wickedness of wicked uncles. Lothar had fathered no children by Theutberga. In this combination of circumstances, historians have found the explanation for Lothar's attempt to get a

44 Regino 864, p. 80. Schmid 1968: 128–34 suggests she came from the Moselle area.
45 His birth-date is uncertain, perhaps as early as 855.
46 Pope Benedict III, *MGH Epp*. V, p. 613. See Genealogy V.

divorce, assuming that his priority was to get his son by Waldrada legitimised.[47] But though political factors account very nicely for the making of the marriage, they do so much less convincingly for its failure. Other queens, Ermentrude for instance, survived large shifts in political circumstances, including the disgrace of close kinsmen. And in fact Lothar rejected Theutberga even *before* any significant shift had occurred – that is, as early as 857.[48] Hence, if Theutberga had no children, she had been given little chance to produce any. In the dossier drawn up against her in 860, where one of the charges was abortion, there could be no allegation of sterility. It seems best to explain Lothar's actions as well-informed contemporaries did: he loved Waldrada[49] and he felt a strong personal aversion to Theutberga.[50] In February 860, a council of Lothar's bishops met at Aachen, and made public what Theutberga had 'voluntarily revealed' in the confessional: before her marriage, she had had anal intercourse with her brother Hubert, and aborted the foetus thus conceived. She begged the bishops (with, adds the verbatim record, 'a bitter look') to let her spend the rest of her life doing penance in a convent: a request the bishops willingly granted.[51] Lothar then set about getting an annulment on the grounds that a woman guilty of incest could not validly enter into a marriage. Subsequently, Theutberga revealed her state of mind: 'I will say whatever they want – not because it's true but because I fear for my life'.[52]

Hubert fled to Charles's kingdom, and later that same year, Theutberga escaped to join him. Both evidently reckoned that protection was most likely to be found in the west. Meanwhile Hincmar produced a lengthy treatise rejecting the judgement of his Lotharingian colleagues: Theutberga's guilt had not been proven, and the whole case must be heard anew.[53] 'Lothar fearing his Uncle Char-

---

47 Konecny 1976: 106–8; Wemple 1981: 84–5.
48 *AB* 857: 84.
49 *AX* 861, for 860. Cf. Lothar's charter of 18 May 863, calling Waldrada his *amantissima coniunx*.
50 *AB* 860: 92.
51 *MGH Capit.* II, no. 306, pp. 466–7.
52 *MGH Epp.* VII, p. 277.
53 *De Divortio Lotharii et Teutbergae, PL* 125, cols. 639–40.

les allied himself with Louis the German and handed him over a part of his kingdom, namely Alsace, on account of that alliance'.[54] Charles at this point probably did not have the whole of the Middle Kingdom in his sights. It looked as if Lothar's divorce plans might well work out, especially when he had drummed his bishops into line so successfully. But Lothar's difficulties could clearly be exploited by his uncles, and his brothers too, to extend their own kingdoms piecemeal at his expense and thereby replenish their stocks of *honores*.[55] Nor was Lothar the only nephew whose realm seemed to offer prospects of rich pickings to his Uncle Charles. Late in 861 some of the local nobles 'invited' Charles to take over the kingdom of Provence, allegedly because their nominal ruler, the epileptic youngest son of Lothar I, was 'useless and unsuited to the office of king'.[56] Though the promised support did not materialise this time (the young king's *bajulus*, Count Gerald of Vienne did not abandon him)[57] Charles's rapid swoop towards the Rhône valley was another straw in the wind. Throughout the rest of his reign, he was going to seek to expand his realm at the expense of Lothar's sons.

The 'wherewithal to reward followers' was not the only consideration a king had to take into account. Royal fathers – unless their descent line was threatened (as Lothar's was) with extinction for lack of legitimate sons – had to meet the demands of legitimate filial ambition. Long reigns, like the lives of adult men in general, tended to fall into two phases: in the first, a king married and worked to secure his inheritance for his sons; in the second, a rising generation of sons challenged their father's position and power. In 861, for instance, Louis the German's eldest son Karlmann was now about thirty, himself married and with his own household and following to support. With help from several of his wife's kinsmen he rebelled against his father. Louis quickly put down the revolt and took revenge: 'he deprived Karlmann's father-in-law Ernest of his *honores*, and expelled him and his (i.e. Ernest's) nephews from his

54   *AB* 860: 93.
55   *AB* 858: 87; 859: 91 record Lothar's grants to his brothers.
56   *AB* 861: 96.
57   Hincmar Ep. 142 indicates that Gerald's own interests were at stake.

kingdom'.[58] (Such detailed information on individual careers is due to Hincmar, who at this point took up authorship of the *AB*.) The twist in this particular story is that the exiles sought refuge with Karlmann's uncle – none other than Charles the Bald, 'who received them warmly and consoled them with *honores*'.[59] This group of highborn 'refugees' were perhaps even more welcome to Charles than Theutberga and Hubert. Not only was their move westwards a blow to Louis the German: they brought with them another of their kinsmen – Adalard, the former seneschal, and uncle of Charles's wife, who since 844 had resided in the Middle Kingdom, acquiring a power-base in the region of Trier. Adalard probably jumped before being pushed. Charles, perhaps with Queen Ermentrude's encouragement, found Adalard the key political role of *bajulus* for Louis the Stammerer. Against this westward flow of noble *honores*-seekers, Lothar managed to tempt into his kingdom Hugh son of Conrad, abbot of St-Germain, in 861. (Hugh was Lothar's first cousin: their mothers were sisters.) Rather than part of a 'Welf' reaction to the revival of 'the queen's party' at Charles's court, Hugh's departure was a personal response to the vacating of Lotharingian *honores*, and to the chance of exploiting his close kin-tie with Lothar, a relationship mentioned by Hincmar. Hugh's brother Conrad did not move with him, however.[60]

If Charles benefited, on balance, from the revolt of his nephew, Louis the German's son, he faced similar problems of his own in 862. In Aquitaine, his son Young Charles married without his permission (the boy had barely reached his fifteenth year) but with the encouragement of Stephen, son of Hugh. The woman he chose was 'the widow of Count Humbert': Hincmar characteristically fails to name the woman concerned (the imposition of anonymity on women was a common symptom of medieval misogyny), yet suggests the marriage's importance. Humbert had perhaps been count of Nevers and Stephen himself may have been his successor.[61] Charles the Bald issued

58 *AB* 861: 94. Cf. *AF* 861, 862: 55. Ernest was duke of Bavaria.
59 *AB* 861: 95. Louis the German may have feared that Charles might 'receive' Karlmann.
60 *AB* 864: 117. Cf. T. 261. See Wollasch 1957a: 209–11.
61 *AB* 862: 99–100. Cf. Auzias 1937: 305–6, n. 3, and 312, n. 18, for another reconstruction.

a peremptory summons to his son. The lad thought it advisable to ask for a safe-conduct before facing his father, and left their meeting 'like a man subdued'.[62] Charles's difficulties with this son were not over: Young Charles and Stephen were probably implicated in the rebellion in Toulouse in 863 of which Raymund was the prime victim. Charles's problems were compounded when the *Marchio* Hunfrid of Gothia, one of the *carissimi* of 859, joined the rebels, seizing Toulouse while Stephen took control of Clermont.[63] Hunfrid had had his own contacts, in 858, with a rebel against Cordoba, the Muslim lord of Zaragoza in north-eastern Spain,[64] and it was perhaps attempts to renew this alliance in 863 that brought an embassy from Cordoba to Charles in the winter of 863–4 to which Charles responded with a return embassy in 864.[65] Again a 'dual of marquises'[66] threatened Charles's authority in a major region and on a frontier. Charles defused both threats, expelling Hunfrid and dismembering his build-up of territorial power.[67] Meanwhile these conflicts had attracted the intervention of Viking warbands, notably active in the early 860s on the coast and rivers of Aquitaine. (In 863, Angoulême was sacked, and its count killed, though the Vikings themselves suffered heavy losses.)[68] With one such warband Pippin II, still in Aquitaine but now evidently bereft of other help, attacked Toulouse.[69] Charles tackled the rebels effectively on the home front: he came to spend Christmas 863 at Nevers and imposed his paternal authority on his namesake in no uncertain terms.[70] Once again Vikings did Charles's work for him: Stephen was killed in a Viking attack on Clermont,[71] while the failure of Pippin II's

62 *AB* 862: 100. Queen Ermentrude was also present at this meeting.
63 Cf. *AB* 863: 105, 864: 111. Calmette 1917: 172.
64 Aimoin, *Translatio SS Aurelii et Georgii* cc. 2, 5, *PL* 115, cols. 941, 943.
65 *AB* 864: 110, 119–20; 865: 129.
66 *AB* 862: 101 and n. 21.
67 *AB* 864: 118. Hincmar's comment that the *missi* 'did little of any use' obscures this key point. Raymund's son Bernard now became count of Toulouse, another Bernard *marchio* of 'part of Gothia'; *AB* 865: 122, 869: 151.
68 *AAng* 863.
69 Aimoin, *Translatio S. Vincentii in Galliam* cc. 11, 12, *PL* 126, col. 1022. Cf. *AB* 864: 111.
70 *AB* 863: 110.
71 *AB* 864: 111.

attack on Toulouse helped seal his fate. In the spring of 864, Ranulf Count of Poitou, captured Pippin 'by a trick' and handed him over to Charles.[72] This time, there would be no escape.

Meanwhile Charles faced another problem as a pater-familias when, in 862, his daughter Judith eloped with Count Baldwin.[73] Control of royal women was a crucial, and sensitive, issue for early medieval kings, and ninth-century Carolingian history had already produced several variations on the theme of liberation.[74] Women through whom men sought *Königsnähe* were not always mere pawns, even when men took the initiatives in the game. Judith's original marriage to Æthelwulf in 856 had been arranged by Charles; her second marriage, as a fourteen-year old widow, to her stepson in Wessex two years later may have been outwith her father's control. Widowed for a second time in 860, Judith had perhaps little option but to return to Francia and her father's custody at Senlis. Count Baldwin had obvious political reasons for showing interest in her (his county included Bruges,[75] and he may have hoped to benefit from Judith's cross-Channel contacts as well as from becoming Charles's son-in-law). But Hincmar in the *AB* makes Judith the subject of the key sentence, suggesting that it was her own choice to respond. Knowing that her father would not consent, she got the consent of her brother Louis the Stammerer instead, subverting correct familial relations, and presenting her father with a *fait accompli*.[76] Charles's furious reaction showed the potential damage of such acts of defiance in the heart of the family. Baldwin and Judith knew just which allies to mobilise: the pope, for moral pressure, and the Viking warlord of Frisia, for pressure of another sort.[77] It took nearly two years be-

---

72 Continuator of Ado of Vienne, *MGH SS* II, p. 324. *AB* 864: 119 is unspecific about which 'Aquitanians' were involved.

73 *AB* 862: 97. Hincmar does not name Baldwin's county; but see below, n. 75.

74 Above 16, 148, 199. Cf. Nelson 1990e.

75 Bruges was in Flanders, an area much smaller than the later medieval county; Dhondt 1948: 106, n. 5.

76 *AB* 862: 97.

77 Nicholas I, *MGH Epp.* VI, pp. 272–5; Hincmar *MGH Epp.* VIII, Epp. 155, 156.

fore Charles acknowledged his daughter's marriage, and 'on the counsel of his faithful men' received Baldwin as his son-in-law.[78] Thereafter, however, Baldwin proved loyal.

Louis the Stammerer imitated not only his sister's action, but also, and more directly, that of his younger brother Charles of Aquitaine. Resentful at being placed under a *bajulus* when he was now an adult (he was 15 on 1 November 861), Louis went into open rebellion against his father at the beginning of 862 and married, again without his father's consent, Ansgard, sister of a favoured supporter in northern Neustria; then he headed towards the Breton March, and with Salomon's help attacked his old rival Robert and ravaged Anjou.[79] The revolt quickly collapsed, thanks in part to Robert's sharp response. By the late summer, Louis the Stammerer was offering his capitulation. For a second time, the projected Neustrian subkingdom had blown up in Charles the Bald's face. Louis was to get no third chance. Already the abbacy of St-Martin, Tours, had been removed from him and granted instead to Theutberga's brother Hubert.[80] Louis and his wife were summoned to Charles's presence, and Louis was assigned the county of Meaux and the lay-abbacy of St-Crispin there.

To understand why this was something other than a consolation-prize, however, the picture needs to be widened to include Vikings, and Bretons too, along with Franks. All were players in the same game. When Salomon and Robert fought each other on the Loire in 862 Salomon 'hired twelve [Danish] ships by a legal hire-contract (*locario iure*)', while Robert 'paid 6,000 lb and exchanged hostages' to secure the services of other Northmen who had recently arrived in the area.[81] Charles had used similar tactics with Ragnar in the 840s, and Bjørn in 858. Exploiting Francia's rich resources, in 860 he offered Weland's Danes, who had earlier ravaged on the Somme, 3,000 lb [of silver] to attack the Vikings on the Seine.[82] The warband based at Oissel since 858 had had plenty of time to become familiar with the 'trading-post' at Chappes on the Seine upstream from

78 *AB* 863: 110.
79 *AB* 862: 97, 100. See Oexle 1969: 193.
80 *AB* 862: 98.
81 *AB* 862: 99.
82 *AB* 860: 92.

Troyes, and in January 861 they came up the river to attack Paris, and burn Melun.[83] Once back at Oissel, they were besieged by Weland's men whose fee Charles now increased to 5,000 lb plus livestock and corn. The Oissel Vikings surrendered after a few months: they had run out of food, but they had enough loot to pay Weland 6,000 lb of gold and silver on their own account.[84] The two groups headed down the Seine together to the sea. Now 'with winter approaching', says Hincmar innocuously, instead of either leaving the Seine altogether, or settling down near the river-mouth to await spring, the Vikings 'split up into their brotherhoods' and came back *upstream* to winter 'at various wharfs [*portus*] along the Seine as far as Paris'. Two special groups, however, came beyond Paris: Weland and his following took up quarters at Melun, while the former Oissel warband under Weland's son 'occupied the monastery of Fossés'. This is the point where Hincmar says that Louis the Stammerer was put 'under the guardianship [*bajulatio*] of Adalard the uncle of Queen Ermentrude and sent to guard the realm against the Northmen'.

The juxtaposition is curious. For Fossés was the family-monastery of Adalard and Queen Ermentrude.[85] Still more curious is the sequel: in January 862, the Fossés Vikings went up the Marne 'with a few ships' by night and looted the *civitas* of Meaux. This attack is recorded very soon after the event by a contemporary, Bishop Hildegar of Meaux, who makes it the occasion of a vitriolic attack on Charles and his men for allowing the Seine basin, 'the Paradise of his realm', to be laid waste. According to Hildegar, not only had the failure at Oissel in 858 made 'the realm of the people of the Franks a most shameful laughing-stock', but the wintering of the Vikings upstream from Paris in 861–2 was the result of 'treachery' [*infidelitas*].[86] He does not say whose. In the *AB*, the attack on Meaux immediately follows Louis the Stammerer's rebellion at the beginning of 862,

83 Lupus Ep. 119; *AB* 861: 94. Late in 858, Wenilo of Sens had got permission from Louis the German 'to take stones from the walls of Melun'; *MGH Conc.* III, no. 47B, c. 11, p. 467.
84 *AB* 861: 95. My account follows Coupland 1987: 56–7.
85 Above, Ch. 7: 176.
86 Hildegar, *Vita Faronis* cc. 123, 125, 127, *MGH SSRM* V, pp. 200–1. Hildegar attributed the survival of the church of Meaux in 862 to St Faro's intervention. See Wylie 1989.

which ended in a settlement whereby Louis was given the county of Meaux. One further juxtaposition has been alleged by a modern critic of Charles to 'border on cynicism:'[87] while Charles summoned an assembly at Pîtres (near Oissel) in June 862 to mobilise 'all the leading men of the realm' in constructing defences on the Seine, the *capitula* of that same assembly prohibited all gatherings and sworn associations that would have promoted self-help.[88]

One man's cynicism may be another's statesmanship. Charles's priorities were to maintain his political control, and to protect his heartlands, in that order. The same Vikings who threatened the second objective could help Charles achieve the first (and the second could be dealt with later). Quartering Vikings at Fossés (whence the monks had fled) could surely only have been done with Adalard's agreement. These warriors were in effect being recruited into Charles's service – as became quite explicit in summer 862 when Weland and his son agreed to be baptised.[89] (It seems to have been about this time too that a Viking named Ansleicus accepted Christianity, joined Charles's military household and then served as a go-between in Charles's efforts to recruit a further Viking warband.)[90] In January Charles was faced with Louis the Stammerer's revolt. Louis's later connection with Meaux, and the peculiar ferocity of Bishop Hildegar's verbal attack on Charles soon afterwards, evoke the suspicion that the bishop was at least a sympathiser with Louis. In that case, if Charles did not actually let the Fossés Vikings loose on Meaux, their activities there would not wholly have displeased him. In the ashes of Meaux's buildings, later in 862, Louis the Stammerer and Hildegar would have seen daily reminders of the wages of sin. The Viking attack on Meaux gave Charles the chance to achieve a notable military success. By stationing guards along the banks of the Marne and quickly rebuilding a barrage across the river behind the attackers, he blocked off their retreat and forced them to terms. They agreed to give Charles ten hostages selected by him, and to

87 Brunner 1979: 133.
88 *AB* 862: 194; *MGH Capit.* II, no. 272, c. 4, p. 309. Cf. above, 100.
89 *AB* 862: 99.
90 *Miracula Sancti Richarii* II, 16, *AA SS* Aprilis III, p. 456.

surrender 'all captives taken since they entered the Marne'.
A date was fixed for them to quit Charles's kingdom, along
with the rest of the Seine Vikings. Before the end of
March, the terms had been carried out.

At the assembly of Pîtres, in June 864, Charles took stock
of his position and tackled a wide range of problems. The
annual gifts swelled the royal coffers.[91] Charles (wearing
his gracious face) thanked the attenders warmly for their
fidelitas, and congratulated 'most if not all of you' for keeping the peace agreed at an assembly on the same spot two
years before. 'It's with all the more confidence that we now
tell you to toil manfully on the fortifications we have begun
building against the Northmen'. What had been laid down
in 862 had been 'made known, heard and received'. This
time Charles wanted everything in writing. He read out (or
had read out for him) 37 *capitula*, plus 3 supplementary
capitula, from a written text, in which Hincmar probably
had a hand. It was legislation on an imposing scale, covering every major aspect of royal power and royal government.[92]

The largest single topic (cc. 8–24) was the coinage re-
form, and associated regulations on markets, weights and
measures. The immediate object was fiscal: a *renovatio monetae* was the king's means of taxing all coin-users.[93] In the
longer run, the revaluation of the coinage would benefit all
those to whom substantial cash-renders were regularly paid.
Charles also addressed three other crucial subjects. First,
on military affairs: the death penalty was introduced for
anyone who sold mail-coats (*bruniae*),[94] weapons, or horses
to foreigners (c. 25); the entire male population were obliged to take part in fortifying *civitates*, building bridges and
causeways, and doing garrison duty – measures inspired by
the legislation of late antiquity and of 'foreign peoples', apparently a reference to the English (c. 27); a royal monopoly of fortification was vigorously asserted and orders were
given for unauthorised strongholds (*castella*) to be disman-
tled (supplementary c. 1). A second major theme was the
maintenance of royal income: all dues and services owed to

91 *AB* 864: 118. Cf. above 49–50.
92 *MGH Capit.* II, no. 273.
93 Above Ch. 2: 33–5.
94 Coupland 1990b: 39 translates 'body armour'.

the king were to be paid and the king's resources and property protected (cc. 5, 28–30, 34 and 37). Thirdly, Charles was concerned to protect and supervise royal agents (cc. 4, 5, 26 and supplementary c. 3). In conveying all these commands to those in the counties, the written word was accorded a vital role (prologue; cc. 35, 36). Was the legislation implemented? Coinage is the one area where surviving evidence gives a clear 'yes'.[95] Yet, if royal agents could operate a uniform system of coin-production and coin-use, why doubt their capacity to organise other generalised services? It can hardly be a coincidence that within a few years of 864, *civitas* fortification is documented at Angoulême as well as at Tours and Le Mans.[96]

The 864 Pîtres assembly also dealt with the affairs of the *regna*. In western Neustria, Charles had reapplied the tactics used for Erispoë and recognised Salomon's rule in Brittany, forging a bond of spiritual kinship probably through the baptismal sponsoring of Salomon's son.[97] At the same time Charles granted Salomon benefices in Anjou. But his Neustrian settlement also entailed the granting of *honores* to leading Franks, some of them former allies of Robert, others his local rivals. Oaths of fidelity were received from all these beneficiaries, notably from Salomon and a large retinue of Breton nobles; and at Pîtres a 50lb. tribute was handed over 'from Salomon's land according to the custom of his predecessors'.[98] Fifty pounds of silver was a small sum compared with the Viking hire-fee of 861, for instance. Nevertheless it had symbolic significance. No Frankish ruler had *ever* ruled Brittany intensively, that is, held royal lands there, stayed there, made grants there, or intervened there directly. Royal government was a matter of indirect authority exercised through a chosen local agent: of confrontations and conversations and offers of security, of facing down individuals' resistance, of imprinting the royal face firmly in the memories of men. Salomon, like Erispoë, came to meet Charles, participated in this political world because he needed the legitimacy Charles could bestow. Charles remained his lord; and grants of regalia streng-

95 Coupland 1985: 713–4; Metcalf and Northover 1989.
96 *AAng.* 868; *AB* 869: 164.
97 See Smith 1992: ch. 4.
98 *AB* 864: 118.

thened rather than weakened Charles's superior status. Salomon was on a par with Charles's Frankish beneficiaries, and with Louis the Stammerer himself, who in 865 was to be sent back to Neustria without any formal royal title but as a recipient of *honores* and royal estates from his father. Charles's authority in Neustria was a reality: having settled a long-running dispute between the see of Le Mans and the monastery of St-Calais in the latter's favour in October 863, he was able to use Bishop Robert of Le Mans as a royal envoy in 864.[99]

In Aquitaine too, Charles's authority was strengthened in 864. Early that year, Young Charles was incapacitated by a terrible accident[100] and his father resumed *de facto* responsibility for Aquitaine. To Pîtres, therefore, came leading Aquitanians; there too Pippin II was brought by his Aquitanian captors and solemnly condemned to death as 'a traitor to the fatherland and to Christendom'.[101] This is the language of Theodosian ideology, just as the content of the 864 Capitulary was inspired by the Theodosian Code. Charles was projecting himself as a ruler who aspired to equal the Christian Roman emperors 'our predecessors': perhaps even hoped to claim (like Justinian with Solomon) that he had surpassed them. The composite nature of Charles's realm lent colour to this idea of imperial rulership: he was a ruler not of one *regnum* alone but of *regna*.

After 864, Charles kept a close eye on developments in Neustria and Aquitaine. The alliance with Salomon was reinforced in 867, and again in 868, when Breton oaths of fidelity were recompensed by a gift of 'royal gear used for liturgical purposes' and concerted action was organised against Vikings on the Loire.[102] Charles had no consistent policy of entrenching 'Robertian power' in Neustria. In 865 Robert was 'transferred' to the countship of Autun in northern Burgundy, and though he returned to Anjou in 866, he was killed fighting against Vikings at Brissarthe later that year, whereupon his young sons were deprived of

---

99   T. 258; *AB* 863: 110, 864: 117.
100 Above Ch. 3: 68.
101 *AB* 864: 119. Pippin was incarcerated at the royal stronghold of Senlis and seems to have died soon after.
102 *AB* 867: 139, 868: 151. The alliance held till Salomon's murder; *AB* 874: 186.

their father's Neustrian *honores*.[103] Charles's cousin 'the cleric Hugh' son of Conrad (he had returned to the western kingdom when Lothar II's patronage proved unrewarding) was installed 'in Robert's place' as holder of the counties of Touraine and Anjou and the abbacy of St-Martin, Tours,[104] and remained Charles's chief supporter in the Loire valley for the rest of the reign.

With his own sons, Charles was unlucky: of the two who had rebelled, Young Charles never recovered from his accident of 864 and died in 866; and by then three others had died in childhood or youth. This left Charles the Bald with only two healthy sons, of whom the younger, Carloman, had been tonsured.[105] As a king, he had to be concerned for the future of his own line. Was he also concerned for the feelings of his wife? Ermentrude had perhaps helped reconcile him with their rebellious offspring[106] and exerted a good deal of political influence, not least in 866, when she was involved in Charles's rapprochement with Lothar II.[107] Perhaps it was the impressive ceremonial of Theutberga's reinstatement which suggested to Ermentrude herself the idea of ritual consecration at the abbey of St-Medard, Soissons and a promise of divinely blessed fecundity.[108] For Charles himself, caught in the cleft stick of an over-narrow descent-line and filial insubordination, the best hope was for new sons 'of the sort to give solace to the church and defence to the realm and desirable help to the faithful men'.[109] Charles meanwhile had to re-deploy those sons he had. After the Young Charles's death in September 866, Louis the Stammerer was installed in Aquitaine early the following year; but Charles kept him on a tight rein, appointing Louis's household officers himself from among his own entourage.[110] This was a new style of Aquitanian subkingdom: Louis never issued coins or charters there. Filial rebellion was no longer associated with an 'Aquitanian

---

103 *AB* 865: 128, 866: 135, 868: 143; Regino 867, for 866: 92–3.
104 *AB* 866: 136.
105 Above Ch. 7: 174.
106 As implied by *AB* 862: 100, and Hincmar Ep. 169, pp. 144– 5.
107 *AB* 866: 132. See Hyam 1990: 163.
108 Stafford 1990: 146–7. For Theutberga, see below 216–17.
109 *MGH Capit.* II, no. 301, p. 454.
110 *AB* 867: 138.

problem'; and once Pippin II had disappeared from the scene, it became clear that the 'problem' had never really been one of separatism.

The disposition of *honores* and the management of magnate interests was always the most delicate part of a ruler's business, as Louis the Pious's reign had shown. At Pîtres in June 864, rivalry between magnates simmered just beneath the surface, and nearly erupted into violence. The man responsible for the trouble was 'Bernard, the son, by both birth and behaviour, of the long-dead tyrant Bernard', that is, the younger son of Bernard of Septimania whom Charles had had executed in 844.[111] The Younger Bernard is famous in modern historiography as 'Hairypaws', meaning 'Foxy', the nickname by which contemporaries knew him later in his career.[112] The baby of whom his mother Dhuoda wrote tenderly in 841 had grown up to seek power in the Autunois, where his father, elder brother and uncle had held *honores* before him.[113] He had made his peace with Charles sometime before June 864, for he attended the Pîtres assembly as count of Autun,[114] and left early with the king's permission. Alarming rumours became rife: 'some said that he planned to assassinate Charles, to avenge his father's death', while others alleged that the intended victims were Counts Robert and Ranulf, then high in royal favour. The upshot was that Charles deprived Bernard 'Hairypaws' of his countship and 'granted it to Robert instead'.[115] This was easier said than done: Bernard had inherited lands and local influence in the Autunois, and he refused to budge. This rebellion in Burgundy became especially serious in 865, and vigorous mobilisation of Charles's supporters in the region was needed.[116] It looks as if Charles's own brother-in-law William had joined the revolt: never a conspicuous beneficiary of *Königsnähe* (he is otherwise totally undocumented), he now became its casualty –

---

111   *AB* 864: 119. Cf. above Ch. 6: 139.
112   *AB* 880: 221.
113   Dhuoda, pref. pp. 84–5; Nithard III, 2; cf. Wollasch 1957b: 187–8. Bouchard 1986: 657 suggests that Bernard 'Hairypaws' had married the daughter of Warin, count of Mâcon.
114   This is indicated retrospectively in *AB* 866: 131.
115   *AB* 864: 119.
116   *MGH Capit.* II, no. 274, pp. 330–3.

captured in Burgundy, and beheaded for treason in September 866.[117] Bernard 'Hairypaws' remained to be dealt with. Probably in 868 he fled Charles's kingdom for Lotharingia.[118] Charles faced similar difficulty in ousting Count Gerald of Bourges in 867 (perhaps for failure to counter a Viking attack). His decision may not have been implemented before 872.[119] But such delay is hardly proof of royal impotence. To 'dishonour' a great man was a major undertaking for *any* early medieval ruler. That Charles was able in the end to force out lay magnates whom he distrusted is a sign of strength.

The positive business of granting *honores* was firmly in the king's hands. Cases of ecclesiastical patronage continue to illustrate this particularly well. Charles pushed through the appointment of his palatine cleric Wulfad to the archbishopric of Bourges quite quickly in 866, assuring the pope that Wulfad's 'prudence and vigour' were indispensable, especially when Vikings still threatened Berry.[120] At around the same time, Charles was surely behind the appointment of the Irishman Elias to the see of Angoulême.[121] Here it was not only the bishopric that Charles could bestow: around 865, he was able to appoint another outsider, Wulfgrin, to the countship. It was Wulfgrin presumably who saw to the rebuilding of the fortifications of Angoulême on royal orders in 868.[122] The career of Archbishop Frotar of Bordeaux, recipient of the abbacies of St-Hilary, Poitiers, in 868, and of Charroux in Poitou a little later, provides further evidence that Charles could deploy patronage in Aquitaine.[123] Three Aquitanian magnates, the *marchiones* of Toulouse, of Gothia and of the Auvergne, obeyed Charles's summons to attend the assembly of Pîtres in August 868.[124]

Charles's position in his Frankish heartlands also held

117   *AB* 866: 134.
118   Inferred from *AB* 869: 165 (and cf. 868: 151 and n. 21).
119   *AB* 867: 143, 868: 143, 872: 177. Cf. Martindale 1990a: 131.
120   *AB* 866: 133–4; *PL* 124, col. 874. Wulfad had been Carloman's tutor.
121   *Sacramentaire d'Angoulême*, p. 312.
122   Above n. 96.
123   *AB* 868: 144; T. 374, 375.
124   *AB* 868: 151 with n. 21. Hincmar, *AB* 869: 153 seems to blame the non-appearance of these three at Cosne-sur-Loire in January 869 not on their disloyalty but on Charles's bad timing.

firm. After the failure of Adalard, then of Robert to mount successful resistance to the Vikings on the Seine in 865–6, Charles himself took the task in hand. Spurred above all by a surprise-attack on St-Denis in October 865 (it was failure to prevent this that cost Adalard and his colleagues their jobs), Charles induced the Vikings to quit the Seine by raising a 4,000 lb tribute-payment through taxation.[125] Graduated impositions on peasant holdings (6d. per free manse, 3d. per servile manse, 1d. per *accola* and ½d. per *hospitium*) were supplemented by a flat rate of 1d. on all manses. Further contributions were required from traders (a tenth levied on their moveable wealth), priests (again a graduated property levy) and free Franks. Though the detailed arrangements are debatable, what is significant is that payments were required from peasants not only on royal or ecclesiastical estates but also on the lands of the lay magnates each of whom was responsible for collecting the contributions from his own *honores*.[126] The relatively small scale of the total 'take' however suggests that only *part* of the realm was required to pay, namely Charles's heartland of Francia. It was Viking access to this area which Charles was determined to block by the construction of a fortified bridge at Pont-de-l'Arche just downstream from Pîtres.[127] There were no further Viking incursions up the Seine during the last decade of Charles's reign. Some Vikings went back to Frisia, while most seem to have turned their attention to England.[128] For his part, Charles thereafter effectively defended the 'paradise' where his main estates and palaces lay. He no longer had to engage in the risky game of playing off one Viking warband against others in his own backyard.

To help him rule Francia, Charles depended on a tight network of loyal counts. A royal judgement happens to survive from 868 with the names of nine counts in attendance on the king at Rouy near Laon in April.[129] Top of the list is the chamberlain Engelram, whose county lay in the north-

---

125 *AB* 865: 128–9. See above Ch. 2.
126 *AB* 866: 130.
127 Ado, *Chron.* 868: 323. See Dearden 1989 and 1990,
128 *AB* 866: 131; *ASC* 866, 'A', p. 47: 'a great army came to the land of the English'.
129 T. 314.

east of the realm, near that of Charles's son-in-law, Count Baldwin. Also on the 868 list are Count Nibelung of the Vexin and Count Aledramn (II) of Troyes. The operations of mints and markets, the summoning of local courts, the mustering of troops, the organisation of local fortifications, and, last but not least, the maintenance of royal vassals on comital benefices, were managed by counts like these. Charles also systematically cultivated and exploited church resources as a reserve of patronage. In the case of St-Denis, he took direct control. After the death of Abbot Louis in 867, Charles became lay-abbot himself and made his own arrangements over benefices granted on St-Denis's lands. There is no sign that the abbey suffered materially during the next decade: on the contrary, the king could protect and favour as well as exploit. It was during these years that the abbey was fortified, while, at the same time, its scriptorium and workshops reached an apogee of skill and output.[130] The monastery of St-Bertin was bestowed in 866 on the noble cleric Hilduin, who paid Charles 30 lb of gold for it, but went down in the abbey's annals as a major benefactor.[131] Other abbacies went to clerics who were also close kinsmen: notably Charles's cousin Hugh who received St-Martin, Tours, and his third son Carloman, who accumulated St-Medard, Soissons (863), St-Germain, Auxerre (866) and St-Amand (c. 866/7), and led a *scara* (rapid-deployment force) into Neustria against the Vikings in 868.[132] Charles's control of episcopal appointments made for effective collaboration between king and bishops in providing for the king's faithful men. Hincmar of Rheims was proud of the consistent record of service rendered from his church to the king.[133] Only with Hincmar of Laon did trouble blow up in 868 precisely over the allocation of benefices on the see's estates: the bishop thought the king had asked for too many; the king, who claimed to have added 2,000 manses to the lands of the see for just this purpose, objected to the arbitrary way the bishop had distributed the grants.[134] The dispute turned dangerous – but

130 Brown 1989: 357–400.
131 Folcuin, *Gesta* c. 69, *MGH SS* XIII, p. 621.
132 See Nelson 1988b: 109
133 Above Ch. 3: 58.
134 See Nelson 1991b.

that was because it had become embroiled in the much larger one of the Lotharingian succession.

The divorce-case of Lothar II had always had large political implications. Acceptance of Lothar's union with Waldrada would make their son Hugh a legitimate heir and so assure the Middle Kingdom's continuance into the next generation. Lothar's brother Emperor Louis II, and his uncles, Louis the German and Charles the Bald, would have to reconcile themselves to the loss of those Frankish heartlands in which Lothar I had seen the very 'wherewithal' of Carolingian power. The aristocracy of the Middle Kingdom had made a choice in 855, in opting for Lothar II's succession against the claims of his elder brother. In the early 860s, the Emperor Louis seemed to align himself with his brother as a fellow-member of Lothar I's descent-line, against their uncles. A likely outcome was that those uncles, for their part, would eventually acknowledge Waldrada's son as Lothar II's heir, striking the best bargains they could and settling for informal influence (like Louis the German's in 855) and marginal territorial gains. Lothar II, manoeuvring his own bishops into line at synods in Aachen (862) and Metz (863) must have felt increasingly confident of getting his way.

Lothar reckoned without Pope Nicholas I – a man determined to extract the maximum authority from his official position. Once the rejected Queen Theutberga had appealed directly to him, Nicholas perceived a test-case of the papacy's moral prestige. Thereafter no legal arguments would wash.[135] When Lothar's two archbishops, Gunther of Cologne and Theutgaud of Trier, came to Rome in 863 with a well-prepared dossier, Nicholas declared them deposed. It was, as the archbishops protested, unheard-of conduct on the pope's part to treat them 'as his clerics instead of his brothers and fellow-bishops'.[136] Nicholas certainly flouted the expectations of many contemporaries – not least of the Emperor Louis II, who had secured his election in 858 and now tried unsuccessfully to pressure him into reinstating the Lotharingian archbishops.[137] For

---

135   Kottje 1988.
136   *AF* 864: 61; cf. *AB* 864: 116.
137   *AB* 864: 112.

Charles, however, this high-handed and high-minded pope was an unexpected ally: both, though for different reasons, were firm defenders of Theutberga. Charles's own attitude had hardened in 863 when Lothar gave support to Judith and Baldwin. Unfortunately for Lothar, his efforts to mobilise Louis the German against Charles coincided with the rebellion of Louis's son Karlmann: Louis, fearing Charles's intervention on Karlmann's behalf, could not risk giving Lothar anything but a lukewarm response. In the end, Lothar's uncles had a common interest in adherence to Pope Nicholas's line; for should Lothar be denied his divorce, then – given his well-known feelings about Theutberga – he was extremely unlikely to father a legitimate heir. His kingdom would then fall into the ready hands of his uncles and their progeny. Both Louis and Charles urgently needed any 'wherewithal' they could come by, to provide for their adult sons.

The old allies of Strasbourg now presented a common front as avuncular pillars of familial propriety. In February 865, Louis (with his sons in tow) and Charles met at Tusey on the Meuse – in Lothar's kingdom.[138] They cited the Biblical text I Timothy 5.8: 'If any provide not for his own, and specially for those of his own house, he hath denied the faith, and is worse than an infidel'. Both Charles and Louis had suffered familial disorder and restored control: their sons now were 'subordinate and obedient as sons ought to be to their fathers and lords'. Louis and Charles promised to love each other's sons 'like their own, in true love'. As for their nephew, they expressed grave concern: he was young, and he had had bad counsellors. He was 'their flesh and blood' (Gen. 2, 23). He had defied God's law on marriage, and must be made to see the error of his ways. The whole text, like Hincmar's brief notice of the meeting,[139] is a masterpiece of innuendo. Only from the *AF* do we learn that a formal pact was agreed, with Hincmar as one of its guarantors.[140] With uncles like Charles and Louis, Lothar II needed no enemies. On 15 August 865, the Feast of the Assumption of the Virgin, he received back Theutberga

138   *MGH Capit.* II, no. 244, pp. 165–7.
139   *AB* 865: 121. ('Douzy' here is an error for Tusey)
140   *AF* 864: 62. Charles's other guarantor was Engilram.

from the hands of the papal legate Arsenius, hotfoot from his uncles' courts. It was probably for this occasion that one of Lothar's craftsmen produced the carved rock-crystal (now in the British Museum) portraying the story of Susannah, wrongfully accused of adultery, and finally vindicated by divine intervention.

Theutberga's reinstatement and its likely eventual result did not prevent both Charles and Louis from trading a little meanwhile on their own accounts. In 866, Lothar yielded to Charles the monastery of St-Vaast, Arras which since 843 had remained an anomalous enclave of Lotharingian territory within Charles's kingdom.[141] In 867, after Louis and Charles had met in early summer at Metz (again in the Middle Kingdom), Lothar made an agreement with Louis, whereby's Waldrada's son Hugh was given Alsace and put under Louis's protection.[142] From the mid-860s, a number of ambitious clerics were drawn from Lothar's realm to Charles's court.[143] Charles also cultivated the goodwill of leading men in the Middle Kingdom: for instance Bishop Adventius of Metz, Archbishop Ado of Vienne, and Count Gerald of Vienne. When Nicholas I's death on 13 November 867 opened the possibility that his successor might prove more accommodating over Lothar's divorce, Louis closed ranks with Charles: meeting in June 868 at Metz, again in Lothar's kingdom, Lothar's uncles made an agreement (whose text, this time, they kept confidential) that 'if God should grant them part of their nephews' realms', they would make a fair division between the two of them, acting 'without deceit, as a brother ought rightly to do towards his brother'. The echo of the Strasbourg Oaths is plangent.[144]

Lothar's desperation and all-too-justified suspicions were reflected in successive visits to his uncles in the summer of 868. From Louis, he extracted an oath 'not to do him [Lothar] harm if he married Waldrada'.[145] Charles was evasive, promising only a further meeting (which never took

141   *AB* 866: 132.
142   *AB* 867: 139.
143   For Hilduin, above 214. For Ratbod and Stephen, see *MGH SS* XV, p. 569.
144   *MGH Capit.* II, no. 245. For the date, see Calmette 1901: 195–200.
145   *AB* 868: 150.

place). It looks as if Lothar tried to bring pressure on Charles. He welcomed Bernard 'Hairypaws', who finally left Autun, and granted him lands in the Ornois to the west of Toul. Lothar seems also to have tried to enlist the support of Bishop Hincmar of Laon, already in dispute with Charles over benefices on church lands.[146] Charles took stern revenge on the bishop, subjecting him to a public dressing-down and confiscating the temporal goods of his see.[147] The bishop had been present at the Metz meeting in June 868: had he dared (or threatened) to divulge its terms to Lothar? When early in 869 Lothar himself went to Rome to plead with the new pope, Hadrian II, Charles refused to give any kind of guarantee to keep out of Lotharingia during Lothar's absence.

In all these developments, Hincmar of Rheims was a key actor. He had been at odds with Charles in 866 over Wulfad's appointment to Bourges. Wulfad had originally been ordained by Ebbo in 840/1: recognition of the validity of his orders called in question the validity of Ebbo's deposition, hence of Hincmar's own consecration to Rheims in 845.[148] By 868, he was back in royal favour, and was present at Metz in June when Charles and Louis made their pact. This time, in writing up the *AB*, not only did Hincmar (as in 865) say nothing about his personal role, but he omitted all reference to the event itself. Hincmar's silence is understandable, for this was the unacceptable face of Carolingian diplomacy, but it warns how much of Carolingian diplomacy has escaped the written record altogether. Hincmar's commitment to Charles's Lotharingian policy was sincere enough, however. The archbishop wanted to extend his metropolitan jurisdiction effectively over the see of Cambrai, which belonged to the province of Rheims yet had been part of the Middle Kingdom since 843. Perhaps too, Hincmar dreamed of a revived papal vicariate of the Gauls, ecclesiastical authority on an imperial scale.

In 869, with Lothar far away in Italy, Charles was busy in Francia, organising the defences of the Seine and holding his summer assembly (as he had several times since 862) at

146 *AB* 868: 150–2.
147 *PL* 125, cols 1035–6.
148 *AB* 866: 132–3, 867: 138.

Pîtres. For help in constructing and garrisoning the bridge-heads there, he had already sent out detailed demands to holders of *honores* and benefices. The fortification of St-Denis had become a further priority. At both Pîtres and St-Denis, stone-defences as well as earthworks were to be built.[149] The everyday business of kingship went on: royal wrath was turned on the recalcitrant bishop of Laon;[150] careful arrangements were made for the liturgical commemoration of the king's vassal Wido, 'most dear to us', who had recently died.[151] Charles knew how to reward fidelity as well as how to punish the disloyal. From Pîtres, he and the queen went to Senlis where 'they distributed alms to holy places'. Here news reached them from Italy: Lothar II had died of fever on 8 August – without having secured his divorce, or his bastard son's inheritance.[152]

Charles wasted no time. He knew – and it is the *AF*, not Hincmar, who report this fact – that Louis the German lay desperately ill at Regensburg. Charles moved eastwards to Attigny, where two kinds of message reached him from Lotharingia. Some of the magnates there argued for delay and time to consult with Louis; others including Bishop Adventius[153] told Charles to come as fast as possible to Metz, promising that supporters would rally to him en route. There was no doubt in Hincmar's mind as to which counsel was wiser and 'more in line with the king's own interests'.[154] With Hincmar in his retinue,[155] Charles moved eastwards reaching Metz on 5 September. It was little more than a year since he and Louis the German had met there to agree a division of Lothar's kingdom: now Louis was far away in Bavaria. On 9 September 869, in the church of St-Stephen, where bishops had solemnly restored his imperial crown to Louis the Pious just 34 years before, Charles was consecrated king of what had been Lothar's kingdom. According to the *AF*, 'he gave orders that he was to be called emperor and augustus on the grounds that

---

149   *AB* 869: 153–4.
150   *AB* 869: 153.
151   T. 325.
152   *AB* 869: 156–7; the news arrived on 23 August.
153   Regino 869: 98.
154   *AB* 869: 157.
155   *PL* 126, col. 584.

now he would possess two realms' (that is, the West Frankish and Middle Kingdoms).[156] Hincmar designed the whole ritual to make very clear that this imperial kingship (imperial in the sense of containing plural *regna*) was Frankish. (Hincmar discounted the imperial regime of Lothar I's son Louis II, who had held the title of emperor since 855: Hincmar referred to him as 'so-called emperor *of Italy*'.)[157] In his address to the assembled nobility, Hincmar claimed that Charles was descended from Clovis (a form of the name Louis), who had been converted to the Catholic Faith 'along with his whole people' and anointed by Hincmar's predecessor St Remigius with oil specially brought from heaven 'of which we still have some'. Blurring the distinction between baptismal anointing and king-making (and drawing on the analogies between the two rites), Hincmar announced the inauguration of a new reign that was at the same time the continuation and climax of the whole mythic history of the Franks.[158] The archbishop intended Rheims as its sacred centre. For Charles, reconstituted Frankish unity signalled a revived Carolingian empire: his sights were set on Aachen, and beyond that, Rome.

156   *AF* 869: 69–70.
157   *AB* 863: 104. See Penndorf 1975.
158   *AB* 869: 161–2.

Chapter 9

869–877: GLITTERING PRIZES

Though Charles assumed no new title after 9 September 869, he took a grip on some traditional heartlands of his dynasty. On the very day of his consecration, Charles made a grant to St-Arnulf, Metz, his father's burial-place, and consigned it to the abbacy of his son Carloman. The charter is dated 'in the first year of succession to Lothar'.[1] There is no evidence that Louis the Stammerer was present at Metz in 869. Nor was Queen Ermentrude. Only a month later, on 6 October, she died at St-Denis. On 9 October (Hincmar is careful to specify the date), Charles was 200 km away at Douzy on the Meuse, with some of his new supporters in attendance, when news of his wife's death reached him. He immediately dispatched one of those Lotharingian recruits, Boso, with an urgent request to two women: Boso's mother, widow of one of Lothar's counts who had held lands in the Ardennes and near Metz, and her sister, Theutberga, widow of Lothar II himself. They were to send Boso's sister Richildis to be betrothed to Charles. There is no evidence of previous acquaintance; but Charles must have been well aware of the political influence of Richildis's kin in the western part of Lotharingia. Boso accomplished his mission, and on 12 October the betrothal ceremony took place. 'Because of his union with Richildis, Charles gave Boso the abbacy of St-Maurice, Agaune.'[2] This strategically-situated abbey had been held a

1   T. 328. Soon after Carloman also received the abbacy of Lobbes; Dierkens 1985: 110, 130.
2   *AB* 869: 164; T. 355. For the political advantages of this match, see Hyam 1990: 156–7.

decade or so earlier by Theutberga's brother Hubert
(maternal uncle, therefore, of Boso and Richildis): it
guarded the main route from Lothar II's realm to Italy.
Charles presumably foresaw that his appropriation of Lothar's kingdom would infuriate the Emperor Louis II. The
imperial couple still had no son, and the succession to *Italy*
must already have been attracting the interest of Louis's
Carolingian uncles and cousins north of the Alps. For the
moment, however, Boso was unable to make good his claim
to St-Maurice, and Louis continued to control the Mons
Iovis pass.

Charles's choice of his second bride had obvious political advantages in the specific circumstances of October
869. Yet Hincmar, who wholeheartedly approved Charles's
move into Lothar's kingdom, clearly disapproved of the
union with Richildis: three times in the *AB* between October 869 and January 870, Hincmar refers to her as the
king's 'concubine'. The three months' delay between betrothal and marriage, perhaps an obligatory period of
mourning for Ermentrude, would have allowed a trial of
Richildis's fertility. Hincmar highlighted the indecent haste
of Charles's new attachment: hence the precise sequence
of dates, with the 9 October – which no ninth-century audience would have failed to recognise as the Feast of St Denis
– implicitly invoking saintly disapproval as well. Perhaps by
the time he wrote up the marriage, Hincmar had come to
resent the influence of Richildis and her brother.[3] For
Charles, it must be said that Ermentrude's death at St-
Denis so soon after the Metz consecration was a piece of
political luck. The arrival of the news on the Feast of St
Denis may well have seemed to Charles a sign that his pa-
tron-saint was favouring his Lotharingian plans, and would
bless the new marriage to Richildis. 'Because of it', Charles,
taking Richildis with him, 'hastened still faster to Aachen
to receive into his authority the rest of those of that region
who had been the men of Lothar, as they had said he
should'.[4] Richildis had a vital part to play in bringing over
supporters to Charles. The relationship between her and
her aunt Theutberga had particular significance: one 'Lotharingian' queen was succeeding another. At this juncture,

3   This is clear in *AB* 876: 190.
4   *AB* 869: 164.

there was special need for a queen to play her part in the government of the palace as dispenser of treasure and nurturer of young warriors. Charles in affirming Theutberga's queenly status, underscored the illegitimacy of Hugh, son of Lothar II by Waldrada. Hugh was a strong potential contender in 869. Two years before, his father had installed him, with guarantees from Louis the German, as Lord of Alsace.[5] There Hugh could expect support from his cousin and namesake Hugh, son of Liutfrid,[6] and from Bernard 'Hairypaws': both seem to have been with Hugh in Alsace in autumn 869, and were won over by Charles in a swift move into that region shortly before the close of the year. Lothar's son therefore could make no bid. As for Louis the German, he was believed to be on the point of death, and so neither he, nor any of his sons, anxious to secure their inheritances further east, was in a position to intervene in Lotharingia.[7] From Italy Louis II and (at his behest) Pope Hadrian sent blasts of protest against Charles's violation of the emperor's 'hereditary right'[8] : the hot air was cool by the time it had crossed the Alps. No-one stood in Charles's way in Lotharingia. He felt confident enough to confiscate benefices from those magnates who would not come over to him,[9] no doubt promising rewards to those who would. After consultation with his Lotharingian supporters, he installed Bertulf, nephew of Bishop Adventius of Metz, as archbishop of Trier.[10] Further south in the Rhône valley, Charles had angled for the support of Count Gerald of Vienne, and secured that of Archbishop Ado of Vienne.[11] He celebrated Christmas 869 at Aachen, the 'capital' (*sedes regni*) of his father and grandfather. As he sat on the throne of Charlemagne, his mind was surely filled with thoughts of empire. Surely now his courtiers' dreams for *Carolus Junior* were to be fulfilled! John the Scot, echoing

---

5 *AB* 867: 139.
6 Strictly a first cousin once removed: Liutfrid (d. 865/6) was Lothar II's maternal uncle, and a supporter of Waldrada; *AB* 862: 102, 869: 165.
7 *AF* 869: 67–9 records their victories against Moravians and Sorbs.
8 *AB* 869: 164; *MGH Epp.* VI, nos. 16, 17, pp. 717–20.
9 *AF* 870: 70.
10 Regino 869: 98. Theutgaud had died in Rome; *AB* 867: 142.
11 T. 309, 329.

Einhard's epithet for Charlemagne, hailed Charles as 'great-hearted hero', his hand 'filled with sceptres'.[12]

Early in the new year, Charles went to Nijmegen and met Roric, the Viking ruler of Frisia; then returned to Aachen for his wedding to Richildis on 22 January. Favours were bestowed on Carloman, and on Charles's son-in-law, Count Baldwin of Flanders. The chamberlain Engelram received the lay-abbacy of Maroilles in Lotharingia.[13] But already Charles's luck was turning. His attempt to install one of his palace clerics, Hilduin, in the see of Cologne seemed well-judged, for Hilduin had plenty of local support, but it was foiled at the last moment by Louis the German who, despite his illness, sent the archbishop of Mainz to block Charles's candidate and consecrate instead a Cologne cleric, Willebert.[14] By February Louis the German, now at the ripe age of 65, had unexpectedly regained his health, and moved north-westwards to Frankfurt, where he was acknowledged as lord by a number of Lotharingian magnates.[15] Charles now received a blunt message: he must quit Aachen and Lothar's kingdom peacefully or his brother would drive him out by force. Charles's position was not strong enough to hold. On 6 March, Engelram and four other close counsellors swore on his behalf to work out with Louis's envoys and 'the faithful men of both together' a partition of Lothar's kingdom.[16] Charles left Aachen for Compiègne, to spend Easter (26 March), and then went to St-Denis, for moral and material reinforcements. The summer assembly met at Attigny in May. Here Louis the German's twelve commissioners arrived, ready to draw up a detailed treaty, but clearly unwilling (any more than Charles had been) to abide by the spirit of the fraternal pact of 868: according to Hincmar, they had been 'made arrogant by Louis's good health'. There were more exchanges, and a change of site. On 8 August Charles and Louis finally met at Meersen on the Meuse: Louis, ever wary, had suggested

12 Herren 1987.
13 T. 333, 334, 337.
14 Regino 869: 99–100. Cf. *AB* 864: 113, 866: 131.
15 *AF* 870: 70.
16 Capit II, no. 250, pp. 191–2. Charles's other envoys were Bishop Odo of Beauvais, and Counts Adalelm (of Laon), Theuderic, and another Adalelm.

that each limit his entourage to 4 bishops, 10 'counsellors' (magnates and holders of major court office) and 30 'ministerials and vassals' (men junior perhaps in terms of age and office but not necessarily of rank).[17] The numbers were similar to those responsible for the peace of Verdun in 843: in other words, a representative group of the elite of the kingdoms concerned.

By the Treaty of Meersen, Charles gained much less than he had hoped for the previous autumn – and Aachen eluded him. He nevertheless gained much. The extant terms of 870 allow a detailed map to be drawn of the new frontier between the realms of Charles and his brother. Charles's acquisitions lay in two main sectors. In the southeast, he gained that part of the kingdom of Provence, that is, the valleys of the Saône and Rhône, which Lothar II had managed to keep out of the hands of Louis II of Italy. Charles had made an unsuccessful bid here in 861: now he received the necessary support from the leading men of the region, notably Count Gerald of Vienne and the archbishops of Vienne, Lyons, and Besançon. Louis II of Italy kept the area around Lake Geneva (Orbe seems to have lain on his frontier), which left Charles's grant of St-Maurice to Boso a dead letter for the time being. The importance of the *civitates* in the Saône/Rhône valley was reflected in the grants of mints and markets Charles now made to churches in Langres, Dijon, Besançon and Tournus.[18]

A still more valuable acquisition lay in the Frankish heartlands, where Charles's northeastern frontier was extended to take in a region of some 50,000 km². One way to gauge the value of Charles's gains here is to recall the course of the negotiations in 842 when Charles had yielded everything beyond the Charbonnière because Lothar needed 'the wherewithal to recompense his followers'.[19] Now, in 870, Charles at last acquired the fertile region of Hesbaye and the lands between the Sambre and the Meuse – the homelands of his ancestors. Another indicator of the value

17 *AB* 870: 167–8.
18 T. 365, 354, 378. Cf. Löwe 1971: 621–7 for the output of scriptoria in this region.
19 Above Ch. 5: 125.

of royal estates here and in the acquired lands further up the Meuse valley and between the Meuse and the Moselle is the number of small mints – upwards of twenty – that began minting here after 870. These functioned as mechanisms of exploitation on the part of the new royal landlord. There was also a group of trading-places (designated *portus* in contemporary texts) in this zone.[20] A curious passage in the *Divisio* text shows the importance of Charles's acquisitions in the Ardennes region: Condroz, assigned to Charles, straddled the agreed boundary of the river Ourthe, and special *missi* had had to be deputed to fix the frontier through the county of Bitburg.[21] Here, on the whole, the allocation favoured Louis the German (he acquired the major abbeys of Prüm, Stavelot and Echternach). Charles gained substantial areas of forest – a major royal resource: like his predecessors he would hunt enthusiastically here.[22]

Charles's aggrandisement was considerable, therefore: sufficient to evoke new ambition in Carloman, the younger of his two surviving sons. Tonsured as a cleric at the age of five, consecrated deacon at eleven, loaded with rich abbacies (not all these communities remembered his regime kindly) and lord of a substantial military following, Carloman had served his father as a loyal aide until 869. Charles's move into Lotharingia, and his second marriage changed not just his own position, but Carloman's prospects as well. Additional grants of abbacies – St-Arnulf, Lobbes, St-Riquier – came Carloman's way; but Charles intended that Richildis should bear a son, whose future kingdom would lie in Francia. The offering of a legitimate son to the church as a means of excluding him from a share in the royal succession was a recent, scarcely-tried strategy. The precedent of Pippin II, forcibly tonsured, then permitted to return to lay status and allocated 'counties and monasteries',[23] could only have encouraged Carloman to hope for a similar concession in his own case. Others had a strong interest in backing him: over the twenty-seven years

---

20 Ghent, Dinant, Huy, Namur and Deventer: see Map 5.
21 *AB* 870: 169.
22 *AB* 869: 162, 872: 180; perhaps 875: 187; *MGH Capit.* II, no. 281, c. 32, p. 361.
23 Above Ch. 7:187. For Carloman's career, see Nelson 1988.

of rule by Lothar I, then Lothar II, a region had become a distinct kingdom, its nobility aware of themselves as its leading men. By 869, that kingdom had a name: the *regnum Lotharii*, 'Lothar's kingdom' (whence modern French 'Lorraine', and German 'Lothringen'). It was claimed in the autumn of 869 by Lothar II's son Hugh. Where he failed, another might succeed. The rich abbey of Lobbes was the base from which Carloman could win support for a bid of his own: so, at least, his father had come to suspect in June 870. None of the charges against Hincmar of Laon mentions complicity with Carloman; but it seems more than a coincidence that on 16 June at the assembly of Attigny where his case was being heard, the bishop was forced to swear an oath of loyalty to Charles, and on 18 June Carloman was arrested and immediately taken by Charles (who now prorogued the Attigny hearing) to the stronghold of Senlis.[24] Stripped of his abbacies, Carloman stayed a prisoner while his father and uncle at Meersen carved up Lotharingia between them.

Carloman was not forgotten. Predictably, his cause was taken up by Pope Hadrian II: the previous year Charles had ignored papal affirmations of the Emperor Louis II's rights to Lothar's realm, and now Hadrian could hit back. His envoys appeared at St-Denis, where Charles was celebrating the saint's feastday on 9 October, to repeat the protests and to urge Carloman's release. Charles was angry. But when 'some of his faithful men', Hincmar probably among them (he was certainly willing a few weeks later to intercede with Charles on Carloman's behalf), also counselled patience, Carloman was released, on condition that he remained under his father's eye. Charles had urgent business in Provence, where he had decided that Count Gerald of Vienne, still in royal favour in July,[25] must be ousted. There is no evidence that Gerald had threatened opposition to Charles; but he had no surviving son, and his position was now being eyed enviously by a new generation seeking the rewards of *Königsnähe*. In November Charles moved to the Rhône valley with Carloman in his retinue. The outcome of the campaign was a success in that Gerald

24 *PL* 124, 1034. See McKeon 1978: 105, 121, 127.
25 T. 342. Cf. T. 309 (868) where Gerald was called *carissimus*.

was driven out, and Vienne handed over to Charles's new brother-in-law, Boso. But by then Carloman had escaped and headed northwards to lands that had been the heart of Lothar's kingdom. Clearly Carloman had won a good deal of support in Lotharingia.[26]

Hincmar reveals the seriousness of the revolt by naming the men Charles relied on to stop it: not just Hincmar himself and the Archchancellor Gauzlin, abbot of St-Germain-des-Prés, but a number of lay magnates based in regions bordering Lotharingia – his chamberlain Engelram, his son-in-law Count Baldwin, and Count Adalelm of Laon.[27] Hincmar wrote to Counts Engelram, Goslin and Adalelm, with the king's instructions to mobilise troops against Carloman, but suggesting that the counts join him in representations to the king to urge a more conciliatory approach. In a second letter to these same three counts, Hincmar repeated his view that they should use persuasion before resorting to force: they must try to 'find some good solution along with Carloman, because he should listen to their and his [Hincmar's] advice'. A third letter from Hincmar, this time 'to Carloman, Goslin and Conrad at the king's command', gave details of the hour, day and place of a meeting of magnates on Charles's orders, but without his presence, to discuss the Carloman affair, and asked Carloman 'to send Goslin and Conrad to that meeting'.[28] These two men were evidently backing Carloman. Goslin was presumably the same man as the addressee of the two previous letters, but Hincmar no longer called him 'count'; Conrad was probably the son of Charles the Bald's uncle Rudolf (died 866), and now made his first appearance on the political scene in the predictable role of a seeker after *Königsnähe* among the next generation of Carolingians.[29] For

---

26 Cf. *Lobbes Annals, MGH SS* IV, p. 15; and *AB* 871:172.
27 For Adalelm, see Werner 1959b: 159. McKeon 1978: 124 misreads *AB* 871: 172 to suggest that Baldwin and Gauzlin were on Carloman's side, when in fact both were serving as Charles's envoys to his son. Gauzlin functioned as archchancellor throughout this period. T. 357 and 361 show him close to Charles in early 872.
28 Summaries of the three letters are given by Flodoard III, c. 26, p. 543.
29 See Genealogical Table IV. This Conrad must be distinguished from his namesake, the count of Auxerre.

Charles, these were significant losses. Nevertheless, there is a notable lack of evidence that any of his leading supporters defected.[30] His determination now hardened against any conciliation with his son.

By 871, Carloman had lost Hincmar's sympathy.[31] Hincmar of Laon had refused to endorse a synodal document, drawn up by his uncle, excommunicating Carloman. For the bishop of Laon this was a desperate act of defiance, and a final one: already embroiled in major disputes with both his uncle and Charles the Bald, and suspected of earlier conspiring with Lothar II, Hincmar of Laon now brought down on himself the full weight of the king's wrath. In August, he was seized by royal agents, deprived of his military following, and brought to the Lotharingian palace of Douzy, where Charles summoned no fewer than 8 archbishops and 22 bishops representing virtually his whole expanded realm.[32] Proceedings were stage-managed by the elder Hincmar: the bishop of Laon was deposed and kept under surveillance. Meanwhile letters had arrived from Pope Hadrian II, who had taken the bishop of Laon's part against Charles in an earlier phase of the dispute. The pope now denounced Charles's harshness towards Carloman, and also wrote to the magnates of Charles's realm, forbidding them to join in suppressing Carloman's revolt.[33] Charles's fiery riposte condemned the pope's interference in the cases of both Carloman and Hincmar of Laon, and presented a strong defence of his own royal rights within his realm.[34] Hadrian's protests were effectively silenced.

By far the most dangerous of Carloman's sympathisers, however, was Louis the German. Charles's success in driving the rebels into Eastern Lotharingia, had thrust Carloman into the waiting arms of his uncle beyond the Rhine.

---

30 The defection of Engelram, associated with this context by Grierson 1939: 309, n. 4, is explicitly assigned to a later date by Hincmar: below: 240.

31 *AB* 871: 173.

32 Eight bishops sent delegates; Mansi XVI, cols. 671–8, and for the entire proceedings, cols. 578–688 (with the accusation about Lothar II at cols. 578–81). Hincmar of Laon's own account (written in 878) is in *MGH Epp.* VII, pp. 94–5. See Devisse 1976: 766–85; McKeon 1978: 124–5.

33 *MGH Epp.* VI, pp. 735–13.

34 *PL* 124, cols 876–96. See Nelson 1991b.

Once again, at a critical moment, Charles's regime, always shadowed by that of his elder brother, was threatened with subversion. Charles was able to respond in kind, for the two-way division of Lotharingia had evoked disappointment on the part of king's sons in East as well as West. In 871, two of Louis the German's sons rebelled against him: they turned – naturally – to their West Frankish uncle for support and travelled to meet him south of Douzy.[35] Charles and his brother were quits: at a hastily-summoned meeting at Maastricht later in August, each agreed to act as honest broker for the other. Hence, 'through Louis the German's good offices', Carloman came to terms with his father at Besançon. He was to remain, again, under Charles's eye. A promise of *honores* was in the wind. It was one Charles had no intention of keeping, though: once back in his own heartlands for the winter, he again incarcerated Carloman at Senlis and ordered the rebel's followers 'each to receive a lord from among the king's faithful men and to state a willingness to live in peace'. Some of those footloose followers, presumably those whom Carloman had beneficed on the lands of St-Germain Auxerre, accepted the lordship of Wala, newly-installed by Charles as bishop of Auxerre.[36]

Charles could have no real security as long as Carloman remained a potential contender for a Lotharingian realm. Despite the dwindling number of Ermentrude's sons, Charles's determination had not changed. His second marriage only confirmed Carloman's exclusion from a royal inheritance; once tonsured, Carloman could never father throne-worthy heirs of his own. By the end of 872 Richildis had given birth to a daughter: Charles had good reason to hope a son would follow, and for this new progeny, he intended his Frankish realm. Meanwhile the acquired Lotharingian lands must reinforce the concentration of power in Charles's own hands. Alleging that Carloman's former supporters were planning to spring him from prison and make him their king, presumably in western Lotharingia, Charles summoned an assembly to Quierzy in January 873 and had his son condemned and blinded, then confined to a mon-

---

35   *AB* 871: 174.
36   *Gesta Epp. Autiss., MGH SS* 13, p. 400.

astic prison at Corbie.[37] Only those contemporaries already hostile to Charles expressed shock, it seems. Pope Hadrian had abandoned Carloman in 872 (and he died in December). His successor John VIII (872–82) said not a word. History, sacred and secular, showed that rebel princes had deserved death. Louis the Pious had blinded his rebellious nephew and that may well have served as Charles's model. At the Quierzy assembly, Charles took measures 'to cut down evil': he threatened malefactors with outlawry and the confiscation of their allodial lands, and since witches had been 'rising up in many places', decreed that 'each count in his county' should arrest men and women suspected of witchcraft and put them to the ordeal. Charles recalled Moses' injunction that witches 'should not be permitted to live' (Exod. xxii.18); he also invoked 'what law and justice teach', that is, the prescriptions of the Theodosian Code which condemned to death those who invoked demons to 'distort the minds of men'.[38] Hincmar of Laon too was blinded in 873, when Charles took vengeance for what he clearly believed was continued complicity with Carloman.[39] Where the clerical tonsure had failed, blinding succeeded in disqualifying Carloman from kingship for ever. Louis the German, having engineered his nephew's escape from Corbie could welcome him only as a pathetic invalid. Hincmar claimed that Louis disapproved of Carloman's wicked conduct:[40] certainly no further political leverage was to be gained there.

Charles's elder surviving son, Louis the Stammerer had inevitably been affected by wider changes in the family scene. In 867 Charles had installed him as king of Aquitaine but with palace-officers chosen for him by his father from his own palace. In May 872, at the assembly of Servais, the countship of Bourges (where Gerald had held out since 868 against Charles's attempts to oust him) was assigned to Boso along with the key posts of chamberlain and master of the doorkeepers in Louis's palace.[41] This meant

---

37 *AB* 873: 181, 183. See Nelson 1988b: 113–5.
38 *MGH Capit.* II, no. 278, pp. 343–7.
39 *MGH Epp.* VI, p. 95. It was alleged in 878 (*AV*, p. 43) that Boso had carried out Hincmar's blinding.
40 *AB* 873: 184.
41 *AB* 867: 138; 872: 177.

giving Boso enormous influence at Louis's court; but at the same time, dividing and ruling as usual, Charles confirmed other magnates in their already extensive regional power, and reinforced the links binding them to his personal service: these were Marquis Bernard of Gothia whose brother Imino served as Charles's count of the palace at about this time,[42] Count Bernard of Toulouse whose *honores* Charles increased,[43] and a third Bernard who can be identified as 'Hairypaws', the son of Bernard 'the tyrant' and of Dhuoda.[44] The third Bernard was a man to watch: his timely acknowledgement of Charles in December 869 had opened the way for his return to the west, but Charles had been in no hurry to restore him to comital status.[45] He was still, so to speak, on trial, though later that year he was granted lands in the Autunois (to which he probably had a hereditary claim) after his men had killed the sitting tenant, yet another namesake of his and also a likely kinsman.[46] Not long after, 'Hairypaws' seems to have acquired the countship of the Auvergne.[47]

Louis the Stammerer's situation in Aquitaine was already unenviable. Soon Charles compelled him to divorce his Neustrian wife Ansgard and to marry instead Adelaide, daughter of Count Adalard, a magnate in northern Burgundy.[48] The result was inevitably to call in question the legitimacy of Louis's two sons by his first wife (that was exactly the charge which Boso was to level when the succession to Louis became an immediate issue, in 879.)[49] These were as yet Charles's only grandsons; but his hopes were pinned on new offspring of his own. There is no record of Louis's resisting his enforced remarriage. His new father-in-law Count Adalard had gained *Königsnähe* whose real reference was to Charles the Bald, not Louis.

42 See Appendix I.
43 Cf. T. 341, and Dhondt 1948: 202, n. 1.
44 *AB* 872: 177. For the nickname, cf. above 211.
45 Note his lack of title in both Hincmar's references to him in *AB* 872: 177, 179.
46 See *AB* 872: 179, n. 14.
47 Cf. what I take to be his first appearance in the *Cartulaire de Brioude*, ed. Doniol, no. 132; and *AB* 877: 201.
48 Werner 1967: 432–3, 437–9. Cf. *AB* 878: 210.
49 Regino 879: 114.

Adalard's position is worth examining more closely. It was not that of a new kind of territorial prince whose consolidated regional power weakened the king's: such is the model of ninth-century political change offered by Dhondt in 1948 and largely accepted by some influential historians since.[50] Adalard had influence in Burgundy, and Charles both acknowledged and exploited it in sending him there as *missus*.[51] Adalard's brother Wulfgrin was appointed by Charles to the distant county of Angoulême.[52] In Burgundy, Adalard's position was offset by that of another magnate, Eccard, who held the three countships of Chalon, Mâcon and Autun, and died without direct heir in 876, whereupon that 'bloc' was dispersed to the benefit not of Adalard, but of Boso and Bernard of Gothia.[53] Charles's own authority in Burgundy did not depend only on secular magnates in any case. One of the most misleading aspects of the 'regional principalities' scenario is the absence of churchmen. Yet it was bishops and abbots who helped Charles to rule his realm effectively both at the centre and in the regions; and any account of Carolingian government, not least in the reign of Charles the Bald, must have room for the interplay of secular and ecclesiastical power. In Burgundy, Charles granted privileges to Bishop Isaac of Langres in 872;[54] in the same year the see of Auxerre went to Wala who paid off the followers of Carloman without (his contemporary biographers stress) causing loss to his church.[55] In 875, the see of Autun was given to Charles's notary Adalgar.[56] Similar points can be made about other

---

50 James 1982: 175; Riché 1983: 188.

51 *Recueil de St-Benôit*, ed. Prou-Vidier ed. no. 31.

52 Werner 1965: 435 cites later evidence; but see Nanglard, *Cartulaire d'Angoulême* no. 37, pp. 62–3 (dated 22 January 868, and subscribed by Count Wulfgrin).

53 Despite Dhondt 1948: 212, there is no evidence that Bernard of Gothia held Berry or Autun in 876–7 thus combining them in 'a solid bloc', nor that Bernard 'Hairypaws' held Toulouse at this time (at least some of the *honores* of Bernard of Toulouse, who died before December 874, went to his kinsmen; Devic and Vaisette II, cols 376–8, 400–3).

54 T. 365.

55 Above, n. 35. Further evidence of Charles's persisting authority at Auxerre, Löwe 1973: 568.

56 Cf. *AB* 876: 195; 877: 200–1.

regions and other leading men. Boso, for instance, held *honores* in Burgundy and Francia as well as in Provence, Aquitaine and Italy – but did not hold them simultaneously. Abbot Hugh regained the abbacy of St-Germain, Auxerre after the downfall of Carloman[57] and kept it while acquiring extensive *honores* in Neustria.[58] His case highlights the special utility to the king of that ecclesiastical anomaly the cleric-abbot, who made no monastic profession, but lived off *honores* and fought like a layman, yet (as a cleric) could leave no legitimate heir. Several abbots, regular or clerical, occupied key posts in the 870s.[59] Last but not least, all these great men, secular and ecclesiastical alike, owed their prominence in the 870s to royal appointment (whether to palatine or to provincial office) and personal service to the king, ties often reinforced by blood-relationship or by marriage into the royal family. Hincmar called these men *speciales*, and he meant the term unkindly because he himself was no longer sure of his place among them. Charles called them his *carissimi*, his *familiares*.

Fortunately, more evidence for Charles's aims and personality survives from the years after c. 869 than before. The young nobles who served as palatine clerics made Charles's court a cradle of bishops;[60] but in Heiric of Auxerre's vignette of a palace 'that deserved to be called an exercise-ground', the focus is on Charles himself, and his 'daily devotion to scholarly as well as to military training'.[61] He wanted fine books. Of those produced for him during this period, two bibles and a Gospel Book have survived. A lively (and perhaps life-like) portrait from the frontispiece to the San Paolo Bible is reproduced on the cover of this book.[62] In Charles's entourage, and in the workshops of churches patronised by him, craftsmen made

---

57 T. 427, 437, 438, and see Wollasch 1957a: 211, 218. Cf. above Ch. 8: 201, 214.

58 See below: 243–4.

59 Cf. Werner 1979: 410–12.

60 Tessier 1955: 46, 81, 87; McKitterick 1990: 326–30.

61 *Vita S. Germani, MGH Poet. Lat.* III, p. 429, ll. 37–8.

62 Detail from throne-portrait on fol. 1r of the Bible of San Paolo fuori le Mura, Hubert 1970: 140, plate 130. Richildis is depicted here at Charles's side: the first full-length portrait of a Carolingian queen.

book-covers of ivory and precious metals encrusted with gems. The ivory plaques on the throne almost certainly commissioned by Charles (and presented to St Peter in 875) depicted the labours of Hercules: a theme with special meaning for a man involved in ceaseless struggle, whose resilience and determination were needed more than ever in the fraught years after 869.[63]

From the late 860s on, Charles's itinerary came to centre on two places. One was Compiègne,[64] the other was St-Denis.[65] The new pattern was significant. Charles was no longer a migratory monarch in quite his old way. More predictable, frequent and prolonged stays meant that scholars and craftsmen could settle down to their work. The artistic output of this period was in part the result. St-Denis, especially now that the king himself was lay-abbot there, was the object of increasing royal largesse as Charles sought the patronage of this *specialis protector* for his family and for his own enterprises. Here were buried Ermentrude in 869, and in 877 an infant son of Richildis; here Charles intended his own burial-place; and here were commemorated his own parents, his dead children, and those of his household (*familiares*) whose devoted service had made them as it were honorary kin.[66] Charles made St-Denis the prime cult-centre and mausoleum of his line. As for Compiègne, he was coming to envisage it as a kind of capital – a successor or rival to, and eventually substitute for, Charlemagne's Aachen. Increasingly during these years, Charles was thinking in imperial terms.

A second letter sent by Charles to Pope Hadrian in February or March 872, answering the pope's angry response to his previous letter,[67] offers a belated unique entrée to an

---

63 The throne, and the ivory portrait-panel depicting Charles himself, are illustrated in Nees 1990: 235–7, 342, 345, plates 21.1; 21.2. For the Hercules ivories, see Gussone and Staubach 1975; and for a different interpretation, Nees 1991.

64 Summer assembly 867; Christmas 868; Easter and autumn 870; Christmas 871; Lent 872; autumn and Christmas 874; Whit 875; 2 visits 876; Lent, Easter and three other stays 877.

65 Lent (wholly or partly) and Easter 868, 869, 871; two visits in 870; Easter 872, 874, 875 and 876; and a visit in early 877.

66 Above Ch. 1: 16; and in general Brown 1989.

67 Above: 229.

extraordinary character: it is the first and only text that can be plausibly ascribed to Charles himself.[68]

'We read in the Book of Chronicles', Charles began, 'that the sons of Israel went forth to battle with a peaceful mind because they fought, not out of vengeful spite, but to gain peace. We say this, because you compel us – dishonoured as we are by letters from you which are unfitting for the royal power – to write to you otherwise than we should have wished, but still with a peaceful mind.'

Charles continued with a self-portrait:

'Bear in mind that we are, though subject to human disturbances, nevertheless a man who walks in the image of God, a man conscious of having been raised up through succession from our grandfather and father, by God's grace, in the title and dignity of a king; and what's more, a Christian, a Catholic practitioner of the Orthodox faith, trained up from infancy in sacred letters and in both ecclesiastical and secular law.'

Yet, Charles complained, Hadrian had condemned him without any formal accusation or trial, let alone conviction. How was he to react to such injustice?

'When some Jews said to the Lord: "Thou hast a devil!" – and He realised that to keep silent would imply assent, He patiently refuted what He heard falsely said, and replied: "I have not a devil." [John viii: 48, 49] In our humble fashion we have followed the example of Him who did not disdain to show through reason that He was no sinner.'

Hadrian had supported Hincmar of Laon's right to appeal to Rome, and had told Charles to 'look after' the property of the see of Laon during the bishop's absence. Charles now repeated what he had asserted the previous year:

68   *PL* 124: 881–96. See Nelson 1991b.

'As Pope Gregory said, we kings of the Franks are not numbered as bishops' bailiffs but lords of the earth.'

In other words, not only was the property of the see (the *spolia*) at the king's disposal during an episcopal vacancy, but Charles was asserting, as Roman Emperors had done, his residual rights (*dominium*) over all temporal wealth in the lands over which he ruled.

He went on to express outrage

'...that I, constituted king by God, endowed with a two-edged sword to take revenge on the wicked and to defend the innocent, should become a supporter of a condemned criminal in sending Hincmar of Laon to Rome. What Hell spewed up this 'universal law'? What Inferno belched it up from its dark depths? . . . What madness has seized you when you know that Christ said:"Through me kings reign!" '.

Charles pressed home his attack along Gelasian lines: public laws promulgated by the authority of princes had to be observed by all bishops, including popes, as

'our predecessors and progenitors the orthodox emperors and kings obeyed the bishop of the Holy See in matters pertaining to his ministry. [But] through the King of Kings, who alone could be both king and priest, "those who lay down laws decree what is just" [Prov viii: 15], and those laws princely powers have termed eternal ones ...'

Hadrian wanted the bishop of Laon to appear at Rome with a 'suitable accuser'. Very well: he, Charles, would be that accuser and with him he would 'bring sufficient suitable witnesses of every order and rank' to prove his case. Meanwhile he begged Hadrian to send no more letters like his last:

'nor to compel us, unwilling as we should be, to turn to that course of action which can be found prescribed for us in the Fifth Universal Council by the Apostolic See . . . . Hitherto we have not wanted to put this in our letters until we had tried to find some other way to turn your harshness to kindness'.

The reference was to the council of 553 whose imperially-designed decrees Pope Vigilius, haled to Constantinople, had been forced to accept. Charles, a new Justinian, was issuing a scarcely veiled threat to march on Rome, with a large following, and put the screws on Vigilius's successor. Hadrian was a shrewd man: in the response he returned in June,[69] 'sensing the throbbing of Charles's cuts and swellings', he 'applied medicinally the oil of consolation, the honey of sweetest charity and the ointment of holy love'. In other words, he accepted that the bishop of Laon's appeal should be heard by a provincial synod, pending which his deposition should stand, thus allowing Charles to deploy the resources of the see of Laon meanwhile. Finally, to complete the king's diplomatic triumph, Hadrian sent assurances that Charles would be his choice to succeed to the imperial title when Louis II of Italy (who had no son) eventually died.

A false rumour of Louis's death had already had Charles the Bald and Louis the German on tenterhooks in 871. Since then intrigues for the imperial succession had intensified, with both Charles and Louis the German negotiating with the influential Empress Engelberga, Louis II's wife. As a *quid pro quo* (probably) for his eldest son Karlmann's acceptance as imperial successor, Louis the German went so far as to offer his share of Lotharingia to the emperor. Charles was able to point out that the consent of the Lotharingians themselves had not been sought.[70] At Gondreville in Burgundy on 9 September 872, the third anniversary of his Lotharingian consecration, Charles held a great assembly at which his bishops undertook, and his lay *fideles* swore, to help the king 'to hold the realm which you have and to gain what God shall grant you hereafter'.[71] Early in 873, Charles's hopes were further raised by the election of John VIII, who clearly meant to continue his predecessor Hadrian's support for Charles's imperial plans. The political situation in southern Italy where Byzantines

69   *MGH Epp.* VI, no. 36, pp. 743–6.
70   *AB* 872: 178.
71   *MGH Capit.* II, no. 277, pp. 341–2.

intruded on the east coast and Arabs on the west, and Lombard princes wheeled and dealt in between, left papal territory dangerously exposed.[72] No wonder that Hadrian and John, for all their rhetoric of papal authority, sought Carolingian strongmen. Louis II had filled that role. He died at Brescia on 12 August 875. Charles must have reacted very fast, for having heard the news at Douzy he reached Pavia before the end of September.[73] En route, at Langres, he had decided who should accompany him to Italy, and who should stay behind. Boso was to go. Richildis (who had given birth prematurely to a short-lived baby boy only five months before)[74] remained in Francia, moving back north to Servais in the heartlands of the realm. More surprisingly, Louis the Stammerer, now at nearly thirty, in effect Charles's only son, was sent to hold recently-acquired Lotharingia.[75] Would he now make the most of this long-deferred chance to prove himself?

Charles moved south to Rome, gaining the support of Italian magnates, and beating off successive rival bids by Louis the German's sons Charles (the future Charles the Fat), then Karlmann. Meanwhile Louis the German himself along with his second son and namesake came from the Rhineland westwards, across Lotharingia, stopped briefly at Metz, and entered Charles's kingdom moving northwest to Attigny. Was it Louis's aim, as in 858, to oust Charles and acquire his kingdom? The contemporary annalist closest to Louis explicitly rejected any such intention: 'Louis meant to force Charles out of Italy'.[76] This was a raid, then, rather than an invasion. But the annalist's judgement was a retrospective one: for the magnates of Charles's kingdom in November 875 the future was uncertain. Louis's presence at Attigny (only some 48 km from Rheims) posed a particular dilemma for Hincmar: 'Keeping Faith', his circular letter to the bishops and lay magnates of his province, combined lukewarm counsels of loyalty with scalding criticisms of Charles (unconvincingly attributed to 'others'), and in effect made the case for yielding to Louis. It seems fairly

---

72 Partner 1972: 66–71.
73 *AB* 875: 187–8; T. 383.
74 *AB* 875: 187.
75 *AB* 875: 187–8.
76 *AF* 875: 84.

clear from the reproaches levelled by John VIII in 876 against 'bishops' (unnamed) 'who wavered in Charles's hour of need' that some of Hincmar's colleagues, and perhaps Hincmar himself, 'caught between hammer and anvil', had indeed yielded.[77]

> 'We voice complaints which we have heard from common people too: that it was not right for our king to leave this realm so unwisely, surrounded as it was on all sides by pagans and disturbed and unstable within .
> . . . Some people are saying, so we have heard, that [Charles] has the whole realm in the hands of himself and his *speciales*, and of those men none will gain or hold onto anything through service, nor through defending nor being of use to the realm, but only by making a payment; and no-one can feel any good faith in [Charles] about *honores* or about his favour when he's dis-honoured and rejected as hateful all whom he used to have most trusty and close.'

Perhaps if God brought him safely back from Italy, Charles might complete whatever good he had begun and change into a new man like St Paul, 'who turned from a savage persecutor into a pious preacher'!

Hincmar also let slip some less than respectable motivations on the part of his addressees: 'Whatever we do, don't let's do it out of greed for abbacies and *honores*'.[78] Elsewhere Hincmar alleged that Louis the German was spurred on by Engelram, Charles's former chamberlain, who had lost his high office and Charles's favour through the hostility of Richildis.[79] The story is plausible; Richildis and her brother Boso had made the most of their new-won *Königsnähe* to amass the benefits of patronage for themselves and their clients. Richildis's influence had probably reached a highpoint during her recent pregnancy; and the shared organisational role of queen and chamberlain in royal household-management[80] could place exceptional strain on that

---

77 *De Fide Servanda, PL* 125, col. 963–80. The following quotations are from cols 979–80.
78 *PL* 125, cols 979, 981A.
79 *AB* 875: 188.
80 Hincmar, *The Government of the Palace* c. 22.

relationship. Hincmar commented scathingly on Richildis's attempts to organise the defence of Charles's kingdom: 'she assembled the magnates who remained there and exacted an oath of loyalty, but . . . they ravaged Charles's kingdom on their own account, in the manner of a hostile army'.[81] Hincmar probably referred here to a particular loss: local magnates with an hereditary claim to the estate of Neuilly, which Charles had lately restored to the church of Rheims, took their chance to have it granted back to them by Richildis. Hincmar was cruelly disappointed.[82] There was no advantage to be gained from this by Louis, however. He had his critics too, even in his own camp: the East Frankish annalist admitted that Louis's men, having 'turned to plundering, and ravaged all they could find', advised Louis to withdraw.[83] Clearly he had gained little support among the West Frankish nobility.[84] Louis and his son barely managed the gesture of spending Christmas at Attigny, then went back eastwards early in 876. What of Charles's son, Louis the Stammerer? Hincmar, silent in the *AB* about his role at this time, reveals in the dossier on Neuilly that Louis as well as his stepmother Richildis sanctioned that estate's re-grant. The Stammerer was trying to make something of his political role. He had failed to stop Louis the German's advance through Lotharingia, however.

The bitterness perceptible in Hincmar's annalistic record did not only arise from regret over his church's losses. There is an aftertaste of sour grapes: after 873, Hincmar had fallen from the heights of royal favour, displaced by a trio of men deeply involved in Charles's imperial plans: Bishop Odo of Beauvais, Archbishop Actard of Tours (transferred from Nantes with papal permission in 871), and Archbishop Ansegis of Sens (former abbot of the Lotharingian abbey of St-Mihiel near Verdun). All three had recently served as Charles's envoys at Rome and been signi-

---

81 *AB* 875: 188.

82 Hincmar, 'The Neuilly Estate' (*De villa Noviliaco*), *PL* 125, col. 1124.

83 *AF* 876: 85. Cf. allegations of severe damage in the Petition presented by the Church of Rheims to the Synod of Ponthion in 876, Mansi XVII, cols 307–18.

84 Cf. letter from John VIII to unnamed defectors, Mansi XVII, cols 233–4.

ficant beneficiaries of royal patronage;[85] their diplomatic
activity had surely contributed to the support Charles
found (as even Hincmar admitted) in Italy late in 875; and
Ansegis, at least, was present on Christmas Day when Charles 'offering precious gifts to St Peter, was anointed and
crowned emperor and took the title "emperor of the Ro-
mans" '.[86] The gifts very probably included 'the *cathedra* of
St Peter' with its famous Hercules-plaques.[87] Charles's Her-
culean patience had indeed found its reward: *Carolus Junior, imperator augustus,* now occupied the place of his
grandfather, Charles Senior (Charlemagne), as a ruler over
the kingdoms: perhaps, at last, he felt he had lived up to
his name.[88] Imperial authority was now to be complemented by an imperial centralisation of church government: within days of his coronation, Charles secured from
John VIII the appointment of Ansegis as papal vicar north
of the Alps.[89] It was the post Hincmar of Rheims had
coveted. His anger made him indiscreet: he was soon having to reassure the pope that contrary to what 'certain
men' alleged, he had not made critical comments about
John's promotion of Ansegis.[90]

Charles secured enough support from the magnates of
central Italy to provide Pope John with a protective alliance;[91] but Rome did not hold him for long. By late
January he was back at Pavia, where at a great assembly he
was formally elected as ruler of the kingdom of Italy. Here
too were unveiled new plans for Boso: he subscribed the
Pavia electoral announcement as 'famous duke, chief min-
ister of the sacred palace and imperial *missus*'. In effect,
Charles was making him viceroy of Italy.[92] Regino says that
'Charles put a crown on his head and ordered him to be
called king, so that he (Charles) should seem to be a lord

---

85 Odo: Grierson 1935: 186–7; Actard, *AB* 871: 174; Ansegis, Charles's
   letter to Nicholas I, *PL* 124, col. 871 and *AB* 870: 171.
86 *AB* 876: 189. Note that Hincmar relegates John VIII and his invitation to a subordinate clause in the last entry for 875.
87 Above: 235.
88 The title is used in T. 400, 401 (dated 26 December 875).
89 On 2 January 876; *PL* 126, col. 660.
90 Flodoard III, c. 21, p. 575.
91 Erchampert of Monte Cassino, *Historia* c. 39, mentions Lambert
   and Guy.
92 *MGH Capit.* II, no. 220, p. 99.

over kings in the manner of ancient emperors'.[93] Such an expression of imperial superiority, foreshadowed in earlier dealings with Breton rulers, fitted the developing Theodosian style of Charles's regime. He also arranged for Boso to strengthen his position in Italy and Provence by marrying Louis II's daughter (and only child).[94] Charles had to leave his newly-acquired realm in strong hands: for himself, news of Louis the German's incursion and Richildis's plight dictated an immediate return to Francia. The speed of Charles's journey was phenomenal: from Vercelli on 1 March, he seems to have reached Besançon in just two weeks. Hardly less impressive was the speed with which Richildis moved south to meet him, travelling from Senlis to Besançon in 10 days.[95] Charles was determined to spend Easter, 15 April, at St-Denis. That rendezvous too was kept. An Easter court offered an occasion for re-establishing Charles's position in Francia and putting the new-won empire, and hoped-for new progeny, under the heavenly protection of his special patron. What Charles said to Louis the Stammerer when they met is not recorded. By then, Richildis was pregnant again.

Hincmar may have been right to see Charles's absence in Italy as an invitation to Viking attacks on Francia; Vikings certainly knew how to exploit Carolingian disputes. Nevertheless, it was unjust to accuse Charles of neglecting his kingdom's protection. In 876, while Abbot Hugh maintained resistance to the Vikings on the Loire, Charles went in May to Bézu in the Vexin to meet the archbishop of Rouen.[96] Threatening Viking movements were in the wind. Charles must have hoped his presence would keep the Seine basin safe, as it had been for the past ten years. That summer's assembly met at Ponthion, near the old frontier with Lotharingia. Only the ecclesiastical side of the assembly's business is documented: the synod sat from 20 June until 16 July, and its ample attendance-list reflected the

---

93 Regino's dating, 877, p. 113, should be corrected to 876. See Fried 1976: 197; Meyer-Gebel 1987: 79.

94 Regino's version is preferable to Hincmar's hint, *AB* 876: 190, that Boso's marriage was directed against Charles: there is no evidence that Boso fell from favour.

95 Details from *AB* 876: 190.

96 T. 406, 407.

scale of an imperial realm.[97] The papal legates played an important role in managing the synod. When envoys, led by Archbishop Willebert of Cologne, arrived on 4 July to present Louis the German's demands for a share in the inheritance of Louis II, they were firmly reminded of Pope John's commitment to Charles. Ansegis's vicariate was confirmed, and a new oath of fidelity required from every bishop. Frotar, another of Charles's clerical *speciales*, was formally transferred (Charles had secured papal approval) from Bordeaux to succeed Wulfad in the key metropolitan see of Bourges.[98] Hincmar's objections on each score were overridden.[99] On the synod's final day, Charles took the opportunity for an imposing display of majesty: 'dressed in Greek fashion and wearing his crown', he and Richildis 'who stood crowned at his side' received *Laudes*, liturgical acclamations, 'according to custom'. A group of newly-baptised Vikings (conveniently sent from the Loire by Abbot Hugh) were led before the emperor.[100] Charles signalled the inauguration of a hoped-for new Justinianic age.

On 28 August 876 Louis the German died at Frankfurt, and within days the news had reached Charles, now at Quierzy. For the first time in his life, no big brother loomed over him. Would he now be able to translate his imperial preeminence into reality? 'He sent envoys to the magnates of his late brother's kingdom', then moved east via Aachen to Cologne.[101] He was not be deflected, even by news that a Viking fleet had appeared at the mouth of the Seine. His priority was the Rhineland, where he intended to face down Louis the German's son Louis the Younger: according to the East Frankish annalist (now more hostile than ever), 'Charles boasted that his horses would drink up the Rhine, and that he would cross by the dry river-bed to lay waste the whole of [his late brother's] realm'. But the same annalist believed that the territory Charles intended to *acquire* was more limited: namely, in addition to the part

97 Map 8. Unfortunately only ecclesiastical participants are named. But oaths were sworn to the emperor by laymen too, 'from Francia, Burgundy, Aquitaine, Septimania, Neustria and Provence'; *MGH Capit.* II, no. 279, p. 348.
98 T. 409.
99 *PL* 125, cols 1125–8; *AB* 876: 192–4.
100 *AB* 876: 194–5.
101 *AB* 876: 195. Richildis was with him, his son Louis apparently not.

of Lotharingia that had eluded him in 870, Louis the German's enclave to the west of the Rhine – the very region around Mainz, Worms and Speyer for which so much diplomatic effort had been expended in 840–3 because it included such important royal centres, palaces and estates.[102] If this was Charles's aim, it was both shrewd and realistic: in the scale of his imperial heartlands he would outdo Lothar I, restore the glories of Ingelheim in the days of his father Louis the Pious.[103] During September, Louis the Younger remained on the east bank of the Rhine at Deutz, with limited support. According to Hincmar, Charles's men across on the west bank mocked the prayers and litanies with which Louis and his companions sought divine help, while Louis put thirty men to the ordeal and secured a divine Judgement that his cause was righteous.[104] Charles, working to gain adherents on the west bank, had quantities of treasure, weapons and horses, and a considerable army. In early October, Louis left his encampment at Deutz intact to deceive Charles's men, and crossed the Rhine to Andernach, some 65 km upstream from Cologne. Charles accepted the challenge. He sent Richildis, now seven months pregnant, back across the Meuse to Herstal, and then advanced towards Louis: though he sent envoys ahead to invite negotiations, he had decided on a surprise attack. On the night of 7 October Charles moved swiftly the last few kilometres to Andernach. His blow was timed for dawn on 8 October – the eve of the feast of St Denis, his special patron. Victory would make a perfect saint's day thank-offering. Unfortunately for Charles, the advantage of surprise was lost: Archbishop Willebert of Cologne had got wind of the plan and sent a messenger to warn Louis. (Charles's failure to place his own man in that see in 870 thus proved even more costly than expected.) It had rained heavily during the night, making the terrain difficult for Charles's horsemen. The result was a military debacle. Not only were some of Charles's leading men killed, and at least four counts taken prisoner, but he lost large amounts

---

102 *AF* 876: 86–7. Cf. above: 116, 135.
103 With one exception (in 868), Louis the German's only recorded visits there were in 876: *MGH DD regum Germaniae* II, nos. 170, 171.
104 *AB* 876: 196.

of treasure and equipment.[105] Charles and his retinue were lucky to escape. On St Denis's day, the grim news reached Richildis at Herstal. Fleeing westwards en route for Rheims, she gave birth to a premature baby boy.

Andernach was a severe blow. But like Alfred of Wessex (beaten at Wilton just five years before), or like Frederick II (beaten at Cuortenuovo some 400 years after) Charles was a man to surmount defeat. With dogged determination, and despite the disruption of his entourage,[106] he pushed on with the business of rulership. An assembly was summoned to Samoussy in late November. Envoys were sent to the lower Seine to arrange terms with the Vikings there, while special troops were deployed in that area.[107] Charles then tried to salvage something from Andernach by cementing the loyalty of supporters recently recruited in eastern Lotharingia. He also tried to rekindle the long-standing rivalry between Louis the Younger and his elder brother Karlmann. In November, however, the three sons of Louis the German agreed on a division of their father's realm which left Louis the Younger in control of all that Charles had hoped to acquire. Shortly before Christmas Charles fell desperately ill. Richildis's baby son, who had clung to life against the odds, died early in the new year.

Once more, Charles fought back against ill-fortune. The release of the prisoners of Andernach in January 877[108] brought Gauzlin back to court. Boso had been in Provence at the time of Andernach, but was back at court for the festive season and stood godfather to his shortlived nephew.[109] Charters in late 876 and early 877 show Charles favouring not only Boso but other *speciales*: Count Conrad, former adherent of Carloman but now firmly bound into Charles's entourage as *carissimus et familiarissimus*,[110] and

---

105 *AB* 876: 197, lists Counts Jerome and Raganar as slain, Counts Aledramn, Adalard, Bernard (probably 'Hairypaws') and Everwin, and Archchancellor Gauzlin, as captives. *AF* 876: 89 stresses the spoils.
106 Perhaps caused by Gauzlin's absence? Cf. Tessier 1955: 428– 9.
107 On this and what follows, see *AB* 876: 198–9.
108 *AF* 877: 89.
109 *Receuil Provence* XVbis; T. 419; *AB* 877: 199.
110 T. 412, suggesting that Conrad's county at this point was Sens; his brother Welf was abbot of St-Colombe Sens, in 877; Tellenbach 1957: 339. Cf. *AB* 876: 198 for Conrad as Charles's negotiator with Vikings.

two brothers named Pippin and Herbert.[111] All these three were Charles's own close kinsmen: Conrad son of Rudolf was his maternal cousin, Pippin and Herbert more distant cousins on the Carolingian side.[112] These men reinforced the support-group Charles had already built up in Francia and Burgundy around Counts Adalard and Adalelm.

A frame of mind very far from defeatist was revealed in the foundation charter for the new chapel at Compiègne, issued by Charles on 5 May and sealed in imperial style with a golden *bulla* (seal).

'Because our grandfather, to whom divine providence granted the monarchy of this whole empire, established a chapel in honour of the Virgin in the palace of Aachen, we therefore, wanting to imitate the pattern set by him, and by other kings and emperors, namely our predecessors, since that part of the *regnum* has not yet come to us by way of share in its division, we have built and completed within the territory under our sway, in the palace of Compiègne, a new monastery, to which we have given the name 'royal', in honour of the glorious mother of God and ever-virgin Mary, and we have decreed that there 100 clerics should continually implore the Lord's mercy for the state of the holy church of God, for our fathers and forefathers, ourselves, our wife and offspring, and for the stability of the whole *regnum*.'[113]

Charles had not abandoned all hope of acquiring Aachen: the vagaries of dynastic politics could never be predicted. He had determined, however, to make Compiègne *his* liturgical centre – on the model, perhaps, not just of Aachen but of Constantinople whose paladin (as Charles surely knew) was the Virgin and whose rulers included such 'imperial predecessors' as Justinian.[114] The resources used for the new foundation were large, the personnel much more numerous than Charlemagne had

111 *AB* 877: 201 names them as Charles's envoys to the pope.
112 Grandsons of King Bernard of Italy: see Genealogical Table 1.
113 T. 425. Cf. the translations of Herren 1987: 596–7; McKitterick 1990: 331. See also Falkenstein 1981: 34.
114 Cf. Wallace-Hadrill 1978: 174–82.

ever envisaged for Aachen. The choice of site, and the new name it now acquired, perfectly expressed the economic and political centrality of the Oise valley in Charles's realm: Compiègne was an apt *Carlopolis*.[115]

In early summer Charles held a meeting at Rheims, attended by 'all the magnates'[116] to arrange for the government of the realm under Louis the Stammerer: arrangements confirmed at a full assembly at Quierzy in mid-June. Charles had decided to return to Italy, partly in response to urgent appeals from John VIII whose lands were increasingly under threat from Arab raiders (Syracuse was to fall in 878, putting Sicily entirely in Arab hands for 200 years), partly because plans for the succession were to be remade in the light of recent events. The Capitulary of Quierzy, drawn up perhaps by Gauzlin, has survived in a unique form.[117] Its first nine *capitula* are couched as a dialogue between Charles and his faithful men: he posed a series of questions about how the internal and external security of his realm north of the Alps could be maintained during his absence, while they gave responses. Its most famous clause (9) provides for a likely enough eventuality: that a count or royal vassal might die back in Francia while his son was with Charles in Italy. In such a case, Charles confirmed that the son should be heir presumptive to the countship or benefice(s). This alleged 'general law' making countships and fiefs heritable has been held responsible for the undermining of Carolingian monarchy in France.[118] In fact filial succession to office and lands was traditional practice: Charles's explicit statement was intended to reassure and encourage the young nobles in his following. The clause's real significance lay in what it revealed of one particular father–son relationship: namely that between Charles and Louis the Stammerer. Charles

115   Lohrmann 1976: 126–7.
116   Hincmar's letter to Louis the Stammerer, *PL* 125, col. 986, mentioning only two absentees: Bernard ('Hairypaws') and Abbot Hugh.
117   *MGH Capit.* II, no. 281, pp. 355–61. Excerpts 'to be read out by Gauzlin' formed a separate text: *MGH Capit.* II, no. 282, pp. 361–3. Manuscripts of both versions survived into modern times, but are now lost.
118   Montesquieu 1989: VI, Book 31, c. 25, pp. 708–9. See above Ch. 1: 13.

was forestalling any redistribution of *honores* by Louis to build up support on his own account. Paternal power was to remain operative from a distance: hence, alongside the provision for temporary arrangements by Louis to ensure short-run administrative continuity, the reservation of Charles's own authority. Charles made that crystal-clear in the case of countships and benefices to which there was no direct heir: Louis and his advisers were to appoint a care-taker and inform Charles, 'and let no-one be angry if we assign the countship (or benefice(s)) to someone other than that caretaker, namely to whom we please'. Signifi-cantly, it is at c. 9 that the capitulary's dialogue-form gives way to that of a traditional royal enactment: Charles pro-poses and also disposes. The faithful men duly answer: 'the rest of the *capitula* need no reply since they have been set out and established by your wisdom'. In keeping control over his adult son (Louis, remember, was now 30 years old), Charles kept control of the distribution of power in his kingdom at large. Facing very similar problems to those of his father Louis the Pious in the late 830s, Charles came up with workable solutions of his own.

Other *capitula* confirm this interpretation. In c. 4, Char-les asks: 'how may we (the royal 'we') be secure concerning our son and concerning you until we return, and how may you be secure concerning our son, and he concerning you?' In their response to this cluster of questions, the faithful men made a far more substantial input than any-where else in the capitulary. As to their own reliability, they rehearsed a series of oaths and promises exchanged be-tween them and Charles, assuring him of their loyalty; as to Louis, 'no-one knows how to take care of him better than you do yourself!'

Charles and his men understood one another: certain named bishops, abbots and counts were to be with Louis 'assiduously' [c.15], as it were *in loco parentis*; Adalard count of the palace was to 'remain with him with the seal' [c.17]; three bishops were made responsible for maintaining com-munications with Charles in Italy [c.25]; last but not least, Charles listed those royal forests in which Louis was forbid-den to hunt (or allowed only restricted rights), and Ada-lelm was assigned the job of checking on Louis's compliance [cc.32, 33]. Louis's performance of every royal function, his use of every royal resource, was to be under the surveillance of his father's faithful men: Counts Adalard, Adalelm, Baldwin, Conrad and Theuderic; the bishops of Paris, Tournai, Beauvais and Soissons; and Abbots Welf of St-Colombe, Sens, Gauzlin of St-Germain, and Fulk of St-Bertin.[119] These were the men left behind, while Charles took others to Italy. But what was to become of Italy, and Louis, in the longer run? The answer was given in c. 14: 'when we return from Rome, he (Louis) is to go there and be crowned king'. God willing, there would be a re-establishment of the familial arrangements of Louis the Pious, and of Lothar: the imperial father would base himself in Francia, the *primogenitus* would take care of Italy – and Italy of him. The longer-term future of Charles's Frankish kingdom remained wide open: c. 13 voiced alternative possibilities for the succession there – a future son by Richildis, or even (ominously for Louis) the choice of a nephew. Such options assured paternal leverage.

In the summer of 877, an exceptionally long series of charters suggests a ruler effectively in charge of Aquitaine and Burgundy as well as Francia itself.[120] The tribute to the Vikings which Charles had agreed to pay over in May was to be raised not only from Francia, 'but also from Burgundy'.[121] The 4,000 lb in silver bullion ('according to weight') paid in 866 had apparently been raised from Francia alone. The taxing of Burgundy helped make 5,000 lb a realistic target. There was a second innovation in the fiscal procedures of 877: whereas in 866 the tenant of a free manse owed 6d., in 877 he owed only 4d., with a further 4d. being diverted from the lord's rent. From the king's standpoint, the total yield per free manse was increased by one third (to 8d.), but the tenant paid one third less than before, while his lord was required not only to collect but to contribute.[122] In other words, the tax-burden was eased for peasants while the state benefited at the expense of

119 Fulk was a former palatine cleric, Schneider 1973: 22–3.
120 T. 430–1, 433–46. In c. 23 of the Quierzy Capitulary, Charles planned to take Brittany back under direct royal authority.
121 *AB* 877: 200, also noting that Neustria was to be taxed separately. (Its yield would be additional to the 5,000 lb)
122 *MGH Capit.* II, no. 280, p. 354; *AB* 877: 200. My inference is that these provisions were to apply only to *honores* given by Charles.

landlords: a remarkable redistribution of wealth entirely in keeping with previous Carolingian efforts to protect and sustain the *pauperes*. The discussion at Quierzy about the *honores* of Boso and Bernard [c. 31] presumably arose from the attempt to implement these arrangements. 'The tribute was raised by those who remained in Francia, and this made the Danes depart.'[123]

In June, Charles 'taking with him his wife and a very large quantity of gold and silver and horses and other goods' began his journey east and south towards Italy.[124] Abbot Hugh was with him at Ponthion in July securing his own Burgundian interests. As Charles journeyed through Burgundy in August, Boso was in attendance at Besançon.[125] It seems that both Hugh and Boso had agreed to come on to Italy in Charles's wake. Early in September Charles was met at Vercelli by a grateful John VIII. The news that his nephew Karlmann was advancing with a large army made Charles all the more impatient to receive reinforcements from across the Alps. But Boso and Hugh never came: instead, according to Hincmar, they conspired against Charles with Count Bernard of the Auvergne and Bernard of Gothia 'and the rest of the lay magnates and bishops, with a few exceptions'. [126]

It is striking that no other contemporary so much as mentions a plot, not even the East Frankish annalist, ever keen to depict Charles's position in the worst possible light. Nevertheless, Hincmar's list of named 'defectors' requires an explanation. Why did these men, hitherto loyal, refuse Charles's summons now? And did their refusal constitute a political catastrophe from which (unlike Andernach) no recovery was possible for Charles? Charles's fiscal experiment had put unprecedented pressure on those with *honores* in Burgundy: Boso, Bernard of the Auvergne (who had hereditary lands in the Autunois) and Hugh. On the other hand, there is no evidence that other Burgundian magnates (the count of the palace Adalard, for instance) opposed Charles. Did Boso in particular resent the loss of

123   *AV* 877: 42.
124   *AB* 877: 200.
125   T. 437, 438 (Hugh); 443, 444 (Boso).
126   *AB* 877: 202.

his viceregal position in Italy which would surely follow if, as Charles evidently intended, Louis the Stammerer were to be set up there as king? In fact Boso's Italian roots were shallow; and he had remained north of the Alps continuously, it seems, between October 876 and September 877. The four dissidents had two things in common: first, none was among the group detailed to remain 'assiduously with Louis', that is permanently in his entourage; second, the main *honores* of all four were located outside Francia proper, in Burgundy, Neustria, and the south, which helps explain why none had been present at Quierzy in June.[127] The dissidents' refusal to join Charles in Italy can be read as a desire to draw him back northwards – to re-establish the *status quo*. Hincmar in the *AB* gives no hint that they supported an alternative Carolingian, and elsewhere shows them actively hostile to Louis the Stammerer.[128] In fact, it was precisely because Louis's regime, as sketched at Quierzy, had included so clear a dividing-line between 'court' and 'country' that Boso and his associates now sensed a loss of *Königsnähe*. It was not that Charles had lost control of the provinces: rather that his absence, coupled with the shift of power within and around the royal family entailed by Louis's establishment, had roused provincial magnates' fears for their own futures. Everyone knew (and the recent fate of Lothar II reminded them) that Franks ran a high risk of mortality in an Italian summer. Suppose Charles did not come back? For Boso, Hugh, and their allies, the prospect of Louis the Stammerer's succession was alarming.

Charles depended on his magnates' help (it was no time to risk an Andernach in the south), but he could also understand their anxieties, and respond positively. His Frankish powerbase had not collapsed. He still had his treasure: he sent Richildis back north with it, and not long afterwards, followed her over the Alps. On the journey he became violently ill. He halted near Maurienne, and sent urgently for Richildis. Charles believed he was dying; he had but one direct heir, and there was no time to contem-

---

127 Hincmar's letter to Louis the Stammerer, *PL* 125, col. 986, says Boso, Bernard and Hugh were absent. The Quierzy Capitulary does not mention Bernard of Gothia.

128 See his letter cited in the previous note.

plate more distant Carolingian claims. To Richildis he entrusted his regalia, 'and the sword known as St Peter's sword': she was to hand these, and the realm, to Louis the Stammerer after all.[129] Charles's last wish was that he be buried at St-Denis. He did not quite live to see another feastday of his patron: on 6 October 877 he died. Though his followers were forced to bury him ('such was the corpse's stench') at Nantua not far from Lyons, his bones were disinterred a few years later and 'taken to St-Denis where they were buried with honour'.[130] There they still remain.

---

129 *AB* 877: 203–4. Hincmar alleges that Charles had been poisoned by his Jewish doctor.

130 Regino 877: 113. The macabre story of the first interment is recorded (without hostile comment) by *AB*, *AF* and *AV*, as well as Regino. A laudatory epitaph was preserved at Nantua; *MGH* Poet. Lat. IV, p. 1001. For the place accorded to Charles by St Louis, see above Ch. 1: 4.

Chapter 10

EPILOGUE

'The last years' of Charles the Bald's reign are often viewed in apocalyptic terms of impending catastrophe. I have avoided that expression – because Charles, unaware that these *were* his last years, continued to work and plan for a future in which he foresaw an expansion of his own power. Hindsight is a mixed blessing for historians: it permits long-run judgements; but it also threatens to impose teleological ones. Only in retrospect does the break-up of Charles's revived empire, the collapse of royal power in his kingdom, seem inevitable. Situate yourself in 877, and move slowly forward in time: it becomes clear that the break-up and the collapse did not precede but followed Charles's death, nor did they follow immediately.

Louis the Stammerer has had a bad press. In personal terms he certainly had had little chance to distinguish himself during his father's lifetime: he and his brothers had been perhaps the main victims of Charles's need to manoeuvre within tight territorial constraints. In political terms, however, Louis was very much Charles's heir. Louis's reign saw no real breakage of links between the heartland of the West Frankish realm and its provinces, its *regna.* Though Italy in practice was totally outwith Louis's control, encouraged by Pope John VIII he set his sights on Rome, and in 878 he made his continuing interest very clear to his East Frankish cousins: 'we still seek and, with God's help, shall seek, our share of the kingdom of Italy'.[1] The rebellion of Bernard of Gothia in 877–8 was hardly a bid

---

1   Treaty of Fouron, *AB* 878: 213. See Fried 1976.

for regional secession, still less the reaction of a territorial principality against monarchic rule:[2] Gothia had been lost to local rivals, and Bernard and his brother Imino spread violence into Aquitaine, Neustria and Francia and finally Burgundy, in what looks like a series of desperate and quite *un*-territorialised bids for an alternative powerbase. Louis showed sound political judgement in his determination to crush these rebels, using some of their former *honores* to win the support of other magnates, especially Bernard of the Auvergne. He provided *Königsnähe* anew for Boso, whose infant daughter married Louis's young son. Rebellion in Neustria was settled in keeping with Carolingian tradition, through mediation exercised at the royal court. Louis responded quickly to an appeal from Abbot Hugh for royal help against the Loire Vikings. The speed with which the aged Hincmar addressed himself to Charles's successor suggests that those who had felt maltreated under the old regime turned hopefully to the new.[3]

The heaviest price Louis had to pay to secure his recognition as king was the loss of direct control of some *honores* in his heartlands: of St-Denis, now granted to Gauzlin; and perhaps also of the countship of Paris, which went to Louis's kinsman Conrad. Even these grants might not have had much long-term significance (neither Gauzlin nor Conrad represented the threat of a territorial dynasty's control) – but for a series of short reigns in the decade that followed. Louis died in April 879, leaving two sons in their early teens. This second change of regime in sixteen months caused a classic sequence of disruption. The dying king had confided his older son, Louis III, as sole successor, to the guardianship of Bernard of the Auvergne, who was allied, in a kind of regency council, with Abbot Hugh and Boso. A rival faction led by Gauzlin of St-Denis[4] summoned the intervention of Louis the German's son and namesake, himself now an experienced ruler in his mid-forties and intent on reviving the Frankish imperial tradi-

2   So, Dhondt 1948: 213; followed by Dunbabin 1985: 14.
3   See *AB* 877–9: 206–16; and Hincmar's letter to Louis, *PL* 125, cols 983–90. Bautier 1978: XXIV–XXXII gives a vivid sketch of Louis's short reign.
4   *AB* 879: 216–17 clearly shows these opposed factions. See Werner 1979.

tion of Charlemagne.[5] The factions in the west reached agreement with each other by dividing the kingdom between Louis the Stammerer's sons, so that each faction had 'its' king; together they reached agreement with Louis the Younger by conceding to him Charles the Bald's Lotharingian gains of 870.[6] Already in 879, 'news of this discord' had drawn Vikings back from England to Francia to overwinter at Ghent.[7]

These threats to royal authority might have been overcome: both Louis III and his brother Carloman showed signs of military talent, and the political will to exclude rival Carolingian contenders (notably Lothar II's bastard son Hugh).[8] Both fell victim to occupational hazards: Louis died in August 882, of internal injuries incurred 'chasing a young woman on his horse for his joke (for he was a young man) while she fled into her father's house', while Carloman died in December 884 after being 'accidentally wounded in the thigh by one of his companions' when 'hunting with young men'.[9] These deaths represented a dynastic catastrophe for the descent-line of Charles the Bald. For that of Louis the German, the deaths of Louis the Younger's little son in 879 (he broke his neck in a fall from a palace window),[10] and of Louis himself in January 882, were similarly disastrous. The result was the reuniting of the whole Carolingian Empire in the hands of Charles the Fat, who, lacking a personal network of support in western Francia, and faced with a Viking attack on Paris itself, conferred key *honores* – the lay-abbacy of St-Denis and the countship of Paris – on Odo, son of the Count Robert of Anjou killed in the skirmish at Brissarthe twenty years before.[11] Charles the Fat himself died at the beginning of 888, leaving no legitimate heir. 'Partly through their deaths while so young, partly through the increasing sterility of

5 Fried 1983.
6 *AB* 880: 220 and n. 1.
7 *AV* 879: 44–6.
8 *AB* 880: 221.
9 *AV* 882: 52, 884: 56.
10 Regino 879: 119: 'a dishonourable death'.
11 Schneidmüller 1979: 106. For Robert, and for Charles the Bald's denial of 'inherited' *honores* to Robert's son after 866, see above Ch. 7: 183–7; Ch. 8: 209–11.

their wives, the royal kindred once so numerous was nar-
rowed to one': Regino of Prüm hardly exaggerated.[12] It was
at this point, 888, that the Carolingian Empire was re-
divided for good, and the beneficiaries included just one
Carolingian, the bastard Arnulf son of Karlmann, who
ruled only in the kingdom of his grandfather Louis the
German. In Italy, Burgundy, and West Francia, Charles the
Fat's successors were, as a shocked Anglo-Saxon contemporary observed, 'not one of them born to their kingdom
on the paternal side'.[13] In what had once been Charles
the Bald's kingdom – and it was a kingdom reduced by the
880 treaty to the boundaries of 869 – the new king was
Odo, count of Paris and lay-abbot of St-Denis.

In the western kingdom, there remained another Carolingian: Charles, later nicknamed *simplex*, meaning (non-pe-
joratively) 'the straightforward',[14] the posthumous son of
Louis the Stammerer. Passed over in the 880s because of
his youth, Charles became the figurehead of rebels against
Odo in 893, and eventually succeeded to the whole western
kingdom in 898 when Odo died leaving no son. In his
charters, many of which were confirmations of grants made
by Charles the Bald, Charles straightforwardly modelled
himself on his grandfather and namesake, imitating his
monogram and seal.[15] Nevertheless it is precisely through
the charters of Charles the Straightforward that changes
can be observed in the bases of royal power since the reign
of Charles the Bald.

First, the pattern of the royal itinerary was different:
Charles the Bald had stayed most often at the palaces of
the Oise and middle Seine valleys, at monasteries whose
abbacies he himself either controlled directly as lay-abbot
or had in his gift, and in *civitates* whose bishops were his
appointees and faithful men. His grandson and namesake
rarely stayed at monasteries or in *civitates*, and among his
grandfather's favoured palaces, visited only Compiègne
relatively often, and then only in his early years and again
in the last years of his reign. During the period from 911–
18, when Charles the Straightforward concentrated on a

12 Regino 888: 117. The 'one' was Arnulf. See Genealogy II
13 *ASC* 887.
14 Schneidmüller 1978.
15 Schneidmüller 1979: 207–9.

vigorous attempt to regain the share of the Lotharingian heartlands acquired by his grandfather in 870 and lost ten years later, his itinerary shifted eastwards, with frequent stays at the palaces of Attigny and Herstal and in a new-built monastic palace at Laon.[16] The bid to recover Lotharingia was justified in terms of dynastic legitimacy, for after 911, the former kingdom of Louis the German had passed out of Carolingian hands. But the bid failed: after 918, the new king 'across the Rhine' Henry of Saxony, grasping the importance of Lotharingia, won crucial aristocratic allies there, and constructed a new legitimacy of his own.[17] Charles the Straightforward had little to fall back on. Further west, in the heartlands of his grandfather's kingdom, once-royal monasteries and *civitates* had, since the 880s, fallen under the domination of local aristocrats. The most significant case in point was the Paris region, where Odo's territorial power had passed, on his death, straight to his brother Count Robert of Anjou.[18] As for Rheims, Archbishop Fulk having assumed the role of arbiter between Odo and Charles, systematically built up his own territorial lordship, complete with fortifications.[19] In other words, Charles the Straightforward was unable in 898 to reverse the alienation of just those resources that had sustained his grandfather's authority.

The beneficiaries of his charters also present a different picture from those of his grandfather's. Their geographical spread is narrower. Gothia apart, few regions other than Francia proper any longer appear as the home-base of those favoured by royal patronage. Another difference is still more significant: where Charles the Bald had made no fewer than 29 grants to faithful men in Francia proper, his grandson made just four. The reduction has been attributed to Charles the Bald's squandering of the fisc, leaving Charles the Straightforward, allegedly, with simply no more to give. This argument, however, fails to take account of the inflow (occasionally documented but now unquantifiable) *into* Charles the Bald's fisc as well as outflow from it;

16 Brühl 1968: 49–50.
17 Reuter 1991a: 140–1.
18 Lauer, *Recueil des Actes de Charles le Simple*, nos. 45, 50.
19 Schneider 1973.

and more important still, it ignores the function of such grants as rewards for faithful service. If would-be beneficiaries continued to attend Charles the Bald's court, that was because they knew benefits were to be had there – just as clerics thronged his palace in hopes of promotion to well-stocked sees. The drastic diminution in the total output of his grandson's charters, and in particular, of grants to lay *fideles,* betoken a fall-off of expectations, hence a slump in fidelity.

These contrasts are symptoms of a political change: the royal palace was ceasing to operate (as Hincmar shows it doing, still, in Charles's reign) as powerhouse, as clearing-house, as distribution-centre for *honores* and largesse. What was new was not the passing of *honores* from one holder to his close kinsman, but the by-passing of the palace in that transfer, the cutting-out of the king from the transmission-process. The specific location of this effectively autonomous hereditary territorial power was significant too. Since Charles the Straightforward no longer had a firm grip on the Seine valley, his dealings with the Viking warlord Rollo, at first glance so reminiscent of Charles the Bald's dealings with Bjørn or Weland, were in fact conducted from a much weaker base. Rollo was granted territory – and territory that included the once major Carolingian centre of Rouen where Rollo settled within a few kilometres of Charles the Bald's fortified bridge at Pîtres. Once the king had made his grant, it was regional magnates who were now Rollo's partners in a new diplomacy in which the king was no longer the central figure.[20] The relationship between magnates and king had been changing in the 880s and 890s, when fortresses – whose unauthorised construction Charles the Bald had fiercely prohibited in 864[21] – proliferated in Francia without any semblance of royal control. By the 920s, the coinage was heading the same way, in Flanders as well as in Aquitaine.[22] A growing political rift came between Charles's former heartlands, and the regions to the west and south. The king no longer went into Neustria or Aquitaine. Ecclesiastical hospitality could not supplement,

---

20   Bates 1982: 9–10.
21   Above Ch. 8: 207.
22   Lafaurie 1970; Metcalf 1979.

or substitute for, permanently maintained royal residences, when sees and monasteries, like the lands formerly assigned to the upkeep of Aquitanian palaces, fell into the hands of the local nobility.[23] Within a year of Charles's death, his appointee as archbishop of Bourges was being denied entry to his own metropolis by a rebel magnate.[24]

The palace had ceased to function as a junction-box in the circuit of power. No longer did the king attempt to intervene in the distribution of *honores*; no longer did magnates move from one post to another at the king's behest; no longer were *missi* sent from the palace; no longer could the king intervene in ecclesiastical appointments in regions distant from his own lands, sending ex-notaries and palace clerks to Aquitanian bishoprics and Burgundian abbacies; no longer did the king along with his nobility, magnates and *minores* alike, promulgate capitularies from assemblies in Francia. A single full capitulary survives from the reign of Charles the Bald's grandson Carloman: that is the last Carolingian capitulary.[25] For most of the aristocracy, *Königsnähe* had been replaced, literally and figuratively, by other kinds of closeness – while the king was permanently remote. He did not, could not, visit the *regna*: more important, great men from the *regna* had no reason to visit him.

The dissolution of political bonds can be traced down to a lower level too. The evidence here is, inevitably, very scrappy: nevertheless it points with remarkable consistency to the maintenance of direct links between the king and the *minores* throughout Charles the Bald's reign, and the disappearance of such links within a generation of Charles's death.[26] Charles's capitularies repeatedly prescribe the activities of *vassi* (or *vassalli*) *dominici*: they constitute the king's *force de frappe* in 864; again perform crucial military roles in 865; are entrusted with peacekeeping in 869; need royal (imperial) permission to transmit benefices to their heirs in 877. [27] In 869, Hincmar reports that *vassi dominici* were instructed to make lists of counts' benefices and

23 Martindale 1985.
24 Letter of John VIII, *MGH Epp.* VII, no. 155.
25 *MGH Capit.* II, no. 287.
26 Cf. Tabacco 1989: 153.
27 *MGH Capit.* II, nos. 273, additional c. 2, p. 328; 274, c. 13, p. 331; 275, cc. 11, 12, p. 336; cf. no. 281, c. 9, p. 358.

report them to the king.[28] An incidental reference in the *Life of Gerald of Aurillac* (written c. 930 within thirty years of its subject's death) indicates what happened to such men later in the ninth century: Gerald, himself a royal *vassus* in the 890s, was pressed to leave the 'royal service' and to commend himself to the leading magnate of his region, William of Aquitaine (son of Bernard 'Hairypaws'). According to the 'Life', William's insistence was characteristic of the *marchiones* whose 'insolence' was 'subjecting royal vassals to itself, now that the condition of the state was disturbed'. Gerald, who refused to transfer his loyalty, and instead 'commended his nephew with a great number of warriors', was the exception who proved the rule. Other vassals, it is implied, no longer acted as agents of the king but became the clients of regional magnates.[29] In Anjou and Burgundy, as in Aquitaine, territorial princes exerted a gravitational pull on the lesser nobility.[30] Free peasants yielded to the 'bad customs' imposed by local lords. In 861, peasants belonging to the lordship of St-Denis still believed that King Charles the Bald might protect their rights and status against the violent exactions of the agents of St-Denis. No more such cases are recorded north of the Alps.[31]

It might be argued that these changes are only apparent, not real, a trick of the evidential light: that the dwindling of capitularies after 877, and their total absence after 884, the drying-up of evidence for church councils after 882, the absence of any sequel to the *AB* as a king-centred record of events, the absence of evidence about assemblies, all simply register the disappearance from the scene of a single colossal multi-media figure – Hincmar of Rheims. Such an argument must be rejected. It is not just that, in Charles the Bald's reign, capitularies and conciliar records were made, and kept, by others as well as Hincmar, nor that charters (a medium outside the control of any one

---

28   *AB* 869: 153.
29   *Vita Geraldi* I, c. 32, *PL* 133, cols 660–1. Gerald still applied to Charles the Straightforward for an immunity for his monastic foundation at Aurillac; Lauer, *Recueil,* no. 21. On this Life, see Airlie 1991.
30   Dunbabin 1985: Ch. 4.
31   Cf. Tabacco 1989: 154–5. For the case of the Mitry peasants, see above Ch. 3: 62–4.

man or single centre) independently tell the same story of waning centripetal force. The whole argument can be turned on its head: the fact that Hincmar's successors did not maintain those traditions is itself a symptom, not cause, of deeper, political, change. A century before, the palace had been the royally-primed pump through which a culture of the written word had been diffused from the top down, from centre to periphery and back again. Charlemagne had personally patronised a palace school, not only for clerics (though ecclesiastical learning was a prime goal) but for young lay nobles too. Louis the Pious and especially Charles the Bald reaped the political benefits in the shape of a literate lay elite – susceptible to messages, ideological as well as practical, purveyed through writing. Because this constituency already existed, Charles the Bald could address it in sermons and histories and capitularies, as well as through the spoken word.[32] The maintenance of the church as an instrument of royal government went hand in hand with the use of literacy as an instrument, and a powerful symbol, of political consensus. This was necessarily a collective exercise; but in Charles the Bald's reign it was promoted and coordinated by the king himself.

Councils and assemblies were not only institutions but associations of men. It was the shared activity of the magnates along with the king at and through these regular meetings which played a key part in shaping political attitudes and establishing a frame of reference for political action. It was also at assemblies that the king could communicate directly with the lesser landholders: royal *adnuntiationes* delivered 'in a loud voice, in the *lingua romana*', that is, the Romance vernacular, translated the high ideals of Charles's *res publica* for the benefit of a broad ruling class. Assemblies did not just happen: they had to be summoned and organised. Once they ceased to be summoned, and to be summoned regularly, other kinds of association replaced them: from the realm-wide level, the coordination of power (along with the uses of literacy) shifted to the regional and local and the pragmatic. What Charles had termed the *societas fidelium* ('the association of [the king's] faithful men') gave way to other groupings

32 See Nelson 1989a; 1991c.

structured around the lordship of magnates: for these, modern historians have had to find their own name, *mouvance*, since no contemporary term is recorded.[33] They represented a privatisation of power, a 'parcellisation of sovereignty'[34] – which came about *after* Charles the Bald's departure from the scene and surely, in part, *because* of it. No realm-wide organisation, whether ecclesiastical or lay, could survive without a large, sustained royal input. That was precisely what was lacking after 877.

Yet something of Charles's *res publica* survived. If the political structures of his kingdom atrophied, the ideology he had championed did not disappear. It included the concepts of fidelity as a public virtue, of office-holding as authority delegated from the king, of the church within the realm as the ally and agent of public authority. Not all of this disappeared in the tenth and eleventh centuries.[35] The church did not wholly lose institutional shape and identity; and its liturgy maintained the generalised practice of prayer for the king, associating kingship with peace. No king after 877 in what had been Charles's realm ever acceeded without being consecrated by bishops. Through the use of royal reign-years to date the charters they drew up for their noble patrons, provincial clergy perpetuated the sense of belonging to a kingdom. The territorial princes of the tenth and eleventh centuries saw themselves, still, as loyal supporters and subordinates of kings they rarely if ever saw. Aristocratic power, 'shockingly unconsecrated and dumb',[36] was legitimised by reference to a superior, royal lordship. The dukes of Normandy, or the counts of Flanders and Poitou, defended their churches, kept public order, controlled castle- building, issued coins, in the name of once-Carolingian royalty. First recorded in the eleventh and twelfth centuries, the genealogies of great magnates link them (through ties of blood or of service) with kings, and sometimes specifically with Charles the Bald. The vernacular epic literature of the twelfth century similarly records older oral traditions: in them, Charlemagne/Charles

---

33 Dunbabin 1985: 59. Cf. Reynolds 1984: Ch. 7.
34 Anderson 1974: 153.
35 Werner 1987 and 1986; Ehlers 1976 and 1983; Nelson 1988a.
36 Southern 1953: 99.

the Bald has become a composite royal figure. If the historic Roland of Charlemagne's reign is the model *fidelis*, the historic Wenilo of Charles the Bald's reign typifies the traitor whose gruesome punishment is visited on him by king and faithful men together. Through their *chansons*, the nobility of the realm that had once been Charles the Bald's achieved a *Königsnähe* of the imagination. Though that realm's permanent identity long postdated Charles the Bald, (Charles the Straightforward was the first even to call himself 'king of the West Franks')[37] it could never have taken shape at all but for the decades in the ninth century during which Charles the Bald ruled it, effectively and vociferously, as a unit. In that sense, though as Charlemagne's grandson he himself always hankered after a larger, imperial realm, Charles was one of the makers of France: a maker in spite of himself, who deserved, nevertheless, his tomb's central place in St Louis's St-Denis.

---

37   Wolfram 1973: 126.

CHARLES THE BALD'S PALACE PERSONNEL

Archchaplain
Ebroin, bishop of Poitiers, 839/40–?853[1]
Hilduin, abbot of St-Germain-des-Prés, ?854–860[2]
? Odo, abbot of Corbie then bishop of Beauvais, 860–877[3]

Archchancellor
Louis, abbot of St-Denis, 840–867[4]
Gauzlin, abbot of St-Germain-des-Prés, 867–877[5]

Chamberlain
Vivian, 843[6]
Engelram, also master of the doorkeepers, 868[7]

Boso, chamberlain and master of the doorkeepers for the kingdom of Aquitaine, 872[8]

Counts of the Palace
Hilmerad, 844–851[9]

1 Oexle 1968: 166, 191.
2 Fleckenstein 1959: 142–5.
3 Grierson 1935: 192–4.
4 Tessier 1955: 38–42.
5 Tessier 1955: 42–6.
6 T. 19, 28. Vivian perhaps held this post until his death in 851: direct evidence is lacking.
7 *AB* 868: 152. Engelram may have held the post since the early 860s. For the years 851–859, information is lacking.
8 *AB* 872: 177. It is possible, but uncertain, that Boso served as chamberlain for Charles's whole kingdom.
9 T. 40: *AFont*: 87.

Fulk, 861–68[10]
Osbert, 863[11]
Imino, 869–874[12]
Adalard, c. 875–877[13]

Other personnel[14]:
Adalard, ? seneschal 840–4[15]
Odacer, ? in charge of imperial chancery 876–7[16]
Gerard and Frederic, subordinates of count of the palace, 877[17]
Adelelm, responsible for forests, 877[18]

10 T. 228, 314.
11 T. 258. Osbert may have been Fulk's deputy.
12 T. 375. Cf. *AB* 878: 207, n.4.
13 Nelson 1986c: 53–5; *MGH Capit.* II, no. 281, c. 17, p. 359.
14 Hincmar, *Government of the Palace* c. 23, lists seneschal, butler, and
    constable, then the officers responsible for accommodating and
    provisioning the itinerant household.
15 Adalard held this office under Louis the Pious; Lot 1908b; but is
    not identified as such in Charles's reign.
16 *AB* 877: 201; Tessier 1955: 92.
17 *MGH Capit.* II, no. 281, c. 17, p. 359.
18 Ibid., c. 33, p. 361.

THE BENEFICIARIES OF THE CHARTERS OF CHARLES THE BALD

Of Charles the Bald's 354 surviving genuine charters approximately 30% (121) are alienations of land or rights by Charles himself: the rest are confirmations either of grants made by his predecessors, or of arrangements (such as exchanges of property) made by the charters' beneficiaries. (This figure for alienations as a percentage of the total number of grants can be compared with approximately 27% for extant charters of Charlemagne, 25% of those of Lothar I, and 38% for those of Louis the German.)[1] Some 42% of Charles's alienations were made to lay beneficiaries, with the remainder to ecclesiastical communities or, more rarely, individual churchmen (usually acting on a community's behalf). Since lands were constantly coming into the fisc as well as leaving it yet such acquisitions are unrecorded, and since grants of benefices were certainly frequent but, again, unrecorded, Charles's charters provide no firm basis for assessing the overall extent of alienation of the fisc in his kingdom.[2] They do, however, give an impression of the range and intensity of Charles's political action (visible in alienations and confirmations alike) in the various parts of his kingdom: the pie-chart shows the distribution of the charter-beneficiaries by their *regnum* of origin.

1 Given the difficulties of categorising this material and great variation in the sizes and values of grants, these figures are necessarily impressionistic. They are based on the editions listed in the Bibliography of Primary Sources. Far more of Charles the Bald's charters survive than of any other Carolingian. This is at least partly attributable to the unusually extensive diffusion of aristocratic literacy, and longstanding, continuous traditions of literate government, in his kingdom; cf. McKitterick 1989; Nelson 1990f.
2 Martindale 1985.

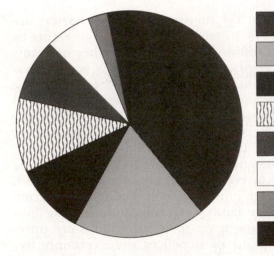

- ■ Francia
- ▨ Neustria
- ■ Aquitaine
- 〰 Burgundy
- ▨ Spanish March
- □ Septimania
- ▨ Lotharingia
- ■ Italy

Distribution of charter-beneficiaries (by *regnum* of origin)

BIBLIOGRAPHY

. . .

PRIMARY SOURCES

A: Narrative, annalistic and biographical texts

1. *Annals of St-Bertin (Annales Bertiniani)*
   Ed. F. Grat, J. Vielliard and S. Clémencet, with intro-
   duction and notes by L. Levillain (Paris 1964). Eng-
   lish translation with introduction and notes by J.L.
   Nelson, *Ninth-Century Histories: the Annals of St-Bertin*
   (Manchester, 1991). Continuation of *Royal Frankish
   Annals* (see below, no. 11). Written in the entourage
   of Louis the Pious from 830 to 840, then kept up by
   Prudentius, former palace cleric of Louis and from
   841 of Charles the Bald, from 843/4 to 861 bishop of
   Troyes. From 861 continued by Hincmar archbishop
   of Rheims until his death in 882. The main annalistic
   work covering the kingdom and reign of Charles the
   Bald.

2. *Annals of Angoulême (Annales Engolismenses)*
   Ed. O. Holder-Egger, *MGH SS* XVI (Hanover, 1859),
   p. 486. Very brief annals written at Angoulême in
   Aquitaine during the ninth century.

3. *Annals of Fontanelle (Annales Fontanellenses; Chronicle of
   St-Wandrille)*
   Ed. (with French translation) by J. Laporte, Société
   de l'histoire de Normandie 15 sér. (Rouen and Paris,
   1951). Brief annals produced at the monastery of Fontanelle (also known as St-Wandrille) near Rouen
   from 840 to 856.

4. *Annals of Fulda (Annales Fuldenses)*
   Ed. F. Kurze, *MGH SRG* (Hanover, 1891). English translation by T. Reuter forthcoming in the companion volume of *Ninth-Century Histories* (Manchester 1991). The main annalistic work in the East Frankish kingdom, from 830 to 901; written at Mainz.

5. *Annals of St-Vaast (Annales Vedastini)*
   Ed. B. von Simson, *MGH SRG* (Hanover, 1909). English translation by S. Coupland forthcoming (Manchester 1992). Annals written at the monastery of St-Vaast, Arras, from 873 to 900.

6. *Annals of Xanten (Annales Xantenses)*
   Ed. B. von Simson, *MGH SRG* (Hanover, 1909). English translation by S. Coupland forthcoming (Manchester 1992). Written in the lower Rhine area (probably Ghent, then Cologne, rather than Xanten). Draws on *RFA* down to 811; then a fuller, and independent, account from 832 to 873.

7. Astronomer, *Vita Hludovici Pii*
   Ed. G. Pertz, *MGH SS* II (Berlin, 1829), pp. 607–48. New *MGH* edition by E. Tremp forthcoming. English translation by Cabaniss, 1961. Anonymous biography of Louis the Pious, written shortly after 840.

8. Flodoard, *Historia Remensis Ecclesiae*
   Ed. I. Heller and G. Waitz, *MGH SS* XIII (Hanover, 1881). History of his church written by a Rheims cleric c. 960, using rich archival materials, and including summaries of letters of Archbishop Hincmar.

9. Nithard, *Historiarum Libri IV (Four Books of Histories)*
   Ed. with French translation by P. Lauer, as *Nithard, Histoire des Fils de Louis le Pieux* (Paris, 1926). English translation Scholz, 1970. Contemporary history, covering 814 to 843, written by participant observer.

10. Regino of Prüm, *Chronicon*
    Ed. F. Kurze, *MGH SRG* (Hanover, 1890). Universal chronicle which becomes fairly full annals from c. 850, written up at Trier in 909, and particularly well-informed on Lotharingia.

11. *Royal Frankish Annals (Annales Regni Francorum)*
     Ed. F. Kurze, *MGH SRG* (Hanover, 1895). English
     translation Scholz, 1970. Main annalistic text covering
     Frankish history from 741 to 830. Kept up in the
     reign of Louis the Pious by chaplains in Louis's en-
     tourage.

12. Thegan, *Gesta Hludowici imperatoris*
     Ed. G. Pertz, *MGH SS* II (Berlin, 1829), pp. 585–604.
     New *MGH* edition by E. Tremp forthcoming. Bio-
     graphy of Louis the Pious written in 837 by Trier
     cleric.

B: Other sources

(i) *Letters*

1. Hincmar of Rheims, *Epistolae*
    Ed. E. Perels, *MGH Epp.* VIII (i) (Berlin, 1939), 206
    letters and summaries (via Flodoard) covering the
    period from 845 down to 868; for letters from 869 to
    882, *PL* 126. The second *MGH* volume is forthcoming.

2. Lupus of Ferrières, *Epistolae*
    Ed. L. Levillain, Loup de Ferrières, *Correspondance*, 2
    vols (Paris, 1927–35), with French translation. (All ci-
    tations in the notes to the present book use Levil-
    lain's numbering.) New ed. by P.K. Marshall (Leipzig,
    1984). English translation by G.W. Regenos, *The Let-
    ters of Lupus of Ferrières* (The Hague, 1966). Collection
    of 133 letters, spanning the period c. 830 to c. 862.

3. Papal correspondence
    Letters of Leo IV, (ed.) A. de Hirsch-Gereuth, *MGH
    Epp.* V (Berlin, 1899); Nicholas I and Hadrian II,
    (ed.) E. Perels, *MGH Epp.* VI (Berlin, 1925); John
    VIII, (ed.) E. Caspar, *MGH Epp.* VII (Berlin, 1928).

4. Eulogius of Toledo, *Epistolae*
    Ed. *PL* 115, cols 841–52. Three letters of archbishop
    of Toledo martyred at Cordoba in 859.

(ii) *Capitularies and conciliar decrees*

Note: for these texts, see above 9, 46, 65.

1. *Capitularia regum Francorum*
    Ed. A. Boretius and V. Krause, *MGH Capit.* II (Hanover, 1897). Edition of the capitularies of Charles the Bald, decrees emanating from meetings between ninth-century Carolingian rulers and from church councils, and other related documents.

2. *Die Konzilien der karolingischen Teilreiches 843–859*
    Ed. W. Hartmann, *MGH Concilia* III (Hanover, 1984). Fine modern edition with discussion of the texts, their sources and contexts.

(iii) *Royal charters*

1. *Receuil des Actes de Charles II le Chauve, roi de France*
    Ed. G. Tessier, 3 vols (Paris, 1943–55). Edition of 354 complete royal charters (with 68 mentions of lost charters also noted), also with a few letters and judgements.

2. *Die Urkunden Lothars I und Lothars II*
    Ed. T. Schieffer, *MGH Diplomata Karolinorum* III (Berlin, 1966). Edition of 145 complete charters of Lothar I (with 50 further mentions of lost charters), and 39 charters of Lothar II (with 11 further mentions of lost charters).

3. *Receuil des Actes de Pépin I et Pépin II, rois d'Aquitaine*
    Ed. L. Levillain (Paris, 1926). Edition of 43 charters (mostly complete) of Pippin I, and 13 of Pippin II; with very full introduction and commentary.

4. *Receuil des Actes de Louis II le Bègue, Louis III et Carloman II, rois de France*
    Ed. R.-H. Bautier (Paris 1978).

5. *Receuil des Actes de Charles le Simple roi de France (893–923)*
    Ed. P. Lauer (Paris, 1949).

(iv) *Private charters*

Note: the following are later medieval cartularies which preserve a few (in the case of no. 5, a substantial number of) ninth-century charters

1. *Cartulaire de l'abbaye de Beaulieu en Limousin*, (ed.) M. Deloche, Paris, 1859.

2. *Cartulaire de l'abbaye de Cysoing*, (ed.) I. de Coussemaker, Lille, 1883.

3. *Cartulaire de l'église d'Angoulême*, (ed.) J. Nanglard, Angoulême, 1900.

4. *Receuil des Chartes de l'abbaye de Saint-Benoît sur Loire (Fleury)*, (ed.) M. Prou and A. Vidier, Paris 1907.

5. *Cartulaire de Brioude*, (ed.) H. Doniol, *Mémoires de l'Académie des Sciences, Belles-Lettres et Arts de Clermont-Ferrand* 3 (1861).

(v) *Translationes and miracula*

Note: A *translatio* is an account of the carrying-away of a saint's body to escape attack. Descriptions of the saint's miracles are often associated with *translationes*.

1. Anonymous, *Translatio Sancti Germani Parisiensis*
   Ed. in *Analecta Bollandiana* 2 (1883), pp. 69–98.
   Translatio with *miracula*, including an account of the Viking attack on St-Germain-des-Prés, Paris, in 845. Written up at St-Germain before 851. Translation by D. Bullough, *The Vikings at Paris*, forthcoming (Manchester, 1992).

2. Ermentarius, *De translationibus et miraculis Sancti Philiberti Libri II*
   Ed. R. Poupardin, *Monuments de l'histoire des abbayes de Saint-Philibert* (Paris, 1905).
   An account of the travels of the community of St-Philibert, Noirmoutier, following Viking attack in 836, to Saumur, Cunauld and then Messay (Poitou). Written up in stages in c. 855 and 863. Translated by D. Herlihy, 1970.

3. Aimoin of St-Germain-des-Prés, *Translatio* of George, Aurelius et Nathalie
   Ed. *PL* 115, cols 939–60.
   Translatio of saints martyred at Cordoba in the early 850s, to St-Germain in 859. Written up at St-Germain c. 875.

4. Aimoin of St-Germain-des-Prés, *Translatio* of Saint Vincent
   Ed. *PL* 126, cols 1011–24.
   Translatio of Cordoban martyr to the monastery of Castres near Albi. Written up c. 875.

5. Aimoin of St-Germain-des-Prés, *Miracula Sancti Germani*
   Ed. *PL* 126, cols 1027–50.
   Revised version, with additional miracles, of *miracula* of St Germain of Paris. Written up c. 875.

6. Adrevald of Fleury, *Miracula Sancti Benedicti*
   Ed. *PL* 124, cols 909–48; extracts (ed.) O. Holder-Egger, *MGH SS* XV (Hanover, 1887), pp. 474–97.
   Written up at St-Benoît, Fleury, c. 870. Contains historical material for the period from Charlemagne onwards.

7. Heiric of Auxerre, *De Miraculis Sancti Germani Episcopi Autissiodorensis Libri II*
   Ed. *PL* 124, cols 1207–70.
   Written up at St-Germain, Auxerre, in later 860s.
   Book II includes miracles from the 850s.

(vi) *Collections of episcopal lives and deeds (gesta):*

1. *Liber Pontificalis*
   Ed. L. Duchesne (revised C. Vogel), 3 vols (Paris, 1955–7). Papal biographies, continued up to 870 (the pontificate of Hadrian II). (The English translation by R. Davis, *The Book of Pontiffs* (Liverpool, 1989) only goes down to 715, but has a valuable introduction.) No English translation exists for the ninth-century lives.

2. *Gesta episcoporum Autissiodorensium*
    Ed. P. Labbe, *Bibliotheca nova manuscriptorum* 1 (Paris, 1657), pp. 411–626, extracts (ed.) G. Waitz, *MGH SS* XIII, pp. 393–400. Deeds of the Bishops of Auxerre, written up in 870s at request of Bishop Wala (872–9) by two Auxerre clerics.

3. Agnellus of Ravenna, *Liber Pontificalis Ecclesiae Ravennatis*
    Ed. O. Holder-Egger, *MGH SRL* (Hanover, 1878), pp. 265–391. Biographies of archbishops of Ravenna written up by local cleric. Earlier part written in 830s, then covers pontificate of Archbishop George (817–46).

(vii) *Miscellaneous*

Note: listed in chronological order.

1. Ermold the Black (Ermoldus Nigellus), *In Honorem Hludowici Pii*
    Ed. E. Faral, *Ermold le Noir. Poème sur Louis le Pieux* (Paris, 1964), with French translation. Extracts in English translation in Godman, 1985. Panegyric verse biography, written in 827/828 by an Aquitanian cleric.

2. Einhard, *Vita Karoli Magni*
    Ed. O. Holder-Egger, *MGH SRG* (Hanover, 1911). English translation L. Thorpe, *Two Lives of Charlemagne* (Harmondsworth, 1969). Biography of Charlemagne written in the reign of Louis the Pious, probably in the early 830s by former confidant of the emperor.

3. Dhuoda, *Liber Manualis*
    Ed. with French translation by P. Riché (Paris, 1975). Handbook of spiritual instruction written in 841–43 by Frankish noblewoman for her son.

4. Walahfrid Strabo, *Carmina*
    Ed. E. Dümmler, *MGH Poet. Lat.* II (Berlin, 1884), pp. 259–423. Selected extracts translated in Godman, 1985. Poems, many of them written at Louis the Pious's court in the 820s and 830s.

5. Walahfrid Strabo, *De Exordiis et Incrementis Quarundam in Observationibus Ecclesiasticis Rerum (The Origins and Development of Ecclesiastical Equipment and Ritual)* Ed. V. Krause, *MGH Capit.* II (Hanover, 1897), pp. 473–516. English translation by A.L.H. Corrêa in preparation.

6. Paschasius Radbertus, *Epitaphium Arsenii* Ed. E. Dümmler, *Abhandlungen der kaiserlichen Akademie der Wissenschaften zu Berlin, phil.-hist. Klasse,* 1900. English translation by Cabaniss, 1967. Life of Abbot Wala of Corbie in dialogue form, written up in the mid-850s by ex-abbot of Corbie.

7. Hildegar of Meaux, *Vita et miracula Sancti Faronis* Extracts (ed.) B. Krusch, *MGH SSRM* V (Hanover, 1910), pp. 171–203. Life of seventh-century bishop of Meaux written by Bishop Hildegar (c. 856–873/76) not long after the Viking attack on Meaux in 862.

8. John the Scot, *Carmina*, (ed.) L. Traube, *MGH Poet.* III (Berlin, 1906), pp. 518–56. Poems, some of them produced at the court of Charles the Bald, written between c. 850 and c. 877.

9. Ado of Vienne, *Chronicon* Extracts (ed.) G. Pertz, *MGH SS* II (Hanover, 1829), pp. 315–23. World history, written up c. 870 by archbishop of Vienne (860–75). Brief section covering ninth century is written from Lotharingian standpoint.

10. Rimbert, *Vita Anskarii* Ed. G. Waitz, *MGH SRG* (Hanover, 1884). English translation by C. H. Robinson, *Anskar, the Apostle of the North* (London, 1921). Life of Anskar, missionary to the Danes and bishop of Hamburg-Bremen, written c. 875 by Anskar's pupil and successor.

11. Notker, *Gesta Karoli Magni* Ed. H. Haefele, *MGH SRG* (Berlin, 1959). English translation by L. Thorpe, *Two Lives of Charlemagne* (Harmondsworth, 1969). Moralising account of deeds of Charlemagne written by St-Gall monk in 880s.

12.   *Anglo-Saxon Chronicle*
      Ed. C. Plummer, 2 vols. (Oxford, 1892–99); translated
      G.N. Garmonsway (London, 1972). First section down
      to 892 compiled in 890s in the circle of Alfred of
      Wessex.

13. and 14. *Gesta Sanctorum Rotonensium* and *Vita Conuuoionis*
      Ed. with English translation, *The Monks of Redon,* by C.
      Brett (Woodbridge, 1989). Hagiographical works pro-
      duced at the east-Breton monastery of Redon, the
      Gesta in the later ninth century, the *Vita,* c. 1000.

15.   *Chronique de Nantes*
      Ed. R. Merlet (Paris, 1896). Chronicle compiled in
      mid-eleventh century in part from earlier materials.

16.   Hariulf, *Chronicon Centulense*
      Ed. F. Lot, *Chronique de l'abbaye de Saint-Riquier* (Paris,
      1894). Monastic chronicle written up in early twelfth
      century, but based on earlier charter material.

17.   Suger, *Oeuvres complètes*
      Ed. A. Lecoy de la Marche (Paris, 1867). The works
      of Abbot Suger of St-Denis include a history of his
      monastery incorporating charter material and high-
      lighting benefactions of Charles the Bald.

18.   William of Malmesbury, *Gesta Pontificum Anglorum* Ed.
      N.E.S.A. Hamilton, Rolls Series (London, 1870). This
      twelfth-century historian knew a good deal about the
      Carolingian period.

(viii)   *Some works of Hincmar of Rheims*

1.   *Explanatio in Ferculum Salomonis* ('The Meaning of
      Solomon's Litter'), 855
      Ed. *PL* 125, cols 817–834.

2.   *De Ecclesiis et Capellis* ('Churches and Chapels'), 857/8
      Ed. M. Stratmann, *MGH Fontes* (Hanover, 1990).

3.   *De Divortio Lotharii regis et Tetbergae reginae* ('The Div-
      orce of King Lothar and Queen Theutberga'), 860
      Ed. *PL* 125, cols 619–772.

4. *De fide Carolo regi servanda* ('Keeping Faith'), 875
    Ed. *PL* 125, cols 961–84.

5. *De Villa Noviliaco* ('The Neuilly Estate'), 876
    Ed. *PL* 125, cols 1121–4.

6. *De iure metropolitanorum* ('The Rights of Metropolitans'), 876
    Ed. *PL* 126, cols 189–210.

7. *Instructio ad Ludovicum Balbum* ('Advice to Louis the Stammerer), 877
    Ed. *PL* 125, cols 938–990.

8. *De Ordine palatii* ('The Government of the Palace'), 881
    Ed. T. Gross and R. Schieffer, *MGH Fontes* (Hanover, 1980).

9. *Ordines* of royal consecration, for Judith (856), Ermentrude (866), Charles the Bald (869) and Louis the Stammerer (877) *MGH Capit.* II, nos. 296, 301, 276 and 302, 304.

SECONDARY WORKS

Airlie, S. (1985), 'The Political Behaviour of Secular Magnates in Francia, 829–879', Oxford University D.Phil. thesis.

Airlie, S. (1990), 'Bonds of power and bonds of association in the court circle of Louis the Pious', in Godman and Collins (eds), *Charlemagne's Heir*, pp. 191–204.

Airlie, S. (1991), 'The anxiety of sanctity: St Gerald of Aurillac and his maker', *Journal of Ecclesiastical History* (forthcoming).

Alibert, D. (1989), 'La majesté sacrée du roi: images du souverain carolingien', in *Histoire de l'Art 5/6*, pp. 23–36.

Anderson, P. (1974), *Passages from Antiquity to Feudalism*, London.

Angenendt, A. (1984a), *Kaiserherrschaft und Königstaufe*. Arbeiten zur Frühmittelalterforschung 15, Berlin and New York.

Angenendt, A. (1984b), 'Theologie und Liturgie der mittel-alterlichen Toten-Memoria', in K. Schmid and J. Wollasch (eds), *Memoria. Der geschichtliche Zeugniswert des liturgischen Gedenkens im Mittelalter*, Munich, pp. 79–199.

Auerbach, E. (1965), *Literary Language and its Public in Late Latin Antiquity and in the Middle Ages*, London.

Auzias, L. (1937), *L'Aquitaine carolingienne*, Toulouse and Paris.

Barrow, J. (1990), 'German cathedrals and the monetary economy in the twelth century', *JMH* 16 (1990), pp. 13–38.

Bates, D. (1982), *Normandy before 1066*, London.

Bautier, R.-H. (1971), *The Economic Development of Medieval Europe*, London.

Bautier, R.-H. (1973), 'Aux origines du royaume de Provence. De la sédition avortée de Boson à la royauté légitime de Louis', *Provence Historique* 23, pp. 41–68.

Bautier, R.-H. (1978), Introduction to *Receuil des Actes de Louis II le Bègue, Louis III et Carloman II rois de France, 877–884*, Paris.

Bernard, H. (1989), Personal communication.

Bishop, J. (1985), 'Bishops as marital advisors in the ninth century', in J. Kirshner and S. Wemple (eds), *Women of the Medieval World*, pp. 54–84.

Bloch, M. (1961), *Feudal Society*, London.

Bolton, J.L. (1980), *The Medieval English Economy 1150–1500*, London.

Borgolte, M. (1986), *Die Grafen Alemanniens im merowingischer und karolingischer Zeit*, Sigmaringen.

Boshof, E. (1990), 'Einheitsidee und Teilungsprinzip in der Regierungszeit Ludwigs des Frommen', in Godman and Collins (eds), *Charlemagne's Heir*, pp. 161–90.

Bouchard, C. (1981), 'The origins of the French nobility: a reassessment', *American Historical Review* 86, pp. 501–52.

Bouchard, C. (1986), 'Family structure and family consciousness among the aristocracy in the ninth to eleventh centuries', *Francia* 14, pp. 639–58.

Bouchard, C. (1988), 'The Bosonids or rising to power in the late Carolingian age', *French Historical Studies* 15, pp. 407–31.

Bourgeois, E. (1885), *Le capitulaire de Kiersy sur Oise (877)*, Paris.

Boussard, J. (1968), 'Les destinés de la Neustrie du ixe au xie siècle', *CCM* 11, pp. 15–28.

Braunfels, W. (ed.) (1965–7), *Karl der Grosse. Lebenswerk und Nachleben*, 5 vols, Düsseldorf.

Brommer P. (1985), *'Capitula episcoporum'. Die bischöflichen Kapitularien des 9. und 10. Jahrhunderts*, Typologie des sources du Moyen Age occidental, Turnhout.

Brown, G. (1989), 'Politics and Patronage at the Abbey of St Denis (814–98): the rise of a Royal Patron Saint', Oxford University D.Phil. thesis.

Brühl, C. (1962), 'Fränkischer Krönungsbrauch', *HZ* 194, pp. 265–326.

Brühl, C. (1968), *Fodrum, Gistum, Servitium Regis*, Cologne.

Brühl, C. (1975), *Palatium und Civitas. Studien zur Profanto-pographie spätantike Civitates vom 3. bis zum 13. Jht*, vol. I: Gallien, Cologne and Vienna.

Brühl, C. (1988), 'The problem of continuity of Roman *civitates* in Gaul', in Hodges and Hobley (eds), *The Rebirth of Towns*, pp. 43–6.

Brunner, H. (1928), *Deutsche Rechtsgeschichte*, vol. II, 2nd edn, Leipzig and Munich.

Brunner, K. (1979), *Oppositionelle Gruppen im Karolingerreich*, Vienna.

Brunterc'h, J.-P. (1985), 'Les découpages administratifs', in P. Périn and L.-C. Feffer (eds), *La Neustrie. Les pays au nord de la Loire de Dagobert à Charles le Chauve*, Paris, pp. 73–5.

Bullough, D. (1962), '"*Baiuli*" in the Carolingian *regnum Langobardorum* and the career of Abbot Waldo (+813)', *EHR* 77, pp. 625–37.

Bullough, D. (1975), '*Imagines regum* and their significance in the early medieval West', in *Studies in Memory of D. Talbot Rice*, Edinburgh, pp. 223–76.

Bullough, D. (1985), '*Albuinus deliciosus Karoli regis*: Alcuin of York and the shaping of the early Carolingian court', in L. Fenske, W. Rösener and T. Zotz (eds), *Institutionen, Kultur und Gesellschaft im Mittelalter. Festschrift für J. Fleckenstein*, Sigmaringen, pp. 73–92.

Bund, K. (1979), *Thronsturz und Herrscherabsetzung im Frühmittelalter*, Bonn.

Cabaniss, A. (1961), *Son of Charlemagne: a Contemporary Life of Louis the Pious*, Syracuse, NY.

Calmette, J. (1901), *La diplomatie caroligienne*, Paris.

Calmette, J. (1917), 'Le siège de Toulouse par les normands en 864 et les circonstances qui s'y rattachent', *AM* 19–20, pp. 153–74.

Calmette, J. (1951), 'Les comtes Bernard sous Charles le Chauve: état actuel d'une énigme historique', in *Mélanges d'histoire du moyen age dédiés à la mémoire de Louis Halphen*, Paris, pp. 103–9.

Campbell, J. (1989), 'The sale of land and the economics of power in early England: problems and possibilities', *Haskins Society Journal* 1, pp. 23–37.

Chadwick, H. (1967), *The Early Church*, Harmondsworth.

Chédeville, A. and Guillotel, H. (1984), *La Bretagne des saints et des rois, Ve-Xe siècle*, Rennes.

Classen, P. (1963) 'Die Verträge von Verdun und Coulaines, 843, als politische Grundlagen des westfränkischen Reiches', *HZ* 196, pp. 1–35.

Classen, P. (1972), 'Karl der Grosse und der Thronfolge im Frankenreich', *Festschrift für H. Heimpel*, 3 vols, Göttingen, iii, pp. 109–34.

Claude, D. (1960), *Topographie und Verfassung der Städte Bourges und Poitiers bis in das 11 Jhdt.*, Lübeck and Hamburg.

Claussen, M. (1990), 'Carolingian spirituality and the Liber Manualis of Dhuoda', *SCH* 27, pp. 43–52.

Coleman, E.R. (1971), 'Medieval marriage characteristics: a neglected factor in the history of serfdom', *Journal of Interdisciplinary History* 2, pp. 205–19.

Coleman, E.R. (1977/8), 'People and property: the structure of a medieval seigneury', in *Journal of European Economic History*, pp. 675–701.

Collins, R. (1983), *Early Medieval Spain*, London.

Collins, R. (1986), *The Basques*, Oxford.

Collins, R. (1990a) 'Charles the Bald and Wifred the Hairy', in Gibson and Nelson (eds), *Charles the Bald*, pp. 169–88.

Collins, R. (1990b), 'Pippin I and the Kingdom of Aquitaine', in Godman and Collins (eds), *Charlemagne's Heir*, pp. 363–89.

Collins, R. and Godman, P. (1990), see Godman, P. and Collins R. (1990).

Coupland, S. (1985), 'L'article XI de l'Edit de Pîtres du 25 juin 864', *Bulletin de la Société française de numismatique* 40, 9, pp. 713–4.

Coupland, S. (1986), *'In palatio nostro:* les monnaies palatines de Charlemagne', *Bulletin de la Société française de numismatique* 41 (7), pp. 87–9.

Coupland, S. (1987), 'Charles the Bald and the defence of the West Frankish Kingdom against the Viking Invasions, 840– 877', Cambridge University Ph.D. thesis.

Coupland, S. (1988), 'Dorestad in the ninth century: the numismatic evidence', *Jaarboek voor Munt- en Penningkunde* 75, pp. 5–26.

Coupland, S. (1990a), 'Money and coinage under Louis the Pious', *Francia,* 17, pp. 23–54.

Coupland, S. (1990b), 'Carolingian Arms and Armor', *Viator* 21, pp. 29–50.

Coupland, S. (1991a), 'The early coinage of Charles the Bald', *Numismatic Chronicle* (forthcoming).

Coupland, S. (1991b), 'The Rod of God's Wrath or the People of God's Wrath? The Carolingians' theology of the Viking invasions', *Journal of Ecclesiastical History* (forthcoming).

Coupland, S. and Nelson, J.L. (1988), 'The Vikings on the Continent', *History Today,* December, pp. 12–19.

D'Abadal, R. (1980), *Els Primers Comtes Catalans,* 3rd edn, Barcelona.

Davies, W. (1983), 'Priests and rural communities in East Brittany in the ninth century', *Etudes Celtiques* 20, pp. 177–97.

Davies, W. (1988), *Small Worlds,* London.

Davies, W. (1990), 'Charles the Bald and Brittany', in Gibson and Nelson (eds), *Charles the Bald,* pp. 98–114.

Davis, R.H.C. (1987), 'Domesday Book: Continental Parallels', in J. Holt (ed.), *Domesday Studies,* Woodbridge, pp. 15–40.

Dearden, B. (1989), 'Charles the Bald's fortified bridge at Pîtres (Seine): recent archaeological investigations', *Anglo-Norman Studies* 11, pp. 107–12.

Dearden, B. (1990), 'Pont-de-l'Arche or Pîtres? a location and archaeomagnetic dating for Charles the Bald's fortifications on the Seine', *Antiquity* 64, pp. 567–71.

Decour, P. (1972), 'Le paludisme provoque la mort de Lothaire II et de Charles le Chauve', *Archives Internationales Cl. Bernard,* no. 2, pp. 13–26.

Delogu, P. (1968a), 'L'istituzione comitale nell'Italia Carolingia', *BISI* 79, pp. 53–114.

Delogu, P. (1968b), 'Strutture politiche e ideologia nel regno di ludovico II', *BISI* 80, pp. 137–89.

Deshman, R. (1980), 'The exalted servant: the ruler-theology of the prayer-book of Charles the Bald', *Viator* 11, pp. 385– 417.

Despy, G. and Verhulst, A. (eds) (1986), *La fortune historiographique des thèses d'Henri Pirenne*, Brussels.

Devic, C. and Vaissete, J. (eds) (1874–6), *Histoire générale de Languedoc*, 3 vols, Toulouse.

Devisse, J. (1962), *Hincmar et la loi*, Dakar.

Devisse, J. (1975, 1976), *Hincmar, archevêque de Reims, 845– 882*, 3 vols, Geneva.

Devroey, J.-P. (1976), '*Mansi absi*: indices de crise ou de croissance?', *MA* 82, pp. 421–51.

Devroey, J.-P. (1979), 'Les services à l'abbaye de Prüm au IXe siècle', *Revue du Nord* 61, pp. 543–69.

Devroey, J.-P. (1981), 'Les méthodes d'analyse démographique des polyptyques du haut moyen âge', *Acta Historica Bruxellensia* 4, pp. 71–88.

Devroey, J.-P. (1984), 'Un monastère dans l'économie d'échanges', *Annales. ESC* 39, pp. 570–89.

Devroey, J.-P. (1985a), 'Réflexions sur l'économie des premiers temps carolingiens (768–877): grands domaines et action politique entre Seine et Rhin', *Francia* 13, pp. 475– 88.

Devroey, J.-P. (1985b), 'Polyptyques et fiscalité à l'époque carolingienne: une nouvelle approche?', *RBPH* 63, pp. 783–94.

D'Haenens, A. (1967), *Les invasions normandes en Belgique au IXe siècle*, Louvain.

D'Haenens, A. (1970), *Les invasions normandes. Une catastrophe?*, Paris.

Dhondt, J. (1948), *Etudes sur la naissance des principautés territoriales en France (IXe – Xe siècles)*, Bruges.

Dierkens, A. (1985), *Abbayes et chapîtres entre Sambre et Meuse (VIIe-XIe siècles)*, Sigmaringen.

Doehaerd, R. (1947), 'Au temps de Charlemagne et des Normands. Ce qu'on vendait et comment on le vendait dans le bassin parisien', *Annales. ESC* 3, pp. 268–80.

Doehaerd, R. (1978), *The Early Middle Ages in the West. Economy and Society*, Amsterdam, New York and Oxford.

Dronke, P. (1984), *Women Writers of the Middle Ages*, Cambridge.

Dubois, J. (ed.) (1965), *Le Martyrologe d'Usuard. Texte et Commentaire*, Brussels.

Dubois, J. and Renaud, G. (eds) (1984), *Le Martyrologe d'Adon*, Paris.

Duby, G. (1968), *Rural Economy and Country Life*, London.

Duby, G. (1974), *The Early Growth of the European Economy*, London.

Duchesne, L. (1910), *Fastes Episcopaux de l'ancienne Gaule*, 3 vols, Paris.

Duchesne, L. (ed.) (1955), *Liber Pontificalis*, revd edn, 3 vols, Paris.

Dümmler, E. (1887–8), *Geschichte des ostfränkischen Reiches*, 3 vols, Leipzig.

Dunbabin, J. (1985), *France in the Making 843–1180*, Oxford.

Dupront, A. (1965), 'L'aprision et le régime aprisionnaire dans le Midi de la France', *MA* 71, pp. 177–213, 375–99.

Durliat, J. (1984), 'Le polyptyque d'Irminon et l'impôt pour l'armée', *BEC* 141, pp. 183–208.

Dutton, P. and Jeauneau, E. (1983), 'The verses of the "Codex Aureus" of St Emmeram', *Studi Medievali* 3rd. ser. 24, pp. 75–120.

Duparc, P. (1951), 'Les cluses et la frontière des Alpes', *BEC* 109, pp. 5–31.

Dvornik, F. (1948), *The Photian Schism*, Oxford.

Dvornik, F. (1966), 'Constantinople and Rome', in *CMH* IV, pp. 431–72.

Ehlers, J. (1976), 'Karolingische Tradition und frühes Nationalbewusstsein in Frankreich', *Francia* 4, pp. 213–35.

Ehlers, J. (1983), 'Kontinuität und Tradition als Grundlage mittelalterlicher Nationsbildung in Frankreich', in H. Beumann (ed.), *Nationes* 4, pp. 15–47.

Eiten, G. (1907), *Das Unterkönigtum im Reiche der Merovinger und Karolinger*, Heidelberg.

Endemann, T. (1964), *Markturkunde und Markt in Frankreich und Burgund vom 9. bis 11. Jhdt.*, Constance.

Engreen, F.E. (1945), 'Pope John VIII and the Arabs', *Speculum* 20, pp. 318–30.

Enright, M. J. (1979), 'Charles the Bald and Æthelwulf of Wessex: the alliance of 856 and strategies of royal succession', *Journal of Medieval History* 5, pp. 291–302.

Erlande-Brandenbourg, A. (1975), *Le roi est mort. Étude sur les funerailles, les sépultures et les tombeaux des rois de France jusqu'à la fin du XIIIe siècle*, Paris-Geneva.

Ewig, E. (1982), 'Remarques sur la stipulation de la prière dans les chartes de Charles le Chauve', in *Mélanges J. Stiennon*, Liège, pp. 221–33.

Falkenstein, L. (1981), *Karl der Große und die Entstehung des Aachener Marienstiftes*, Paderborn.

Felten, F. (1980), *Äbte und Laienäbte im Frankenreich. Studie zum Verhältnis Staat und Kirche im früheren Mittelalter*, Stuttgart.

Fichtenau, H. (1984), *Lebensordnungen des 10 Jahrhundert*, Stuttgart.

Folz, R. (1969), *The Concept of Empire*, London.

Fossier, R. (1968), *La terre et les hommes en Picardie jusqu'à la fin du XVIIIe siècle*, Paris.

Fossier, R. (1978), *Polyptyques et censiers*, Typologie des sources du Moyen Age occidental, Turnhout.

Fossier, R. (1981), 'Les tendances de l'économie: stagnation ou croissance?', *SS Spoleto* 27, pp. 261–90.

Fossier, R. (1986), 'L'économie du haut moyen age entre Loire et Rhin', in Despy and Verhulst (eds), *La fortune historiographique des thèses d'Henri Pirenne*, pp. 51–9.

Fouracre, P. (1985), 'The context of the OHG *Ludwigslied*', *Medium Ævum* 54, pp. 87–103.

Fournier, G. (1962), *Le peuplement rural en Basse-Auvergne durant le haut Moyen Age*, Paris.

France, J. (1979), 'La guerre dans la France féodale', *Revue Belge d'Histoire Militaire* 23, pp. 177–98.

France, J. (1985), 'The military history of the Carolingian period', *Revue Belge d'Histoire Militaire* 26, pp. 81–99.

Fried, J. (1976), 'Boso von Vienne oder Ludwig der Stammler? Der Kaiserkandidat Johannes VIII', *DA* 32, pp. 193–208.

Fried, J. (1982), 'Der karolingische Herrschaftsverband im 9 Jhdt.', *HZ* 235, pp. 1–43.

Fried, J. (1983), 'König Ludwig der Jüngere in seiner Zeit', *Geschichtsblätter für den Kreis Bergstraße* 16, pp. 5–32.

Fried, J. (1990), 'Ludwig der Fromme, das Papsttum und die fränkische Kirche', in Godman and Collins (eds), *Charlemagne's Heir*, pp. 231–73.

Fuhrmann, H. (1958), 'Eine im Original erhaltene Propagandaschrift des Erzbischofs Gunthar von Köln (865)', *Archiv für Diplomatik, Schriftsgeschichte, Siegel- und Wappenkunde* 4, pp. 1–51.

Fuhrmann, H. (1972–4), *Einfluß und Verbreitung der pseudoisidorischen Fälschungen*, Schriften der MGH 24, 3 vols, Munich.

Fuhrmann, H. (1990), 'Fälscher unter sich: zum Streit zwischen Hinkmar von Reims und Hinkmar von Laon', in Gibson and Nelson (eds), *Charles the Bald*, pp. 224–34.

Gaehde, J.E. (1977), see Mütherich, F. and Gaehde, J.E.

Ganshof, F.L. (1927), 'La "tractoria". Contribution à l'étude des origines du droit de gîte', *Tijdschrift voor Rechtsgeschiedenis* 8, pp. 69–91.

Ganshof, F.L. (1949), 'Notes critiques sur les "Annales Bertiniani"', in *Mélanges dédiés à la mémoire de F. Grat*, 2 vols, Paris, vol. ii, pp. 159–74.

Ganshof, F.L. (1956), 'Zur Entstehungsgeschichte und Bedeutung des Vertrags von Verdun (843)', *DA* 12, pp. 313–30, translated in Ganshof 1971.

Ganshof, F.L. (1959), 'À propos du tonlieu à l'époque carolingienne', *SS Spoleto* 6, pp. 485–508.

Ganshof, F.L. (1970), 'L'historiographie dans la monarchie franque sous les Mérovingiens et les Carolingiens', in *SS Spoleto* 17 (ii), pp. 631–85.

Ganshof, F.L. (1971), *The Carolingians and the Frankish Monarchy*, London.

Ganz, D. (1979), Review of Devisse 1975–6, in *Revue Belge de Philologie et d'Histoire* 57, pp. 711–18.

Ganz, D. (1989), 'Humour as history in Notker's *Gesta Karoli Magni*', in E.B. King et al. (eds), *Monks, Nuns and Friars in Medieval Society*, University of the South.

Ganz, D. (1990a), 'The debate on Predestination', in Gibson and Nelson (eds), *Charles the Bald*, pp. 283–302.

Ganz, D. (1990b), *Corbie in the Carolingian Renaissance*, Sigmaringen.

Geary, P. (1991), *Furta Sacra*, 2nd edn Princeton.

Gibson, M.T. and Nelson, J.L. (1990), *Charles the Bald. Court and Kingdom*, 2nd revised edn, London.

Gillingham, J. (1990), 'Ademar of Chabannes and the history of Aquitaine in the reign of Charles the Bald', in Gibson and Nelson (eds), *Charles the Bald*, pp. 41–51.

Gillmor, C. (1988), 'War on the rivers: Viking numbers and mobility on the Seine and Loire, 841–886', *Viator* 19, pp. 79–109.

Gillmor, C. (1989), 'The logistics of fortified bridge building on the Seine under Charles the Bald', *Anglo-Norman Studies* 11, pp. 87–106.

Godman, P. (1985), *Poetry of the Carolingian Renaissance*, London.

Godman, P. (1987), *Poets and Emperors*, Oxford.

Godman, P. and Collins, R. (1990), *Charlemagne's Heir. New Perspectives on the Reign of Louis the Pious*, Oxford.

Goffart, W. (1966), *The Le Mans Forgeries*, Cambridge, Mass.

Goffart, W. (1989), *The Narrators of Barbarian History*, Princeton.

Gorissen, P. (1949), 'Encore la clause ardennaise du traité de Meersen', *MA* 55, pp. 1–4.

Grierson, P. (1934), 'Hugues de S.-Bertin: était-il archichapelain de Charles le Chauve?', *MA* 44, pp. 241–51.

Grierson, P. (1935), 'Eudes de Beauvais', *MA* 45, pp. 161–98.

Grierson, P. (1937), 'The early abbots of St-Bavo's of Ghent', *RB* 49, pp. 29–61.

Grierson, P. (1938), 'La maison d'Evrard de Frioul et les origines du comté de Flandre', *Revue du Nord* 96, pp. 241–66.

Grierson, P. (1939a), 'Les origines des comtés d'Amiens, Valois et Vexin', *MA* 49, pp. 81–123.

Grierson, P. (1939b), 'The identity of the unnamed fiscs in the *Brevium Exempla*', *Revue Belge de Philologie et d'Histoire* 13, pp. 437–59.

Grierson, P. (1940), 'Abbot Fulco and the date of the *Gesta abbatum Fontanellensium*', *EHR* 55, pp. 275–84.

Grierson, P. (1965), 'Money and coinage under Charlemagne', in W. Braunfels (ed.), *Karl der Grosse*, vol. I, pp. 501–36.

Grierson, P. (1981), 'The Carolingian Empire in the eyes of Byzantium', *SS Spoleto* 27 (ii), pp. 885–918.

Grierson, P. (1990), '*The Gratia Dei Rex* coinage of Charles the Bald', in Gibson and Nelson (eds), *Charles the Bald*, pp. 52–64.

Guillotel, H. (1975–6), 'L'action de Charles le Chauve vis-à-vis de la Bretagne, 843–851', *Mémoires de la Société d'Histoire et Archéologie de la Bretagne* 53, pp. 5–32.

Guillotel, H. and Chédeville, A. (1984), see Chédeville, A. and Guillotel, H.

Gussone, N. and Staubach, N. (1975), 'Zur Motivkreis und Sinngehalt der *Cathedra Petri'*, *FMS* 9, pp. 334–50.

Hallam, E.M. (1982), 'Royal burial and the cult of kingship in England and France, 1060–1330', *Journal of Medieval History* 8, pp. 359–80.

Halphen, L. and Lot, F. (1909), see Lot, F. and Halphen, L.

Halphen, L. (1977), *Charlemagne and the Carolingian Empire*, Amsterdam, New York and London.

Hannig, J. (1983), *'Pauperiores vassi de infra palatio?* Zur Entstehung der karolingischen Königsbotenorganisation', *MIÖG* 91, pp. 309–74.

Hartmann, W. (ed.) (1984), *MGH Concilia* III. *Die Konzilien der karolingischen Teilreiche 843–859*, Hanover.

Hartmann, W. (1989), *Die Synoden der Karolingerzeit im Frankenreich und in Italien*, Paderborn.

Hassall, J. and Hill, D. (1970), 'Pont-de-l'Arche: Frankish influence on the West Saxon burh?', *Archaeological Journal* 197, pp. 188–95.

Head, T. (1990), *Hagiography and the Cult of Saints*, Cambridge.

Hendy, M.F. (1988), 'From public to private: the western barbarian coinages as a mirror of the disintegration of late Roman state structures', *Viator* 19, pp. 29–78.

Hennebicque, R. (1981), 'Structures familiales et politiques au IXe siècle: un groupe familial de l'aristocratie franque', *RH* 265, pp. 289–333.

Herlihy, D. (1970), *The History of Feudalism*, New York.

Herren, M. (1987), 'Eriugena's "Aulae sidereae", the "Codex Aureus", and the palatine church of St. Mary at Compiègne', *Studi Medievali*, 3rd ser. 28, pp. 593–608.

Herrin, J. (1988), *The Formation of Christendom*, Princeton.

Hill, D. (1988), 'Unity and diversity – a framework for the study of European towns', in Hodges and Hobley (eds), *The Rebirth of Towns*, pp. 8–15.

Hill, D. and Hassall, J. (1970), see Hassall, J. and Hill, D.

Hlawitschka, E. (1960), *Franken, Alemannen, Bayern und Burgunder in Oberitalien 774–962*, Freiburg.

Hodges, R. (1989), *The Anglo-Saxon Achievement*, London.

Hodges, R. (1990a), 'Trade and market origins in the ninth century: relations between England and the Continent', in Gibson and Nelson (eds), *Charles the Bald*, pp. 203–23.

Hodges, R. (1990b), *Dark Age Economics*, 2nd edn, London.

Hodges, R. and Hobley, B. (eds) (1988), *The Rebirth of Towns in the West AD 700–1050*, London.

Hodges, R. and Whitehouse, D. (1983), *Mohammed, Charlemagne and the Origins of Europe*, London.

Hubert, J., Porcher, J. and Volbach, W.F. (1970), *Carolingian Art*, London.

Hyam, J. (1990), 'Ermentrude and Richildis', in Gibson and Nelson (eds), *Charles the Bald*, pp. 154–68.

Jacob, A. (1972), 'Une lettre de Charles le Chauve au clergé de Ravenne', *RHE* 67, pp. 402–22.

James, E. (1982), *The Origins of France*, London.

Jarnut, J. (1985), 'Die frühmittelalterliche Jagd unter rechts- und sozialgeschichtlichen Aspekten', *SS Spoleto* 31(ii), pp. 765–808.

Jarnut, J. (1990), 'Ludwig der Fromme, Lothar I. und das *Regnum Italiae*', in Godman and Collins (eds), *Charlemagne's Heir*, pp. 349–62.

Jäschke, K.-U. (1970), 'Die karolingergenealogien aus Metz und Paulus Diaconus. Mit einem Exkurs über Karl "den Kahlen"', *Rheinische Vierteljahrsblätter* 34, pp. 190–218.

Jeauneau, E. and Dutton, P. (1983), see Dutton, P. and Jeauneau, E.

Johanek, P. (1987), 'Der fränkische Handel der Karolingerzeit im Spiegel der Schriftquellen', in K. Düwel *et al.* (eds), *Untersuchungen zu Handel und Verkehr der vor- und frühgeschichtlichen Zeit in Mittel- und Nordeuropa*, Abhandlungen der Akademie der Wissenschaften in Göttingen, Phil.-Hist. Klasse, 156, part IV, pp. 7–68.

Joranson, E. (1923), *The Danegeld in France*, Rock Island, Illinois.

Kaiser, R. (1981), *Bischofsherrschaft zwischen Königtum und Fürstenmacht. Studien zur bischöflichen Stadtherrschaft im westfränkish-französischen Reich im früheren und hohen Mittelalter*, Bonn.

Kantorowicz, E.H. (1946), *Laudes Regiae. A Study in Liturgical Acclamations and Medieval Ruler Worship*, Berkeley, California.

Keller, H. (1967), 'Zur Struktur des Königsherrschaft im karolingischen und nachkarolingischen Italien. Der "consiliarius regis" in den italienischen Königsdiplomen des 9. und 10. Jhdts.', *Quellen und Forschungen aus Italienischen Archiven und Bibliotheken* 47, pp. 123–223.

Kelly, J. (1986), *The Oxford Dictionary of Popes*, Oxford.

Keynes, S. and Lapidge, M. (1983), *Alfred the Great. Asser's Life of Alfred and Other Contemporary Sources*, Harmondsworth.

Kienast, W. (1968), *Studien über die französischen Volksstämme des Frühmittelalters*, Stuttgart.

King, P.D. (1987), *Charlemagne. Translated Sources*, Kendal.

Konecny, S. (1976), *Die Frauen des karolingischen Königshauses*, Vienna.

Kottje, R. (1988), 'Kirchliches Recht und päpstlicher Autoritätsanspruch. Zu den Auseinandersetzungen über die Ehe Lothars II', in Mordek, H. (ed.), *Aus Kirche und Reich: Studien zu Theologie, Politik und Recht im Mittelalter. Festschrift für F. Kempf*, Sigmaringen, pp. 97–103.

Kuchenbuch, L. (1978), *Bäuerliche Gesellschaft und Klosterherrschaft im 9 Jhdt. Studien zur Sozialstruktur der Familia der Abtei Prüm*, Wiesbaden.

Lafaurie, J. (1970), 'Numismatique de Carolingiens aux Capétiens', *CCM* 13, pp. 117–37.

Lair, J. (1897), 'Les Normands dans l'île d'Oscelle', *Mémoires de la société historique et archéologique de Pontoise et du Vexin* 20, pp. 9–40.

Latouche, R. (1961), *The Birth of Western Economy*, London.

Lebecq, S. (1989), 'La Neustrie et la mer', in H. Atsma (ed.), *La Neustrie*, Beiheft der *Francia* 16/1, pp. 405–40.

Le Goff, J. (1969), *Les intellectuels au moyen âge*, Paris.

Le Maître, P. (1980), 'L'oeuvre d'Aldric du Mans et sa signification', *Francia* 8, pp. 43–64.

Lesne, E. (1910–1943), *Histoire de la propriété ecclésiastique en France*, 6 vols, Lille.

Levillain, L. (1903), 'Le sacre de Charles le Chauve à Orléans', *BEC* 64, pp. 31–53.

Levillain, L. (1923), 'L'archichapelain Ebroin, évêque de Poitiers', *MA* 34, pp. 177–222.

Levillain, L. (1926), Introduction to *Receuil de Actes de Pépin I et Pépin II, rois d'Aquitaine (814–848)*, Paris.

Levillain, L. (1937a), 'Essai sur le comte Eudes, fils de Harduin et de Guérinbourg, 845–871', *MA* 46, 47, pp. 153–82, 233–71.

Levillain, L. (1937b), 'Les Nibelungen historiques et leurs alliances de famille', *AM* 49, pp. 337–407.

Levillain, L. (1938), 'Les Nibelungen historiques et leurs alliances de famille' (suite), *AM* 50, pp. 5–52.

Levillain, L. (1939), Review of Auzias 1937, in *MA* 49, pp. 131–46.

Levillain, L. (1941), 'Les comtes de Paris à l'époque franque', *MA* 50, pp. 137–205.

Levillain, L. (1946), 'De quelques personnages nommés Bernard dans les Annales d'Hincmar', in *Mélanges dédiés à la mémoire de Félix Grat*, 2 vols, Paris, vol. i, pp. 169–202.

Levillain, L. (1947), 'Les personnages du nom de Bernard dans la seconde moitié du IXe siècle', *MA* 53, pp. 197–242.

Levillain, L. (1948), 'Les personnages du nom de Bernard dans la seconde moitié du IXe siècle' (suite), *MA* 54, pp. 1–35.

Levillain, L. (1964), Introduction and notes to Grat, F. (ed.), *Annales de Saint-Bertin*.

Leyser, K.J. (1968), 'The German aristocracy from the ninth century to the early twelfth century', *Past and Present* 41, pp. 25–53.

Leyser, K.J. (1979), *Rule and Conflict in an Early Medieval Society: Ottonian Saxony*, London.

Leyser, K.J. (1982), *Medieval Germany and its Neighbours 900–1250*, London.

Lohrmann, D. (1976), 'Trois palais royaux de la vallée de l'Oise d'après les travaux des érudits mauristes: Compiègne, Choisy-au-Bac et Quierzy', *Francia* 4, pp. 121–40.

Lohrmann, D. (1989), 'Le moulin à eau dans le cadre de l'économie rurale de la Neustrie, VIIe-IXe siècles', in H. Atsma (ed.), *La Neustrie*, Beiheft der *Francia* 16/1, pp. 367–404.

Longnon, A. (1886, 1895), *Polyptyque de l'abbaye de S.-Germain-des-Prés*, 2 vols, Paris.

Lot, F. (1902), 'Une année du règne de Charles le Chauve: année 866', *MA* 15, pp. 394–438, repr. in Lot (1970), pp. 415–60.

Lot, F. (1904a), 'Le Pont de Pitres', *MA* 2nd sér. 18, pp. 1–27, repr. Lot (1970a), pp. 535–61.

Lot, F. (1904b), 'Pons Liadi', *MA* 2nd sér. 18, pp. 127–39, repr. in Lot (1970a), pp. 569–78.

Lot, F. (1906), 'Aleran comte de Troyes', *MA* 19, pp. 199–204, repr. in Lot (1970a), pp. 582–7.

Lot, F. (1908a), 'La grande invasion normande de 856–862', *BEC* 69, pp. 5–62, repr. in Lot (1970a), pp. 713–70.

Lot, F. (1908b), 'Note sur le sénéchal Alard', *MA* 2nd sér. 12, pp. 185–201, repr. in Lot (1970a), pp. 591–607.

Lot, F. (1915), 'La Loire, l'Aquitaine et la Seine de 862 à 866: Robert le Fort', *BEC* 76, pp. 473–510, repr. in Lot (1970a), pp. 781–818.

Lot, F. (1921), 'Conjectures démographiques sur la France au IXe siècle', *MA* 23, pp. 1–27, repr. in Lot (1973), pp. 465–521.

Lot, F. (1924), 'Les tributs aux normands et l'église de France au IXe siècle', *BEC* 85, pp. 58–78, repr. in Lot (1973), pp. 699–719.

Lot, F. (1941), 'I: Les comtes d'Auvergne entre 846 et 877. II. Les comtes d'Autun entre 864 et 878', *BEC* 102, pp. 282–91, repr. in Lot (1970a), pp. 664–73.

Lot, F. (1968, 1970a, 1973), *Receuil des travaux historiques*, 3 vols, Geneva and Paris.

Lot, F. (1970b), 'Roric. Ses incursions', in *Receuil* ii, pp. 678–85.

Lot, F. (1970c), 'Godfred et Sidroc sur la Seine', in *Receuil* ii, pp. 686–90.

Lot, F. (1970d), 'Sidroc sur la Loire', in *Receuil* ii, pp. 691–704.

Lot, F. and Halphen, L. (1909), *Le règne de Charles le Chauve*, i. 840–851, Paris.

Louis, R. (1946), *Girard, comte de Vienne (...819–877)*, 3 vols. Auxerre.

Löwe, H. (1951), 'Studien zu den Annales Xantenses', *DA* 8, pp. 59–99.

Löwe, H. (1957), see Wattenbach, W., Levison, W. and Löwe, H.

Löwe, H. (1967), 'Die Geschichtsschreibung der ausgehenden Karolingerzeit', *DA* 23, pp. 1–30.

Löwe, H. (1972), 'Hinkmar von Reims under der Apokrisiar', in *Festschrift für H. Heimpel*, 3 vols, Göttingen, vol. iii, pp. 197–225.

Löwe, H. (1973), *Die Karolinger vom Vertrag von Verdun bis zum Herrschaftsantritt der Herrscher aus dem sächsischen Hause. Das Westfränkische Reich*, Heft V of Wattenbach, Levison and Löwe, *Deutschlands Geschichtsquellen im Mittelalter*, Weimar.

Löwe, H. (1988), 'Die Apostasie des Pfalzdiakons Bodo (838) und das Judentum der Chasaren', in G. Althoff, D. Geuenich, O.G. Oexle and J. Wollasch (eds), *Person und Gemeinschaft im Mittelalter. Festschrift für K. Schmid*, Sigmaringen, pp. 157–69.

Loyn, H. and Percival, J. (1975), *The Reign of Charlemagne*, London.

Lynch, J. (1986), *Godparents and Kinship in Early Medieval Europe*, Princeton.

Maddicott, J.R. (1989), 'Trade, industry and the wealth of King Alfred', *Past and Present* 123, pp. 3–51.

Magnou-Nortier, E. (1976), *Foi et fidelité. Recherches sur l'évolution des liens personnels chez les Francs du VIIe au IXe siècle*, Toulouse.

Magnou-Nortier, E. (1987), 'Le grand domaine: des maîtres, des doctrines, des questions', *Francia* 15, pp. 659–700.

Magnou-Nortier, E. (1989), 'La gestion publique en Neustrie', in H. Atsma (ed.), *La Neustrie*, Beiheft der *Francia* 16/1, pp. 271–320.

Malbos, L. (1964), 'Du surnom de Plantevelue', *MA* 70, pp. 5–11.

Malbos, L. (1966), 'L'annaliste royal sous Louis le Pieux', *MA* 72, pp. 225–33.

Malbos, L. (1970), 'La capture de Bernard de Septimanie', *MA* 76, pp. 7–13.

Marenbon, J. (1981), 'Wulfad, Charles the Bald and John Scottus Eriugena', in Gibson and Nelson (eds), *Charles the Bald*, 1st edn, pp. 375–83.

Marenbon, J. (1990), 'John Scottus and Carolingian Theology: from the *De Praedestinatione*, its background and its critics, to the *Periphyseon*', in Gibson and Nelson (eds), *Charles the Bald*, 2nd edn, pp. 303–25.

Martindale, J. (1977), 'The French aristocracy in the early Middle Ages: a reappraisal', *Past and Present* 75, pp. 5–45.

Martindale, J. (1985), 'The kingdom of Aquitaine and the dissolution of the Carolingian fisc', *Francia* 11, pp. 131– 91.

Martindale, J. (1990a), 'Charles the Bald and the government of the kingdom of Aquitaine', in Gibson and Nelson (eds), *Charles the Bald*, pp. 115–38.

Martindale, J. (1990b), 'The nun Immena and the foundation of the abbey of Beaulieu: a woman's prospects in the Carolingian Church', *SCH* 27, pp. 27–42.

McCormick, M. (1984), 'The liturgy of war in the early Middle Ages: crises, litanies and the Carolingian monarchy', *Viator* 15, pp. 1–23.

McCormick, M. (1986), *Eternal Victory. Triumphal Rulership in Late Antiquity, Byzantium and the Early Medieval West*, Cambridge.

McKeon, P. (1970), 'Le Concile d'Attigny', *MA* 80, pp. 401–25.

McKeon, P. (1974a), 'The Carolingian Councils of Savonnières (859) and Tusey (860) and their background', *Revue Bénédictine* 84, pp. 75–110.

McKeon, P. (1974b), 'Archbishop Ebbo of Rheims', *Church History* 43, pp. 437–47.

McKeon, P. (1978), *Hincmar of Laon and Carolingian Politics*, Urbana, Chicago and London.

McKitterick, R. (1977), *The Frankish Church and the Carolingian Reforms*, London.

McKitterick, R. (1980), 'Charles the Bald and his library: the patronage of learning', *EHR* 95, pp. 28–47.

McKitterick, R. (1983), *The Frankish Kingdoms under the Carolingians*, London.

McKitterick, R. (1989), *The Carolingians and the Written Word*, Cambridge.

McKitterick, R. (1990), 'The palace school of Charles the Bald', in Gibson and Nelson (eds), *Charles the Bald*, pp. 326–39.

Metcalf, D.M. (1979), 'Coinage and the rise of the Flemish towns', in M.J. Mayhew ed., *Coinage in the Low Countries (880–1500)*, British Archaeological Reports 54, Oxford, pp. 1–24.

Metcalf, D.M. (1990), 'A sketch of the currency in the time of Charles the Bald', in Gibson and Nelson (eds), *Charles the Bald*.

Metcalf, D.M. and Northover, J.P. (1989), 'Coinage alloys from the time of Offa and Charlemagne to c. 864', *Numismatic Chronicle* 159, pp. 101–20.

Metz, W. (1960), *Das karolingische Reichsgut. Eine verfassungs- und verwaltungsgeschichtliche Untersuchung*, Berlin.

Meyer-Gebel, M. (1987), 'Zur annalistischen Arbeitsweise Hinkmars von Reims', *Francia* 15, pp. 75–108.

Montesquieu, C.L.S. (1989), *The Spirit of Laws* (trans. and ed.) A.M. Cohler, B.C. Miller and H.S. Stone, Cambridge.

Montesquiou-Fézensac, B. de (1963), 'Le tombeau de Charles le Chauve à Saint-Denis', *Bulletin de la Société des Antiquaires de France*, pp. 84–8.

Morrison, K.F. (1964), *The Two Kingdoms. Ecclesiology in Carolingian Political Thought*, Princeton.

Mühlbacher, E. (1896), *Deutsche Geschichte unter den Karolingern*, Berlin.

Musset, L. (1965), *Les invasions. II. Le second assaut contre l'Europe chrétienne (VIIe-XIe siècle)*, Paris.

Musset, L. (1974), 'La renaissance urbaine des Xe et XIe siècles dans l'ouest de la France: problèmes et hypothèses', in *Mélanges E.-R. Labande*, Poitiers, pp. 563–75.

Mütherich, F. (1971), 'Der Elfenbeinschmück des Thrones', in M. Maccarrone *et al* (eds), *La Cattedra lignea di S. Pietro in Vaticano*, Atti della Pontificia Accademia Romana de Archeologia, ser. iii, Memorie X, Vatican City, pp. 253–73.

Mütherich, F. (1975), 'Die Reiterstatuette aus der Metzer Kathedrale', in *Studien zur Geschichte der europäischen Plastik. Festschrift für T. Müller*, Munich, pp. 9–15.

Mütherich, F. and Gaehde, J.E. 1977), *Carolingian Painting*, London.

Nees, L. (1990), 'Charles the Bald and the *Cathedra Petri*', in Gibson and Nelson (eds), *Charles the Bald*, pp. 340–7.

Nees, L. (1991), *A Tainted Mantle. Hercules and the Classical Tradition at the Carolingian Court*, Philadelphia.

Nelson, J.L. (1971), 'National synods, kingship as office and royal anointing: an early medieval syndrome', *SCH* 7, pp. 41–59, repr. in Nelson (1986a), pp. 239–57.

Nelson, J.L. (1977a), 'Kingship, law and liturgy in the political thought of Hincmar of Rheims', *EHR* 92, pp. 241–79, repr. in Nelson (1986a), pp. 133–72.

Nelson, J.L. (1977b), 'Inauguration Rituals', in P.H. Sawyer and I.N. Wood (eds), *Early Medieval Kingship*, Leeds, pp. 50–71, repr. in Nelson (1986a), pp. 283–308.

Nelson, J.L. (1979), 'Charles the Bald and the Church in town and countryside', *SCH* 16, pp. 103–18, repr. in Nelson (1986a), pp. 75–90.

Nelson, J.L. (1980), 'The earliest surviving royal *Ordo*: some liturgical and historical aspects', in B. Tierney and P. Linehan (eds), *Authority and Power. Studies in Medieval Law and Government presented to Walter Ullmann*, Cambridge, pp. 29–48, repr. in Nelson (1986a), pp. 341–60.

Nelson, J.L. (1983a), 'Legislation and consensus in the reign of Charles the Bald', in P. Wormald (ed.), *Ideal and Reality. Studies in Frankish and Anglo-Saxon Society presented to J.M. Wallace-Hadrill,* Oxford, pp. 202–27, repr. in Nelson (1986a), pp. 91–116.

Nelson, J.L. (1983b), 'The church's military service in the ninth century: a contemporary comparative view?', *SCH* 20, pp. 15–30, repr. in Nelson (1986a), pp. 117–32.

Nelson, J.L. (1985), 'Public *Histories* and private history in the work of Nithard', *Speculum* 60, pp. 251–93, repr. in Nelson (1986a), pp. 195–238.

Nelson, J.L. (1986a), *Politics and Ritual in Early Medieval Europe,* London.

Nelson, J.L. (1986b), '"A king across the sea": Alfred in Continental perspective', *Transactions of the Royal Historical Society* 36, pp. 45–68.

Nelson, J.L. (1986c), 'Dispute settlement in Carolingian West Francia', in W. Davies and P. Fouracre (eds), *The Settlement of Disputes in Early Medieval Europe,* Cambridge, pp. 45–64.

Nelson, J.L. (1987), 'Carolingian royal ritual', in D. Cannadine and S. Price (eds), *Rituals of Royalty. Power and Ceremonial in Traditional Societies,* Cambridge, pp. 137–80.

Nelson, J.L. (1988a), 'Kingship and empire', in J.H. Burns (ed.), *The Cambridge History of Medieval Political Thought,* Cambridge, pp. 211–51.

Nelson, J.L. (1988b), 'A tale of two princes: politics, text and ideology in a Carolingian annal', *Studies in Medieval and Renaissance History* 10, pp. 105–41.

Nelson, J.L. (1989a), 'Ninth-century knighthood: the evidence of Nithard', in C. Harper-Bill, C. Holdsworth and J.L. Nelson (eds), *Studies in Medieval History presented to R. Allen Brown,* Woodbridge, pp. 255–66.

Nelson, J.L. (1989b), 'Translating images of authority: the Christian Roman emperors in the Carolingian world', in M.M. Mackenzie and C. Roueché (eds), *Images of Authority. Papers presented to Joyce Reynolds on the occasion of her 70th birthday,* Cambridge, pp. 194–205.

Nelson, J.L. (1990a, 'The reign of Charles the Bald: a survey', in Gibson and Nelson (eds), *Charles the Bald,* pp. 1– 22.

Nelson, J.L. (1990b), ' The Annals of St Bertin', in Gibson and Nelson (eds), *Charles the Bald,* pp. 23–40.

Nelson, J.L. (1990c), 'The last years of Louis the Pious', in Godman and Collins (eds), *Charlemagne's Heir*, pp. 147–60.

Nelson, J.L. (1990d), 'Hincmar of Reims on king-making: the evidence of the Annals of St. Bertin', in J.M. Bak (ed.), *Coronations*, Berkeley and Los Angeles, pp. 16–34.

Nelson, J.L. (1990e). 'Perceptions du pouvoir chez les historiennes du haut moyen-âge', in M. Rouche and J. Heuclin (eds), *La femme au moyen âge*, Maubeuge, pp. 75–85.

Nelson, J.L. (1990f). 'Literacy in Carolingian Government', in R. McKitterick (ed.), *The Uses of Literacy in Early Medieval Europe*, Cambridge, pp. 258–96.

Nelson, J.L. (1991a), *Ninth-Century Histories: the Annals of St-Bertin*, Manchester.

Nelson, J.L. (1991b), ' "Not bishops' bailiffs but lords of the earth": Charles the Bald and the problem of sovereignty', in D. Wood (ed.), *The Church and Sovereignty. Essays in Honour of Michael Wilks*, Oxford.

Nelson, J.L. (1991c), 'Charles le Chauve et les utilisations du savoir', in D. Iogna-Prat, C. Jeudy and G. Lobrichon (eds), *L'école carolingienne d'Auxerre de Murethach à Remi*, Paris, pp. 37–54.

Nightingale, J. (1988), 'Monasteries and their Patrons in the Dioceses of Trier, Metz and Toul, 850–1000', Oxford University D. Phil. thesis.

Nineham, D. (1989), 'Gottschalk of Orbais', *Journal of Ecclesiastical History* 40, pp. 1–18.

Odegaard, C. (1941), 'Carolingian oaths of fidelity', *Speculum* 16, pp. 284–96.

Odegaard, C. (1945a), 'The concept of royal power in Carolingian oaths of fidelity', *Speculum* 20, pp. 279–89.

Odegaard, C. (1945b), *Vassi and Fideles in the Carolingian Empire*, Cambridge, Mass.

Odegaard, C. (1951), 'The Empress Engelberge', *Speculum* 26, pp. 77–103.

Oexle, O.G. (1967), 'Die Karolinger und die Stadt des heilige Arnulf', *FMS* 1, pp. 250–364.

Oexle, O.G. (1969), 'Bischof Ebroin von Poitiers und seine Verwandten', *FMS* 3, pp. 138–210.

Oexle, O.G. (1988), 'Haus und Ökonomie im früheren Mittelalter', in G. Althoff *et al* (eds), *Person und Gemeinschaft im Mittelalter. Festschrift für K. Schmid*, Sigmaringen, pp. 101–22.

Orlowski, T. (1989), 'La statue équestre de Limoges et le sacre de Charles l'Enfant. Contribution à l'étude de l'iconographie politique carolingienne', *CCM* 30, pp. 131–44.

Parisot, R. (1899), *Le royaume de Lorraine sous les Carolingiens, 843–923*, Paris.

Partner, P. (1972), *The Lands of St. Peter*, London.

Penndorf, U. (1975), *Das Problem der 'Reichseinheitsidee' nach der Teilung von Verdun*, Munich.

Percival, J. and Loyn, H. (1975), see Loyn, H. and Percival, J.

Pirenne, H. (1939), *Mohammed and Charlemagne*, English trans. B. Miall, London.

Prinz, J. (1965), 'Ein unbekanntes Aktenstück zum Ehestreit König Lothars II', *DA* 21, pp. 249–63.

Prinz, J. (1977), 'Der Feldzug Karls des Kahlen an dem Rhein im September 876', *DA* 33, pp. 543–5.

Randsborg, K. (1980), *The Viking Age in Denmark*, London.

Reuter, T. (ed.) (1978), *The Medieval Nobility*, Amsterdam and New York.

Reuter, T. (1985), 'Plunder and tribute in the Carolingian Empire', *Transactions of the Royal Historical Society* 35, pp. 75–94.

Reuter, T. (1990), 'The end of Carolingian military expansion', in Godman and Collins (eds), *Charlemagne's Heir*, pp. 391–405.

Reuter, T. (1991a), *Germany in the Early Middle Ages*, London.

Reuter, T. (1991b), *Ninth-Century Histories: The Annals of Fulda*, Manchester.

Reynolds, S. (1984), *Kingdoms and Communities in Western Europe, 900–1300*, Oxford.

Richard, A. (1893), 'Observations sur les mines d'argent et l'atelier monétaire de Melle sous les Carolingiens', *Revue Numismatique*, 3rd sér. 11, pp. 194–225.

Riché, P. (ed.) (1975), *Dhuoda. Manuel pour mon fils*, Paris.

Riché, P. (1977), 'Charles le Chauve et la culture de son temps', in *Jean Scot Eriugène et l'histoire de la philosophie*, Colloques internationales du CNRS 561, Paris, pp. 37–46, repr. in Riché 1981.

Riché, P. (1981), *Instruction et vie religieuse dans le haut moyen âge*, London.

Riché, P. (1982), 'Les Irlandais et les princes carolingiens', in H. Löwe (ed.), *Die Iren und Europa im früheren Mittelalter*, 2 vols, Stuttgart, vol. 2, pp. 735–45.

Riché, P. (1983), *Les Carolingiens. Une famille qui fit l'Europe*, Paris.

Rouche, M. (1984), 'Les repas de fête à l'époque carolingienne', in D. Menjot (ed.), *Manger et boire au Moyen Age*, Actes du Colloque de Nice (15–17 octobre 982), 1: Aliments et Société, Nice, pp. 265–96.

Rouche, M. (1990), 'Géographie rurale du royaume de Charles le Chauve', in Gibson and Nelson (eds), *Charles the Bald*, pp. 189–202.

Sanchez-Albornoz, C. (1969), 'El tercer rey de España', *Cuadernos de Historia de España* 49–50, pp. 5–49.

Sassier, Y. (1991), 'Les carolingiens et Auxerre', in D. Iogna-Prat, C. Jeudy and G. Lobrichon (eds.), *L'école carolingienne d'Auxerre*, Paris, pp. 21–36.

Sawyer, P.H. (1982), *Kings and Vikings*, London.

Sawyer, P.H. and Wood, I.N. (eds) (1977), *Early Medieval Kingship*, Leeds.

Schieffer, R. (1979), 'Möglichkeiten und Grenzen der biographischen Darstellung frühmittelalterlichen Persönlichkeiten. Zu dem neuen Hinkmar-Buch von J. Devisse', *HZ* 229, pp. 85–95.

Schieffer, R. (1986), 'Hinkmar von Reims', *Theologische Realenzyklopadie* 15, pp. 355–60.

Schieffer, R. (1990), 'Väter und Söhne im Karolingerhause', in *Beiträge zur Geschichte des Regnum Francorum*, Beihefte der *Francia*, Band 22, Paris, pp. 149–64.

Schieffer, T. (1982), 'Ludwig "der Fromme"'. Zur Entstehung eines karolingischen Herrscherbeinamens', *FMS* 16, pp. 58–75.

Schieffer, T. (1960), 'Karl von Aquitanien', in L. Lenhart (ed.) *Universitas. Festschrift für A. Stohr*, 2 vols, Mainz, ii, pp. 42–54.

Schieffer, T. (1966), Introduction to *MGH Diplomata Karolingorum 3: Die Urkunden Lothars I und Lothars II*, Berlin and Zurich.

Schleidgen, W. (1977), *Die Überlieferungsgeschichte der Chronik des Regino von Prüm*, Mainz.

Schlesinger, W. (1970), 'Zur Erhebung Karls des Kahlen zum König von Lothringen, 869 in Metz', in G. Dröge *et al.* (eds), *Landschaft und Geschichte. Festschrift für F. Petri*, Bonn, pp. 173–98.

Schmid, K. (1968), 'Ein karolingischer Königseintrag im Gedenkbuch von Remiremont', *FMS* 2, pp. 96–134.

Schneider, G. (1973), *Erzbischof Fulco von Reims (883–900) und das Frankenreich*, Munich.

Schneidmüller, B. (1978), 'Die "Einfältigkeit" Karls III von Westfrankreich als frühmittelalterliche Herrschertugend. Überlegungen zu den cognomen *simplex*', *Schweizerische Zeitschrift für Geschichte* 28, pp. 62–6.

Schneidmüller, B. (1979), *Karolingische Tradition und frühes französisches Königtum. Untersuchungen zur Herrschaftslegitimation der westfränkisch-französischen Monarchie im 10. Jahrhundert*, Frankfurt.

Scholz, B. (1970), *Carolingian Chronicles*, Ann Arbor.

Schramm, P.E. (1954–6), *Herrschaftszeichen und Staatssymbolik*, Schriften der *MGH* 13, 3 vols, Stuttgart.

Schramm, P.E. (1960), *Der König von Frankreich. Das Wesen der Monarchie vom 9. zum 16. Jahrhundert*, 2 vols, 2nd edn, Darmstadt.

Schramm, P.E. (1968), *Kaiser, Könige und Päpste*, 4 vols, Stuttgart.

Schramm, P.E. and Mütherich, F. (1962), *Denkmale der deutschen Könige und Kaiser*, Munich.

Schramm, P.E. and Mütherich, F. (1983), *Die deutschen Kaiser und Könige in Bildern ihrer Zeit*, rev. edn, Munich.

Smith, J.M.H. (1982), 'The archbishopric of Dol and the ecclesiastical politics of ninth-century Brittany', *SCH* 18, pp. 59–70.

Smith, J.M.H. (1985), 'Carolingian Brittany', Oxford University D.Phil. thesis.

Smith, J.M.H. (1992), *Province and Empire. Brittany and the Carolingians*, Cambridge.

Smyth, A.P. (1977), *Scandinavian Kings in the British Isles 850–880*, Oxford.

Southern, R.W. (1953), *The Making of the Middle Ages*, London.

Spufford, P. (1988), *Money and its Use in Medieval Europe*, Cambridge.

Stafford, P. (1981), 'The king's wife in Wessex', *Past and Present* 91, pp. 5–27.

Stafford, P. (1983), *Queens, Concubines and Dowagers. The King's Wife in the Early Middle Ages*, Athens, Georgia

Stafford, P. (1990), 'Charles the Bald, Judith and England', in Gibson and Nelson (eds), *Charles the Bald*, pp. 139–53.

Staubach, N. (1982), *Das Herrscherbild Karls des Kahlen. Formen und Funktionen monarchischer Repräsentation im früheren Mittelalter*, Münster.

Staubach, N. and Gussone, N. (1975), see Gussone, N. and Staubach, N.

Staubach, N. (1990), '"Des großen Kaisers kleiner Sohn": zum Bild Ludwigs des Frommen', in Godman and Collins (eds), *Charlemagne's Heir*, pp. 701–22.

Stratmann, M. (ed.) (1990), *Hincmar, Collectio de Ecclesiis et Capellis*, MGH Fontes 14, Hannover.

Tabacco, G. (1989), *The Struggle for Power in Medieval Italy*, Cambridge.

Taeger, B. (1977), 'Zum *Ferculum Salmonis* Hinkmars von Reims', *DA* 33, pp. 153–67.

Tellenbach, G. (1957), 'Über die ältesten Welfen im West- und Ostfrankenreich', in G. Tellenbach ed. *Studien and Vorarbeiten zur Geschichte des großfränkischen Adels*, Freiburg, pp. 335–40.

Tessier, G. (1955), Introduction to *Receuil des Actes de Charles II le Chauve* (vol. iii), Paris.

Ullmann, W (1962) *The Growth of Papal Government in the Middle Ages*, 2nd edn, London.

Ullmann, W. (1972) *A Short History of the Papacy in the Middle Ages*, London.

Van Caenegem, R.C. and Ganshof, F.L. (1978), *Guide to the Sources of Medieval History*, Amsterdam and New York.

Van Es, W.A. and Verwers, W.J.H. (1980), *Excavations at Dorestad 1:* The Harbour, Hoogstraat 1, Nederlandse Oudheden no. 9, Amersfoort.

Van Rey, M. (1972), 'Die Münzprägen Karls des Kahlen und die westfränkische Königslandschaft', in W. Besch, K. Fehn, D. Höroldt, F. Irsigler and M. Zender (eds), *Die Stadt in der europäischen Geschichte. Festschrift Edith Ennen*, Bonn, pp. 153– 84.

Vercauteren, F. (1935–36), 'Comment s'est-on défendu au IXe siècle dans l'empire franc contre les invasions normandes?', *Annales du XXXe congres de la fédération archéologique et historique de Belgique*, pp. 117–32.

Verhulst, A. (1989), 'The origins of towns in the Low Countries and the Pirenne Thesis', *Past and Present* 122, pp. 3–35.

Verhulst, A. and Despy, G. (1986), see Despy, G. and Verhulst, A.

Verwers, W.J.H. (1988), 'Dorestad: a Carolingian town?', in Hodges and Hobley (eds), *The Rebirth of Towns*, pp. 52–6.

Verwers, W.J.H. and Van Es, W. (1980), see Van Es, W.A. and Verwers, W.J.H.

Vlasto, A.P. (1970), *The Entry of the Slavs into Christendom*, Cambridge.

Vogel, W. (1906), *Die Normannen und das fränkische Reich bis zur Gründung der Normandie (799–911)*, Heidelberg.

Waitz, G. (ed.) (1883), *Annales Bertiniani, MGH SSRG*, Hanover.

Wallace-Hadrill, J.M. (1960), *The Fourth Book of the Chronicle of Fredegar with its continuations*, Oxford.

Wallace-Hadrill, J.M. (1971), *Early Germanic Kingship in England and on the Continent*, Oxford.

Wallace-Hadrill, J.M. (1975), *The Vikings in Francia*, The Stenton Lecture for 1974, Reading, reprinted in Wallace-Handrill 1976.

Wallace-Hadrill, J.M. (1976), *Early Medieval History*, Oxford.

Wallace-Hadrill, J.M. (1978), 'A Carolingian Renaissance Prince: the Emperor Charles the Bald', *Proceedings of the British Academy* 64, pp. 155–84.

Wallace-Hadrill, J.M. (1981), 'History in the mind of Archbishop Hincmar', in J.M. Wallace-Hadrill and R.H.C. Davies (eds), *The Writing of History in the Middle Ages. Essays presented to R.W. Southern*, Oxford, pp. 43–70.

Wallace-Hadrill, J.M. (1983), *The Frankish Church*, Oxford.

Ward, E. (1990a), 'Caesar's wife: the career of the Empress Judith, 819–29', in Godman and Collins (eds), *Charlemagne's Heir*, pp. 205–27.

Ward, E. (1990b), 'Agobard of Lyons and Paschasius Radbertus as critics of the Empress Judith', *SCH* 27 pp. 15–25.

Wattenbach, W., Levison, W. and Löwe, H. (1952, 1953, 1957, 1963, 1973), *Deutschlands Geschichtsquellen im Mittelalter*, 5 vols, Weimar.

Weidemann, M. (1989), 'Bischofsherrschaft und Königtum in Neustrien . . . am Beispiel des Bistums Le Mans', in H. Atsma (ed.), *La Neustrie*, Beiheft der *Francia* 16/1, pp. 161–94.

Weinrich, L. (1963), *Wala. Graf, Monch und Rebell*, Hamburg.

Wemple, S.F. (1981), *Women in Frankish Society*, Philadelphia.

Werner, K.F. (1958), 'Untersuchungen zur Frühzeit des französischen Fürstentums (9.-10. Jht.), I-III', *WaG* 18, pp. 256–89.

Werner, K.F. (1959a), 'Zur Arbeitsweise Reginos von Prüm', *WaG* 19, pp. 96–116.

Werner, K.F. (1959b), 'Untersuchungen zur Frühzeit des französischen Fürstentums (9.-10. Jht.), IV', *WaG* 19, pp. 146–93.

Werner, K.F. (1960), 'Untersuchungen zur Frühzeit des französischen Fürstentums (9.-10. Jht.), V-VI', *WaG* 20, pp. 87–119.

Werner, K.F. (1965), 'Bedeutende Adelsfamilien im Reiche Karls des Grossen', in W. Braunfels (ed.), *Karl der Grosse*, vol. I, pp. 83–142.

Werner, K.F. (1967), 'Die Nachkommen Karls des Grossen', in W. Braunfels (ed.), *Karl der Grosse*, vol. IV, pp. 403–79.

Werner, K.F. (1978), 'Important noble families in the kingdom of Charlemagne', in T. Reuter (ed.), *The Medieval Nobility*, pp. 137–202.

Werner, K.F. (1979), 'Gauzlin von Saint Denis und die westfränkische Reichsteilung von Amiens (880)', *DA* 35, pp. 395–462.

Werner, K.F. (1980), 'Missus-marchio-comes: entre l'administration centrale et l'administration locale de l'empire carolingien', in W. Paravicini and K.F. Werner (eds), *Histoire comparée de l'administration (IVe-XVIIIe siècle)*, Beihefte der *Francia* 9, Munich, pp. 191–239.

Werner, K.F. (1984), *Les origines (avant l'an mil), Histoire de la France*, vol. 1, general ed. J. Favier, Paris.

Werner, K.F. (1985), 'Qu'est-ce que la Neustrie', in P. Périn and L.-C. Feffer (eds), *La Neustrie*, Rouen, pp. 29–38.

Werner, K.F. (1987), 'Gott, Herrscher und Historiograph. Der Geschichtsschreiber als Interpret des Wirkens Gottes in der Welt und Ratgeber des Könige', in E.-H. Hehl *et al.*, *Deus qui mutat tempora. Menschen und Institutionen im Wandel des Mitttelalters. Festgabe für A. Becker,* Sigmaringen, pp. 1–31.

Werner, K.F. (1990), *'Hludovicus Augustus:* Gouverner l'empire chrétien – idées et réalités', in Godman and Collins (eds), *Charlemagne's Heir*, pp. 3–124.

Wervers, W.J.H. (1988), 'Dorestad: a Carolingian town?', in Hodges and Hobley (eds), *The Rebirth of Towns*, pp. 52–6.

Wickham, C. (1981), *Early Medieval Italy*, London.

Wickham, C. (1984), 'The other transition: from the Ancient World to Feudalism', *Past and Present* 103, pp. 3–36.

Wickham, C. (1988), *The Mountains and the City. The Tuscan Apennines in the Early Middle Ages*, Oxford.

Wickham, C. (1990), 'European forests in the early Middle Ages: landscape and land clearance', *SS Spoleto* 37, pp. 479– 548.

Wolfram, H. (1973) 'Lateinische Herrschertitel im neunten und zehnten Jhdt.', in Wolfram ed., *Intitulatio II. Lateinische Herrscher- und Fürstentitel im neunten und zehnten Jhdt.*, Vienna-Cologne-Gras, pp. 19–178.

Wolfram, H. (1987), *Die Geburt Mitteleuropas*, Vienna and Berlin.

Wollasch, J. (1957a), 'Das *Patrimonium Beati Germani* in Auxerre', in G. Tellenbach (ed.), *Studien und Vorarbeiten zur Geschichte des großfrankischen und frühdeutschen Adels*, Freiburg, pp. 185–224.

Wollasch, J. (1957b), 'Eine adlige Familie des frühen Mittelalters, ihr Selbstverständnis und ihre Wirklichkeit', *Archiv für Kulturgeschichte* 39, pp. 150–88.

Wollasch, J. (1959), 'Königtum, Adel und Kloster im Berry während des 10. Jhdt.', in G. Tellenbach (ed.), *Neue Forschungen über Cluny und die Cluniacenser*, Freiburg, pp. 20–49.

Wollasch, J. (1984),'Kaiser und Könige als Brüder der Mönche. Zum Herrscherbild im liturgischen Handschriften des 9. bis 11. Jhdts', *DA* 40, pp. 1–20.

Wood, I.N. (1986), 'Disputes in the late fifth- and sixth-century Gaul: some problems', in W. Davies and P. Fouracre (eds), *The Settlements of Disputes in Early Medieval Europe*, Cambridge, pp. 7–22.

Wood, I.N. (1987), 'Christians and pagans in ninth-century Scandinavia', in B. Sawyer, P. Sawyer and I. Wood (eds), *The Christianization of Scandinavia*, Alingsås, pp. 36–67.

Wood, I.N. and Sawyer, P.H. (1977), see Sawyer, P.H. and Wood, I.N.

Wormald, P. (1982), 'The Ninth Century', in J. Campbell (ed.), *The Anglo-Saxons*, pp. 132–59.

Wylie, N. (1989), 'The *Vita Faronis* of Bishop Hildegar of Meaux', University of London B.A. dissertation.

GENEALOGICAL TABLES

Genealogy I
The descendants of Charlemagne

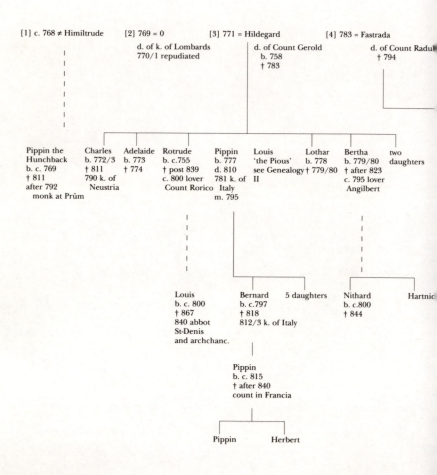

[1] c. 768 ≠ Himiltrude   [2] 769 = 0   [3] 771 = Hildegard   [4] 783 = Fastrada

d. of k. of Lombards
770/1 repudiated

d. of Count Gerold
b. 758
† 783

d. of Count Radu[...]
† 794

Pippin the
Hunchback
b. c. 769
† 811
after 792
monk at Prūm

Charles
b. 772/3
† 811
790 k. of
Neustria

Adelaide
b. 773
† 774

Rotrude
b. c.755
† post 839
c. 800 lover
Count Rorico

Pippin
b. 777
d. 810
781 k. of
Italy
m. 795

Louis
'the Pious'
see Genealogy
II

Lothar
b. 778
† 779/80

Bertha
b. 779/80
† after 823
c. 795 lover
Angilbert

two
daughters

Louis
b. c. 800
† 867
840 abbot
St-Denis
and archchanc.

Bernard
b. c.797
† 818
812/3 k. of Italy

5 daughters

Nithard
b. c.800
† 844

Hartnic

Pippin
b. c. 815
† after 840
count in Francia

Pippin   Herbert

306

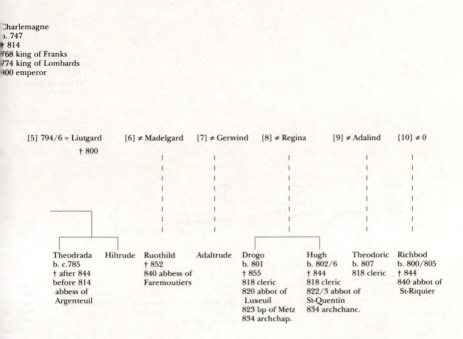

Charlemagne
b. 747
† 814
768 king of Franks
774 king of Lombards
800 emperor

[5] 794/6 = Liutgard   [6] ≠ Madelgard   [7] ≠ Gersvind   [8] ≠ Regina   [9] ≠ Adalind   [10] ≠ 0
         † 800

Theodrada	Hiltrude	Ruothild	Adaltrude	Drogo	Hugh	Theodoric	Richbod
b. c.785		† 852		b. 801	b. 802/6	b. 807	b. 800/805
† after 844		840 abbess of		† 855	† 844	818 cleric	† 844
before 814		Faremoutiers		818 cleric	818 cleric		840 abbot of
abbess of				820 abbot of	822/3 abbot of		St-Riquier
Argenteuil				Luxeuil	St-Quentin		
				823 bp of Metz	834 archchanc.		
				834 archchap.			

Genealogy II
The descendants of Louis the Pious

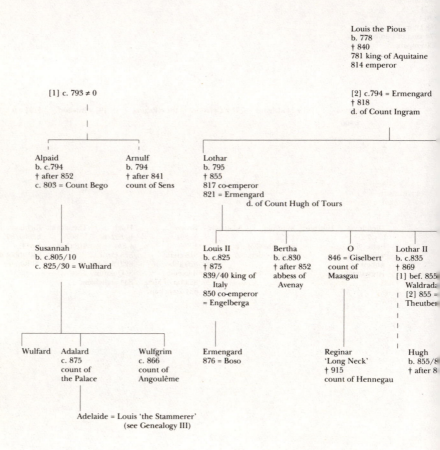

Louis the Pious
b. 778
† 840
781 king of Aquitaine
814 emperor

[1] c. 793 ≠ 0

[2] c.794 = Ermengard
† 818
d. of Count Ingram

Alpaid
b. c.794
† after 852
c. 803 = Count Bego

Arnulf
b. 794
† after 841
count of Sens

Lothar
b. 795
† 855
817 co-emperor
821 = Ermengard
d. of Count Hugh of Tours

Susannah
b. c.805/10
c. 825/30 = Wulfhard

Louis II
b. c.825
† 875
839/40 king of
Italy
850 co-emperor
= Engelberga

Bertha
b. c.830
† after 852
abbess of
Avenay

O
846 = Giselbert
count of
Maasgau

Lothar II
b. c.835
† 869
[1] bef. 855
Waldrad
[2] 855 =
Theutber

Wulfard

Adalard
c. 875
count of
the Palace

Wulfgrim
c. 866
count of
Angoulême

Ermengard
876 = Boso

Reginar
'Long Neck'
† 915
count of Hennegau

Hugh
b. 855/8
† after 8

Adelaide = Louis 'the Stammerer'
(see Genealogy III)

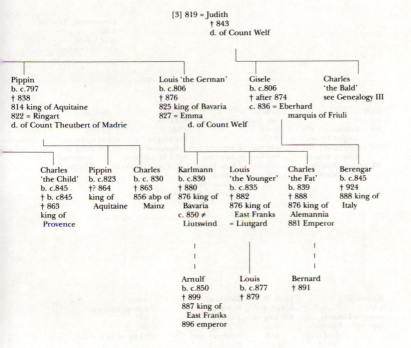

[3] 819 = Judith
† 843
d. of Count Welf

Pippin	**Louis 'the German'**	**Gisele**	**Charles**
b. c.797	b. c.806	b. c.806	'the Bald'
† 838	† 876	† after 874	see Genealogy III
814 king of Aquitaine	825 king of Bavaria	c. 836 = Eberhard	
822 = Ringart	827 = Emma	marquis of Friuli	
d. of Count Theutbert of Madrie	d. of Count Welf		

Charles	**Pippin**	**Charles**	**Karlmann**	**Louis**	**Charles**	**Berengar**
'the Child'	b. c.823	b. c. 830	b. c.830	'the Younger'	'the Fat'	b. c.845
b. c.845	†? 864	† 863	† 880	b. c.835	b. 839	† 924
† b. c845	king of	856 abp of	876 king of	† 882	† 888	888 king of
† 863	Aquitaine	Mainz	Bavaria	876 king of	876 king of	Italy
king of			c. 850 ≠	East Franks	Alemannia	
Provence			Liutswind	= Liutgard	881 Emperor	

Arnulf
b. c.850
† 899
887 king of
East Franks
896 emperor

Louis
b. c.877
† 879

Bernard
† 891

Genealogy III
The descendants of Charles the Bald

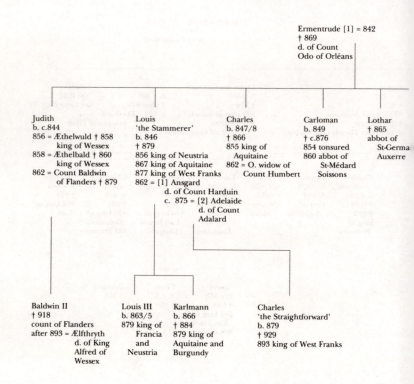

Ermentrude [1] = 842
† 869
d. of Count
Odo of Orléans

Judith
b. c.844
856 = Æthelwuld † 858
  king of Wessex
858 = Æthelbald † 860
  king of Wessex
862 = Count Baldwin
  of Flanders † 879

Louis
'the Stammerer'
b. 846
† 879
856 king of Neustria
867 king of Aquitaine
877 king of West Franks
862 = [1] Ansgard
  d. of Count Harduin
c. 875 = [2] Adelaide
  d. of Count
  Adalard

Charles
b. 847/8
† 866
855 king of
  Aquitaine
862 = O. widow of
  Count Humbert

Carloman
b. 849
† c.876
854 tonsured
860 abbot of
  St-Médard
  Soissons

Lothar
† 865
abbot of
  St-Germa
  Auxerre

Baldwin II
† 918
count of Flanders
after 893 = Ælfthryth
  d. of King
  Alfred of
  Wessex

Louis III
b. 863/5
879 king of
  Francia
  and
  Neustria

Karlmann
b. 866
† 884
879 king of
  Aquitaine and
  Burgundy

Charles
'the Straightforward'
b. 879
† 929
893 king of West Franks

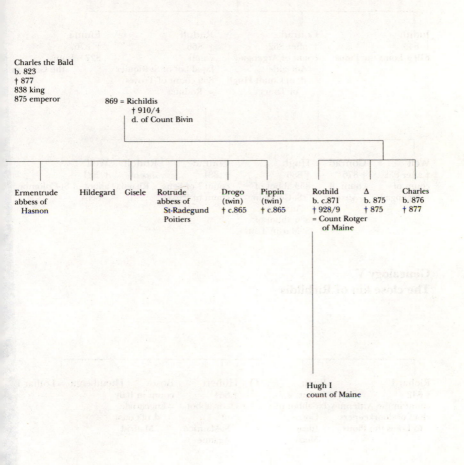

Charles the Bald
b. 823
† 877
838 king
875 emperor

869 = Richildis
      † 910/4
      d. of Count Bivin

| Ermentrude abbess of Hasnon | Hildegard | Gisele | Rotrude abbess of St-Radegund Poitiers | Drogo (twin) † c.865 | Pippin (twin) † c.865 | Rothild b. c.871 † 928/9 = Count Rotger of Maine | Δ b. 875 † 875 | Charles b. 876 † 877 |

Hugh I
count of Maine

Genealogy IV
The close kin of Judith

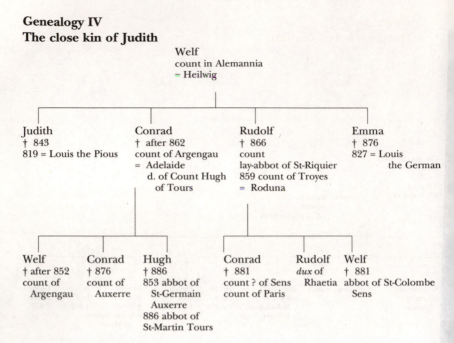

Welf
count in Alemannia
= Heilwig

Judith
† 843
819 = Louis the Pious

Conrad
† after 862
count of Argengau
= Adelaide
d. of Count Hugh
of Tours

Rudolf
† 866
count
lay-abbot of St-Riquier
859 count of Troyes
= Roduna

Emma
† 876
827 = Louis
the German

Welf
† after 852
count of
Argengau

Conrad
† 876
count of
Auxerre

Hugh
† 886
853 abbot of
St-Germain
Auxerre
886 abbot of
St-Martin Tours

Conrad
† 881
count ? of Sens
count of Paris

Rudolf
dux of
Rhaetia

Welf
† 881
abbot of St-Colombe
Sens

Genealogy V
The close kin of Richildis

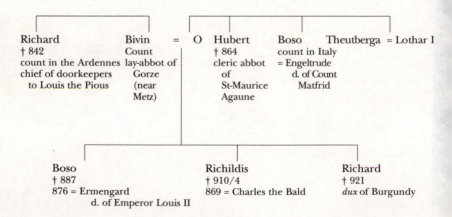

Richard
† 842
count in the Ardennes
chief of doorkeepers
to Louis the Pious

Bivin = O
Count
lay-abbot of
Gorze
(near
Metz)

Hubert
† 864
cleric abbot
of
St-Maurice
Agaune

Boso
count in Italy
= Engeltrude
d. of Count
Matfrid

Theutberga = Lothar I

Boso
† 887
876 = Ermengard
d. of Emperor Louis II

Richildis
† 910/4
869 = Charles the Bald

Richard
† 921
dux of Burgundy

Genealogy VI
The close kin of Bernard

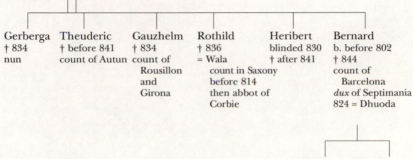

William
† 806
count of Toulouse
founder of monastery of Gellone
=

Cunegund [1]   = [2] Witberga

Gerberga	Theuderic	Gauzhelm	Rothild	Heribert	Bernard
† 834	† before 841	† 834	† 836	blinded 830	b. before 802
nun	count of Autun	count of	= Wala	† after 841	† 844
		Rousillon	count in Saxony		count of
		and	before 814		Barcelona
		Girona	then abbot of		*dux* of Septimania
			Corbie		824 = Dhuoda

William
b. 826
† 849

Bernard
'Hairypaws'
b.841
† 886

Genealogy VII
The close kin of Ermentrude

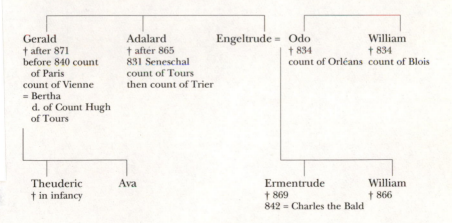

Gerald	Adalard	Engeltrude =	Odo	William
† after 871	† after 865		† 834	† 834
before 840 count	831 Seneschal		count of Orléans	count of Blois
of Paris	count of Tours			
count of Vienne	then count of Trier			
= Bertha				
d. of Count Hugh				
of Tours				

Theuderic	Ava		Ermentrude	William
† in infancy			† 869	† 866
			842 = Charles the Bald	

MAPS

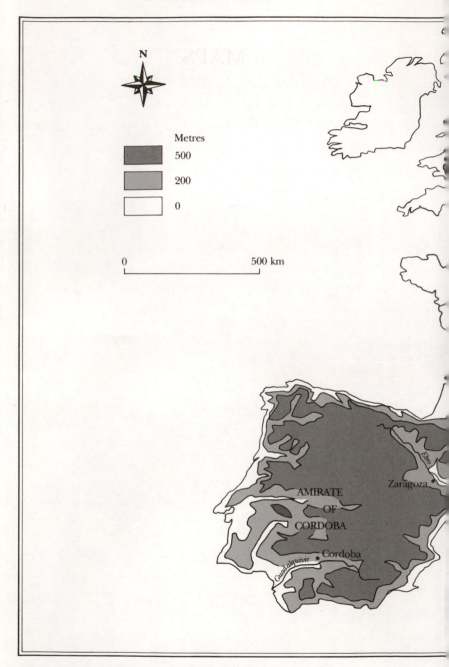

Map 1: General map of the Carolingian world

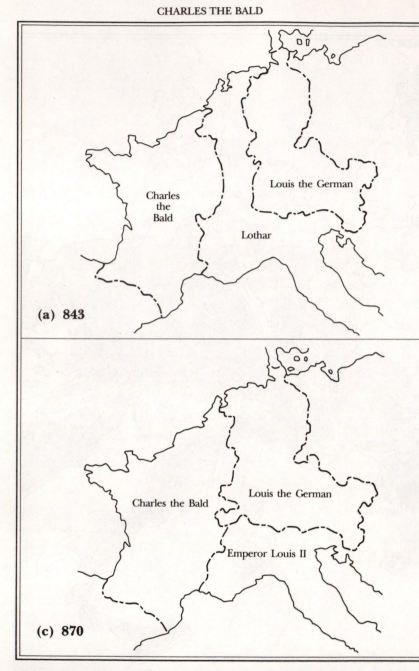

Map 2: Divisions of the Carolingian world, 843–880

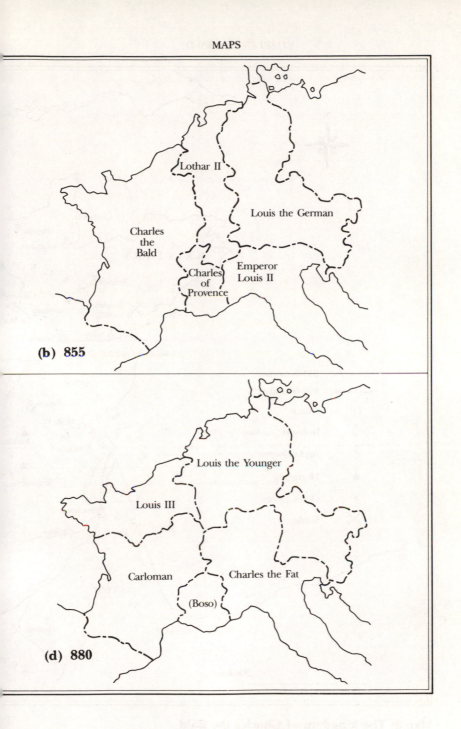

(b) 855

Lothar II

Louis the German

Charles
the
Bald

Charles
of
Provence

Emperor
Louis II

(d) 880

Louis the Younger

Louis III

Carloman

Charles the Fat

(Boso)

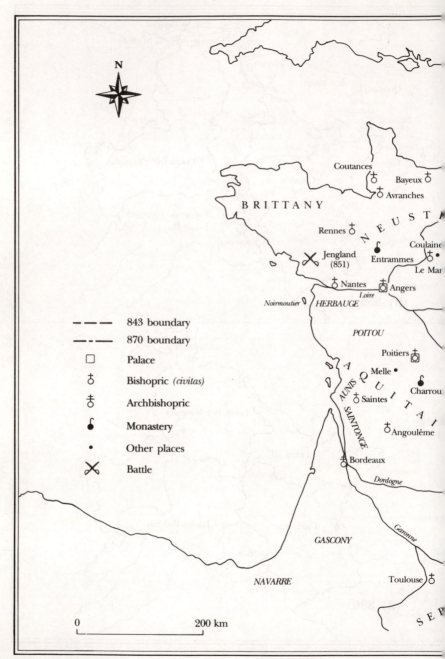

Map 3: The kingdom of Charles the Bald

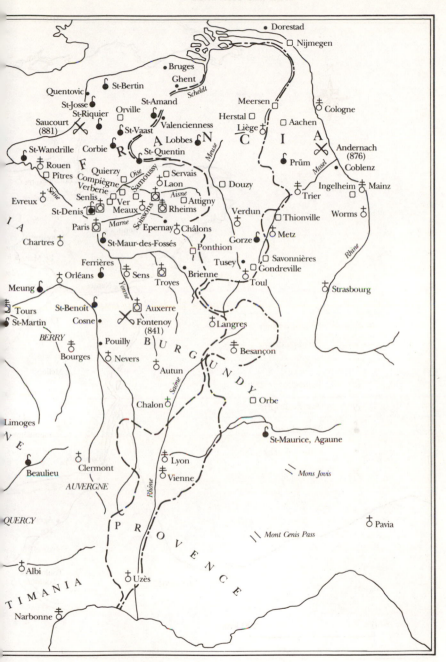

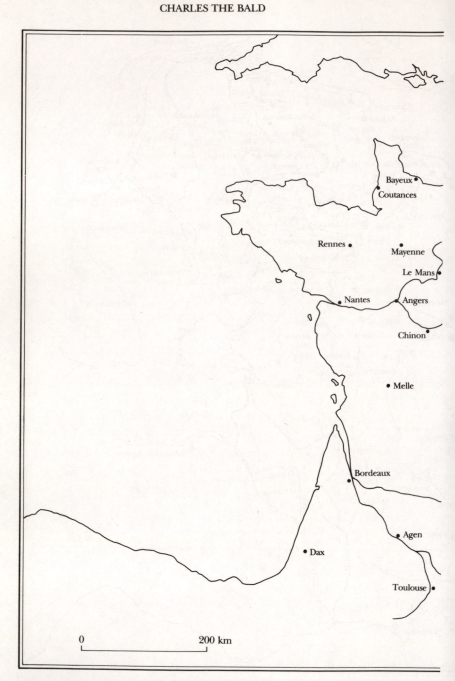

Map 4: The mints of Charles the Bald

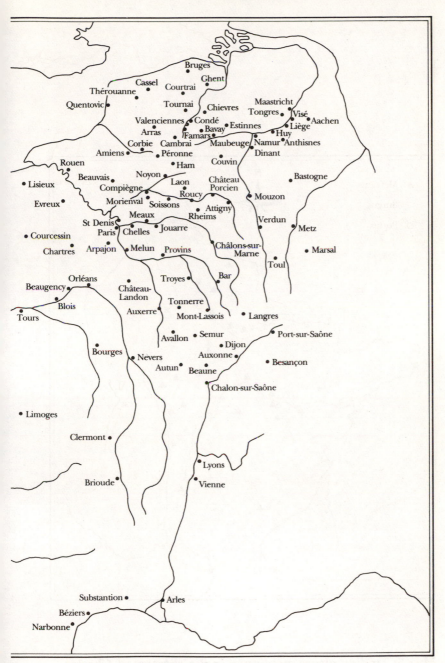

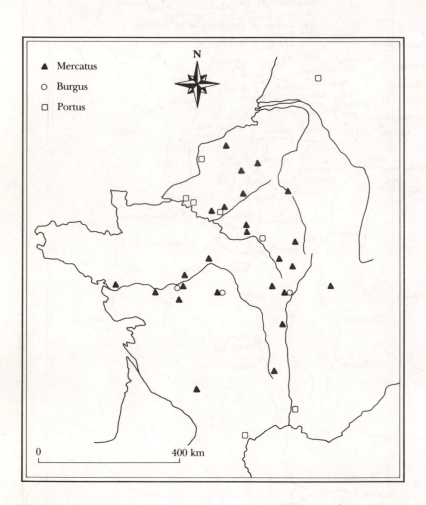

Map 5: Trading places mentioned in the charters of Charles the Bald

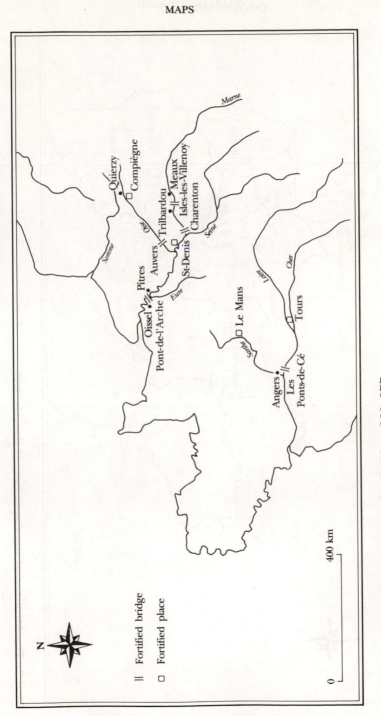

Map 6: Fortifications of Charles the Bald, c. 860–877

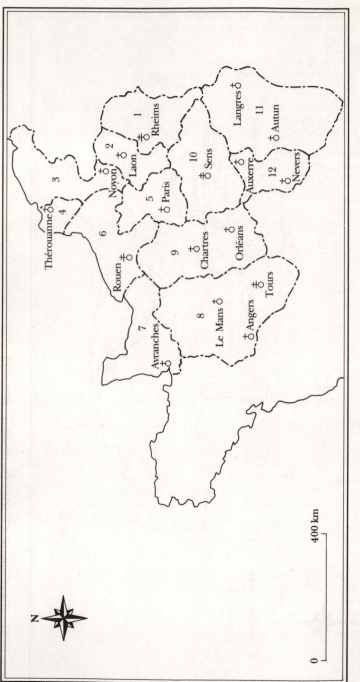

Map 7: The *Missatica* of the Capitulary of Servais, 853

Missaticum 1
Rheims, Voncq, Atenois, Perthes, Bar-le-Duc, Chanzy, Vertus, Binson, Tardenois
Missi: Bishop Hincmar [of Rheims], Ricuin, Engilscalc

Missaticum 2
Laon, Porcien, Soissons, Orxois, Valois
Missi: Bishop Pardulus [of Laon], Altmar, Theodacrus

Missaticum 3
Noyon, Vermandois, Arras, Courtrai, Flanders, the counties of Engilramn and the
counties of Waltcaud
Missi: Bishop Immo [of Noyon], Abbot Adalard [of St-Bertin], Waltcaud, Odalric

Missaticum 4
The counties of Berengar, Engiscalc, Gerard and the counties of Reginar
Missi: Bishop Folcuin [of Thérouanne], Adalgar, Engiscalc and Berengar

Missaticum 5
Paris, Meaux, Senlis, Vexin, Beauvais, Vendeuil
Missi: Abbot Louis [of St-Denis], Bishop Irminfrid [of Beauvais], Ingilwin, Got-
selm

Missaticum 6
Rouen, Talou, Vimeu, Ponthieu, Amiens
Missi: Bishop Paul [of Rouen], Bishop Hilmerad [of Amiens], Herloin, Hungar

Missaticum 7
Avranches, Coutances, Bayeux, Cotentin, *Otlingua Saxonia* and Harduin's [part of
that area], Eu, Lisieux
Missi: Bishop Eirard [of Lisieux], Abbot Theuderic [of Jumièges], Herloin, Harduin

Missaticum 8
Le Mans, Angers, Tours, Corbonnais, Sées
Missi: Bishop Dodo [of Angers], Robert and Osbert

Missaticum 9
Blois, Orléans, Vendôme, Chartres, Dreux, Châteaudun, Evreux, Arpajon, Poissy,
Madrie
Missi: Bishop Burchard [of Chartres], Rodulf, Abbot Henry

Missaticum 10
Sens, Troyes, Gâtinais, Melun, Provins, Arcis-sur-Aube, Brienne
Missi: Bishop Wenilo [of Sens], Odo and Donatus

Missaticum 11
Counties of Milo and counties of Isembard, namely Autun, Mâcon, Châlon, [land
of] Chattuarii, Tonnerre, Beaune, Duesme, the county of Attela, and the
county of Romold
Missi: Bishop Theutbold [of Langres], Bishop Jonas [of Autun], Isembard, Abbot
Abbo, and Daddo

Missaticum 12
Nevers, Auxerre, Avallon
Missi: Hugh, Gozso, Nibelung

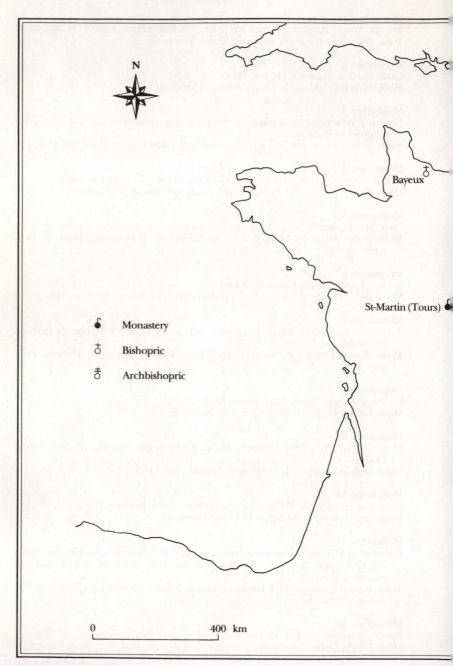

N

Bayeux

St-Martin (Tours)

Monastery

Bishopric

Archbishopric

0   400 km

Map 8: Attendance of the Synod of Ponthion, 876

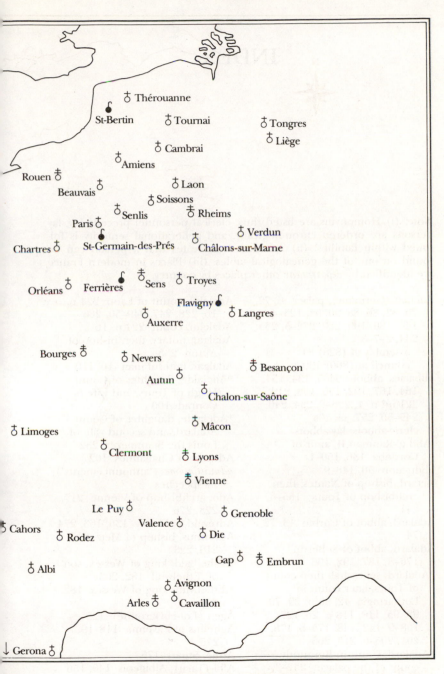

Thérouanne
St-Bertin
Tournai
Tongres
Liège
Cambrai
Amiens
Rouen
Laon
Beauvais
Soissons
Senlis
Rheims
Paris
Verdun
St-Germain-des-Prés
Châlons-sur-Marne
Chartres
Orléans
Ferrières
Sens
Troyes
Flavigny
Langres
Auxerre
Bourges
Nevers
Besançon
Autun
Chalon-sur-Saône
Mâcon
Limoges
Clermont
Lyons
Vienne
Le Puy
Grenoble
Cahors
Valence
Die
Rodez
Gap
Embrun
Albi
Avignon
Arles
Cavaillon
Gerona

INDEX

Note: (i) Homonyms are listed thus: clerical personnel precede lay, lay persons are ordered chronologically, and generational seniority is followed within families. (ii) An asterisk indicates that a person can be found on one of the genealogical tables. (iii) Places in modern France are identified by *département*; other places by country.